# Study Guide

## For

## Cole and Smith's

# The American System of Criminal Justice

### Media Edition
### Tenth Edition

**Scott Johnson**
*Frostburg State University*

THOMSON

WADSWORTH ™

Australia • Canada • Mexico • Singapore • Spain • United Kingdom • United States

Printed in the United States of America
1  2  3  4  5  6  7  06  05  04  03

Printer: Globus Printing

ISBN: 0-534-61534-1

For more information about our products, contact us at:
**Thomson Learning Academic Resource Center**
**1-800-423-0563**

**For permission to use material from this text,**
**contact us by:**
**Phone:** 1-800-730-2214
**Fax:** 1-800-731-2215
**Web:** http://www.thomsonrights.com

Cover Image: © Cameron Heryet/ Getty Images

**Asia**
Thomson Learning
5 Shenton Way #01-01
UIC Building
Singapore 068808

**Australia/ New Zealand**
Thomson Learning
102 Dodds Street
South Street
Southbank, Victoria 3006
Australia

**Canada**
Nelson
1120 Birchmount Road
Toronto, Ontario M1K 5G4
Canada

**Europe/Middle East/South Africa**
Thomson Learning
High Holborn House
50/51 Bedford Row
London WC1R 4LR
United Kingdom

**Latin America**
Thomson Learning
Seneca, 53
Colonia Polanco
11560 Mexico D.F.
Mexico

**Spain/ Portugal**
Paraninfo
Calle/Magallanes, 25
28015 Madrid, Spain

# TABLE OF CONTENTS

# INTRODUCTION

By using this study guide, you can learn and review the material in the textbook. The summaries and outlines for each chapter highlight the important topics covered in the text. In addition, the review questions will reinforce the key terms and people from each chapter. By reviewing the study guide as you complete each chapter and prior to each exam, you should be able to put forth your best effort on exams and, more importantly, you should be able to absorb, understand, and retain more ideas and information from the course. Each chapter also includes General Practice questions, Multiple Choice questions, True and False questions and "Worksheet" assignments. If your instructor does not assign them to you, you may want to do them on your own to expand your knowledge.

This study guide is not the only resource available to support your study of criminal justice. In conjunction with your textbook, you can find a wealth of information about criminal justice on the World Wide Web. By exploring and utilizing web sites, you can study materials from your textbook while obtaining a wealth of additional information. Wadsworth Publishing's criminal justice web site (**http://cj.wadsworth.com**) provides a valuable resource, including links to hundreds of web sites containing information about criminal justice. Use this web site as your starting point to undertake research, explore career options, or simply keep up to date with developments in criminal justice. Contemporary criminal justice is being shaped by new technologies and instant access to world-wide sources of information. Here is your chance to step into the twenty-first century by gaining valuable knowledge and skills involving computers and new information technologies.

## *Practical Advice for Students*

A study guide is a useful tool for improving one's academic performance. However, a study guide cannot "rescue" those who have neglected their assignments and failed to make a solid effort to succeed throughout the entire semester. You can best achieve your academic goals by approaching this course -- and every other course -- with a few important principles in mind. These principles, if taken to heart, can help any student achieve better grades and gain greater benefits from his or her education.

1. Complete all reading assignments **before** the materials are covered in class.

You will have a much better understanding of lectures and class discussions if you have become familiar with assigned topics beforehand. Although today's students lead busy lives with jobs, family responsibilities, active social lives, and community involvement, it is possible for nearly any student to fulfill class reading assignments merely by making such assignments a regular part of his or her weekly schedule. If you set aside specific hours each week for reading and studying criminal justice materials, just as you may set aside certain hours each week for friends or favorite television shows, you will automatically become well-prepared for class as part of your regular weekly routine.

2. Take notes as you read just as you would during a lecture.

You will gain much greater understanding of the material in the textbook if you merely spend the extra time that it takes to write notes as you read. The process of writing notes forces you to organize material and it reinforces in your memory the important points from the reading assignments. In addition, when it is time to study for exams, you will have additional notes to assist your reviewing process.

3. Be active in class. Even if you do not think you have important comments to contribute, think of questions to ask that will expand your knowledge about the material in the textbook.

The greatest regret of many former students, including this author, is that they did not take a more active role in their own education. It can be very easy to be passive in the classroom, especially in large classes. However, students who make an effort to participate actively in class discussions gain huge benefits. By asking questions or volunteering to participate in discussions, you keep your mind actively involved in exploring the topics of the course. Passive students merely receive and record information, while active students gain analytical insights by questioning and exploring ideas. In addition, you will have an easier time learning and remembering concepts in any course if you are actively involved in discussing them.

Moreover, as a practical matter, active students attract the attention of instructors. This attention can provide many additional benefits. Such students are most likely to develop relationships with instructors that enable them to meet and discuss freely the course material, career planning, and other useful subjects. Instructors often formally or informally give extra credit toward high grades to students who make regular contributions to class discussions. Active students also will inevitably receive better letters of recommendation if they ever need to use a professor as a reference for a job or graduate school application.

It is very easy to be active in class, even if you are struggling to understand or to generate your own interest in specific course topics. As you do the reading for each assignment, think of three or four comments and questions to take to class. Write them down and raise them at appropriate times during class discussions. Even students who do not feel confident about their abilities to contribute significantly to class discussions can become actively involved by planning their comments and questions before they arrive at class. After consciously preparing comments and questions for a few classes, most students find that they start to think of additional questions and gain new insights as they participate in each class. Eventually students feel so "connected" to the lectures and discussions that their interest and enthusiasm generate questions and comments during each class whether or not they formally prepared specific comments beforehand.

4. Push yourself to go above and beyond the minimum expectations for the course.

You will learn much more and get better grades if you push yourself to go beyond the minimum expectations for the course. When you encounter a topic that interests you in the textbook, go to the library and read more about the subject by using the sources listed at the end of each textbook chapter. If you receive a writing assignment, after checking with the instructor to make sure that there is no *maximum page limit*, write a longer paper than required for the assignment. Pushing yourself to do extra work will add to your knowledge and interest, give you more information and understanding to exhibit in the exams, and impress the instructor with your enthusiasm and effort. Many students throughout the country who are not naturally "gifted" consistently receive higher grades than so-called "smarter" students simply by out-working them. Virtually every college instructor has had students who achieved 'A's through determination, willpower, and consistent effort, while naturally gifted students may receive lower grades by choosing to coast through their courses rather than apply themselves. You never know how well you can do in your studies until you really make the effort to do your best work. Many students will surprise themselves and find that they are "smarter" than they thought when they get high grades from making the effort to go above and beyond minimum course requirements. Even if you do not receive an 'A' after putting forth maximum effort, at least you can rest easy knowing that you gave your best effort. This is a much better feeling than receiving a 'B-' and always wondering whether or not you could have done better if you had tried harder.

5. Take pride in your work.

Do not hand in sloppy work. Proofread your papers. Have friends or family members read your work to check for silly errors in spelling, typing, and grammar. Everyone makes mistakes, especially in their formal writing assignments. The strong students are often separated from the weak students by taking the extra time to double-check for errors. As you check for errors, you will often notice ways in which you can add additional material or otherwise make your writing stronger. The development of good work habits will carry over into your professional career. When you write a memo for your boss in a law enforcement agency, business, or government agency, you will be judged by your presentation as well as by the content of your analysis. Take the extra step necessary to present your best work to your instructors.

<u>6. Talk to your classmates.</u>

Even if your instructor wants you to complete all assignments on your own, you can still gain great benefits by talking to your classmates about interesting topics that emerge from the textbook and lectures. As many former students look back on their college experiences, they recognize that some of the most valuable and educational moments during college came while discussing, debating, and analyzing issues with their classmates. The process of interacting with others forces us to reexamine and clarify our own thoughts. This process helps to reinforce concepts and provides a stronger basis for good performances on exams, papers, and other academic assignments.

<u>7. Go to see your instructor during his or her office hours.</u>

Students gain many benefits from seeking one-on-one contacts with their instructors. You can ask additional questions about the course material. You can clarify expectations about class assignments. More importantly, personal contacts with instructors can make the instructor better able to understand how well students understand the course material. Such contacts can provide feedback to enable the instructor to review material or reinforce specific topics. In addition, personal contact with instructors also permits instructors to provide advice about careers and graduate school possibilities when instructors become personally acquainted with their students.

<u>8. Try to connect the course material to your own life.</u>

Spend time thinking about the implications of the topics covered in the textbook. Do not file the course away in one section of your mind for the limited purpose of passing exams and earning a grade. Criminal justice subjects are important to all of us. As citizens and voters, we must choose the legislators, governors, judges, and presidents who will shape criminal justice policy. Someday *you* might be a leader who will make decisions about criminal justice. Thus, it is especially important that you read newspapers, read news magazines, watch television news, and keep yourself informed about what is happening in the world. As you view the news, think about how contemporary events fit with the topics and analysis contained in the textbook. The material that you learn in this course should enable you to gain a better understanding of developments in American society and help you to evaluate the campaign promises and policy proposals of politicians who present themselves to you during each election season.

If you are interested in a criminal justice career, use the textbook and course material to analyze your own interests and aspirations. For example, many students want to be FBI agents or police officers. They frequently focus on the most "exciting" aspects of those jobs, such as apprehending dangerous lawbreakers through fascinating investigations. However, you must get beyond the *image* of law enforcement officers in order to make good choices about careers. Just as the television show "Law and Order" does not provide an accurate presentation of the daily lives of lawyers, most television images of law enforcement officers, prosecutors, and other criminal justice actors provide incomplete if not inaccurate images.

To choose a career, you must first examine *yourself.* How do you want to spend eight to ten hours each working day for (potentially) thirty or more years? What kinds of tasks are of interest to you? Do you want to work with people? Do you want to work in an office? What kind of organization do you want to work for? As you examine yourself, think about the daily lives of professionals in the criminal justice system. Remember, for example, police officers can spend significant amounts of time directing traffic, getting cats out of trees, or just watching activity on several city blocks. Every job has its "boring" aspects and those aspects must be recognized in order to make a wise choice about careers. Some students also use the material in this course to think about different kinds of jobs that are less visible than those of police officers and prosecutors. For example, how many students have really examined opportunities for becoming parole officers, court administrators, or counselors in a correctional setting? By applying the course topics to yourself, you can use the textbook to help shape your own life if you have an interest in a criminal justice career.

If you begin to identify jobs that may be of interest to you, think about how you can learn more about those jobs. You could make an appointment with a local criminal justice professional to ask him or her about how to begin a career as, for example, a probation officer. Although students may initially feel too shy to seek appointments with prosecutors or police chiefs or other justice professionals, they soon discover that these professionals often enjoy talking about their careers, backgrounds, and life experiences. Remember, all of these people were once students who had to think about what careers to pursue. They remember how difficult it can be to gain enough understanding about various careers in order to make wise choices about which directions to pursue.

## 9. Enjoy your studies.

College can be a very burdensome time of life, as students juggle classes, jobs, and family responsibilities while trying to make ends meet. College is, however, one of the few moments in life when people have the opportunity to focus their attention on *ideas*. College courses force you to learn about ideas, but it is up to you to think deeply about these ideas. This is your moment to question the things that you have always taken for granted. This is your moment to clarify your values, beliefs, and goals. College will not shape you into a certain kind of person. It merely provides the opportunity for you to explore, to wonder, to debate, and to discuss as you learn relevant concepts and theories about specific subjects. When you stop attending college classes and undertaking reading assignments, it is more difficult to take the time to encounter new ideas and to analyze your place in the world. Seize the opportunity that college presents for you to expand your mind. Although you may ultimately conclude that your beliefs, values, and world-view suit you just fine, you can have greater confidence in that conclusion by recognizing and seizing the opportunity that college presents for exploring ideas with the assistance of your instructors and classmates. Even if you feel burdened at this moment by seemingly impossible workloads and financial strains, do not lose sight of the *opportunity for education* that you are experiencing. Make the most of it. Enjoy it. For most people, the same opportunity may not present itself again at another stage in life.

# CHAPTER 1

# CRIME AND JUSTICE IN AMERICA

## LEARNING OBJECTIVES

After covering the material in this chapter, students should understand:

1.  public policy concerning crime is determined in political arenas;

2.  crime control in a democracy involves balancing the value of safety and security with protection of individuals' rights;

3.  the comparison and reality of Packer's Crime Control Model and Due Process Model.

4.  categorization of crime, including *mala in se*, *mala prohibita*, occupational, organized, visible, victimless, and political;

5.  the extent of crime, crime trends, and related demographic influences;

6.  the sources for measuring crime and the weaknesses of those sources (especially UCR and NCVS).

## CHAPTER SUMMARY

This chapter explores the problems of dealing with crime and justice in a democracy. The public policy issues of crime and justice require the enforcement of the law and the protection of freedoms at the same time which can be problematic. Herbert Packer's two models of the criminal justice process provide an ideal version, the due process model, with its emphasis upon freedom and justice, and the reality-based version, the crime control model, with its emphasis efficiency and order.

Another problem in dealing with crime in a democracy is the issue of defining crime. While some acts are easily defined as criminal, such as murder, others are not so easily defined, such as euthanasia or abortion. Mala in se refers to acts that are wrong in themselves where the public can reach a consensus upon the criminality of the act. However, mala prohibita are acts that the government defines as criminal but the public might find conflictual. Examples are smoking marijuana or public drunkenness. Many scholars argue that the government use the law to impose values upon the public.

There are many different types of crime, such as occupational, organized, visible, political, crimes without victims, hate crimes, and cybercrime. Law enforcement authorities focus largely upon visible crime, which involves street crimes such as burglary or homicide, because people fear this type of crime more than any other. However, occupational crime, also known as white-collar crime, and political crimes can impose great costs upon society financially.

The crime problem today is a difficult issue for researchers because data on crime are not reliable. The Uniform Crime Reports provides data reported to police but does not track the dark figure of crime which is not reported to the police officials. The National Crime Victimization Survey involves interview of samples of the U. S. population by the government but people often inaccurately report their experiences to the government.

## CHAPTER OUTLINE

I. INTRODUCTION

A.    After the terrorist attacks on September 11, 2001, a Gallup Poll reported that terrorism, national security and fear as the most important problem in the U. S.
Despite the terrorist attacks, Americans are still preoccupied with crime. Why? Terrorism is itself a crime and crime remains a focus of Americans as a major social problem.
B.    What Americans Think: What do you think is the most important problem facing this country today?

## II. THEMES OF THE BOOK

## III. CRIME AND JUSTICE AS PUBLIC POLICY ISSUES
Reiman argues that our system is designed not to reduce crime but to project a visible image of the threat of crime. In a democracy, political leaders are greatly influenced by public opinion. However, legislators also know that they can cater to the American public's anxiety about crime and community safety. As a result, policies often appear to be enacted that are popular with the general public but that are thought by researchers to have little potential impact on the crime problem.

THE POLICY DEBATE: Have Tough Crime Control Policies Caused a Decline in Crime?

A.    Crime and Justice in a Democracy
  1.    Difficult to achieve the goal of enforcing laws and protecting rights of individuals. Unlike in an authoritarian state, rights must be respected in a democracy.

B.    Crime Control versus Due Process
  1.    Herbert Packer's two competing models; ideal types designed to organize thinking about the criminal justice system. Packer recognizes that the administration of criminal justice operates within the contemporary American society and is therefore influenced by cultural forces that, in turn, determine the models' usefulness.
  2.    Crime Control Model: Order as a Value
      a.    Goal: Repression of Criminal Conduct
      b.    Value: Efficiency
      c.    Nature of Process: Administrative and filtering
      d.    Decision Point: Police and Prosecutor (i.e., plea bargaining, discretionary dismissals)
      e.    Basis for Decision Making: Discretion
      f.    Analogy: Assembly Line
  3.    Due Process Model: Law as a Value
      a.    Goal: Preserve individuals' liberty
      b.    Value: Reliability (i.e., accurate decisions about guilt and innocence)
      c.    Nature of the Process: Adversarial
      d.    Decision Point: Courtroom (i.e., trial)
      e.    Basis for Decision Making: Law
      f.    Analogy: Obstacle course

C.    The Politics of Crime and Justice
  1.    Criminal justice policies are developed in national, state, and local political arenas.
  2.    There are risks that politicians will enact laws that they believe the people want even though the resulting policies will have little or no impact on crime.
  3.    The clearest link between politics and criminal justice can be seen in the competing statements and promises of Republicans and Democrats who run against each other for office.
  4.    Politics and politicians also control the budgets for criminal justice agencies. Large amounts are allocated for the war on drug but limits are placed on spending for poor people's defense attorneys.

5.  Local prosecutors and judges are elected to office through political campaigns.
6.  What Americans Think: Contrast in public's emphasis on spending for crime control and spending for social welfare.

IV. DEFINING CRIME
A.  *Mala in se* crimes, wrongs in themselves (murder, rape, assault), based on shared values: consensus.
B.  *Mala prohibita* crimes are not wrongs in themselves but are punished because they are prohibited by government. There is often a lack of consensus about whether such actions should be illegal (e.g., use of marijuana; gambling, etc.).
C.  What Americans Think: Lack of consensus about criminalizing marijuana, homosexual relations, and assisted suicide.
D.  American criminal laws may clash with religious and cultural practices of immigrants.

V.  TYPES OF CRIME
Crimes can be categorized as *mala in se* v. *mala prohibita*; felonies v. misdemeanors. Other categories based on level of risk and profitability, degree of public disapproval, and cultural characteristics of offenders:

A.  Occupational Crime
Violation of law committed through opportunities created in the course of a legal business or profession. Sometimes referred to as "white collar crime" although that does not encompass all categories of occupational crime. Despite sizable sums of money illegally obtained, often does not receive stiff punishments.
1.  Crimes for the benefit of the employing organization: price fixing, theft of trade secrets, etc.
2.  Crimes through the exercise of state-based authority: politicians taking bribes, police officers stealing from the evidence room, etc.
3.  Crime by professionals in their capacity as professionals: lawyers stealing from clients, stockbrokers engaged in insider trading, doctors sexually exploiting patients.
4.  Crimes committed by individuals as individuals where opportunities are not based on governmental power or professional position: employee theft from the organization, filing false expense claims, etc. Total losses due to employee theft are greater than all business losses from shoplifting, burglary, or robbery.
    a.  Most such crimes do not come to public attention. Many businesses and professional organizations "police" themselves by firing employees who commit offenses.

B.  Organized Crime
Social framework for the perpetration of criminal acts rather than specific acts themselves. Organized criminals provide goods and services to people, and will engage in any illegal activity as long as it is low risk and high profit (e.g., pornography, money laundering, illegal disposal of toxic waste).
1.  Organized crime has been associated with many different ethnic and immigrant groups as they struggled to gain access to legitimate economic opportunities when they became more accepted in American society.
2.  Increasing problem of transnational criminal groups.
3.  Close-Up: The Russian Mafiya of Brighton Beach

C.  Visible Crime
Street crime or ordinary crime primarily by lower classes and run the gamut from shoplifting to homicide (i.e., violent crimes, property crimes public order crimes).
1.  Visible crimes make up the FBI's Uniform Crime Reports

2.     Theorists have argued that the predominantly lower class composition of correctional institutions reflects society's bias toward enforcing and punishing street crimes committed by the lower classes to a much greater extent than the crimes committed by people possessing greater status, wealth, and power.

D.     <u>Crimes Without Victims</u>
Offenses involving a willing and private exchange of goods or services, such as gambling, pornography, drug use, prostitution, etc. They are also called public order crimes.
1.     Claimed justification for criminalizing such activities is the protection of society as a whole, including its moral fibre. Are these crimes really victimless if these people harm themselves?
2.     Because these cases flood the courts, it is costly for society to enforce these laws.

E.     <u>Political Crime</u>
Includes activities such as treason, sedition (rebellion), and espionage which are carried out for an ideological purpose. American examples include acts of violence by those opposed to legal abortions.
1.     Crimes such as the Oklahoma City bombing may be politically motivated, but they are prosecuted as visible crimes rather than political crimes.

F.     <u>Cybercrime</u>
The use of the computer or Internet to commit acts against persons, property, public order, or morality.
1.     The Internet is used to disseminate child pornography. Hackers create viruses that cause significant economic harm to businesses and government.
2.     Government has been slow to respond with new laws addressing newly developing harmful behaviors based on technology.

G.     <u>CLOSE-UP: You Could Get Raped</u>
Example of woman victimized by a stalker who posted phony information about her on the Internet.

H.     <u>CLOSE-UP: Hate Crimes: A New Category of Personal Violence</u>
Laws in most states target violent acts directed at victims because of their race, ethnicity, gender, religion, or sexual orientation. Controversies arise concerning whether such laws violate freedom of speech and association.

VI.     THE CRIME PROBLEM TODAY

A.     <u>What Americans Think</u>
Americans believe (erroneously) that there is more crime than in the prior year.

B.     <u>The Worst of Times?</u>
1.     The amount and types of crime may change during different historical eras. The United States experienced outbreaks of violence at various points throughout history.
2.     The murder rate reached a high in 1933, fell to a low in the 1950s, rose to a new high in 1980 and then fell again in the 1990s.

C.     <u>The Most Crime-Ridden Nation?</u>
1.     Comparisons between nations require the selection of similar nations (i.e., similar governing systems and levels of economic development) and use of reliable data.
2.     Homicide rates in the United States are much higher than those for other countries, but victimization rates for assault and robbery are higher in some other countries.
3.     Property crime rates are higher in Australia, Canada, and some other countries than in the United States.

4.      Just as in the United States, crime rates in some other countries showed declines in the late 1990s.

D.      Keeping Track of Crime
Difficult to measure actual amount of crime because of the "dark figure of crime," namely large numbers of crimes that are not reported

1.      Homicide and auto theft regularly reported because, respectively, missing persons and located bodies must be accounted for, and crime reports are necessary for recovery on auto insurance.

2.      Rape, thefts, and other crimes reported less because of victims' and witnesses' fears, relationships with perpetrators, and unwillingness to get involved with police.

3.      Uniform Crime Reports (UCR)
Flawed measure of crime because:
   a.      Only counts crimes reported to police;
   b.      Events labeled as crimes defined differently in different jurisdictions.
   c.      However, changes are being instituted in the late 1990s using the National Incident-Based Reporting System (NIBR) which will provide detailed information on 46 offenses in 22 crime categories. The NIBRS will distinguish between attempted and completed crimes.

4.      National Crime Victimization Surveys (NCVS) Surveys of households on crime victimization has enhanced knowledge about crime and probability of victimization. Valuable because has established stable patterns of victimization rates. However, flawed measure of crime because:
   a.      People will not report their own participation in such crimes as prostitution, gambling, drug trafficking, and purchasing stolen property.
   b.      Definition of criminal event depends on victim's perception of event.
   c.      Memories of precise year in which event happened may fade over time.

E.      Comparative Perspective: Iceland -- Little Crime
Urban, homogeneous country with little crime; geographically isolated from drugs and other problems; primary problem of alcohol abuse treated harshly.

F.      Trends in Crime
Crime trends changed during 1980s

1.      UCR showed steady increase in crime rates until 1980, but NCVS showed stable victimization rates with declines during the 1980s.
   a.      Since 1993, both the UCR and NCVS show declines in violent crimes, including homicides.
   b.      Increased UCR crime rates attributable to increased willingness of citizens to report crimes, the availability of "911" numbers, and neighborhood-level watch and police patrol programs, so we cannot be certain about what increases show us about actual criminal behavior.

2.      Age: Demographic Influences on Crime Trend
Crime trends affected by demographic trends, especially the number of people in the crime-prone age group, fourteen to twenty-four years.
   a.      The number of legal abortions since 19 has decreased the number of people in the crime prone years in the late 1990s.
   b.      Experts warned that of a projected increase in the number of teenage males at the start of the twenty-first century may lead to significant increases in crime. Such a rise in crime has not occurred.

3.      Crack Cocaine
Increases in violent crime and homicide in the 1980s are generally attributed to killings by young people under age 25. Killings were produced by spread of crack cocaine and availability of powerful handguns. The decline in crack use has apparently contributed to a reduction in violent crime.

## REVIEW OF KEY TERMS

Fill in the appropriate term for each statement:

crime
public policy
crimes without victims
fear of crime
mala in se
mala prohibita
due process model
crime control model
occupational crime
organized crime
visible crime
political crime
cybercrime
hate crime
National Incident-Based Reporting System (NIBRS)
Uniform Crime Reports (UCR)
National Crime Victimization Survey (NCVS)
dark figure of crime

1. _____ is the metaphor for the amount of crime that goes unreported to the police.

2. _____ is generated from a compilation of reports from law enforcement agencies throughout the country.

3. _____ is also known as street crime or ordinary crime.

4. _____ involve the willing and private exchange of illegal goods and services.

5. _____ are offenses that are wrong by their very nature.

6. _____ measures the amount of crime from the perspective of victims.

7. _____ is the means through which each police officer will record and report each offense in a crime incident instead of merely describing the most serious crime in the incident.

8. _____ is conduct committed through opportunities created through professional or employment activities.

9. _____ are acts, such as treason and sedition, that constitute threats against the state.

10. _____ are offenses that are banned by statute but are not inherently wrong.

11. _____ a social framework for the perpetration of criminal acts, often on a basis that crosses state and national boundaries.

12. _____ distorts the accuracy of the public's perceptions of the extent of the crime problem and affects many people's daily behavior.

13. _____ is a specific act of commission or omission in violation of the law, for which a punishment is prescribed

14. _____ depicts the criminal justice system as emphasizing reliable decisions that protect individuals' liberty through an adversarial process based on law.

15. _____ depicts the criminal justice system as one that emphasizes efficient repression of crime through the exercise of discretion in administrative processing of cases.

16. Crime and Justice are _____ issues.

17. An offense committed through the use of computers is called a _____.

18. Violent acts aimed at individuals because of their race are called _____ crimes.


## REVIEW OF KEY PEOPLE

Edwin Sutherland
Herbert Packer
Megan Kanka
John Gotti
James Kopp
Jeffrey Reiman

1. _____ developed the crime control and due process models as the means to provide new insights into the nature of the criminal justice system.
2. _____ : developed the concept of "white collar crime" and led criminal justice scholars away from an exclusive focus on criminal behavior by lower class people. Also developed differential association theory.
3. _____ argues that our system to project to the American people a visible image of the threat of crime, not to reduce crime.
4. Megan's law requires sex offenders who have served their sentences to report their addresses for display on an Internet web site for the public to peruse. This law is named for _____ who was murdered by a convicted sex offender.
5. _____, who died in June 2002, was the boss of New York's Gambino crime "family" and the most important gangster since Al Capone.
6. _____ is an example of someone who committed a political crime. He was arrested for the murder of Dr. Barnett Slepian near Buffalo, New York because he performed abortions.


## GENERAL PRACTICE QUESTIONS

Although it does not accurately characterize the processing of most cases in the criminal justice system, the ____1____ was developed by ____2____ to illustrate how the system's primary goal in some cases could be to preserve individual liberty through careful, reliable determinations of guilt or innocence.

Acts that are wrong by nature are called ___3____ while acts prohibited by law but not wrong by themselves are called ____4_____.

Two sources of data on crime are a reporting system where police describe each offense called the _____5_____ and interviews of samples of the U. S. population called _____6_____. The ____7____ cannot adequately measure ____8____ because reports from police departments are limited to crimes that are reported to or discovered by law enforcement officials.

# SELF-TEST SECTION

## MULTIPLE CHOICE QUESTIONS

1.1. Which of the following is stressed by the crime control model ?
a) freedom
b) order
c) law
d) socialism
e) all of the above

1.2. Which of the following is stressed by the due process model ?
a) democracy
b) order
c) law
d) efficiency
e) all of the above

1.3. Which of the following refers to acts that are wrong by nature?
a) mala in se
b) dark figure of crime
c) victimology
d) mala prohibita
e) mala mala

1.4. Which of the following refers to acts prohibited by government?
a) mala in se
b) dark figure of crime
c) victimology
d) mala prohibita
e) mala mala

1.5. What law requires sex offenders to register with the authorities?
a) Crime Control Bill of 1994
b) Omnibus Crime Control Act
c) Sex and Justice Act of 1999
d) Uniform Crime Reports Act
e) Megan's Law

1.6. Which of the following refers to an organized crime syndicate usually associated with "families"?
a) occupational crime
b) victimless crime
c) visible crime
d) organized crime
e) cybercrime

1.7. Which of the following refers to crime committed using one or more computers?
a) online crime
b) high-tech crime
c) visible crime
d) cybercrime
e) intelcrime

1.8. The "war on drugs" is associated with what type of crime?
a) occupational crime
b) crimes without victims
c) visible crime
d) organized crime
e) cybercrime

1.9. What type of crime is the murder of an abortion doctor ?
a) occupational crime
b) victimless crime
c) visible crime
d) organized crime
e) political crime

1.10. What type of crime is homicide?
a) occupational crime
b) victimless crime
c) visible crime
d) organized crime
e) political crime

1.11. What type of crime is using "insider" stock trading information for personal gain?
a) occupational crime
b) victimless crime
c) visible crime
d) organized crime
e) political crime

1.12. What type of crime is burning a cross?
a) occupational crime
b) victimless crime
c) hate crime
d) organized crime
e) cybercrime

1.13. What is the name for crime not reported to the police?
a) subtle crime
b) victimless crime
c) invisible crime
d) silent crime
e) dark figure of crime

1.14. What is the most accurate measure of crime in America?
a) Uniform Crime Reports
b) dark figure of crime
c) National Incident-Based Reporting System
d) National Crime Victimization Survey
e) there is no accurate measure

1.15. In which of the following places in the U. S. is gambling a legal business?
a) Nevada
b) New Jersey
c) Michigan
d) Indian reservations
e) all of the above

1.16. In which of the following places in the U. S. is prostitution a legal business?
a) Nevada
b) New Jersey
c) Michigan
d) Indian reservations
e) all of the above

1.17. Which measure of crime relies upon more detailed reports of crime by police agencies?
a) FBI Statistics Data
b) dark figure of crime
c) National Incident-Based Reporting System
d) National Crime Victimization Survey
e) there is no such measure

1.18. What percentage of Americans believe that marijuana should be legal?
a) 10
b) 28
c) 50
d) 76
e) 97

1.19. Which age group commits the most crime?
a) 15 and under
b) 16-24
c) 25-34
d) 35-44
e) 45 and over

1.20. Why was there an increase in violent crime in the late 1980s and early 1990s?
a) spread of crack cocaine
b) greater use of semi-automatic handguns
c) fewer law enforcement personnel on the streets
d) a and b
e) none of the above

1.21. The homicide rate in the U. S. is _____ as large as Canada.
a) twice
b) three times
c) four times
d) five times
e) ten times

1.22. What percentage of Americans believe that homosexual relations between consenting adults should be legal?
a) 10
b) 28
c) 50
d) 76
e) 97

1.23. Which of the following is TRUE about Iceland?
a) Iceland has a very high crime
b) Iceland has a high crime rate
c) Iceland has an average rate of crime
d) Iceland has very little crime
e) Iceland has the same rate of crime as the U. S.

1.24. The rate of serious property crime in the U. S. is…
a) higher than most countries
b) about the same as most countries
c) lower than most countries
d) the U. S. does not measure property crime because it is a capitalist nation
e) the U. S. has the highest property crime rate of any country

1.25. The risk of lethal violence in the U. S. is…
a) higher than most countries
b) about the same as most countries
c) lower than most countries
d) the U. S. does not measure lethal crime
e) the U. S. has the lowest risk of lethal violence of any country

## TRUE/FALSE QUESTIONS

1.1. The news media rarely exaggerate crime in America.

1.2. Crime and justice are public policy issues because they are addressed by government.

1.3. Reiman urges criminalizing the acts of the poor and less affluent.

1.4. There have been significant decreases in every types of violent crime in the U. S. in recent years.

1.5. political leaders are not influenced by public opinion in a democracy.

1.6. Laws in the U. S. begin with the premise that only the innocent have rights, not the guilty.

1.7. The crime control model emphasizes order as a value.

1.8. The due process model emphasizes law as a value.

1.9. Megan's Law was designed to prosecute white-collar criminals.

1.10. Americans are not in agreement about which acts are criminal.

1.11. Mala prohibita are acts prohibited by government.

1.12. Mala in se are acts wrong by nature.

1.13. The U. S. has only one source of data on crime, the Uniform Crime Reports.

1.14. Law enforcement officials focus largely upon visible crime.

1.15. Edwin Sutherland developed the term, "white-collar crime."

1.16. The Iran-Contra scandal is an example of a political crime.

1.17. Iceland has very high crime rates compared to the United States.

1.18. Persons usually provide accurate information when interview about their experiences with crime.

1.19. Organized crime is associated with many different ethnic and racial groups.

1.20. Cybercrime is not a problem yet because only middle and upper-income persons have computers and they usually do not commit crimes.

# ANSWER KEY

Key Terms
1.    dark figure of crime
2.    Uniform Crime Reports
3.    visible
4.    crimes without victims
5.    mala in se
6.    National Crime Victimization Survey
7.    National Incident-Based Reporting System
8.    occupational crime
9.    political crime
10.   mala prohibita
11.   organized crime
12.   fear of crime
13.   crime
14.   due process model
15.   crime control model
16.   public policy
17.   cybercrime
18.   hate crime

Key People
1.    Herbert Packer
2.    Edwin Sutherland
3.    Jeffrey Reiman
4.    Megan Kanka
5.    John Gotti
6.    James Kopp

General Practice Questions
1.    due process model
2.    Herbert Packer
3.    mala in se
4.    mala prohibita
5.    National Incident-Based Reporting System
6.    National Crime Victimization Survey
7.    Uniform Crime Reports
8.    dark figure of crime

Multiple Choice Questions
1.1.    b
1.2.    c
1.3.    a
1.4.    d
1.5.    e
1.6.    d
1.7.    d
1.8.    b
1.9.    e
1.10.   c
1.11.   a
1.12.   c
1.13.   e
1.14.   e
1.15.   e

1.16.   a
1.17.   c
1.18.   b
1.19.   b
1.20.   d
1.21.   a
1.22.   c
1.23.   d
1.24.   c
1.25.   a

<u>True/False</u>
1.1.    F
1.2.    T
1.3.    F
1.4.    T
1.5.    F
1.6.    F
1.7.    T
1.8.    T
1.9.    F
1.10.   T
1.11.   T
1.12.   T
1.13.   F
1.14.   T
1.15.   T
1.16.   T
1.17.   F
1.18.   F
1.19.   T
1.20.   F

WORKSHEET 1.1: CONSENSUS OR NOT?

For each of the following activities, explain whether you believe the criminal law is based on a consensus in American society about which behaviors should be punishable as crimes.

Prostitution_____

_____

_____

_____

Smoking Marijuana_____

_____

_____

_____

Income Tax Evasion_____

_____

_____

_____

Copying Computer Software Without
Permission_____

_____

_____

_____

# CHAPTER 2

## VICTIMIZATION, AND CRIMINAL BEHAVIOR

### LEARNING OBJECTIVES

After covering the material in this chapter, students should understand:

1.     the existence of differences in criminal behavior patterns of men and women;

2.     the role of victims in precipitating crimes;

3.     classical and positivist theories about the causes of crime, including biological, psychological, and sociological approaches;

4.     the policy implications of the respective theories about the causes of crime.

### CHAPTER SUMMARY

Victimology surfaced in the 1950s as a field of criminology that studied the role of the victim in the criminal act. Young male residents of lower-income communities are the most likely to be victimized by crime. Because of the connection between race and social status in the United States, African Americans are more frequently victimized by crime than are whites. Most crime is intraracial. A significant percentage of crimes are committed by acquaintances and relatives of victims, especially crimes committed against women. Crime has a significant impact on all of society when one recognizes the financial and emotional costs it produces. Government agencies have begun to be more sensitive to the needs of crime victims. Thus, there are now programs in many places to provide services and compensation. Scholars have begun to study the role that victims may play in facilitating crimes. The classical school of criminology emphasized reform of the criminal law, procedures, and punishments. The rise of science led to the positivist school, which viewed behavior as stemming from social, biological, and psychological factors. Positivist criminology has dominated the study of criminal behavior in the twentieth century. The criminality of women has only recently been studied. It is argued that, as women become more equal with men in society, crimes committed by females will increase in number.

### CHAPTER OUTLINE

I.     INTRODUCTION
       During the summer of 2002, the media gave constant attention to child abduction and murder cases, but FBI statistics show that such cases have not increased but have remained steady at about 115 per year. This raises significant questions about understanding the causes of the criminal behavior by the perpetrator as well as the effects upon the victims and their families.

II.    CRIME VICTIMIZATION

A.     Who Is Victimized?
       Victimology subfield emerged in the 1950s and 1960s to focus attention on who is victimized, the impact of victimization, and role of victims in precipitating attacks.

1.    Lifestyle-exposure theory: i.e., urban poverty: Violent crime primarily is an urban phenomenon, in areas with high incidence of physical deterioration, economic insecurity, poor housing, family disintegration, and transiency.

2.    African-Americans more likely than whites to be victims; most violent crime is intraracial (i.e., offender and victim are same race. Young more likely than old to be victims. Men and low-income city dwellers more likely to be victims.

B.    The Impact of Crime

1.    Estimates of total tangible losses from crime(medical bills, lost property, work time) are put at $105 billion.  The intangible costs to victims (pain, trauma, lost quality of life) are put at $450 billion.

2.    The cost of operating the criminal justice system is over $146 billion per year to taxpayers.

3.    The foregoing costs estimates do not include consideration of the costs to consumers of organized and occupational crime.

4.    Fear as an Impact of Criminality

    a.    Fear of crime rose sharply from the 1960s until 1973 and then stabilized.

    b.    Fear of crime greatest in urban areas; stimulates movement of jobs and businesses outside of cities and limits activities of city residents, especially at night.

    c.    Women, elderly, and upper-income suburbanites more frightened than the average citizen.

    d.    Fear exceeds reality; fear may be fed by television, news media, personal communication in social networks, etc.

5.    Level of fear also affected by both likelihood of victimization and seriousness of offense. Thus in some places people are more fearful of burglary than murder since burglary is more likely to occur.

6.    Reduction in crime rates has not reduced fear of crime. News and entertainment on television and movies emphasize crime and may contribute to fear.

7.    Disorderly behavior in neighborhoods can contribute to fear of crime and lead people to curtail their normal activities.

8.    It is easier for wealthy people to take measures to protect themselves against crime.

C.    The Experience of Victims in the System

1.    Victims traditionally overlooked and forgotten; often felt interrogated and poorly treated by criminal justice officials in addition to their emotional, economic, and physical injuries.

2.    During past two decades, justice agencies have taken new interest in the treatment and welfare of crime victims.

3.    Proposed "Victim's Rights" constitutional amendment and various other state and federal enactments have placed more emphasis on victims.

4.    Programs of counseling, compensation, and assistance have been instituted.

D.    The Role of Victims in Crime

1.    Victims may voluntarily act in ways that invite crime or the opportunity for crime.

2.    Conclusions of studies:

    a.    Some citizens do not take proper precautions

    b.    People can provoke or entice criminal act

    c.    Victims in certain nonstranger crimes are unwilling to assist officials with investigation and prosecution.

III.    CAUSES OF CRIME

A.    Classical and Positivist Theories

1. The Classical School: Up through the 18th century, most Europeans saw criminal behavior in religious terms: wrongdoers were under the devil's influence.

2. Cesare Beccaria's *Essay on Crimes and Punishments* published in Italy in 1764. First, secular explanation for crime caught the attention of thinkers in Europe and North America. Beccaria argued that crime is rational behavior and that most people have the potential to engage in criminal behavior. It is fear of punishment that keeps people in check. Argued for a rational link between gravity of crime and severity of punishment: the punishment should fit the crime.

3. Classical notions remain of interest among scholars who argue that crime results from rational choices and lawbreakers weighing the risks and benefits of crime.

4. Neoclassical Criminology: In the 1980s, new interest in classical criminology emerged has some scholars argued that crimes may result from rational choices by people weighing the costs and benefits of illegal activities. These ideas have influenced sentencing reform, criticisms of rehabilitation, and greater use of incarceration.

5. Positivist Criminology: The dominant approach. New focus in nineteenth century assumed:
   a. Human behavior is controlled by physical, mental, and social factors, not by free will.
   b. Criminals are different from noncriminals.
   c. Science can be used to discover the causes of crime and to treat deviants.

6. The particular theory of crime causation accepted by society will affect the definition of laws and crime policies.

B. Biological Explanations

Cesare Lombroso claimed that criminals are born criminal and have traits that mark them as more primitive and savage than other people. Some genealogical studies have found many lawbreakers within individual family trees. Led to policies favoring sterilization of institutionalized persons.

1. Biological explanations rejected as racist following World War II, but gained renewed exposure in 1970s through sociobiology theories.

2. James Q. Wilson and Richard Herrnstein's book *Crime and Human Nature* (1985) reviewed the scholarly literature and claimed that certain "constitutional factors" such as sex, age, body type, intelligence, and personality, predispose some people to crime.

3. Research gives some support to notion that certain factors may be related to violent behavior in some people.

4. Policy implications: A policy based on biological explanations would attempt to identify people with specific traits and then treat them with drug therapy, supervision, or incapacitation.

5. Proposals calling for the chemical castration of repeat sex offenders are erroneously based on biological explanations.

C. Psychological Explanations

1. Henry Maudsley (1835-1918), English psychologist who believed that criminals were "morally insane."

2. Sigmund Freud's (1856-1939) proposed theories of early childhood experiences in the unconscious and also developed psychoanalysis, a technique for the treatment of personality disorders. Freud's personality theory said that the personality is comprised of three parts: id, ego, and superego.

3. Psychiatrists have linked criminal behavior to such concepts as innate impulses, psychic conflict, and the repression of personality.

4. Psychopathology: Related theories claimed that some people were "psychopaths," "sociopaths," or has anti-social personalities." Critics, however, have noted that it is difficult to identify and measure emotional factors in order to isolate people thought to be criminogenic.

5.      Policy Implications: Develop policies to and treat people with personality disorders

D.    <u>Sociological Explanations</u>

    1.      Sociological explanations of crime assume that the offender's personality and actions are molded by contact with the social environment and such factors as race, age, gender, and income.

    2.      Emile Durkheim believed that crime was a natural component of social life.

    3.      University of Chicago researchers in the 1920s looked closely at the ecological factors that gave rise to crime: poverty, inadequate housing, broken families, and the problems of new immigrants.

    4.      Social Structure Theory: attribute criminal behavior to the stratified nature of Western societies, giving particular prominence to the fact that classes control very different amounts of wealth, status, and power. Thus deprivations and inequality lead the lower classes to crime.

        a.      Robert Merton extended Durkheim's idea that the structure of society often permits the situation of *anomie* to develop: social conditions in which rules or norms to regulate behavior have weakened or disappeared. Deviant behavior may appear for individuals who are anomic or frustrated because they are unable to achieve their aspirations.

    5.      Policy Implications: Society should take actions to address the social conditions that breed crime by, for example, expanding education, job training, urban development, and health care.

    6.      Social Process Theory: Because criminal behavior is not limited to the poor, social process theorists believe that criminality results from the interactions of people with the institutions, organizations, and processes of society. Thus everyone has the possibility of being a criminal, regardless of social status or education. There are subgroups of social process theories:

        a.      Learning theories: Criminal activity is normal learned behavior with family and peers as primary influences. Differential association theory, for example, states that criminal behavior is learned through interactions with other persons, especially family members and other close associates.

        b.      Control theories: All members of society have the potential to commit crimes, but most people are restrained by their ties to such conventional institutions and individuals as family, church, school, and peer groups. Criminality results when these primary bonds are weakened and the person no longer follows the expected norms for behavior.

        c.      Labeling theories: By breaking rules, certain individuals come to be labeled as deviant by society. The stigmatized individuals then come to believe that the label is true and they assume a criminal identity and career. By arguing, in effect, that the criminal justice system creates criminals by labeling individuals as such, this approach advocates the decriminalization of certain offenses to avoid needlessly placing labels on people.

    7.      Policy Implications: If crime is learned behavior, then people must be treated in ways that build conventional bonds, develop positive role models, and avoid labeling. Thus there should be policies to promote stable families and develop community agencies to assist those in need.

    8.      Social Conflict Theory: Argues that criminal law and criminal justice are mainly the means of controlling society's poor and have-nots. The rich commit crimes but are much less likely to be punished.

        a.      Critical, radical, or Marxist criminologists argue that the class structure of society results in certain powerless groups in society being labeled as deviant. When the status quo is threatened, criminal laws are altered to label and punish threatening groups and deviant criminals.

9.    Policy Implications: Develop policies to reduce class-based conflict and injustice. Give equal enforcement attention and punishment to crimes committed by upper-class offenders.

E.    Women and Crime
1.    Most theories about the causes of crime are based almost entirely on observations of males. Except with respect to prostitution and shoplifting, little crime research focused on women prior to the 1970s. It was assumed that women did not commit serious crimes because of their nurturing, dependent nature. Women offenders were viewed as moral offenders: "fallen women."
2.    Freda Adler's work stressed the role of the women's movement in changing women's roles and making their criminal behavior more similar in the 1970s and thereafter.
3.    Rita Simon emphasized greater freedom and opportunities in the job market as the source of changes in women's criminality
4.    Research shows that the number of women being arrested seems to be growing faster than the growth of men in crime. However, the number of women arrested is still relatively small.
5.    Some researchers believe that women will become more involved in economic and occupational crimes as more women pursue careers in business and industry.
6.    In general, like male offenders, women arrested for crimes tend to come from poor families in which physical and substance abuse are present.

F.    Assessing Theories of Criminality
All of the theories focus on the visible crimes of the poor, but pay less attention to organized crime and white-collar crimes. Theorists have also paid primary attention to criminality by males. There is a need for a theory that can help integrate various explanations that seem to apply to certain kinds of crimes or offenders.


**REVIEW OF KEY TERMS**

Fill in the appropriate term for each statement

sociological explanations
differential association
victimology
classical criminology
positivist criminology
biological explanations
psychological explanations
social structure theories
anomie
social process theories
learning theories
control theories
labeling theories
social conflict theories
criminogenic factors


1. _____ assert that crime is normal behavior which may be undertaken by anyone depending on the social forces and groups that influence their behavior.

2. _____ asserts that criminal behavior stems from free will, and therefore the system should demand accountability from offenders through deterrence-oriented punishments.

3. _____ assert that certain individuals are treated as criminals by the system, and thus these individuals receive a message from the system that leads them to act as lawbreakers.

4. _____ assert that criminal law and the criminal justice system are primarily means of controlling the poor.

5. _____ is a state of normlessness caused by a breakdown in the rules of social behavior.

6. _____ assert that is crime learned behavior.

7. _____ assert that criminal behavior is caused by physiological and neurological factors.

8. _____ assert that crime is the creation of a lower-class culture as poor people respond to poverty and deprivation.

9. _____ assert that criminal behavior results when the bonds that tie an individual to others in society are broken.

10. _____ includes the study of how victims may precipitate crimes.

11. _____ asserts that criminal behavior stems from social, biological, and psychological factors.

12. _____ are influences that are thought to bring about criminal behavior in an individual.

13. _____ assert that mental processes and associated behaviors are the cause of criminal behavior.

14. _____ assert that people become criminals when they identify with family members and individuals who regard criminal activity as normal and usual.

15. _____ assert that social conditions that bear on the individual are the causes of crime.


## REVIEW OF KEY PEOPLE

Edwin Sutherland
Cesare Lombroso
Cesare Beccaria
Sigmund Freud
Robert Merton
James Q. Wilson & Richard Hernnstein

1. _____ : associated with the theory that criminality is biologically determined.

2. _____ : wrote book examining research on links between biological factors and criminal behavior.

3. _____ : associated with social structure theories of criminality and the idea that anomie within society influences criminal behavior.

4. _____ : developed theory that behavior can be caused by mental activity that takes place outside of our conscious awareness

5. _____ : developed the concept of "white collar crime" and led criminal justice scholars away from an exclusive focus on criminal behavior by lower class people. Also developed differential association theory.

6. _____ : regarded as the originator of classical criminology.

## GENERAL PRACTICE QUESTIONS

____1____ established the groundwork for ____2____ by arguing that people choose to commit crimes and that fear of punishment keeps people in check.

With the development of ____3____, science-based theories emerged about the causes of criminal behavior, including ____4____ drawing from ____5____'s assertions about the influence of mental processes over behavior.

Among the ____6____, ____7____ posits that criminals identify and emulate people who view crime as normal, acceptable activity and ____8____ asserts that criminal behavior stems from the deterioration of ties between an individual and conventional institutions and people that support and reinforce society's rules and values.

# SELF-TEST SECTION

## MULTIPLE CHOICE QUESTIONS

2.1. The field of victimology emerged in the...
a) 1950s
b) 1960s
c) 1970s
d) 1980s
e) 1990s

2.2. Which of the following is TRUE about crime and race?
a) most violent crimes are interracial but property crimes are intraracial
b) most property crimes are interracial but violent crimes are intraracial
c) both property and violent crimes are mostly intraracial
d) both property and violent crimes are most interracial
e) race is not a factor in property or violent crimes

2.3. Which of the following is TRUE about victims and their offenders?
a) most victims and offenders are of a different race and social class
b) most victims and offenders are of a different race but the same social class
c) most victims and offenders are of the same race but different social class
d) most victims and offenders are of the same race and social class
e) all of the above are FALSE

2.4. Which of the following is a consequence of crime?
a) higher taxes
b) higher prices
c) increased levels of fear in society
d) all of the above
e) none of the above

2.5. Which of the following is TRUE about victims?
a) victims are most often elderly women
b) the criminal justice system in the U. S. focuses more on the victim than the offender
c) victims are a key source of evidence in a criminal investigation
d) victims are protected by a Victims Bill of Rights in the U. S Constitution
e) all of the above are TRUE

2.6. Which of the following is FALSE about victims?
a) most victims of crime are young males who are nonwhite
b) many victims behave in ways that invite crime
c) victims of crimes of nonstrangers are more willing to help in the investigation
d) all of the above are TRUE
e) all of the above are FALSE

2.7. Which of the follow is an example of a person who is criminogenic?
a) person becomes a criminal because of a dysfunctional childhood
b) person becomes a criminal because of poverty
c) person becomes a criminal because of a personality disturbance
d) person becomes a criminal because of huge jaws
e) all of the above

2.8. Which twentieth century thinker proposed a psychoanalytic theory of criminal behavior?
a) Cesare Lombroso
b) Cesare Beccaria
c) Sigmund Freud
d) Henry Goddard
e) Ada Jukes

2.9. Which of the following is TRUE concerning social process theory?
a) the poor are the only people who commit crimes
b) criminal behavior is abnormal behavior
c) people commit crimes because of the circumstances in their lives
d) social process theory gained recognition in the nineteenth century
e) all of the above are TRUE

2.10. Which of the following is TRUE concerning social structure theory?
a) the poor are the only people who commit crimes
b) criminal behavior is inborn
c) people commit crimes because of their physical traits
d) social structure theory is associated with social class
e) all of the above are TRUE

2.11. Which of the following is TRUE concerning social conflict theory?
a) the poor are the only people who commit crimes
b) criminal behavior is abnormal behavior
c) people commit crimes because of personality disorders
d) one type of social conflict theory is Marxism
e) all of the above are TRUE

2.12. Which of the following is TRUE about women and crime?
a) there has been more research about women as opposed to men
b) women commit the same types of crime as men
c) the number of crimes committed by women has increased recently
d) women account for one-half of all arrests
e) all of the above are TRUE

2.13. Which of the following is TRUE about theories of criminality?
a) they focus on both the rich and the poor
b) they focus on visible and less visible crimes
c) some theories can predict criminality
d) they overemphasize the role of women
e) all of the theories contain a bit of truth

2.14. Which of the following is an example of the problems faced by victims?
a) emotional stress
b) missed work
c) defense attorneys may attempt to question their credibility
d) all of the above
e) none of the above

2.15. Which of the following is TRUE about crime?
a) the fear of crime is low compared to the reality of crime
b) the fear of crime is high compared to the reality of crime
c) the fear of crime is about right when compared to the reality of crime
d) there has been no research on the fear of crime in relation to the reality of crime
e) the media plays an insignificant role in regard to the public's fear of crime

2.16. Which of the following is most likely to be victimized?
a) elderly person watching television at home alone
b) white female shopping during the day
c) young black male at a nightclub
d) all of the above are likely to be victimized
e) none of the above are likely to be victimized

2.17. Which of the following is TRUE about the impact of crime?
a) the costs are mainly economic
b) the costs are mainly psychological
c) the costs are mainly to the operation of the criminal justice system
d) all of the above are costs
e) none of the above are costs

2.18. Which of the following are psychological or emotional costs of crime?
a) cost of medical care
b) lost property
c) lost quality of life
d) all of the above
e) none of the above

2.19. Which of the following are economic costs of crime?
a) cost of medical care
b) pain
c) lost quality of life
d) trauma
e) all of the above

2.20. Which of the following links criminal behavior to innate impulses, psychic conflict, and repressed personalities?
a) biological theories
b) psychological theories
c) sociological theories
d) legal theories
e) conflict theories

2.21. Which of the following links criminal behavior to heredity?
a) biological theories
b) psychological theories
c) sociological theories
d) legal theories
e) conflict theories

2.22. From 1972 to 1993, what percent of respondents indicated that fear of crime limited their freedom?
a) 10
b) 25
c) 40
d) 75
e) 90

2.23. Who argues that as women and men become more equal than the gender differences in criminal behavior will decrease?
a) Rita Simon
b) Sigmund Freud
c) Freda Adler
d) Robert Merton
e) Henry Maudsley

2.24. Who argues that gender differences in criminal behavior will decrease as women gain more freedom and become less dependent on men?
a) Rita Simon
b) Sigmund Freud
c) Freda Adler
d) Robert Merton
e) Henry Maudsley

2.25. What U. S. Supreme Court decision declared sterilization unconstitutional as a form of criminal punishment?
a) Freud v. Adler (1945)
b) Lombroso v. Beccaria (1867)
c) Skinner v. Oklahoma (1942)
d) Vacco v. Quill (1997)
e) Durkheim v. Chicago (1920)

## TRUE/FALSE QUESTIONS

2.1. Women commit less crime than men.

2.2. There is general agreement within among criminologists that biological explanations of criminal behavior are the best.

2.3. An elderly women who is wealthy has a greater risk of becoming a victim of crime.

2.4. Crime does not impose any costs on the operation of the criminal justice system.

2.5. There is not a field of criminology that studies the role of victims.

2.6. Most people experience crime indirectly

2.7. The "Crime Victims' Bill of Rights" was ratified in April 2002 as the 28th Amendment to the U. S. Constitution .

2.8. The criminal justice system focuses upon finding and prosecuting the offender.

2.9. People cannot take precautions to protect themselves against criminals.

2.10. Classical criminology portrays crime as rational.

2.11. Classical criminologists argue that laws and punishments should be hidden from the public.

2.12. Learning theory is a biological explanation for criminal behavior.

2.13. Sigmund Freud is most often associated with psychological explanations for criminal behavior.

2.14. Residents in small towns and rural areas are more afraid to walk the streets than those residents in large cities.

2.15. Positivist criminologists argue that criminals are different from noncriminals.

2.16. According to a Seattle study, residential burglary is the most feared crime.

2.17. Theories about the causes of crime do affect how crimes are punished.

2.18. Theories about the causes of crime do affect how guilt or innocence is determined.

2.19. The persons most likely to be victimized by crime are whites and people with high-incomes.

2.20. Demographic factors (age gender, and income) affect lifestyle which, in turn, affects people's exposure to dangerous places.

# ANSWER KEY

Key Terms
1.  social process theories
2.  classical criminology
3.  labeling theories
4.   social conflict theories
5.  anomie
6.  learning theories
7.  biological explanations
8.  social structure theories
9.  control theories
10. victimology
11. positivist criminology
12. criminogenic factors
13. psychological explanations
14. differential association theories
15. sociological explanations

Key People
1.  Cesare Lombroso
2.  James Q. Wilson & Richard Hernnstein
3.  Robert Merton
4.  Sigmund Freud
5.  Edwin Sutherland
6.  Cesare Beccaria

General Practice Questions
1.  Cesare Beccaria
2.  classical criminology
3.  positivist criminology
4.  psychological explanations
5.  Sigmund Freud
6.  social process theories
7.  differential association theory
8.  control theory

Multiple Choice
2.1.    a
2.2.    c
2.3.    d
2.4.    d
2.5.    c
2.6.    c
2.7.    d
2.8.    c
2.9.    c
2.10.   d
2.11.   d
2.12.   c
2.13.   e
2.14.   d
2.15.   b
2.16.   c

2.17.    d
2.18.    c
2.19.    a
2.20.    b
2.21.    a
2.22.    c
2.23.    c
2.24.    a
2.25.    c

True/False
2.1.    T
2.2.    F
2.3.    F
2.4.    F
2.5.    F
2.6.    T
2.7.    F
2.8.    T
2.9.    F
2.10.    T
2.11.    F
2.12.    F
2.13.    T
2.14.    F
2.15.    T
2.16.    T
2.17.    T
2.18.    T
2.19.    F
2.20.    T

WORKSHEET 2.1: THEORIES ABOUT THE CAUSES OF CRIME

On his way home from school, a fourteen-year-old boy from a poor family stops at a convenience store. When he thinks the clerk is not looking, he puts a bottle of orange juice under his coat and heads for the door. The clerk catches him and calls the police. How might one explain the boy's criminal action according to each of the following theories about causes of crime?

Biological Explanations _____

_____

_____

_____

_____


Psychological Explanations _____

_____

_____

_____

_____


Social Structure Theory _____

_____

_____

_____

_____


Social Process Theory _____

_____

_____

_____

_____

WORKSHEET 2.2: MULTIDISCIPLINARY PERSPECTIVE

Discuss how the following persons have contributed to the study of criminal behavior:

Emile Durkheim_____

_____

_____

_____

_____

Robert Merton_____

_____

_____

_____

_____

Cesare Lombroso_____

_____

_____

_____

_____

Cesare Beccaria_____

_____

_____

_____

_____

Freda Adler _____

_____

_____

_____

Rita Simon _____

_____

_____

_____

_____

# CHAPTER 3

## THE CRIMINAL JUSTICE SYSTEM

### LEARNING OBJECTIVES

After covering the material in this chapter, students should understand:

1.   the goals of criminal justice include doing justice, controlling crime, and preventing crime;

2.   the existence, organization, and jurisdiction of national and state criminal justice systems, including the dual court system;

3.   criminal justice as a "system," with specific characteristics: discretion, resource dependence, sequential tasks, and filtering;

4.   the primary agencies of criminal justice, and the prevalence of local agencies and institutions;

5.   the flow of decision making in the criminal justice system, including the thirteen steps in the decision making process;

6.   the criminal justice wedding cake.

7.   crime and justice in a multicultural society

### CHAPTER SUMMARY

The three goals of criminal justice are doing justice, controlling crime, and preventing crime. The dual court system contains a national system and state systems of criminal justice that enforce laws, try cases, and punish offenders. Criminal justice is a system made up of a number of parts or subsystems--police, courts, corrections. Exchange is a key concept for the analysis of criminal justice processes. The four major characteristics of the criminal justice system are discretion, resource dependence, sequential tasks, and filtering. The processing of cases in the criminal justice system involves a series of decisions by police officers, prosecutors, judges, probation officers, wardens, and parole board members. The criminal justice system consists of thirteen steps that cover the stages of law enforcement, adjudication, and corrections. The four-layered criminal justice wedding cake model indicates that not all cases are treated equally. The existence of unequal treatment of people within the criminal justice system would clash with the American values of equality, fairness, and due process. Racial disparities in criminal justice are explained in one of three ways: minorities commit more crimes; the criminal justice system is racist; the criminal justice system expresses the racism of society.

### CHAPTER OUTLINE

#### I. INTRODUCTION
On November 3, 2000, Gregory McKnight allegedly kidnapped Emily Murray, a Kenyon College student. McKnight allegedly shot her to death and her body was found six weeks later. As McKnight's case moved through the various stages of the criminal justice system, the trial judge ruled that the county prosecutor could not seek the death penalty against McKnight because a capital punishment trial would be too expensive. Unfortunately, this illustrates how the processes used by the American system of criminal justice cannot guarantee that a convicted person will receive the most severe possible punishment.

II.     THE GOALS OF CRIMINAL JUSTICE

A.     Goals for the System
1.     In 1967, the President's Commission on Law Enforcement and Administration of Justice described the criminal justice system as an apparatus society uses to "enforce the standards of conduct necessary to protect individuals and the community." Underneath this statement are three underlying goals:

B.     Doing Justice
1.     Without a system founded on *justice* there would be little difference between criminal justice in the United States and that in authoritarian countries. Elements of the goal:
    a.     Offenders will be held fully accountable for their actions.
    b.     The rights of persons who have contact with the system will be protected.
    c.     Like offenses will be treated alike.
    d.     Officials will take into account relevant differences among offenders and offenses.

C.     Controlling Crime
1.     The criminal justice system is designed to control crime by apprehending, prosecuting, convicting, and punishing those members of the community who do not live according to the law.
2.     Constraint on the goal: Efforts to control crime must be carried out within the framework of law.

D.     Preventing Crime
1.     The deterrent effect of the doing justice and crime control goals. Punishing those individuals who violate the law provides examples that are likely to deter others from committing wrongful acts.
2.     The actions of citizens in taking simple precautions. Unfortunately many people leave homes and cars unlocked, and take other actions that facilitate crime.
3.     Question of Ethics: Has a storeowner who has repeatedly been victimized by burglaries gone too far when he creates a booby-trap that electrocutes a burglar?

E.     Value Conflicts
1.     Decisions must be made that reflect legal, social, political, and moral values. There are possible conflicts among these values and there are implications from choosing one value over another.

III.     CRIMINAL JUSTICE IN A FEDERAL SYSTEM

A.     U.S. Constitution
1.     The U.S. Constitution gives the federal government specific powers over taxation, commerce, and national defense. Although it does not specifically discuss criminal justice institutions, there are federal law enforcement agencies and other aspects of national government involved in crime policy and the administration of justice.

B.     Two Justice Systems
1.     Criminal laws are written and enforced primarily by agencies of the states (including counties and municipalities), yet the rights of defendants are protected by the constitutions of both state and national governments.
2.     Although the large majority of criminal cases are heard in state courts, certain offenses (e.g., drug violations and transportation of a kidnap victim across state lines) are violations of *both* state and federal laws.

3.    Example: when President Kennedy was assassinated in 1963, Lee Harvey Oswald was prosecuted for violating Texas law because Congress had not yet made it a federal offense to kill the President.

C.    Expansion of Federal Involvement
1.    Congress has expanded the powers of the FBI and other federal agencies. Now the federal government pursues organized crime gangs dealing with drugs, pornography, and gambling on a national basis
2.    The FBI also has authority to help local police in certain situations, such as stolen property that may have been transported across state lines.
3.    Disputes over jurisdiction may occur so federal and state officials need cooperation.
4.    The existence of multiple criminal justice systems makes criminal justice in the United States highly decentralized.

IV.    CRIMINAL JUSTICE AS A SYSTEM

A.    The System Perspective
1.    The concept of system helps us to recognize that the agencies and processes of criminal justice are linked. One result is that the actions of the police, for example, have an impact on the other parts of the system prosecution, courts, and corrections.
2.    One key concept is *exchange*, meaning the mutual transfer of resources among individual actors, each of whom has goals that he or she cannot accomplish alone.
    a.    Plea bargaining is an obvious example of exchange.
    b.    The prosecutor and defense attorney reach agreement on the plea and sentence. Each actor, including the defendant and the judge, gains a benefit as a result.
    c.    The concept of exchange reminds us that decisions are the products of interactions among individuals in the system and that the subsystems of criminal justice are linked together by the actions of individual decision makers.

B.    Characteristics of the Criminal Justice System
1.    Discretion: At all levels of the justice process officials have significant ability to act according to their own judgment and conscience.
    a.    Police officers, prosecutors, judges, and correctional officials may consider a wide variety of circumstances and exercise many options as they dispose of a case.
    b.    The need for discretionary power has been justified primarily on two counts:
        i.    Resources: If every violation of the law were to be formally processed, the costs would be staggering.
        ii.    Justice: Criminal justice practitioners believe that in many cases justice can be more fully achieved through informal procedures. For example, a judge may believe that justice is better served if a sex offender is sent to a mental hospital rather than to prison.
2.    Resource Dependence: Criminal justice does not produce its own resources but is dependent on others for them. It must therefore develop special links with people responsible for the allocation of resources--that is, the political decision makers.
    a.    Criminal justice actors must be responsive to the legislators, mayors, and city council members who hold the power of the purse. Justice officials seek to maintain a positive image in news reports and seek to keep voters happy.
2.    Sequential Tasks: Every part of the criminal justice system has distinct tasks that are carried out sequentially.
    a.    Because a high degree of interdependence characterizes the system, the actions of one part of the system directly affect the work of the others.

     b.  The courts can deal only with the cases brought to them by the prosecutor, who can deal only with persons arrested by the police.

   4.  <u>Filtering</u>: The criminal justice process may be viewed as a filtering process through which cases are screened: some are advanced to the next level of decision making, and others are either rejected or the conditions under which they are processed are changed.

     a.  Persons who have been arrested may be filtered out of the system at various points; very few of the suspects arrested are prosecuted, tried, and convicted.

     b.  At each stage in the process decisions are made by officials as to which cases will proceed to the next level.

     c.  The "funnel like" nature of the criminal justice system results in many cases entering at the top but only a few making it all the way to conviction and punishment.

## V.  OPERATIONS OF CRIMINAL JUSTICE AGENCIES

 A.  <u>Criminal Justice Subsystems</u>

   1.  The subsystems encompassing the police, prosecution and defense, courts, and corrections consist of over 60,000 public and private agencies that utilize an annual budget of over $146 billion, and a staff of more than 2 million people.

 B.  <u>Police</u>

   1.  Complexity and fragmentation characterize the number and jurisdiction of the 18,769 public organizations in the United States engaged in law enforcement activities.

   2.  Only fifty are federal law enforcement agencies; the rest are state and local.

   3.  The responsibilities of police organizations fall into four categories:

     a.  Keeping the peace: The protection of rights and persons in a wide variety of situations, ranging from street-corner brawls to domestic quarrels.

     b.  Apprehending law violators and fighting crime: This responsibility actually accounts for only a small proportion of law enforcement agencies' time and resources.

     c.  Engaging in crime prevention: Educating the public about the threat of crime and by reducing the number of situations in which crimes are most likely to be committed.

     d.  Providing a variety of social services: Recover stolen property, direct traffic, provide emergency medical aid, get cats out of trees, help people who have locked themselves out of their apartments, etc.

 C.  <u>Courts</u>

   1.  Dual court system: Separate judicial structure for each state in addition to a national structure.

   2.  Interpretation of the law can vary from state to state. Judges have discretion to apply the law as they feel it should be applied until they are overruled by a higher court.

   3.  Courts are responsible for adjudication--determining if defendants are guilty according to fair procedures.

 D.  <u>Corrections</u>

   1.  On any given day about 6 million Americans are under the supervision of the corrections system.

   2.  Only about a third of convicted offenders are actually incarcerated; the remainder are under supervision in the community through probation, parole, community-based halfway houses, work release programs, and supervised activities.

   3.  The federal government, all the states, most counties, and all but the smallest cities are engaged in the corrections enterprise.

4. Increasingly, nonprofit private organizations such as the YMCA have contracted with governments to perform correctional services.

5. For-profit businesses have undertaken the construction and administration of institutions through contracts with governments.

VI. THE FLOW OF DECISION MAKING IN THE SYSTEM

A. Discretionary Decisions

1. The disposition of cases in the criminal justice system involves a series of decisions made by police officers, prosecutors, judges, probation officers, wardens, and other officials who decide whether a case will move on to the next point or be dropped from the system.

B. Steps in the Decision Making Process
Remember that the formal procedures outlined may not always depict reality. The system looks like an assembly line as decisions are made about defendants. The process is shaped by the concepts of system, discretion, sequential tasks, filtering, and exchange.

1. Investigation: Police are normally dependent on a member of the community to report the offense.

2. Arrest: Taking a person into custody when police determine there is enough evidence indicating a particular person has committed a crime.

  a. Under some conditions, arrests may be made on the basis of a warrant; an order issued by a judge who has received information pointing toward a particular person as the offender.

  b. In some states, police officers may issue a summons or citation that orders a person to appear in court on a particular date, thus eliminating the need to hold the suspect physically until case disposition.

3. Booking: Procedure by which an administrative record is made of the arrest; a suspect may be fingerprinted, photographed, interrogated, and placed in a lineup for identification by the victim or witnesses. Bail may be set.

  a. All suspects must be warned that they have the right to counsel, that they may remain silent, and that any statement they make may later be used against them.

4. Charging: Prosecuting attorneys determine whether there is reasonable cause to believe that an offense was committed and whether the suspect committed it.

5. Initial Appearance: Suspects must be brought before a judge to be given formal notice of the charge for which they are being held, to be advised of their rights, and to be given the opportunity to post bail. The judge determines if there is sufficient evidence to hold the suspect for further criminal processing.

  a. The purpose of bail is to permit the accused to be released while awaiting trial. To ensure that the person will be in court at the appointed time, surety (or pledge), usually in the form of money or a bond, is required.

  b. The amount of bail is usually based primarily on the judge's perception of the seriousness of the crime and the defendant's record.

  c. For minor crimes, suspects may also be released on their own recognizance--a promise to appear in court at a later date.

  d. Some suspects may be kept in custody if they are viewed as a threat to the community.

6. Preliminary Hearing/Grand Jury

  a. The preliminary hearing, used in about half the states, allows a judge to determine whether probable cause exists to believe that the accused committed a known crime within the jurisdiction of the court. The case against the defendant may be dismissed or the accused is bound over for arraignment on an information.

  b. In federal system and other states, the prosecutor appears before a grand jury composed of citizens who decide if there is enough evidence to allow the prosecutor to file an indictment.

   c. The preliminary hearing and grand jury deliberations are designed to prevent hasty and malicious prosecutions, to protect persons from mistakenly being humiliated in public, and to discover if there are substantial grounds upon which a prosecution may be based.

  7. Indictment/Information: The prosecutor prepares the formal charging document and enters it before the court.

  8. Arraignment: The accused person is next taken before a judge to hear the indictment or information read and is asked to enter a plea. The judge must determine if a guilty plea is made voluntarily and whether the person has full knowledge of the possible consequences of the plea.

  9. Trial: For the relatively small percentage of defendants who plead not guilty, the right to a. trial by an impartial jury is guaranteed by the Sixth Amendment for defendants facing charges which carry six months or more of imprisonment.

   a. Most trials are summary or bench trials conducted by a judge without a jury.

   b. It is estimated that only about 10-15 percent of cases go to trial and only about 5 percent are heard by juries.

  10. Sentencing: The judge's intent is to make the sentence suitable to the particular offender within the requirements of the law and in accordance with the retribution (punishment) and rehabilitation goals of the system.

  11. Appeal: Defendants found guilty may appeal their convictions to a higher court based on claims that the rules of procedure were not properly followed or that the law forbidding the behavior is unconstitutional. Defendants lose about 80 percent of appeals. A successful appeal typically leads to a new trial rather than release.

  12. Corrections: Probation, intermediate sanctions, incarceration are the sanctions most generally impose and supervised by the corrections subsystem.

   a. Probation allows convicted offenders to serve their sentences in the community under supervision. Violations of probation conditions can lead to imprisonment.

   b. Intermediate sanctions include intensive probation supervision, boot camp, home confinement, and community service.

   c. Incarceration: Offenders convicted of misdemeanors usually serve their time in city or county jails, while felons serve their time in state prisons.

  13. Release: Release may be accomplished through serving the full sentence imposed by the court or by returning to the community under supervision of a parole officer with restrictive conditions.

  14. Close Up: The Christopher Jones Case
    Illustrating the stages of the process in an actual criminal case.

 C. The Criminal Justice Wedding Cake

  1. The key concept for differentiating cases according to the way in which criminal justice officials and the public react to it.

  2. Layer 1: Very few "celebrated" cases that are exceptional, get great public attention, result in a jury trial, and often have extended appeals.

  3. Layer 2: Felonies that are deemed to be serious by officials, e.g., crimes of violence committed by persons with long criminal records against victims unknown to them.

  4. Layer 3: Felonies by offenders who are seen as of lesser concern than those in Layer 2; many cases are filtered out of the system, and plea bargaining is encouraged.

  5. Layer 4: Misdemeanors encompassing 90 percent of all cases handled in the criminal justice system; processes are speedy and informal, and fines, probation, or short jail sentences result. Assembly-line justice reigns.

VII. CRIME AND JUSTICE IN A MULTI-CULTURAL SOCIETY

A.     African-Americans, Hispanics, and other minorities are drawn into the criminal justice system at much higher rates than the white majority.
1.     African-Americans account for 1/3 of arrests and 1/2 of incarcerations.
2.     Since 1980, the proportion of Hispanic-Americans among all inmates in U.S. prisons has risen from 7.7 percent to 16 percent.
3.     About 1/3 of all African-American males in their twenties are under criminal justice supervision.
4.     The crime victimization rate is 260 per 1,000 Hispanic households versus 144 per 1,000 non-Hispanic households.

B.     Disparity is a difference between groups that can be explained by legitimate factors. But discrimination occurs when people are treated differently without regard to their behavior or qualifications.

C.     Three frequent explanations for racial disparities.
1.     Theory 1: African-Americans and Hispanics Commit More Crimes.
    a.     However, there is no evidence of an ethnic link to criminal behavior. Criminal behavior is evident among all groups.
    b.     There is a link between crime and economic disadvantages which disproportionately affect these minority groups. Unemployment rates are higher and average family income is lower among these minority groups.
    c.     Because most crime is intraracial rather than interracial, minority group members in poor neighborhoods also suffer from more significant victimization rates.
    d.     African-Americans and Hispanics are arrested more often and for more serious crimes on average than whites. Analysts question whether crime control efforts should shift to an emphasis on reducing social problems that may contribute to crime.
2.     Theory 2: The Criminal Justice System Is Racist
    a.     Research indicates that people of color are arrested more often for drug offenses even though they do not engage in drug use more often than whites. Also, unfounded arrests of African-Americans occur at four times the rate of unfounded arrests of whites.
    b.     The rate of incarceration for poor and minority citizens is greater than even their higher offense rates would justify.
    c.     Disparities need not be the result of overt racism. For example, if police patrols concentrate on poor neighborhoods, more arrests will be made there than elsewhere.
    d.     Poor people are less likely to make bail or hire their own attorneys, two factors that may contribute to a higher imprisonment rate.
3.     Theory 3: America Is A Racist Society.
    a.     There is some evidence of racism in the way that society asks the criminal justice system to operate. For example, federal sentencing guidelines punish users of crack cocaine about one hundred times more harshly than users of powder cocaine, even though the drugs are nearly identical. The only difference is that whites tend to use the powder form while people of color tend to use crack
    b.     Sentencing studies find a stronger link between unemployment and sentencing than between crime rates and sentencing. This suggests that prisons are being used to confine people who cannot find jobs.
    c.     Drug law enforcement is aimed primarily at low-level dealers in minority neighborhoods.

d.    Numerous examples of African-American and Hispanic professionals who have been falsely arrested when police saw a person of color whom they believed was "out of place."

## REVIEW OF KEY TERMS

Fill in the appropriate term for each statement:

crime
political considerations
system
booking
exchange
plea bargain
discretion
filtering process
dual court system
adjudication
arrest
warrant
information
indictment
felony
misdemeanor
Crime Control Model
preliminary hearing
Due Process Model
"wedding cake"
resource dependence
grand jury
arraignment
decentralization
bail
doing justice
controlling crime
preventing crime
U.S. Constitution
federal law enforcement agencies
Congress
bench trial
jury trial
sequential tasks

1. _____ is the authority to make decisions by using one's own judgment and conscience which provides the basis for individualization and informality in the administration of justice.

2. _____ is a primary goal of criminal justice that provides the basis for distinguishing the American system from those of authoritarian countries.

3. _____ is an adjudication process presided over by a judge that handles most criminal cases in which there is no successful plea bargain.

4. _____ is a document charging an individual with a specific crime prepared by a prosecuting attorney and presented to a court at a preliminary hearing.

5. _____ is a characteristic of the criminal justice system that leads criminal justice officials to be responsive to elected officials and legislative bodies.

6. _____ consists of separate judicial structures for states and for the national government.

7. _____ is intended to permit the release of defendants pending the processing of their cases if they do not pose a threat to the community.

8. _____ is the physical taking of a person into custody on the ground that there is probable cause to believe that he or she has committed a criminal offense.

9. _____ possess the authority to investigate and apprehend suspects for crimes that are related to powers granted by the U.S. Constitution to Congress.

10. _____ is a complex whole consisting of interdependent parts whose operations are directed toward goals and are influenced by the environment within which they function.

11. _____ is a characteristic of the organization of law enforcement and other criminal justice agencies in the United States.

12. _____ is a characteristic of the criminal justice system that describes how one subsystem must complete its responsibilities before a case is passed to the authority of another subsystem.

13. _____ is a specific act of commission or omission in violation of the law, for which a punishment is prescribed

14. _____ is the system characteristic through which some cases are moved out of the criminal justice system and others are pushed ahead to later stages in the system.

15. _____ is a primary goal of criminal justice that involves apprehending, prosecuting, and punishing those who violate criminal laws.

16. _____ is the stage in the criminal justice process in which formal charges are read and the defendant enters a plea.

17. _____ is the institution that enacts criminal laws for the federal government.

18. _____ is a stage in the criminal justice process in which defendants are normally photographed and fingerprinted.

19. _____ is an adjudication process in which a group of citizens determine the guilt or innocence of a criminal defendant.

20. _____ depicts the cases within the criminal justice system as having specific characteristics that lead various categories of cases to be processed in different ways.

21. _____ is a court order authorizing law enforcement officials to take certain actions, for example, to arrest suspects or to search premises.

22. _____ is a stage in the criminal justice process in which a judge determines whether or not there is sufficient evidence for a case to move forward for prosecution.

23. _____ depicts the criminal justice system as emphasizing reliable decisions that protect individuals' liberty through an adversarial process based on law.

24. _____ is a primary goal of criminal justice that relies on citizens to take precautions in their daily lives.

25. _____ is the fundamental basis for the American governing system that provides the general outlines for the structure of the government and specifies the rights possessed by individuals.

26. _____ is a collection of citizens responsible for hearing evidence concerning the likelihood that a crime was committed and a specific individual committed the crime in order to return an indictment that will permit a prosecution to move forward.

27. _____ are matters taken into account in the formulation of public policies and in making choices among competing values.

28. _____ are serious crimes carrying penalties of one year or more imprisonment.

29. _____ is the process of determining whether or not a defendant is guilty.

30. _____ is a mutual transfer of resources or information that underlies the motivations and decisions of actors within the criminal justice system.

31. _____ is a document returned by a grand jury as a "true bill" charging an individual with a specific crime.

32. _____ provides the basis for establishing guilt and setting punishments in the majority of cases in the criminal justice system.

33. _____ are less serious offenses carrying penalties of no more than one year of incarceration.

34. _____ depicts the criminal justice system as one that emphasizes efficient repression of crime through the exercise of discretion in administrative processing of cases.

## REVIEW OF KEY PEOPLE

Timothy McVeigh
O. J. Simpson
Lee Harvey Oswald
Christopher Jones
Michael Kennedy

1. In 1997 reports surfaced indicating that the late _____, then a thirty nine year old lawyer and nephew of the late President John F. Kennedy, had carried on an affair with his children's 14 year old baby sitter.
2. Because Congress had not made killing the president a federal offense in 1963, the suspected assassin of John Kennedy, _____, would have been charged under Texas laws had he lived.
3. _____, a thirty-one-old man from Battle Creek, Michigan, was arrested, charged, and convicted of serious crimes arising from the police investigation of a series of robberies.
4. The case of Oklahoma City bomber _____ and the celebrated trial of football legend _____ on double murder charges are layer one cases in the criminal justice wedding cake.

## GENERAL PRACTICE QUESTIONS

One example of the way in which ____1____ affect the development of criminal justice policies is the power of elected officials serving in ____2____ to enact criminal laws and allocate budgetary resources for criminal justice agencies on behalf of the federal government.

Prosecutors exercise ____3____ in making decisions about which cases will leave the criminal justice system through the ____4____ and which cases will be discussed with criminal defense attorneys in the ____5____ process that obtains convictions without taking cases to trial.

In states that do not initiate formal charges by having a prosecutor file an ____6____, a group of citizens, known as the ____7____, decides whether or not there is sufficient evidence to pursue a case. If they find the existence of sufficient evidence, they issue an ____8____.

Among the primary goals of criminal justice, ____9____ relies on the deterring effect of punishing offenders as well as the actions of private citizens.

Criminal justice agencies throughout the United States are characterized by ____10____ and fragmentation. In the judicial branch, this is evident in the ____11____ which is very different from the unified, national systems that exist in many other countries.

# SELF-TEST SECTION

## MULTIPLE CHOICE QUESTIONS

3.1. Which of the following is a goal of the American criminal justice system?
a) consolidating power at the local level
b) preventing crime
c) consolidating power at the federal level
d) dramatizing crime
e) all of the above are goals of the criminal justice system

3.2. Which of the following is TRUE about the American criminal justice system?
a) citizens have authority to enforce the law
b) most people take steps to protect themselves against crime
c) there is little difference between the U. S criminal system and authoritarian countries
d) criminal justice officials are limited by the constitutional rights of individuals
e) criminal justice officials never fall short of doing justice

3.3. Which of the following is TRUE about discretion within the American system of criminal justice?
a) discretion not exist within the American system of criminal justice
b) discretion exists but for only a few participants
c) discretion exists for all participants but it does not limit the values of the American system
d) discretion exists and its use limits the values of the American system
e) discretion exists for only judges

3.4. Which of the following is TRUE about the American system of criminal justice?
a) very few suspects who are arrested are then prosecuted, tried, and convicted
b) all suspects who are arrested are then prosecuted, tried, and convicted
c) no suspects who are arrested are then prosecuted, tried, and convicted
d) a large percentage of suspects who are arrested are then prosecuted, tried, and convicted
e) none of the above are TRUE

3.5.  Which of the following is an attribute of the American system of criminal justice?
a) mandatory actions
b) resource dependence
c) independence of actors
d) rigidity of institutions
e) independent subsystems

3.6. How many state and local law enforcement agencies exist within the American system of criminal justice?
a) roughly 5,000
b) roughly 10,000
c) roughly 12,000
d) roughly 18,000
e) roughly 35,000

3.7. How many federal law enforcement agencies exist within the American system of criminal justice?
a) 5
b) 20
c) 30
d) 50
e) 120

3.8. Which state does NOT have a state law enforcement agency?
a) California
b) Ohio
c) New York
d) South Dakota
e) Hawaii

3.9. What is the annual budget of the state and local law enforcement agencies within the American system of criminal justice?
a) more than $50 billion
b) more than $100 billion
c) more than $500 billion
d) more than $1 trillion
e) less than $100 million

3.10. Which of the following are major duties of police agencies?
a) keeping the peace
b) apprehending criminals
c) providing social services
d) preventing crime
e) all of the above

3.11. Which of the following duties is being performed if a police officer "directs traffic"?
a) solving crime
b) apprehending criminals
c) providing social services
d) preventing crime
e) all of the above

3.12. Which of the following duties is being performed if a police officer "provides emergency aid"?
a) solving crime
b) apprehending criminals
c) providing social services
d) preventing crime
e) all of the above

3.13. Which of the following accounts for the smallest amount of an officer's time?
a) keeping the peace
b) apprehending criminals
c) providing social services
d) preventing crime
e) all of the above account for a great deal of an officer's time

3.14. Which of the following engage in corrections?
a) federal government
b) state government
c) most counties
d) most cities
e) all of the above

3.15. What is the ratio of American adults who are under the supervision of state and federal corrections systems to the entire
adult population?
a) one in three
b) one in ten
c) one in fifteen
d) one in twenty-three
e) one in thirty-four

3.16. The right to a trial by an impartial jury is guaranteed by the...
a) First Amendment
b) Fifth Amendment
c) Sixth Amendment
d) Eighth Amendment
e) Tenth Amendment

3.17. How many percent of criminal cases go to trial?
a) five
b) ten to fifteen
c) twenty
d) thirty to forty
e) fifty

3.18. How many percent of criminal cases go before a jury?
a) five
b) ten to fifteen
c) twenty
d) thirty to forty
e) fifty

3.19. What layer of the criminal justice wedding cake would include Timothy McVeigh's trial for bombing the federal building in Oklahoma
City?
a) layer one (celebrated case)
b) layer two (serious felony case)
c) layer three (less important felony case)
d) layer four (misdemeanor case)
e) layer five (federal case)

3.20. What layer of the criminal justice wedding cake would prosecutors refer to as "heavy" cases with "tough" sentences?
a) layer one (celebrated cases)
b) layer two (serious felony cases)
c) layer three (less important felony cases)
d) layer four (misdemeanor cases)
e) layer five (federal cases)

3.21. What layer of the criminal justice wedding cake contains ninety percent of all cases?
a) layer one (celebrated cases)
b) layer two (serious felony cases)
c) layer three (less important felony cases)
d) layer four (misdemeanor cases)
e) layer five (federal cases)

3.22. Which of the following is NOT a layer of the criminal justice wedding cake?
a) layer one (celebrated case)
b) layer two (serious felony case)
c) layer three (less important felony case)
d) layer four (misdemeanor case)
e) layer five (federal case)

3.23. Which group was on the minds of those who framed the Fourteenth Amendment's equal protection clause?
a) women
b) white men
c) African-Americans
d) handicapped persons
e) homosexuals

3.24. In what case did the U. S. Supreme Court declare that segregation (separate but equal) was unconstitutional?
a) Marbury v. Madison (1803)
b) Plessy v. Ferguson (1896)
c) Shelley v. Kramer (1948)
d) Brown v. Board of Education (1954)
e) Roe v. Wade (1973)

3.25. The link between crime and economic disadvantage is...
a) non-existent
b) slight
c) moderate
d) significant
e) a universal law of causal and effect


**TRUE/FALSE QUESTIONS**

3.1. All laws are applied fairly in the United States

3.2. The easiest goal of the American system of criminal justice is to do justice.

3.3. The U. S. Constitution does not provide for a national police force.

3.4. There are no federal law enforcement agencies in the U. S.

3.5. Under the National Stolen Property Act, the FBI may investigate thefts of more than $5,000 in value.

3.6. Two-thirds of all criminal justice employees work for local government.

3.7. Discretion is not an important concept within the American system of criminal justice.

3.8. The subsystems of the American system of criminal justice are interdependent.

3.9. Eighty percent of American police are found at the federal level.

3.10. African-Americans are treated fairly within the American system of criminal justice.

3.11. All fifty states in the U. S. have state law enforcement agencies.

3.12. The U. S. criminal justice system processes most of its cases at the federal level.

3.13. State courts are required by the U. S. Supreme Court to decide all cases in a similar fashion.

3.14. Trial judges and other officials are ruled to have acted properly in eighty percent of appeals.

3.15. Christopher Jones was arrested for loitering.

3.16. Ninety percent of criminal cases involve serious felonies.

3.17. The drafters of the Fourteenth Amendment's equal protection clause were concerned solely with women's rights.

3.18. There is a large disparity between the sentences imposed upon those convicted for crack cocaine and those convicted for powder cocaine.

3.19. Michael Tonry argues that the "War on Drugs" was designed to disadvantage black youths.

3.20. The link between crime and economic disadvantage is not significant.

**ANSWER KEY**

Key Terms

1.      discretion
2.      doing justice
3.      bench trial
4.      information
5.      resource dependence
6.      dual court system
7.      bail
8.      arrest
9.      federal law enforcement agencies
10.     system
11.     decentralization
12.     sequential tasks
13.     crime
14.     filtering process
15.     controlling crime
16.     arraignment
17.     Congress
18.     booking
19.     jury trial
20.     "wedding cake"
21.     warrant
22.     preliminary hearing
23.     due process model
24.     preventing crime
25.     U.S. Constitution
26.     grand jury
27.     political considerations
28.     felonies
29.     adjudication
30.     exchange
31.     indictment
32.     plea bargaining
33.     misdemeanors
34.     crime control model

Key People
1.      Michael Kennedy
2.      Lee Harvey Oswald
3.      Christopher Jones
4.      Timothy McVeigh and O. J. Simpson

General Practice Questions

1.      political considerations
2.      Congress
3.      discretion
4.      filtering process
5.      plea bargaining
6.      information
7.      grand jury
8.      indictment

9.   preventing crime
10.  decentralization
11.  dual court system

<u>Multiple Choice</u>
3.1.   b
3.2.   d
3.3.   d
3.4.   a
3.5.   b
3.6.   d
3.7.   d
3.8.   e
3.9.   a
3.10.  e
3.11.  c
3.12.  c
3.13.  b
3.14.  e
3.15.  e
3.16.  c
3.17.  b
3.18.  a
3.19.  a
3.20.  b
3.21.  d
3.22.  e
3.23.  c
3.24.  d
3.25.  d

<u>True/False</u>
3.1.   F
3.2.   F
3.3.   T
3.4.   F
3.5.   T
3.6.   T
3.7.   F
3.8.   T
3.9.   F
3.10.  F
3.11.  F
3.12.  F
3.13.  F
3.14.  T
3.15.  F
3.16.  F
3.17.  F
3.18.  T
3.19.  T
3.20.  F

## WORKSHEET 3.1  SYSTEM ATTRIBUTES

Imagine that you are a county prosecutor.  Briefly describe how the attributes of the criminal justice system (discretion, resource dependence, sequential tasks, and filtering) would affect your relationships, decisions, and actions with respect to each of the following.

Police_____

_____

_____

_____

Defense
Attorneys_____

_____

_____

_____

Trial Judges_____

_____

_____

_____

News Media_____

_____

_____

_____

County
Commissioners_____

_____

_____

_____

WORKSHEET 3.2  STEPS IN THE PROCESS

Briefly describe what happens at each of the following steps in the justice process.

Booking_____

_____

_____

Preliminary
Hearing_____

_____

_____

_____

Grand Jury
Proceeding_____

_____

_____

_____

Arraignment_____

_____

_____

_____

Trial_____

_____

_____

_____

Sentencing_____

_____

_____

_____

Appeal_____

# CHAPTER 4

## CRIMINAL JUSTICE AND THE RULE OF LAW

---

## LEARNING OBJECTIVES

After covering the material in this chapter, students should understand:

1.  the development of American criminal law from the English common law system;

2.  the sources of criminal law;

3.  the principles of substantive criminal law;

.4.  the accepted defenses and their justifications in substantive criminal law;

5.  the importance of procedural due process;

6.  the expansion of the meaning of the Bill of Rights and its protections for criminal defendants.


## CHAPTER SUMMARY

Criminal law focuses on prosecution and punishment by the state of people who violate specific laws enacted by legislatures, while civil law concerns disputes between private citizens or businesses. Criminal law is divided into two parts: substantive law that defines offenses and penalties, and procedural law that defines individuals' rights and the processes that criminal justice officials must follow in handling cases. The common law tradition, which was inherited from England, involves judges' shaping law through their decisions. Criminal law is found in written constitutions, statutes, judicial decisions, and administrative regulations.

Substantive criminal law involves seven important elements that must exist and be demonstrated by the prosecution in order to obtain a conviction: legality, *actus reus,* causation, harm, concurrence, *mens rea,* punishment. The *mens rea* element, concerning intent or state of mind, can vary with different offenses, such as various degrees of murder or sexual assault. The element may also be disregarded for strict liability offenses that punish actions without considering intent. Criminal law provides opportunities to present several defenses based on lack of criminal intent: entrapment, self-defense, necessity, duress (coercion), immaturity, mistake, intoxication, and insanity. Standards for the insanity defense vary by jurisdiction with various state and federal courts using several different tests: M'Naghten Rule, Irresistible Impulse Test, Durham Rule, Comprehensive Crime Control Act Rule, the Model Penal Code rule.

The provisions of the Bill of Rights were not made applicable to state and local officials by the U.S. Supreme Court until the mid-twentieth century, when the Court incorporated most of the Bill of Rights' specific provisions into the due process clause of the Fourteenth Amendment. The Fourth Amendment prohibition on unreasonable searches and seizures has produced many cases questioning the application of the exclusionary rule. Decisions by the Burger and Rehnquist Courts during the 1970s, 1980s, and 1990s have created several exceptions to the exclusionary rule and given greater flexibility to law enforcement officials. The Fifth Amendment provides protections against compelled self-incrimination and double jeopardy. As part of the right against compelled self-incrimination, the Supreme Court created *Miranda* warnings that must be given to suspects before they are questioned. The Sixth Amendment includes the right to counsel, the right to a speedy and public trial, and the right to an impartial jury.

The Eighth Amendment includes protections against excessive bail, excessive fines, and cruel and unusual punishments. Many of the Supreme Court's most well-known Eighth Amendment cases concern the death penalty, which the Court has endorsed, provided that states employ careful decision-making procedures that consider aggravating and mitigating factors.

**CHAPTER OUTLINE**

I.      INTRODUCTION

A.     <u>Michael Pangle: Vehicular Homicide</u>
Michael Pangle was arrested for drunk driving and the police released Pangle into the custody of a friend. Pangle was driven back to his automobile and, while attempting to drive himself home, he crashed into another automobile killing himself and another motorist. Who should be responsible for this vehicular homicide? Should Pangle be the only person held responsible? Should his friend bear some of the blame? Should the police for releasing him? This case raises questions about which behaviors should be punished as crimes.
    1.    Law defines those behaviors that are labeled criminal and the individuals who are culpable. This is called substantive criminal law.
    2.    Law describes the procedures to be followed under our adversarial system by those with the responsibility for law enforcement, adjudication, and corrections. This is called procedural criminal law. Thus, the criminal justice system operates as an administrative system influenced by political, social, *and legal* forces.

II.    FOUNDATIONS OF THE CRIMINAL LAW

A.    <u>Substantive Law and Procedural Law</u>
    1.    Law must proscribe an act before it can be regarded as a crime and have accompanying punishment. Civil law concerns contracts, property, and personal injuries. Criminal law concerns conduct that is punished by the government.
    2.    Criminal law is divided into substantive and procedural law:
        a.    Substantive law: stipulates the types of conduct that are criminal and the punishments to be imposed.
        b.    Procedural law: sets forth the rules that govern the enforcement of the substantive law.

B.    <u>Sources of Criminal Law</u>
    1.    Earliest known codes are the Sumerian (3100 B.C.) and the Code of Hammurabi (1750 B.C.): written codes divided into sections to cover different types of offenses. Greeks and Romans also had earlier codes.
    2.    Common Law: U.S. uses the Anglo-American common law system which originated in England as primary source of its legal values and law.
        a.    Common Law: Anglo-American system of uncodified law, in which the judges follow precedent set by earlier decisions when they decide new but similar cases. The substantive and procedural law originally developed in this manner but was later codified by legislatures.
        b.    Common law system relies on doctrine of following earlier court rulings when making judicial decisions.
    3.    Written Law
        a.    Constitutions: provides the fundamental principles and procedural safeguards that serve as guides for the enactment of laws and the making of decisions. The U.S. Constitution includes the Bill of Rights and most state constitutions similarly list protections for individuals in the criminal process.
        b.    Statutes: laws passed by legislative bodies, usually contain the substantive and procedural laws of a state. Federal criminal laws are passed by Congress and deal with violations on federal land, involving the national interest (e.g., treason), or multiple jurisdictions (e.g., kidnapping across state lines).
           i.    Penal codes: each state's penal code provides the statutory definition of that state's crimes.
    c.    Case law: judicial decisions guided by precedents from previous court cases.

d.    Administrative regulations: laws and rulings made by federal, state, and local agencies, such as a health department. Frequently concern such matters as pollution, industrial safety, traffic.

C.    Felony and Misdemeanor
1.    Felony: punishable by more than one year incarceration or harsher sentence; also carries with it certain rights, such as right to counsel for indigent defendants and right to trial by jury. Also may bar convicted offenders from specific occupations and professions in various states.
2.    Misdemeanor: punishable by one year or less; often in a local jail rather than in a state prison, which may be reserved for longer felony sentences.

D.    Criminal Law versus Civil Law
1.    Criminal law: defines an offense against society; state punishes violations.
2.    Civil law: defines relationships between individuals within society; civil wrongdoers pay compensation for the harms they cause.
3.    Both Civil and Criminal: some acts can be both a civil and criminal matter if the state prosecutes the defendant and a victim sues the defendant for damages.
    a.    Increasingly may be lawsuits against others whose non-criminal conduct contributed to a crime, such as a rape victim suing an apartment complex for lax security.
4.    Civil forfeiture: involves the government taking property, which may be connected to or separate from a criminal proceeding.
    a.    *In rem* actions concern the guilt or innocence of the property itself.
    b.    *In personam* forfeiture action against person
    c.    1996 U.S. Supreme Court decision permits forfeiture of car co-owned by innocent spouse

III.    SUBSTANTIVE CRIMINAL LAW

A.    Seven Principles of Criminal Law
1.    Legality: existence of a law defining the crime; the U.S. Constitution prohibits *ex post facto* laws.
2.    *Actus reus*: behavior of either commission or omission; bad intentions alone or status alone (i.e., such as being a drug addict) is insufficient; must have act or omission
3.    Causation: causal relationship between the act and the harm suffered.
4.    Harm: damage inflicted on legally protected value (e.g., person, property, reputation); also includes the potential for harm: inchoate offenses when conspire to commit offense even if harm does not actually occur.
5.    Concurrence: the simultaneous occurrence of the intention and the act.
6.    *Mens rea* (a guilty state of mind): guilty mind requires intention to commit the act.
7.    Punishment: the stipulation in the law of sanctions to be applied against persons found guilty of the forbidden behavior.

B.    Comparative Perspective: Islamic Criminal Law
Proofs and punishments for various crimes, including adultery, defamation, apostasy, use of alcohol, and theft; based on the *Shari'a*, Islamic law.

C.    Elements of a Crime
1.    Attendant circumstances
2.    *Actus rea* (the act)
3.    *Mens rea* (state of mind)

a.      Burglary example: entering a building or occupied structure (*actus rea*), with the intent to commit a crime (*mens rea*), when the premises are not open to the public or the actor is not privileged to enter (attendant circumstances).

D.      Statutory Definitions of Crimes
1.      Definitions of crimes vary from state to state.
2.      Murder and Nonnegligent Manslaughter: murder requires "malice aforethought" or some other requirement of a higher level of intent.
3.      Rape: difficulties with finding corroborating evidence and with the public humiliation of the victim; in some jurisdictions, an absence of visible physical injury has been taken to mean that there was no force used and therefore there was consent.
4.      Close-Up: Acquaintance Rape. Oakland Raiders professional football player, Darrell Russell is accused of date rape.

E.      Responsibility for Criminal Acts
1.      *Mens rea*: key element for establishing perpetrator's responsibility; not necessarily whether person acted with consciousness of guilt, but whether a reasonable man in the defendant's situation and with his physical characteristics would have had a consciousness of guilt ("objective *mens rea*").
2.      Accidents are not crimes because of the absence of *mens rea*, although acts of extreme negligence or recklessness may be criminal. Different levels of intent in criminal law. Depending on the statute, criminal acts may be done either intentionally, knowingly, recklessly, or negligently.
3.      Also strict liability offenses or public welfare liability: legislature can criminalize acts without showing of intent, such as pure food and drug laws, housing laws, sanitation laws; such offenses usually do not lead to incarceration unless there is a refusal to comply after given notice of violation.
     a.      Concept upheld in Justice Jackson's opinion in *Morissette v. United States* (1952).
4.      Entrapment is a defense claiming the absence of intent when the defendant lacks predisposition and government induced a law-abiding citizen to commit a crime.
     a.      1992 Supreme Court found entrapment in case of federal agents sending solicitations to Nebraska farmer to offer to sell him child pornography. According to Justice White's opinion: the government may not "originate a criminal design, implant in an innocent person's mind the disposition to commit a criminal act, and then induce commission of the crime so that the government may prosecute."
5.      Self-Defense: person who feels in immediate danger of being harmed by another's unlawful use of force may ward off the attack in self-defense; generally must use only the force level necessary to defend yourself.
     a.      Bernard Goetz, the New York City "subway vigilante," argued self-defense in shooting: state court clarified its standard to emphasize that Goetz had to *believe* that deadly force was necessary and his belief had to be reasonable.
6.      Necessity: for one's own preservation or to avoid a greater evil, inflict a harm on a person who was not responsible for the imminent danger (i.e., person speeding in order to take a sick child to the hospital): famous example of survivors in lifeboat killing and eating cabin boy in order to survive
7.      Duress (Coercion): a person who has been forced or coerced to commit an act has acted under duress.
     a.      Missouri prison escapee unsuccessful in claiming duress as defense when he claimed that he escaped in order to avoid further homosexual assaults against him

8. Immaturity: traditionally Anglo-American law has excused criminal behavior by children under the age of seven on the ground that they are immature and not responsible for their actions; arguments could be made concerning the capacity of seven- to fourteen-year-olds to contest whether they had sufficient maturity to be responsible for their actions.

9. Mistake: under the Model Penal Code a reasonable mistake of law or fact may be a defense.

10. Intoxication: voluntary intoxication is normally not a defense unless the crime required specific rather than general intent; a person tricked into consuming an intoxicating substance can use intoxication as a defense.
   a. 1996 U.S. Supreme Court decision approved Montana statute barring introduction of evidence of intoxication to negate intent element of crime.

11. Insanity: controversial and relatively rare defense successful in only about one percent of cases. Usually accompanied by civil commitment statute permitting insane acquittee to be hospitalized until condition improves. Five variations on insanity rule used by various states:
   a. M'Naghten Rule: did not know what he was doing or did not know it was wrong.
   b. Irresistible Impulse: could not control his own conduct.
   c. Durham Rule: the criminal act was caused by his mental illness.
   d. Model Penal Code (Substantial capacity test): lacks substantial capacity to appreciate the wrongfulness of his conduct or to control it.
   e. Federal rule: lacks capacity to appreciate the wrongfulness of his conduct or wrongfulness of act a result of severe mental disease or defect. Implemented through the Comprehensive Crime Control Act of 1984.

12. Close-Up: The Insanity Defense and Its Aftermath: A former teacher who tortured a student to death might be released from a mental facility after being acquitted through the insanity defense. By contrast, a man who broke a window in Virginia still held in a mental hospital thirteen years later a much longer period of confinement than if convicted of the crime.

13. After John Hinckley's assassination attempt on the life of President Ronald Reagan, the insanity defense was reexamined and eight states adopted the defense of "guilty but mentally ill" that allows conviction but requires psychiatric care during imprisonment. Federal law shifted burden of proof to defendant to prove insanity.

14. It remains difficult to present successful insanity defense (e.g., Jeffrey Dahmer was unsuccessful despite gruesome cannibalism).

15. Insanity acquittees usually committed to mental hospital where they may actually stay longer than if they had been convicted and served a term in prison.

IV. PROCEDURAL CRIMINAL LAW

A. Procedural Due Process of Law
Accused persons in criminal cases must be accorded certain rights and protections in keeping with the adversarial nature of the proceeding and they must be tried according to legally established procedures.
   1. Procedures may seek to advance truth seeking (e.g., trial by jury) or to prevent improper governmental actions (e.g., unreasonable searches and seizures).
   2. What Americans Think: College freshman increasingly believe that courts show too much concern for the rights of criminals.

B. Bill of Rights
Ten amendments added to the U.S. Constitution in 1789 including protections against self-incrimination and double jeopardy.
   1. *Barron v. Baltimore* (1833): initially determined that Bill of Rights only provided protection for individuals against actions by the federal government, not actions by state

governments. The constitutions of many states contained their own lists of protections for people within those states.

C.   The Fourteenth Amendment and Due Process
    1.    Post-Civil War amendment stating that "no State shall" deprive people of:
        a.    the privileges and immunities of citizenship
        b.    life, liberty, or property without due process of law
        c.    equal protection of the laws
        These vague terms are subject to interpretation by the U.S. Supreme Court.
    2.    During the twentieth century the Supreme Court gradually made most of the provisions of the Bill of Rights applicable against the states by saying that individual rights had been incorporated into the 14th Amendment right to due process which was good against actions by states. This process was called incorporation.
        a.    Several early cases caused the Supreme Court to identify due process rights possessed by people against the states: *Moore v. Dempsey* (1923) and *Powell v. Alabama* (1932) concerning quick death sentences given to African-American defendants in unfair proceedings and *Brown v. Mississippi* (1936) in which defendants were beaten until they confessed.
        b.    Concept of "fundamental fairness" to determine which specific rights were applicable against the states as a component of the 14th Amendment right to due process.

D.   The Due Process Revolution
Supreme Court applied specific provisions of the Bill of Rights against the states by incorporating into due process right of the 14th Amendment; most of the criminal defendants' rights in the Bill of Rights were incorporated during the 1960s.
    1.    Earl Warren, Chief Justice from 1953 to 1969.
    2.    *Mapp v. Ohio* (1961) applied the exclusionary rule against state and local law enforcement officials after Cleveland police made a warrantless search of a home.
    3.    Warren Burger, Chief Justice from 1969 to 1986.

E.   Fourth Amendment: Unreasonable Searches and Seizure
    1.    What is Unreasonable?
    2.    Problems of the Exclusionary Rule: applicable against federal government in 1914 (*Weeks*; against state and local in 1961 (*Mapp*); exceptions created during the Burger and Rehnquist Court eras (e.g., *Leon*-good faith exception).
        a.    Conservatives argue that exclusion is not effective against police misconduct and that it exacts a high price from society.
        b.    Liberals argue that it is better for a few guilty people to go free than to permit police to engage in misconduct.
    3.    Recent Supreme Court decisions give greater flexibility to police for conducting searches.

F.   Fifth Amendment: Self-Incrimination & Double Jeopardy
    1.    Self-Incrimination: Warren Court era decisions shifted focus from courtroom to defendants' initial contacts with police; thus require access to counsel (*Escobedo v. Illinois*, 1964) and to be informed of rights, including right to remain silent (*Miranda v. Arizona*, 1966).
        a.    Statements obtained in violation of *Miranda* warnings can be excluded from evidence unless they fall under one of the exceptions created by the Burger Court (e.g., public safety; inevitable discovery rule).
    2.    Suspects continue to confess. Police have adapted their interrogation techniques.

3.     Double Jeopardy: a person charged with a criminal act may be subjected to only one prosecution or punishment for that offense in the same jurisdiction; if a case dismissed before trial, a subsequent prosecution is permissible.

    a.     Does not preclude the possibility of successive prosecutions in different (i.e., state or federal) jurisdictions. (Rodney King case had subsequent federal prosecution of police officers after initial state court acquittal).

G.    Sixth Amendment: Right to Counsel and Fair Trial

1.     Right to Counsel: *Gideon v. Wainwright* (1963) required appointed counsel for indigent state court defendants facing six months or more of incarceration. Right to counsel extended to other points in the process (preliminary hearings, etc.). However, no right to counsel for discretionary appeals or in trial with only fine as sentence.

2.     Speedy and Public Trial: public trial is to protect defendant from arbitrary conviction.

3.     Impartial Jury: jury is supposed to serve a representative function; jury trial must be available in states to defendants facing serious charges (*Duncan v. Louisiana*, 1968). Jury is supposed to be drawn from fair cross-section of the community. There is no guarantee that the jury will be representative. Impartiality best achieved through random selection of jury pool; avoids exclusion of identifiable groups.

H.    Eighth Amendment: Fines, Bail, and Punishment

1.     Release on Bail: release not required, bail simply cannot be "excessive"; federal statute permits holding defendants in jail after a finding that they may be dangerous to the community or that no conditions of release may prevent flight from the jurisdiction (*United States v. Salerno and Cafero*).

2.     Excessive Fines: *Austin v. United States* (1993), justices unanimously returned to the lower court for re-hearing a case involved the forfeiture of an estimated $40 million in real estate and businesses. In 1998, the Court actually identified an excessive fine when a traveler at an airport forfeited $357,000 for failing to report that he was transporting more than $10,000.

3.     Cruel and Unusual Punishment: Supreme Court determined in 1958 (*Trop v. Dulles*) that the term "cruel and unusual punishments" must be defined according to contemporary standards. In 1972, (*Furman v. Georgia*) the death penalty, as administered at that time, found cruel and unusual for being too arbitrary. States rewrote their laws to create more extensive deliberative procedures and Supreme Court    approved such capital punishment statutes in 1976 (*Gregg v. Georgia*).

    a.     New procedures include consideration of aggravating and mitigating factors.

    b.     In 1987, *McCleskey v. Kemp*, the Court rejected the use of statistics to show systemic racial discrimination.

    c.     Although the Court has found the death penalty to be constitutional, it still addresses cases concerning the procedures to be used for appeals and other post-conviction reviews.

    d.     Question of Ethics: is the use of electroshock devices on defendants a violation of the Constitution?

    e.     Supreme Court did rule in *Atkins v. Virginia (2002)* that it violates the Eighth Amendment to execute a mentally retarded person.

I.    The Supreme Court Today

1.     Supreme Court composition changed during the 1970s, 1980s, and 1990s as conservative Republican presidents (Richard Nixon, Ronald Reagan, George Bush) appointed a total of nine members before the first Democratic president (Bill Clinton) to make appointments since the 1960s made appointments of two justices in 1993 and 1994.

    a.     The Republican appointees, who were more conservative than their Warren Court predecessors, made decisions narrowing the scope of many rights for criminal defendants and prisoners -- they did not, however, engage in the wholesale elimination of basic rights established in prior case decisions.

b.    Many state courts have used their state constitutions to make decisions about criminal defendants' rights that are more expansive than those of the U.S. Supreme Court.


## REVIEW OF KEY TERMS

Fill in the appropriate term for each statement

civil forfeiture
felony
common law
misdemeanor
United States v. Leon
Weeks v. United States
Trop v. Dulles
Morissette v. United States
The Queen v. Dudley & Stephens
Escobedo v. Illinois
United States v. Salerno and Cafaro
Barron v. Baltimore
Sitz v. Michigan Dept. of State Police
Mapp v. Ohio
Gideon v. Wainwright
Austin v. United States
Furman v. Georgia
Powell v. Alabama
Wyoming v. Houghton
Miranda v. Arizona
civil law
self-defense
statutes
defendant
substantive criminal law
constitution
inchoate offenses
administrative regulations
*mens rea*
*ex post facto*
*actus reus*
causation
strict liability
necessity
procedural due process
duress
incorporation
immaturity
exclusionary rule
M'Naghten Rule
Durham Rule
Irresistible Impulse Test
insanity defense

burglary
murder
manslaughter
rape
malice aforethought
intoxication
Islamic law
Bill of Rights
Fourth Amendment
self incrimination
Fifth Amendment
capital punishment
Sixth Amendment
double jeopardy
Eighth Amendment
Atkins v. Virginia
right to counsel
Fourteenth Amendment
entrapment

1. _____ defines the undesirable behaviors that the government will punish.

2. _____ is forcible sexual contact without a woman's consent or with a female who is too young to consent.

3. _____ may be used with reasonable force to protect against criminal attacks.

4. _____ is the underlying legal document for a state or country that provides its basic laws.

5. _____ is the portion of the Constitution used by the Supreme Court to apply rights against infringement by states.

6. _____ is a crucial element of intent for murder charges.

7. _____ is the claim that someone lacked the appropriate mental capacity to be held responsible for a criminal act.

8. _____ is the body of rules that regulate conduct between individuals in their private relationships.

9. _____ is a constitutional right that attempts to assure that criminal defendants' rights are protected during the processing of cases.

10. _____ are rules written by agencies within the government.

11. _____ is a homicide that lacks the highest level of intent.

12. _____ is the process by which the Supreme Court applied provisions of the Bill of Rights against the states.

13. _____ is a defense with its historical roots in sailors' cannibalism while lost at sea.

14. _____ is a defense that is rarely available unless someone unwittingly ingested alcohol.

15. _____ prevents the use of torture and mutilation as punishment.

16. _____ is the intent element of a crime.

17. _____ is a criminal law written to punish an act that has already occurred.

18. _____ is the required action component of criminal laws.

19. _____ provides a defense in some jurisdictions when a defendant could not control his own conduct.

20. _____ is a person charged with a crime.

21. _____ permits the assignment of criminal responsibility without a showing of criminal intent.

22. _____ is a defense when someone physically forces someone else to commit a crime.

23. _____ provides the right against double jeopardy.

24. _____ is a felony that requires a specific act, attendant circumstances, and state of mind.

25. _____ is an intentional homicide.

26. _____ is divided into three categories, with punishments determined either by religious rules, victims' claims, or judges' discretion.

27. _____ is the necessary relationship in criminal law between an action and a harm.

28. _____ is the production of damaging testimony against one's self.

29. _____ is the constitutional provision that seeks to make people feel secure against unwarranted intrusions into their homes and property.

30. _____ provides assurances that accused persons in criminal cases will be accorded certain rights and will be tried according to legally established procedures.

31. _____ is the most severe punishment in the American criminal justice system which is governed by rules against cruel and unusual punishments.

32. _____ provides a defense when law enforcement officers are too aggressive in seeking to induce a particular individual to commit a crime.

33. _____ provides a defense in some jurisdictions when a defendant did not know what he was doing or did not know that was he was doing was wrong.

34. _____ is the term for less serious offenses that are punishable by one in jail or lesser punishments.

35. _____ is the seizure of property by the government.

36. _____ is the legal system that the United States inherited from Great Britain.

37. _____ is the term for serious offenses punishable by one year or more of imprisonment.

38. _____ affects the evidence when police violate Fourth or Fifth Amendment rights.

39. _____ are laws enacted by legislatures.

40. _____ provides the right to trial by jury.

41. _____ contains a list of rights added to the Constitution and initially applicable only against the federal government.

42. _____ is a defense when someone is considered too young to form the necessary intent to be held responsible for a criminal act.

43. _____ provides the right against excessive fines.

44. _____ provides a defense in some jurisdictions when the criminal act was caused by mental illness.

45. _____ is a right against being tried twice for the same offense.

46. _____ are crimes that include conspiracies and attempts.

47 _____ is the case that forbade police from denying defendants the opportunity to consult with their attorneys.

48 _____ is the case that required states to provide attorneys for indigent defendants who faced serious criminal charges.

49 _____ is the case in which the Supreme Court applied the exclusionary rule against the states in cases of improper searches and seizures.

50._____ is the case in which the Supreme Court found that the application of capital punishment violated the Eighth Amendment.

51. _____ is a case that created an exception to the exclusionary rule.

52. _____ is the case that required police officers to inform suspects of their rights upon arrest

53. _____ is the case in which the Supreme Court determined that the Excessive Fines Clause of the Eighth Amendment applies to seizures of property by the government.

54. _____ is the case that examined the necessity defense for cannibalism on the high seas.

55. _____ is the first case to interpret the scope and coverage of the Bill of Rights.

56. _____ is the case that endorsed criminalization of actions that lacked criminal intent.

57. _____ is the case that involved the application of due process rights for a controversial rape charge.

58. _____ is the case that excluded a coerced confession when the defendants were beaten and forced to confess.

59. _____ is the case in which the Supreme Court upheld the Bail Reform Act which permits federal judges to detain without bail suspects considered dangerous to the public.

60. _____ is the case in which the Supreme Court approved the revised death penalty statutes enacted by various states during the 1970s after the application of capital punishment had been declared unconstitutional in a previous case.

61. _____ is the case in which the U.S. Supreme Court decided that sobriety checkpoints do not violate the Fourth Amendment.

62. _____ is the case from 1914 that decided evidence must be excluded when federal law enforcement officials conduct an improper search.

63. _____ is the case that decided police can search auto passengers' purses, suitcases, and other containers if the driver of the car is found in possession of drugs or other contraband.

64. _____ is the case that decided the meaning of the Eighth Amendment's cruel and unusual punishments clause shall be defined by evolving societal standards.

65. The U. S. Supreme Court declared in _____ that it violates the Eighth Amendment to execute the mentally retarded.


**REVIEW OF KEY PEOPLE**

Earl Warren
Warren Burger
Bill Clinton
King John of England
William Rehnquist

1. The current Chief Justice on the U. S. Supreme Court is _____.

2. Chief Justice _____ led a liberal revolution that included expanding the rights of criminal defendants.

3. _____ issued the Magna Carta, promising that "no free man shall be arrested, or imprisoned, or disseized, or outlawed, or exiled, or in any way molested; nor will we proceed against him unless by the lawful judgment of his peers or by the law of the land."

4. _____ was chief justice of the U. S. Supreme Court from 1969-1986.

5. President _____ appointed Justices Ruth Bader Ginsburg and Stephen Breyer to the U. S. Supreme Court.


**GENERAL PRACTICE QUESTIONS**

Fill in the blanks with appropriate term, case, or person

When judges follow case precedents, they are adhering to the ____1____ system that the United States inherited from England.

When a defendant wishes to claim that he or she is not guilty by reason of ____2____, the rule applied by the court for determining capacity of criminal responsibility will vary from state to state.

When a defendant wishes to claim that he or she is not guilty by reason of _____3_____, the court will determine whether the level of force used was based on a reasonable fear and did not exceed the perceived threat.

Society has many rules for the behavior of its citizens. Under _____4_____, the government defines rules that make violators subject to punishment by the government. By contrast, the rules known as _____5_____, govern disputes between individuals. Although there are formal rules that govern the processing of all cases, _____6_____ rules are especially important for the protection of the rights of people who face criminal punishment.

Police behavior is controlled by a number of legal rules. For example, under the defense of _____7_____ in substantive criminal law, a defendant may show that the police essentially initiated the commission of the crime. Procedural due process rules provide other controls by applying, for example, the _____8_____ when police obtain evidence without following proper procedures for respecting the Fourth or Fifth Amendment rights of suspects.

Under the leadership of Chief Justice Earl Warren, the Supreme Court decided a variety of cases, such as _____9_____, which provided a right to counsel for indigent defendants facing serious charges, through the process of _____10_____ in which rights from the _____11_____ were recognized as applying to the states through the _____12_____. Under subsequent Chief Justices, such as Chief Justice William Rehnquist, who was appointed to be Chief Justice by President Reagan, the Supreme Court was less supportive of rights for criminal defendants.

# SELF-TEST SECTION

## MULTIPLE CHOICE QUESTIONS

4.1. What do most people fear about the powers of government in the wake of the September 11th terrorist attacks?
a) government will not be powerful enough to protect our national security
b) government will be too powerful and violate freedoms
c) government will ignore the problem
d) people are not in fear of the government
e) none of the above

4.2. What type of law governs business deals, contracts, and real estate?
a) civil law
b) criminal law
c) authoritarian law
d) substantive law
e) common law

4.3. What type of law is based upon custom and tradition as interpreted by judges?
a) civil law
b) criminal law
c) authoritarian law
d) substantive law
e) common law

4.4. What did the American Law Institute develop to make state laws more uniform?
a) Model Penal Code
b) The Bill of Rights
c) Victim's Bill of Rights
d) The Fourteenth Amendment
e) American Bar Association

4.5. How are crimes classified within the American system of criminal justice?
a) media attention
b) seriousness
c) victims
d) federal or state
e) crimes are not classified

4.6. A felony charge usually means that the offender may be given a prison sentence of more than...
a) one week
b) one month
c) one year
d) one decade
e) one life sentence

4.7. Which of the following is NOT something that a person who committed a felony can be barred from doing in society?
a) serving on a jury
b) voting
c) practicing law
d) practicing medicine
e) getting married

4.8. What is the burden of proof in a civil trial?
a) reasonable doubt
b) reasonable suspicion
c) probable cause
d) preponderance of the evidence
e) totality of the circumstances

4.9. Which of the following permits law enforcement agencies to sell seized property and use the money for themselves?
a) search warrant
b) indictment
c) forfeiture law
d) arrest warrant
e) guilty verdict in a criminal trial

4.10. The U. S. Supreme Court struck down a California law that made it a crime to be addicted to drugs in the case of...
a) Cohen v. California (1971)
b) Rochin v California (1954)
c) Chimel v. California (1969)
d) O. J. Simpson v. California (1995)
e) Robinson v. California (1962)

4.11. Why are there alcohol restrictions in the state of Utah?
a) history of alcohol-related traffic accidents
b) high rate of underage drinking
c) high rate of liver disease
d) Mormon religion
e) high rate of domestic violence associated with alcohol

4.12. Under Islamic law, what is the punishment for adultery?
a) probation
b) six months in jail
c) stoning to death
d) financial penalties up to $1000
e) there is no punishment

4.13. Which of the following is NOT associated with Islamic criminal law?
a) the safety of the public from physical attack, insult, and humiliation
b) the stability of the family
c) the protection of property against theft, destruction, or unauthorized interference
d) the protection of the government and the Islamic faith against subversion
e) all of the above are associated with Islamic criminal law

4.14. Which of the following is an example of a mitigating circumstance?
a) premeditation
b) waiving the right to remain silent
c) lying about the crime
d) a crime in the heat of passion
e) showing indifference to life

4.15. The level of force used in self-defense cannot exceed the...
a) police's reasonable perception of the threat
b) person's (using self-defense) reasonable perception of the threat
c) judge's reasonable perception of the threat
d) average person's reasonable perception of the threat
e) threat as perceived by the person who is the attacker (not the person exercising self-defense)

4.16. In the case of The Queen v. Dudley and Stephens, what was the defense's argument in the murder of a young sailor?
a) insanity
b) self-defense
c) necessity
d) entrapment
e) duress

4.17. In what case did the U. S. Supreme Court rule that states could hold sexually violent predators in mental hospitals after they have finished serving prison sentences?
a) Kansas v. Hendricks (1997)
b) Robinson v. California (1962)
c) Durham v United States (1954)
d) Mapp v. Ohio (1961)
e) In re Gault (1967)

4.18. Who issued the Magna Carta?
a) King Edward
b) King George
c) King John
d) Queen Victoria
e) Prince Alfred

4.19. In what case did the U. S. Supreme Court rule that the Bill of Rights did not apply to the states?
a) Marbury v. Madison (1803)
b) Barron v. Baltimore (1833)
c) Durham v United States (1954)
d) Mapp v. Ohio (1961)
e) Gibbons v. Ogden (1824)

4.20. What three amendments were added to the U. S. Constitution immediately after the Civil War?
a) First, Second, and Third
b) Fourth, Fifth, and Sixth
c) Tenth, Eleventh, and Twelfth
d) Thirteenth, Fourteenth, and Fifteenth
e) Twentieth, Twenty-First, and Twenty-Second

4.21. Which of the following landmark U. S. Supreme Court cases stated that "cruel and unusual punishments" must be
defined according to contemporary standards?
 a) Mapp v. Ohio (1961)
b) Weeks v. United States (1914)
c) Trop v. Dulles (1958)
d) Gideon v. Wainwright (1963)
e) Powell v. Alabama (1932)

4.22. Which of the following landmark U. S. Supreme Court cases stated that jury trials must be available in states to defendants facing serious charges?
a) Duncan v. Louisiana (1968)
b) Weeks v. United States (1914)
c) Trop v. Dulles (1958)
d) Gideon v. Wainwright (1963)
e) Powell v. Alabama (1932)

4.23. Which of the following best explains Chief Justice Rehnquist's  application of criminal defendants' rights?
a) Rehnquist has expanded the rights of criminal suspects
b) Rehnquist has eliminated the rights of criminal suspects
c) Rehnquist has narrowed the rights of criminal suspects
d) Rehnquist has created new rights for criminal suspects
e) Rehnquist has refused to hear cases dealing with the rights of criminal suspects

4.24. Which of the following rights has not been nationalized upon the states?
a) right against double jeopardy
b) right against unreasonable seizure
c) right to an attorney
d) right to a grand jury trial
e) all of the above have been nationalized

4.25. In what case did the U. S. Supreme Court declare that the death penalty was being used in an arbitrary and discriminatory way?
a) Furman v. Georgia (1972)
b) Payne v. Tennessee (1991)
c) McClesky v. Kemp (1985)
d) Atkins v. Virginia (2002)
e) Gregg v. Georgia (1976)


## TRUE/FALSE QUESTIONS

4.1. In a criminal trial, guilt must be established beyond a reasonable doubt.

4.2. The U. S. criminal justice system operates according to common law.

4.3. A lawsuit involving slander or defamation is an example of civil law.

4.4. Precedent is the title given to the leader of the British system.

4.5. A misdemeanor is a very serious offense.

4.6. A felony is not a serious offense.

4.7. A person convicted of a felony may lose the right to vote.

4.8. A person cannot be arrested for simply being under the influence of drugs.

4.9. Islamic law has no penalty for adultery.

4.10. The Bill of Rights was nationalized through the Fifteenth Amendment.

4.11. Chief Justice Earl Warren narrowed the interpretation of criminal defendants' rights.

4.12. Self-defense is based on the defending person's perception of the threat.

4.13. The criminal defendants' rights are found in the Fourth, Fifth, Sixth, and Seventh Amendments.

4.14. Only a few of the Bill of Rights have been nationalized upon the states.

4.15. The Bill of Rights was ratified by the states at the same time as the U. S. Constitution.

4.16. The Fourth Amendment contains the right against unreasonable search and seizure.

4.17. The death penalty can be used by states against juveniles.

4.18. The death penalty can be used by states against the mentally retarded.

4.19. The Bill of Rights was influenced by the Magna Carta.

4.20. Chief Justice William Rehnquist is liberal.

**ANSWER KEY**

Key Terms

1. substantive criminal law
2. rape
3. self-defense
4. constitution
5. Fourteenth Amendment
6. malice aforethought
7. insanity defense
8. civil law
9. right to counsel
10. administrative regulations
11. manslaughter
12. incorporation
13. necessity
14. intoxication
15. Eighth Amendment
16. *mens rea*
17. *ex post facto*
18. *actus reus*
19. Irresistible Impulse Test
20. defendant
21. strict liability
22. duress
23. Fifth Amendment
24. burglary
25. murder
26. Islamic law
27. causation
28. self-incrimination
29. Fourth Amendment
30. procedural due process
31. capital punishment
32. entrapment
33. M'Naghten Rule
34. misdemeanor
35. civil forfeiture
36. common law
37. felony
38. exclusionary rule
39. statutes
40. Sixth Amendment
41. Bill of Rights
42. immaturity
43. Eighth Amendment
44. Durham Rule
45. double jeopardy
46. inchoate offenses
47. Escobedo v. Illinois
48. Gideon v. Wainwright
49. Mapp v. Ohio
50. Furman v. Georgia
51. United States v. Leon

52. Miranda v. Arizona
53. Austin v. United States
54. The Queen v. Dudley & Stephens
55. Barron v. Baltimore
56. Morissette v. United States
57. Powell v. Alabama
58. Brown v. Mississippi
59. United States v. Salerno and Cafaro
60. Gregg v. Georgia
61. Sitz v. Mich. Dept of State Police
62. Weeks v. United States
63. Wyoming v. Houghton
64. Trop v. Dulles
65. Atkins v. Virginia

Key People

1. William Rehnquist
2. Earl Warren
3. King John of England
4. Warren Burger
5. Bill Clinton

General Practice Questions

1. common law
2. insanity
3. self-defense
4. substantive criminal law
5. civil law
6. procedural due process
7. entrapment
8. exclusionary rule
9. Gideon v. Wainwright
10. incorporation
11. Bill of Rights
12. Fourteenth Amendment

Multiple Choice

| 4.1. | b |
| 4.2. | a |
| 4.3. | e |
| 4.4. | a |
| 4.5. | b |
| 4.6. | c |
| 4.7. | e |
| 4.8. | d |
| 4.9. | c |
| 4.10. | e |
| 4.11. | d |
| 4.12. | c |
| 4.13. | e |
| 4.14. | d |
| 4.15. | b |
| 4.16. | c |

4.17.    a
4.18.    c
4.19.    b
4.20.    d
4.21.    c
4.22.    a
4.23.    c
4.24.    d
4.25.    a

True/False
4.1.     T
4.2.     F
4.3.     T
4.4.     F
4.5.     F
4.6.     F
4.7.     T
4.8.     T
4.9.     F
4.10.    F
4.11.    F
4.12.    T
4.13.    T
4.14.    F
4.15.    F
4.16.    T
4.17.    T
4.18.    F
4.19.    T
4.20.    F

# WORKSHEET 4.1: PRINCIPLES OF CRIMINAL LAW

Acting in response to complaints about smokers gathering in the lobby of the library, the Board of Trustees of the Jonesville Public Library approves the following new rule on the evening of February 6th. The new rule states:

"It shall be unlawful for anyone to smoke at the public library. This rule shall take effect as soon as the Jonesville City Council meets to approve it."

The Jonesville City Council is scheduled to consider the new rule at its 7 p.m. meeting on February 15th. The Library's new smoking rule is the third item scheduled for discussion on the Council's agenda. At 7:05 p.m. on February 15th, Sam Johnson leaves the public library. At the front door to the library he encounters his brother John. John is struggling while using both hands to carry ten overdue books. He has a lighted cigarette dangling from his mouth. "Hey, John," says Sam, "I don't think that you're supposed to smoke in the library anymore." "Really, I hadn't heard that," said John. "Say, while you're holding the door for me, Sam, can you take this cigarette and put it in that ashtray in the lobby? Thanks a million." As Sam took the cigarette from his brother's lips and walked toward the ashtray, a police officer coming out of the lobby arrested him for violating the library's anti-smoking rule.

You are asked to serve as Sam's attorney. Use four of the seven principles of criminal law to formulate arguments on Sam's behalf about why he should not be found guilty of violating the rule.

1._____

_____

_____

_____

2._____

_____

_____

_____

3._____

_____

_____

_____

4._____

_____

_____

# WORKSHEET 4.2: INSANITY DEFENSE

Over the course of seven years, a mother has five babies and they all die during the first months of their lives. Doctors conclude that each child died from Sudden Infant Death Syndrome (SIDS) -- commonly known as "crib death" -- the unexplainable cause of death for 7,000 to 8,000 American babies each year. The woman's family doctor publishes an article about her family to show how SIDS tragically seems to run in families, perhaps for unknown genetic reasons. Years later a prosecutor notices the article and charges the woman with murdering all of her children. The woman initially confesses during police questioning but later claims that the police pressured her to confess. You are hired as her defense attorney. A psychiatrist friend of yours tells you that your client might suffer from a psychiatric condition known as "Munchausen's syndrome by proxy." You hope to use this information to consider presenting an insanity defense.

1. Go to the library and locate a book on medicine or psychiatry that can define for you "Munchausen's syndrome by proxy." What is the definition?

_____

_____

_____

2. Briefly explain whether or not your client's condition can fulfill the requirements of the various tests for the insanity defense.

M'Naghten:_____

_____

_____

Irresistible Impulse:_____

_____

_____

Durham:_____

_____

_____

Substantial Capacity:_____

_____

_____

Federal Comprehensive Crime Control Act:_____

_____

_____

76

## WORKSHEET 4.3: FOURTH AMENDMENT AND EXCLUSIONARY RULE

A woman called the police to her home after her daughter was severely beaten earlier in the day by the daughter's boyfriend. The daughter agreed to use her key to let the officers into the apartment where the man was sleeping. The officers did not seek to obtain either an arrest warrant or a search warrant. After the daughter unlocked the apartment door, the officers entered and found a white substance, which later proved to be cocaine, sitting on a table. They arrested the sleeping man and charged him with narcotics offenses. The defendant sought to have the drugs excluded from evidence because the officers' warrantless search was based on permission from the girlfriend who had moved out of the apartment several weeks earlier and therefore had no authority to give the officers permission to enter and search.

As the prosecutor, think about possible exceptions to the exclusionary rule, such as those discussed for the Fourth and Fifth Amendments, to make arguments about why the evidence should not be excluded.

1. _____

_____

_____

2. _____

_____

_____

Now, imagine that you are the judge. Decide whether the evidence obtained in the warrantless search should be excluded. Provide reasons for your decision. Consider the words of the Fourth Amendment, the purposes of the Amendment, and the potential effects on society from the rule you formulate for this case.

_____

_____

_____

_____

_____

_____

_____

_____

[Compare with *Illinois v. Rodriguez*, 110 S.Ct. 2793 (1990)].

WORKSHEET 4.4: FIFTH AND SIXTH AMENDMENTS

After arresting a suspect for burglary, police officers learned that the suspect's nickname was "Butch." A confidential informant had previously told them that someone named "Butch" was guilty of an unsolved murder in another city. The police in the other city were informed about this coincidence and they sent officers to question the suspect about the murder. Meanwhile, the suspect's sister secured the services of a lawyer to represent her brother on the burglary charge. Neither she nor the lawyer knew about the suspicions concerning the unsolved murder case. The lawyer telephoned the police station and said she would come to the station to be present if the police wished to question her client. The lawyer was told that the police would not question him until the following morning and she could come to the station at that time. Meanwhile, the police from the other city arrived and initiated the first of a series of evening questioning sessions with the suspect. The suspect was not informed that his sister had obtained the services of a lawyer to represent him. The suspect was not told that the lawyer had called the police and asked to be present during any questioning. During questioning, the suspect was informed of his *Miranda* rights, waived his right to be represented by counsel during questioning, and subsequently confessed to the murder.

1. If you were the defense attorney, what arguments would you make to have the confession excluded from evidence?

_____

_____

_____

_____

_____

2. If you were the judge, would you permit the confession to be used in evidence? Provide reasons for your decision.

_____

_____

_____

_____

_____

_____

_____

[Compare your decision with *Moran v. Burbine*, 475 U.S. 412 (1985)]

# CHAPTER 5

## POLICE

---

### LEARNING OBJECTIVES

After covering the material in this chapter, students should understand:

1. the English origins from which American police eventually developed;

2. the history of American police, including the Political Era, the Professional Model era, and the Community Model era;

3. organization of the police in the American federal system, including federal, state, and local;

4. styles of policing, including watchman, legalistic, and service;

5. police functions and the extent of those functions, including order maintenance, law enforcement, and service;

6. the nature of police work, including citizen-police encounters and the role of discretion;

7. the underlying issues and development of practices to address domestic violence.

### CHAPTER SUMMARY

The police in the United States have their roots in the early nineteenth-century developments of policing in England. Similar to England, the American police have limited authority, are under local control, and are organizationally fragmented. Three eras of American policing are: the political era (1840-1920), the professional era (1920-1970), and the community policing era (1970-present). In the U.S. federal system of government, police agencies are found at the national, state, county, and municipal levels. Improvements have been made during the past quarter-century in recruiting more officers who are women, racial and ethnic minorities, and well-educated applicants. The functions of the police are order maintenance, law enforcement, and service. Police executives develop policies on how they will allocate their resources according to one of three styles: the watchman, legalistic, or service styles. Discretion is a major factor in police actions and decisions. Patrol officers exercise the greatest amount of discretion. The problem of domestic violence demonstrates the connection between police encounters with citizens, their exercise of discretion, and police actions. Police face challenges in dealing with special populations, such as the mentally ill and homeless, who need social services, yet often attract the attention of police because they disturb or offend other citizens as they walk the streets. Policing in a multicultural society requires an appreciation of the attitudes, customs, and languages of minority-group members. For police to be effective they must maintain their connection with the community.

### CHAPTER OUTLINE

I. INTRODUCTION.
   The terrorist attacks on September 11, 2001 demonstrated that we are not completely secure in our society. Before the destruction of the World Trade Center, most Americans had little reason to recognize the number of agencies with law enforcement responsibilities and their particular

areas of emphasis. As a result of September 11th, we are more aware and appreciative of the law enforcement agencies at all of levels of the American criminal justice system.

II.    THE DEVELOPMENT OF THE POLICE IN THE UNITED STATES

A.    The English Roots of the American Police
  1.    Three major traditions passed from England to the United States:
    a.    limited authority
    b.    local control
    c.    organizational fragmentation
  2.    In early England, frankpledge system required that groups of ten families, called tithings, agree to uphold the law, maintain order, and commit to court those who had violated the law. Every male above the age of twelve was required to be part of the system. The tithing was fined if members did not perform their duties.
  3.    Parish constable system established in England in 1285 under the Statute of Winchester. All citizens required to pursue criminals under direction of constables. Traditional system of community law enforcement maintained well into the eighteenth century.
  4.    Bow Street Runners, amateur volunteer force in London impressed authorities with their effectiveness, but concept unable to spread around the country after death of founder, Henry Fielding, in 1754.
  5.    In 1829, under Home Secretary Sir Robert Peel, Parliament established the Metropolitan Constabulary for London, which was structured along the lines of a military unit. The Home Secretary was responsible for supervising the "bobbies" (named after Robert Peel).
  6.    Early English police mandate was to maintain order while keeping a low profile; attempted to use nonviolent methods and minimize conflict between police and public. Leaders feared that if the police were too powerful or too visible, they might threaten civil liberties. Four-part mandate:
    a.    Prevent crime without repressive use of force and avoid military intervention in community disturbances;
    b.    Manage public order nonviolently, using force to obtain compliance only as last resort;
    c.    Minimize and reduce conflict between the police and the public;
    d.    Demonstrate efficiency by means of the absence of crime and disorder rather than by physical evidence of police actions in dealing with problems.

B.    Policing in the United States
  1.    Before the Revolution, Americans shared English belief that community members had a basic responsibility to help maintain order. Over time, ethnic diversity, local political control, regional differences, the opening up of the West, and the violent traditions of American society were factors that brought about a different development of police in the United States compared with that in England.
  2.    The Political Era: 1840-1920
    a.    Growth of cities led to pressure for modernization of police forces. Cities faced ethnic conflicts as a consequence of massive immigration, hostility toward non-slave African-Americans, mob actions against banks and other institutions during economic declines: raised fears about the survival of democratic institutions.
    b.    Large cities, such as Boston and Philadelphia, took first steps toward adding daytime police force to supplement night watchmen.
    c.    In urban North, close ties developed between police and local political leaders; political party machine recruited and maintained the police and the police acted on behalf of local politicians. Police performed crime prevention,

order maintenance, and service functions in decentralized manner by responding to problems individually as they encountered them.

  d.   In the South, first organized police patrols in cities with large slave populations because whites feared revolts. "Slave patrols" had full powers to search, arrest, and administer corporal punishment against African-Americans.

  e.   The frontier West often governed by vigilante justice. Local sheriffs depended on the assistance of men in the community. Federal marshals were primarily responsible for courtroom security and custody of prisoners.

3.   The Professional Model Era: 1920-1970

  a.   Progressive reform movement pushed by upper-middle-class, educated Americans sought to rid government of party politics and patronage. Reformers influenced by the Progressive movement sought to professionalize police and remove the connections between police and local politicians. Two primary goals of Progressives were to create efficient government and us e government services to improve services for the poor.

  b.   Six elements emphasized in model of professional policing:
    i.   Police force should stay out of politics.
    ii.  Members should be well-trained, highly disciplined, and tightly organized.
    iii. Laws should be equally enforced.
    iv.  Police should take advantage of technological developments;
    v.   Merit rather than political patronage should be the basis of personnel decisions;
    vi.  Crime fighting should be prominent.

  c.   Switch to crime fighting emphasis from order maintenance emphasis did more to change the nature of American policing than did any of the other aspects of the professionalism model.

  d.   Reformers such as August Vollmer and O.W. Wilson introduced motorized patrols, radio communication, rapid response plans, and rotating beat assignments. Diminished connections between individual police officers and specific neighborhoods and citizens. The emphasis on professionalism encouraged the creation of national organizations such as the International Association of Police Chiefs.

  e.   By the 1930s and thereafter, police emphasized their concern with serious crimes as the police increased their reliance on technology, centralized decision making, and equal enforcement of the laws.

  f.   During the 1960s, the civil rights and anti-war movements as well as urban riots raised questions about the professional model. Police were isolated from the communities that they were supposed to serve and their attempts to maintain order appeared to focus on maintaining the status quo at the expense of political minorities, such as inner-city residents.

4.   The Community Model Era: 1970-Present

  a.   Research questioned the professional model's effectiveness. Important research findings clashed with major tenets of the professional crime-fighter model. These findings included:
    i.   Increasing number of police officers in neighborhood was found to have little effect on crime rate.
    ii.  Rapid response to calls for service does not greatly increase the arrest of criminals.
    iii. It is difficult if not impossible to improve rates of solving crimes.

  b.   Critics argued that professional model, especially use of motorized patrol, isolated police from the community.

  c.   James Q. Wilson and George Kelling argued in their "broken windows thesis" that a reorientation to little problems, such as maintenance of order, provision of services, and strategies to reduce the fear of crime, would be most beneficial for reducing community fear and improving quality of life by preventing neighborhood disorder and deterioration. Also would improve public attitudes toward the police by moving to a problem-oriented approach.

     d.    Remains to be seen whether this new orientation, which has its critics, will increase police effectiveness. Much depends on exactly what the public and government leaders expect police to accomplish.

## III.  LAW ENFORCEMENT AGENCIES

A.    <u>Federal Agencies</u>
Have taken dominant role in eyes of media and public although fewer in number than state and local agencies.

    1.    FBI:  broadest range of control; investigates all crimes not under control of other federal agencies.

        a.    J. Edgar Hoover became Director in 1924; made major changes to increase professionalism and reduce reputation for corruption and violation of civil liberties. After Hoover, the FBI has been criticized for its responsiveness to the policies of particular presidential administrations.

    2.    Other agencies:

        a.    Drug Enforcement Administration (DEA)
        b.    Bureau of Alcohol, Tobacco, and Firearms (BATF)
        c.    Secret Service; Div. of Treasury Dept. (responsible for counterfeiting, forgery, protection of the president).
        d.    Internal Revenue Service
        e.    Bureau of Postal Inspection
        f.    Border Patrol; Div. of Immigration and Naturalization Service
        g.    U.S. Coast Guard
        h.    National Parks Service

    3.    Internationalization of U.S. Law Enforcement:
The U.S. government has increasingly stationed officers overseas to address terrorism, drug trafficking, and other trans-border problems. U.S. officials have limited authority on foreign soil. Yet agents have been successful in tracking down terror and drug suspects abroad.

    4.    International agency: INTERPOL, headquartered in France, coordinates U.S. and other nations. The U.S. Interpol unit is the U.S. National Central Bureau which facilitates communication between foreign and U.S. law enforcement agencies. American police organizations have assisted in United Nations peacekeeping operations around the world.

B.    <u>State Agencies</u>
Every state except Hawaii has state police; in many states they fill the void for enforcement in rural areas; also may have state crime lab available for all local law enforcement agencies.

C.    <u>County Agencies</u>
Sheriffs are found in almost all of the 3,100 counties in the U.S.; traditionally have had responsibility for rural policing; sheriff often also has responsibility for local jail; may be selected by election or by political appointment depending on state.

D.    <u>Native American Tribal Police</u>:
Native American tribes have significant autonomy. Tribal law enforcement agencies may enforce laws on Native American reservations.

E.    <u>Municipal Agencies</u>:

Law enforcement departments exist in 1,000 cities and 20,000 towns, but only in cities do they fulfill all four functions; in large metropolitan areas many agencies engage in cross-jurisdiction cooperation

F.  Comparative Perspective: Organization of the Police in France: centralized national police force enforcing national criminal code.

IV.  POLICE FUNCTIONS

A.  General Functions
Complete list includes protect constitutional guarantees of free speech and assembly, facilitate movement of people and vehicles, resolve conflicts, identify problems, create and maintain feeling of security in community, and assist those who cannot care for themselves.

B.  Order Maintenance
Order Maintenance: prevent disturbances and threats to public peace. It requires the exercise of significant discretion when officers decide how to handle situations as they arise.

C.  Law Enforcement
Situations in which the law has been violated and only the identity of the guilty needs to be determined. Victims frequently delay calling the police, thereby reducing the likelihood of apprehending the offender.

D.  Service
First aid, rescuing animals, and extending social welfare services, especially to lower class citizens. Most calls to police are unrelated to crime and many are merely seeking information. Many of these functions may assist crime control, such as checking the doors of buildings, dealing with runaways and drunks, etc.

E.  Implementing the Mandate
　　1.　Police administrators have learned that they can gain greater support for their budgets by emphasizing the crime-fighting function.
　　2.　David Bayley argues that police do not prevent crime.
　　　　a.　There is no connection between number of officers and the crime rate.
　　　　b.　Primary strategies adopted by the police have not been shown to affect crime. These core strategies are patrolling the street by uniformed officers, rapid response to emergency calls, and expert investigation by detectives.

V.  POLICE POLICY
Police use their discretion in determining how to deploy resources and which criminal behaviors to address or overlook.

A.  Styles of Policing
Community influence on policing: James Q. Wilson found that political culture, reflecting socioeconomic characteristics of city and the organization of city government exerted major influence over police operational style:
　　1.　Watchman style: emphasize order maintenance in declining industrial town, partisan mayor-council form of government; ignore minor violations, especially traffic and juvenile.
　　2.　Legalistic style: emphasize law enforcement in good government council-manager form of government; police acted as if there was a single standard of community conduct; police professionalism; large number of traffic tickets and misdemeanor arrests.

3.  Service style: emphasize balance between maintaining order and law enforcement; less likely than the legalistic to make arrests in suburban communities; burglaries and assaults taken seriously, but seek to avoid arrests for minor offenses.

VI.  POLICE ACTIONS

A.  Encounters Between Police and Citizens
1.  The accessibility of the police to the citizen, the complainant's demeanor and characteristics, and the type of violation all structure official reaction and the probability of arrest. However, many people fail to call the police to report crimes because they believe that it is not worth the effort and the cost to the citizens' time. Thus citizens exercise control over police work by the decisions about whether or not to call the police.
2.  What Americans Think: Americans appear to have confidence in police.

B.  Police Discretion
Discretion is a characteristic of organizations: officials are given the authority to base decisions on their own judgment rather than on a formal set of rules.
1.  Discretion increases as one moves *down* the organizational hierarchy: patrol officers have the greatest amount of discretion in maintaining order and enforcing highly ambiguous laws (e.g. disorderly conduct, public drunkenness, breach of the peace, etc.)
2.  Officers exercise discretion in a number of ways: noninvolvement, arrest, informal handling of incident, etc.
3.  Four factors especially important in affecting officers' exercise of discretion:
    a.  Characteristics of crime.
    b.  Relationship between the alleged criminal and the victim.
    c.  Relationship between the police and the criminal or victim.
    d.  Departmental policies.
4.  Formal rules cannot cover all situations; officers must have a shared outlook that provides a common definition of situations they are likely to encounter.

C.  Domestic Violence
1.  Domestic violence perpetrated by men against women is consistent across racial and ethnic boundaries. African-American women, women aged 16-24 , from urban areas, and from lower income families are the most likely to be victims of violence by an intimate. Thirty percent of all female murder victims were killed by an intimate.
2.  Until mid-1970s, often not treated as serious criminal matter despite the fact that many women are victimized repeatedly. Concerns were expressed that police would make the situation worse for the victim by intervening into a "private family matter."
3.  Intervention in domestic disputes was also dangerous to police officers: volatile, emotional situations; police officer in field feels challenged to choose appropriate response to the situation.
4.  Close-up: Battered women, Reluctant Police: Joanne Tremins and Tracey Thurman cases in Torrington, Connecticut.
5.  In the past, officers tried to calm the couple and make a referral to social service agencies. Police departments began to reconsider their practices after research in Minneapolis and other cities found that abusive husbands who were arrested and briefly jailed were less likely to commit acts of domestic violence again.
6.  Research in Milwaukee indicated that factors such as the victim's injuries and the defendant's arrest record influenced the prosecutor's decision to charge.
7.  Policy changes were also enacted as a result of lawsuits against departments by injured women who claimed that police ignored evidence of criminal assaults. Police agencies have developed training programs for their officers concerning domestic violence.

VII. POLICE AND THE COMMUNITY

A.      Special Populations.
        1. Urban police have the complex task of working with social service agencies in dealing with special populations such as the homeless, runaways, mentally ill, drugs addicts, and alcoholics.

B.      Policing a Multicultural Society
        1.      Circumstances for effective police functions difficult, especially in urban areas where there is distrust of police and a lack of cooperation among some citizens.
        2.      The United States is growing more ethnically diverse, partly through immigration. Police relations with citizens may be hampered by stereotypes, cultural differences, and language barriers.
        3.      Two reasons that some urban residents resent the police are permissive law enforcement in poor neighborhoods that provides residents with unequal police protection, and allegations of police brutality.
        4.      Studies show that many police have biased attitudes toward the poor and members of racial minority groups.
        5.      The military organization of police and the "war on crime" mentality many encourage violence by police toward inner city residents.
        6.      CLOSE-UP: Living Under Suspicion
                Frequent experience of African Americans being hassled and even framed by the police.
        7.      Difficulties in police relationship to minority communities. Police may not strictly enforce some laws, yet be more aggressive in treating poor people or minority group members as potential suspects for other kinds of crimes.
C.      CLOSE-UP: Driving While Black

D.      Community Crime Prevention
        1.      There is now recognition that control of crime and disorder cannot rest on police; requires community cooperation and involvement: thus citizens' crime watch groups have proliferated.
        2.      Neighborhood watch; crime stopper programs on television and radio, other mechanisms for community involvement. Baltimore example of residents in a neighborhood working to improve area and reduce crime.


## REVIEW OF KEY TERMS

Fill in appropriate term for each statement

frankpledge
clearance rate
order maintenance function
service function
law enforcement function
watchman style
legalistic style
Bow Street Runners
Political Era
Statute of Winchester
FBI
Secret Service
federal agencies
state police
U.S. marshal

"posse comitatus"
Professional Model Era
Community Policing Era
"broken windows thesis"
discretion
service style
Gendarmerie Nationale
domestic violence
sheriff

1. _____ are responsible for many crimes that cross state boundaries.

2. _____ emphasizes strict enforcement of all laws.

3. _____ constitutes the contemporary era in American policing history that seeks to reconnect law enforcement officers with the citizens.

4. _____ emphasizes order maintenance and arrests only for major infractions but historically associated with discriminatory practices.

5. _____ exists everywhere except Hawaii and serves useful functions for law enforcement on highways and in rural areas.

6. _____ was the name commonly applied to the London law enforcement group established by Henry Fielding in the eighteenth century.

7. _____ was associated with law enforcement in the frontier West but is currently primarily responsible for federal courthouse security and guarding prisoners.

8. _____ is the French national police organization.

9. _____ emphasizes that fear of crime grows from disorder in society.

10. _____ is the primary federal law enforcement agency that deals with such crimes as bank robbery and kidnapping.

11. _____ is the historical era in which modern technologies were developed and applied to policing.

12. _____ is employed by police in dealing with tense confrontations and disputes on the streets.

13. _____ is the function that the public often believes is the primary focus of police resources.

14. _____ was formed upon the call of local law enforcement officials in frontier areas who needed the citizens' help in fighting crime.

15. _____ is a style which creates avoidance of arrests for minor offenses and use of nonarrest sanctions because the police emphasize other goals and activities.

16. _____ provided the early English system of families committing themselves to protect each other and their communities.

17. _____ emphasizes the prevention of behavior that either disturbs or threatens to disturb the public peace.

18. _____ constituted the earliest era in the American policing history.

19. _____ is the primary federal agency that deals with counterfeiting.

20. _____ is often an elected official.

21. _____ has been a problem area that has challenged police departments' biases and effectiveness as experimental policies are developed for fair decision making that will prevent future problems.

22. _____ frequently encompasses the largest number of tasks performed by police officers on a daily basis.

23. _____ is the percentage rate of crimes that police believe they have resolved by making arrests.

24. _____ established the parish constable system in England.

## REVIEW OF KEY PEOPLE

Fill in the appropriate name

Henry Fielding
J. Edgar Hoover
August Vollmer
James Q. Wilson & George Kelling
Sir Robert Peel
O.W. Wilson

1. _____ was responsible for professionalizing the FBI.

2. _____ developed the "broken windows thesis."

3. _____ established the first unofficial police force in London.

4. _____ advocated professionalization of police and police intervention into the lives of citizens before they entered into crime.

5. _____ oversaw the development of the official police force in England.

6. _____ was an ardent proponent of motorized patrols and rapid response as the means to facilitate effective crime fighting.

## GENERAL PRACTICE QUESTIONS

Although many Americans believe the police devote their primary efforts to the ____1____ function, in part because the police created this image with the emphasis they developed during the ____2____ era, most scholars recognize that officers devote more time and tasks to the ____3____ function.

Among the ____4____ concerned with law enforcement responsibilities, the ____5____ has the broadest responsibilities. However, they do not have responsibilities for as many crimes as local officials, such as the county ____6____.

When police officers perform their ____7____ function, such as when they are called to ____8____ situations, they must use ____9____ to determine whether or not make arrest.

## SELF-TEST SECTION

## MULTIPLE CHOICE QUESTIONS

5.1. How many families were in a tithing?
a) one
b) two
c) five
d) seven
e) ten

5.2. Why did an organized police force develop in England during
the eighteenth century?
a) growth of commerce and industry
b) decline of farming
c) social disorder in the large cities
d) all of the above
e) none of the above

5.3. Federal law enforcement agencies are part of what branch of government?
a) judiciary
b) executive
c) legislative
d) local
e) state

5.4. When was the Bureau of Investigation (later renamed the FBI) established?
a) 1908
b) 1924
c) 1972
d) 1980
e) 1994

5.5. Where is the International Criminal Police Organization (Interpol) based in the world?
a) Stuttgart, Germany
b) New York, New York
c) Brussels, Belgium
d) Moscow, Russia
e) Lyons, France

5.6. Which of the following best describes police organization in France?
a) decentralized
b) highly centralized
c) highly decentralized
d) somewhat centralized
e) there is no police organization in France

5.7. For the most part, what role is emphasized by the police?
a) crime fighter
b) social service provider
c) crime preventer
d) crime investigator
e) social service investigator

5.8. What community would you most likely find the legalistic style of policing?
a) reform-minded city
b) middle class suburban
c) mixed racial/ethnic composition
d) blue collar
e) all of the above

5.9. What community would you most likely find the service style of policing?
a) reform-minded city
b) middle class suburban
c) mixed socio-economic
d) blue collar
e) all of the above

5.10. What community would you most likely find the watchman style of policing?
a) blue collar
b) mixed racial/ethnic composition
c) declining industrial city
d) all of the above
e) none of the above

5.11. What community would you most likely find the legalistic style of policing?
a) blue collar
b) middle class suburban
c) mixed socio-economic
d) blue collar
e) all of the above

5.12. The beating of Rodney King is an example of an abuse resulting from the...
a) watchman style
b) service style
c) legalistic style
d) all of the above
e) none of the above

5.13. Who developed the three styles of policing-watchman, legalistic, and service?
a) Robert Peel
b) James Q. Wilson
c) J. Edgar Hoover
d) Henry Fielding
e) August Vollmer

5.14. Who was chief of police in Berkeley, California (1909-1932) and a leading advocate of professional policing?
a) Robert Peel
b) James Q. Wilson
c) J. Edgar Hoover
d) Henry Fielding
e) August Vollmer

5.15. Who wrote the book, Fixing Broken Windows, about strategies to restore order and reduce crime in the U. S.?
a) Robert Peel and James Q. Wilson
b) O. W Wilson and August Vollmer
c) J. Edgar Hoover and Henry Fielding
d) George Kelling and Catherine Coles
e) Wyatt Earp and Mark Moore

5.16. What are the three historical periods of policing?
a) political, professional, and community model
b) pre-colonial, colonial, and post-colonial
c) crime fighter, crime preventer, and service provider
d) watchman, legalistic, and service
e) crime control, crime and order, and order

5.17. As chief of police of Wichita, Kansas, who promoted the use of motorized patrols and rapid response?
a) Robert Peel
b) James Q. Wilson
c) J. Edgar Hoover
d) O. W. Wilson
e) August Vollmer

5.18. Who wrote the article, "Broken Windows: The Police and Neighborhood Safety" about how police should work more on little problems?
a) Robert Peel and Bat Masterson
b) O. W Wilson and August Vollmer
c) J. Edgar Hoover and Henry Fielding
d) George Kelling and James Q. Wilson
e) Wyatt Earp and Mark Moore

5.19. What year did the Fraternal Order of Police form?
a) 1896
b) 1902
c) 1915
d) 1924
e) 1972

5.20. What year did the International Order of Chiefs of Police form?
a) 1896
b) 1902
c) 1915
d) 1924
e) 1972

5.21. Where did the term "posse" originate?
a) Latin term for " police"
b) French term for "public"
c) Old English term for "possessing the convict"
d) Latin term for "power of the country"
e) German term for "capture of prisoners"

5.22. During what policing era does fingerprinting develop?
a) political
b) professional
c) community
d) all of the above
e) none of the above

5.23. During what policing era does close personal contact between officers and citizens occur?
a) political
b) professional
c) community
d) all of the above
e) none of the above

5.24. During what policing era does the use of motorcycle units occur?
a) political
b) professional
c) community
d) all of the above
e) none of the above

5.25. During what policing era do political machines dominate?
a) political
b) professional
c) community
d) all of the above
e) none of the above

**TRUE/FALSE QUESTIONS**

5.1. The roots of American policing derive largely from England.

5.2. The organization of police in France is decentralized.

5.3. British police did not have to deal with ethnic diversity.

5.4. The professional era of policing involved staying out of politics.

5.5. The urban riots of the 1960s did not affect the assumptions of the professional model.

5.6. Community policing involved more foot patrols.

5.7. Within the United States, Native Americans tribes have no sovereignty.

5.8. Providing first aid is an example of a service function.

5.9. The service style of policing is most likely found in a declining industrial city.

5.10. American policing did not develop differently in the South as opposed to the Northeast.

5.11. British police are called "bobbies" after Sir Robert Peel.

5.12. In the United States, police power resides with the federal government.

5.13. One aspect of American policing is limited authority.

5.14. Community policing began in the 1920s.

5.15. A tithing is a group of two families.

5.16. The political era of policing involved police corruption.

5.17. France has a stable history and, therefore, maintaining order is not a priority.

5.18. The service style of policing places a balance between law enforcement and order maintenance.

5.19. The watchman style of policing emphasizes law enforcement.

5.20. Public confidence is important for police if they are to do their job well.

# ANSWER KEY

## Key Terms
1.     federal agencies (or FBI)
2.     legalistic style
3.     Community Policing era
4.     watchman style
5.     state police
6.     Bow Street Runners
7.     U.S. marshal
8.     Gendarmerie Nationale
9.     "broken windows thesis"
10.    FBI
11.    Professional Model era
12.    discretion
13.    law enforcement function
14.    "posse comitatus"
15.    service style
16.    frankpledge
17.    order maintenance function
18.    Political era
19.    Secret Service
20.    sheriff
21.    domestic violence
22.    service function
23.    clearance rate
24.    Statute of Winchester

## Key People
1.     J. Edgar Hoover
2.     James Q. Wilson & George Kelling
3.     Henry Fielding
4.     August Vollmer
5.     Sir Robert Peel
6.     O.W. Wilson

## General Practice Questions
1.     law enforcement
2.     Professional Model
3.     service
4.     federal agencies
6.     sheriff
7.     order maintenance
8.     domestic violence
9.     discretion

## Multiple Choice
5.1.     e
5.2.     d
5.3.     b
5.4.     a
5.5.     e
5.6.     b
5.7.     a
5.8.     a

| | |
|---|---|
| 5.9. | b |
| 5.10. | d |
| 5.11. | c |
| 5.12. | a |
| 5.13. | b |
| 5.14. | e |
| 5.15. | d |
| 5.16. | a |
| 5.17. | d |
| 5.18. | d |
| 5.19. | c |
| 5.20. | b |
| 5.21. | d |
| 5.22. | b |
| 5.23. | c |
| 5.24. | b |
| 5.25. | a |

True/False

| | |
|---|---|
| 5.1. | T |
| 5.2. | F |
| 5.3. | T |
| 5.4. | T |
| 5.5. | F |
| 5.6. | T |
| 5.7. | F |
| 5.8. | T |
| 5.9. | F |
| 5.10. | F |
| 5.11. | T |
| 5.12. | F |
| 5.13. | T |
| 5.14. | F |
| 5.15. | F |
| 5.16. | T |
| 5.17. | F |
| 5.18. | T |
| 5.19. | F |
| 5.20. | T |

WORKSHEET 5.1: ORGANIZATION OF THE POLICE

Imagine that you are a member of Congress. One of your staff assistants brings you a proposal to nationalize law enforcement throughout the United States. The proposal calls for abolishing state police agencies, county sheriffs, and local police departments. Instead, Congress would create a new U.S. Department of Law Enforcement. A Secretary of Law Enforcement would oversee a national police agency which would have units established in each state, county, city, and town. Your assistant argues that the new organization would save resources by coordinating the work of every law enforcement officer in the nation and creating a standard set of law enforcement policies and priorities. In addition, the plan would standardize training, salary, and benefits for police officers everywhere and thus raise the level of professionalism of police, especially in small towns and rural areas.

Before you decide whether or not to present this proposal to Congress, respond to the following questions.

1. Are there any undesirable consequences that could develop from putting this plan into action?

_____

_____

_____

_____

_____

2. As a politician, you are concerned about how others will react to the plan. How do you think each group would react and why?

a. Voters_____

_____

_____

b. State and local politicians_____

_____

_____

c. Police officers_____

_____

_____

3. Will you support the proposal? Why or why not?

_____

_____

WORKSHEET 5.2:  POLICE POLICY

You are a retired police chief.  A state government has hired you to provide advice on the appropriate police policy to implement in several jurisdictions.  You advise them on whether to choose the watchman, legalistic, or service style.  Explain why.

A.  A city of 100,000 that contains a diverse mixture of Whites, African-Americans, Asian-Americans, and Hispanics.  The unemployment rate is high.  Few wealthy people live in the city.  Most people are middle-class, but 25 percent of the citizens qualify for government assistance.  The police department reflects the racial/ethnic mix of the city's population.

B.  A small town of 2,000 residents.  Most residents work in one lumber mill or in businesses that serve loggers and farmers who live in the area.  The town's population is almost entirely white, except when large numbers of people from various minority groups arrive in the summer and fall to work on local farms.

C.  A suburb with 15,000 residents.  Twenty percent of the residents are members of minority groups.  Nearly all of the town's residents are white-collar or professional workers with high incomes.  Most people commute to a big city to work.

A._____

_____

_____

_____

_____

_____

B._____

_____

_____

_____

_____

_____

C._____

_____

_____

_____

_____

_____

### CHAPTER 6

# POLICE OFFICERS AND LAW ENFORCEMENT OPERATIONS

## LEARNING OBJECTIVES

After covering the material in this chapter, students should understand:

1.      the recruitment, training, and socialization of police officers;

2.      the recruitment and integration of women and minority officers;

3.      the police subculture, including the working personality and the elements of danger and authority;

4.      the organization of police departments and their allocation of resources;

5.      police action and decision making, including organizational response and productivity issues;

6.      the role of detectives and the investigation function, including the apprehension process and forensic techniques;

7.      the role of specialized operations in traffic, vice, and drug enforcement.

## CHAPTER SUMMARY

The police must recruit and train individuals who will uphold the law and receive citizen support. Improvements have been made during the past quarter- century in recruiting more officers who are women, racial and ethnic minorities, and well-educated applicants. The police work in an environment greatly influenced by their subculture. The concept of the working personality helps us understand the influence of the police subculture on how individual officers see their world. The isolation of the police strengthens bonds among officers but may also add to job stress. Police operations are shaped by their formal organizational structures and also influenced by social and political processes both within and outside the department. The police are organized along military lines so that authority and responsibility can be located at appropriate levels. Police services are delivered through the work of the patrol, investigation, and specialized operations units. The patrol function has three components: answering calls for assistance, maintaining a police presence, and probing suspicious circumstances. The investigation function is the responsibility of detectives in close coordination with patrol officers. The felony apprehension process is a sequence of actions that includes crime detection, preliminary investigation, follow-up investigation, clearance, and arrest. Specialized units dealing with traffic, drug, and vice are found in large departments .

## CHAPTER OUTLINE

I.      INTRODUCTION
        Officer John Reilly was shot in May 1996 in Bristol, Connecticut. This demonstrates the dangers associated with police work. . In America, law enforcement agencies face these dangerous and difficult situations as they deal with crime, violence, racial tensions, and drugs. Handling such situations, often without warning or with incomplete information, is problematic for patrol officers--especially since they must try to do so within the limits of the law.

II.    WHO ARE THE POLICE?

A.    Recruitment
1.    People have various motivations in seeking a career in law enforcement:  public service, secure government work, adventure, etc.
2.    Minimum standards and low pay will attract only those unable to enter more attractive occupations.  Need to have desirable pay and benefits.
3.    Increasingly departments are able to attract college educated recruits.
   a.    Recruits must pass physical exam, background check, physical fitness test, and psychological tests.
4.    Federally funded Police Corps program provides reimbursement of college expenses for college grads who agree to serve for four years on a police force.

B.    Training
1.    Police academy run by large departments or by the state for rural and town recruits.
2.    Recruits told that real learning will take place on the job.
3.    Process of *socialization* includes learning informal practices as well as formal rules.
4.    Officers work in an organizational framework in which rank carries privileges and responsibilities.
   a.    Performance measured by their contribution to the group's success.
5.    Patrol officers are expected to handle a multitude of difficult situations.

C.    The Changing Profile of the Police
1.    Changes away from all white, all male police forces spurred by:
   a.    Police-community relations problems.
   b.    Urban riots of the 1960s that were caused by conflict between white police and minority communities.
   c.    Equal opportunity laws.
2.    Minority Police Officers
   a.    Studies show increased representativeness in many of the country's largest departments.
   b.    Election of African-American or Hispanic mayor does not necessarily mean that the police department will become more open and representative.
3.    Women on the Force
   a.    First woman officer in 1905 in Portland, Oregon.  Only 1.5 percent of officers women in 1970; up to only 10 percent twenty years later.  Women may make up 16 percent of force in large cities of 250,000 or more, but about half of U.S. police agencies employ no women.
   b.    Most women have easily met performance requirements, but it is at the social level that they have met their greatest resistance.  Male officers often doubt that women can physically back them up in a crime situation or disturbance.
   c.    Resistance may also be based on cultural expectations by male officers and public about women's role and behavior.  Women may be subjected to sexual harassment.
   d.    Comparative Perspective: Women Police Officers and the Status of Women in Society Opportunities for women to serve as law enforcement officers are typically affected by a society's views about the appropriate roles for women.
   e.    CLOSE-UP:  Patrol Officer Cristina Murphy

III.    THE SUBCULTURE OF THE POLICE

A.    Subculture Defined
1.    Subculture is a subdivision of national culture defined by occupation, ethnicity, class, and residence: forms functioning group unity of shared values, beliefs, and attitudes -- leads police to have shared expectations about human behavior.

2. The police subculture produces a working personality: a complex of emotional and behavioral characteristics developed by members of an occupational group in response to the work situation and environmental influences.

B. The Working Personality
   1. One's occupational environment shapes the way one interprets events. Two important elements in police working personality: danger and authority.
   2. Danger
      a. Police are especially attentive to signs of potential violence because they work in dangerous situations.
      b. Socialization process teaches recruits to be cautious and suspicious. Orientation toward watching and questioning can contribute to tension and conflict in contacts with the public.
      c. Police officers constantly on edge watching for unexpected dangers, on duty and off duty.
   3. Authority
      a. Police officers, a symbol of authority with low occupation status, must often be assertive in establishing authority with citizenry. This can lead to conflict, hostility, and perhaps overreaction and police brutality.
      b. Officer expected to remain detached, neutral, and unemotional even when challenged and in situations of conflict.
   4. Public Morality: High sense of morality in the law enforcement subculture. Morality helps police overcome dilemmas. Dilemma of contradiction between the goal of preventing crime and police inability to do so. Dilemma of using discretion to handle situations that do always strictly follow established procedure. Dilemma of police must invariably act against at least one person's interest, including the possibility of injuring or killing someone. Morality is helpful in encouraging police to serve the public under difficult conditions, but may also lead to negative impact if police use morality to engage in stereotyping in categorizing people.
   5. Police Isolation
      a. Public generally supportive of police, but police perceive public to be hostile; officers tend to socialize primarily with other officers.
      b. Officers' contacts with the public are frequently during moments of conflict, crisis, and emotion.
      c. Because police officers are so identified with their jobs, members of the public frequently treat them as police, even when off-duty. Increases the need for bonding and socializing between officers, officers' families, and families of other officers. Develop group identity.
      d. Officers may be unable to step back from jobs and separate their professional and personal lives.
      What Americans Think: Racial differences in Americans' assessments of police honesty and ethics.
   6. Job Stress
      a. Working environment and subculture affect physical and mental health in form of marital problems, health problems, and drinking problems. Suicide can be a problem.
         i. External stress: real threats and dangers on the job.
         ii. Organizational stress: produced by paramilitary character of police forces -- odd hours, changing schedules, detailed rules and procedures.
         iii. Personal stress: may be affected by racial or gender status, or by not adjusting to group-held values.
         iv. Operational stress: total effect of the need to confront daily the tragedies of urban life.

b.       Police departments had been slow to address issue of stress, but many have
         developed counseling, liberal disability rules and other mechanisms.

IV.    ORGANIZATION OF THE POLICE

A.     Organization of Departments
   1.      Police have traditionally been organized in a military manner with a hierarchical
           structure of ranks in order to make discipline, control, and accountability primary
           values. This is thought to assist in efficient mobilization of police and as a means to
           control police in order to protect civil liberties.
   2.      The structure of a well-organized police department is designed to fulfill five functions:
           a.       Apportion workload among members and units according to a logical plan
           b.       Ensure that lines of authority and responsibility are as definite and direct as
                    possible.
           c.       Specify a unit of command throughout so that there is no question as to which
                    orders should be followed.
           d.       Place responsibility, accompanied by commensurate authority. If the
                    authority is delegated, hold the user accountable.
           e.       Coordinate efforts of members and units so that all will work harmoniously to
                    accomplish the mission.
   3.      Districts and precincts may be established throughout city. Separate functional units may
           be established for: patrol, investigation, traffic, vice, and juvenile.
   4.      Usually only middle-sized to large cities maintain specialized vice and juvenile units.
   5.      The role of the police bureaucracy in the broader criminal justice system:
           a.       Police are the gateway to the justice system through which information and
                    individuals enter. Officers' use of discretion in arresting individuals and
                    investigating cases defines the nature and quality of cases entered.
           b.       Police officers' administrative decisions are influenced by the fact that others
                    determine the ultimate outcome of the case. Officers may feel that they are
                    ignored or looked down upon by prosecutors, lawyers, or judges.
           c.       Police officers are expected to observe rules and obey superiors while
                    simultaneously exercising independent, discretionary judgments.

V.     POLICE RESPONSE AND ACTION

A.     Organizational Context
   1.      Police in democracy organized mainly to be *reactive* (citizen-invoked calls for service)
           rather than *proactive* (police-invoked).
   2.      Police arrive after the fact, thus reports by victims and observers define the boundaries of
           policing.
   3.      The public has come to expect that police will respond to every call. This results in
           incident-driven policing.
   4.      Police employ proactive strategies such as surveillance in some contexts. As more police
           personnel are allocated to proactive operations, the number of resulting arrests are likely
           to rise.

B.     Organizational Response
   1.      Administrative environment and organization of department affect the way in which calls
           are processed as well as the nature of police response.
   2.      Centralization of communications (i.e., 911 numbers and two-way radios) has altered
           past practices of individual officers observing and addressing crime problems in
           neighborhoods. Now police react to instructions from communications center and can
           report back for further instructions and assistance.

3. Police departments use *differential response strategies* for calls. Dispatchers make decisions about whether or not a patrol car needs to rush to the scene of each call. A delayed response may be just as effective depending on the nature of the call.

4. Advocates of community policing believe that advances in communication technology further isolate the officers from the community and prevent them from building rapport.

5. Close-Up: Holding the 911 Line

C. Productivity
1. Following the lead of New York City's Compstat program, several cities now emphasize accountability at the precinct level. Local commanders must explain the results of their efforts to combat crime.

2. Police have difficulty in measuring the quantity and quality of their work.

3. Crime rates and clearance rates are problematic measures of police productivity.

4. The clearance rate varies by the nature of the offense.

5. Police often use "activity" as a measure (i.e., tickets issued, arrests made, suspects stopped for questioning), although this does not necessarily reflect, for example, the complete range of order maintenance functions. It may actually be more beneficial for society when police spend their time calming conflicts, becoming acquainted with citizens, and providing services and information for people.
What Americans Think: Favorable attitudes toward the ability of the police to combat crime.

VI. DELIVERY OF POLICE SERVICES

A. Division of Responsibilities
1. Line units: directly involved in operational activities, accounts for approximately 84 percent of personnel. Patrol bureau generally the largest, accounting for two-thirds of all sworn officers. Staff functions supplement or support the line functions.

B. Patrol
1. Patrol officers make up two-thirds of all sworn officers. In small communities, the patrol force constitutes the entire department.

2. Patrol function has three components.
   a. Answering calls for assistance
   b. Maintaining a police presence.
   c. Probing suspicious circumstances.

3. When not responding to calls, officers engage in preventive patrol--making the police presence known to deter crime and to be available to respond to calls.

4. Patrol officers' presence in a community can be major factor in reducing *fear* of crime. Patrol may also improve community relations and increase citizen cooperation with police.

5. Patrol work is low status, entry level, often viewed as boring, thankless and taken for granted, yet patrol officers carry the major burden of the criminal justice system in confronting difficult conflict situations and making discretionary decisions.

C. INVESTIGATION

1. Detective Responsibilities All units usually involved with investigation, but patrol unit's preliminary investigation is crucial because success in some cases is linked to the speed of identifying and arresting the offender. When offender not immediately apprehended, then investigation often transferred to detectives: higher status and pay, less supervision, and devoted to crime fighting rather than other functions

2. Detectives often organized by type of crime that they investigate (homicide, robbery, etc.). One criticism of detectives is that they may duplicate work of patrol or break continuity of investigation by transferring case to separate unit. Detectives in small departments must be generalists.

102

3. Detectives involved when:
   a. Serious crime occurs and offender immediately identified and apprehended. Detective prepares case for prosecutor.
   b. Offender is identified but not apprehended, so detective tries to locate individual.
   c. When offender is not identified but there are several suspects, the detective conducts investigation aimed at either confirming or disproving suspicions.
   d. When there is no suspect, the detective must start from scratch.
4. Detectives rely on technical expertise in their department and from cooperating police forces.

B. Apprehension
   Stages in Process:
   1. Crime detected.
   2. Preliminary investigation, usually by patrol officer. Information gathered in this immediate phase is crucial; need accurate identification of victim and witnesses. So-called "hot search" immediately at crime scene.
   3. Follow-up investigation, often by detective in larger cities. Incidents other than murder, rape, and suicide often receive little attention from detectives. Investigations involve a number of discretionary decisions by detectives. "Cold search" may involve reinterviewing witnesses after the fact and searching for additional evidence.
   4. Clearance and arrest: a crime is cleared when evidence supports the arrest of a suspect or when suspect admits committing the offense. Clearance does not mean that the suspect will eventually be found guilty.

C. Forensic Techniques
   1. Use of science to aid in gathering evidence: fingerprints, blood sample analysis, DNA analysis. Forensic component of investigation hampered if there is a lack of facilities that can do the complete range of tests. Localities often rely on state crime lab or on FBI crime lab.
   2. Full implementation of DNA fingerprinting must wait until enough labs fully equipped for such analysis. Hold great potential for investigating various crimes.
   3. New Directions in Criminal Justice Policy National DNA Database: Many states and the federal government are building a national database of DNA records that is maintained by the FBI. The project is known as CODIS, which stands for Combined DNA Index System

D. Research on Investigation
   1. Research suggests that the police have overrated the importance of investigation as a means of solving crimes and shows that most crimes are cleared because of arrests made by the patrol force at or near the scene. Response time -- time from commission of crime to arrival of police -- is very important element in apprehension as is the identification of the suspect by the victim.
      1. Detectives important because high status gives patrol officers a goal to seek and fulfills public's expectation that police will conduct investigations.

E. Special Operations
   1. Traffic: authorities disagree about whether or not to create separate units for traffic responsibilities. Traffic work is highly discretionary and essentially proactive, and the level of enforcement can be considered a direct result departmental policies and norms. Traffic enforcement is one area in which departments enforce norms of productivity.
   2. Vice: enforcement against prostitution, gambling, narcotics, etc. depends on proactive police work. Because of the nature of the crimes, political influence is sometimes brought to bear to dampen enforcement.

Increasingly police are using electronic surveillance and undercover work. Frequent reliance on informants creates problems. Critics fear that such operations move away from opening policing and thereby threaten civil liberties.

3. Drug Enforcement: many large cities have separate drug bureaus within police departments. Different strategies employed, including flooding "drug market" areas with police officers aggressively making arrests. Police activities may only move drug dealers to different location. Law enforcement efforts have not stopped sales and use of illegal drugs.

4. War on Drugs has consumed significant resources. There are questions about whether law enforcement is the best approach to addressing society's drug problems.

## REVIEW OF KEY TERMS

Fill in the appropriate term for each statement
line functions
sworn officers
directed patrol
differential response
aggressive patrol
problem-oriented policing
arrest
reactive patrol
proactive patrol
detectives
vice unit
traffic unit
productivity
staff functions
preventive patrol
response time
foot patrol
community-oriented policing
preliminary investigation
clearance rate
forensic techniques

1. _____ is an approach in which officers seek to identify, analyze, and respond to the underlying circumstances that create the incidents that generate citizens' calls for police assistance.

2. _____ are basic police operations performed by units such as patrol and traffic.

3. _____ is something difficult to measure because of the varied responsibilities of police officers, although arrests, traffic tickets, and other indicators have been used for this purpose.

4. _____ is the typical American patrol strategy that involves officers responding to citizens' calls.

5. _____ is a critical component of police performance in the eyes of the public although, depending on the nature of the crime, the police will not necessarily make more arrests by doing a more impressive job with respect to this measure.

6. _____ is a strategy designed to direct patrol resources in a proactive manner against known high crime areas

7. _____ is viewed by many as a critical element in community-oriented policing because it brings officers into closer contact with the public.

8. _____ is the initial examination of witnesses and crime scene by patrol officers.

9. _____ are police employees who have taken an oath and been given powers by the state to make arrests and use force in accordance with their duties.

10. _____ is the police subdivision responsible for enforcement of laws against prostitution.

11. _____ involves the use of scientific testing including chemical testing of substances and DNA analysis.

12. _____ is the general patrol strategy in which officers actively seek to identify and apprehend lawbreakers; used heavily for traffic and vice enforcement.

13. _____ is a measure of police productivity based on arrests supported by evidence rather than ultimate convictions and sentences for crimes.

14. _____ is a strategy involving dispatchers prioritizing calls for service and using various response options.

15. _____ are the high status officers responsible for investigation after patrol officers have completed preliminary investigation.

16. _____ is the police subdivision which can have its productivity most easily measured.

17. _____ is a philosophy of patrol and resource allocation that emphasizes closer contact between officers and citizens and the development of officers' knowledge about the conditions, needs, problems, and personalities in specific neighborhoods.

18. _____ are performed by supplemental police staff not involved in direct operations.

19. _____ is a proactive patrol strategy which may involve greater numbers of on-street interrogations and traffic stops.

20. _____ is the job stress produced by entering a dark building or responding to a report of "a man with a gun."

21. _____ is the process by which the rules, symbols, informal practices, and values of a group are learned by its members.

22. _____ is the job stress produced by the need to confront daily tragedies and feel unappreciated for facing danger in the public interest.

23. _____ is a key element of the police working personality which makes officer continuously cautious and on guard.

24. _____ is the job stress inherently produced by paramilitary character of police forces and the constant adjustment to changing schedules.

## REVIEW OF KEY PEOPLE

George W. Bush
Lola Baldwin
Cristina Murphy

1. The first female police officer was _____ in 1905 in Portland, Oregon.
2. President _____ created a Department of Homeland Security that produced job changes within federal agencies, such as the movement of officers from various agencies into the expanded Sky Marshals program to provide security on airline flights.
3. Patrol Officer _____ stated that "women, they sometimes just can't stand the idea that a woman exists who can have power over them. They feel powerless and expect all women to feel that way too. As I said, everyone has an opinion."

## GENERAL PRACTICE QUESTIONS

When police decide to allocate resources to crime "hot spots," they use ____1____, which is a form of ____2____ because it involves police initiative rather than reaction.


Police may directly address problems in a community through ____3____, which involves in-depth examination recurring problems, and through ____4____ which will bring officers in closer contact with citizens in their neighborhoods.


_____5_____ is not a particularly good measure of ____6____ because it is so heavily dependent on prompt reports from victims and witnesses and because impressive performance will not necessarily increase the rate of arrests.


There are two elements in the ____7____ which affect police officers' views and interpretations of situation. One element, ____8____, leads officers to be suspicious and cautious, and the other element, ____9____, leads officers to feel isolated from a society in which people always see the officer as enforcer of the law, even in off-duty hours.


After many problems with police-community relations in inner-city neighborhoods, many departments sought to recruit ____10____ in the hope that, among other things, officers' discretionary decisions would produce a reduction in the corrupt behavior classified as ____11____ in which groups of citizens are treated unequally.

# SELF-TEST SECTION

## MULTIPLE CHOICE QUESTIONS

6.1. What bars state and local governments from discriminating in their hiring practices?
a) Equal Employment Opportunity Act of 1972
b) Civil Rights Act of 1866
c) Jim Crow laws
d) Equal Access Employment Act of 1987
e) Article V of the U. S. Constitution

6.2. Which of the following is a line function?
a) patrol
b) investigation
c) traffic control
d) vice
e) all of the above

6.3. What is the clearance rate for prostitution arrests?
a) 10 %
b) 25%
c) 50%
d) 75%
e) 100%

6.4. Which of the following is TRUE of police work?
a) working personality and occupational environment are closely linked and have a major impact on police work
b) working personality and occupational environment are closely linked and have a minor impact on police work
c) working personality and occupational environment are not linked and have no impact on police work
d) working personality and occupational environment are closely linked and have no impact on police work
e) working personality and occupational environment are not linked and have a major impact on police work

6.5. What type of stress is produced by real threats and dangers?
a) external stress
b) organizational stress
c) personal stress
d) operational stress
e) none of the above

6.6. What type of stress is produced by the nature of police work?
a) external stress
b) organizational stress
c) personal stress
d) operational stress
e) none of the above

6.7. What type of stress is produced by gender status among peers?
a) external stress
b) organizational stress
c) personal stress
d) operational stress
e) none of the above

6.8. What type of stress is produced by being lied to on the job by a thief?
a) external stress
b) organizational stress
c) personal stress
d) operational stress
e) none of the above

6.9. What is TRUE about the profile of the American police officer in
the 21st century?
a) there are fewer women than in the past
b) there are fewer nonwhites than in the past
c) officers are better educated than in the past
d) all of the above are TRUE
e) all of the above are FALSE

6.10. In Baltimore, what is the system designed to reduce the number of nonemergency calls to 911?
a) 211 system
b) 311 system
c) 411 system
d) 007 system
e) 611 system

6.11. What is the origin of the word "patrol"?
a) from a Scottish word meaning "rolling police"
b) from a German word meaning "police action"
c) from a French word meaning "to tramp around in the mud"
d) from a Spanish word meaning "to dance in the streets"
e) from a Latin word meaning "walking with authority"

6.12. How many instances does rapid police response really make a difference?
a) none
b) a small fraction
c) about one-half
d) a great many
e) all

6.13. Which of the following delays slow the process of calling the police?
a) ambiguity delays
b) coping delays
c) conflict delays
d) all of the above
e) none of the above

6.14. In the past, patrols were organized by "beats" because it was assumed that...
a) crime could happen anywhere
b) police could "beat" criminals at their game
c) police could use timing techniques to solve crimes
d) criminals were all "deadbeats"
e) all of the above

6.15. Which of the following is NOT a function of a well-organized police department?
a) clear lines of authority
b) division of labor
c) each working separately to achieve goals
d) unity of command
e) link duties with appropriate authority

6.16. Urban police departments are divided into...
a) units
b) wards
c) precincts
d) classes
e) categories

6.17. Which of the following is an example of a proactive strategy?
a) responding to a citizens' call
b) undercover work
c) citizen approaching police on the street with information
d) all of the above
e) none of the above

6.18. Which of the following is an example of a reactive strategy?
a) surveillance
b) undercover work
c) waiting for a citizen to approach police on the street with information
d) all of the above
e) none of the above

6.19. How can a police officer best handle stress?
a) work harder
b) keep to yourself
c) seek counseling
d) all of the above
e) none of the above

6.20. Which of the following is a change in the profile of police in the past thirty years?
a) more women are police officers
b) more nonwhites are police officers
c) police officers are better educated
d) all of the above are examples of changes in the past thirty years
e) none of the above are examples of changes in the past thirty years

6.21. Which of the following is TRUE about police work and stress?
a) more police die by their own hands than are killed in the line of duty
b) stress is not a problem today for police, but it was in the past
c) police are less likely to commit suicide than a member of the general public
d) all of the above are TRUE
e) all of the above are FALSE

6.22. If a police officer feels uncomfortable because of his/her race, this is an example of...
a) external stress
b) organizational stress
c) personal stress
d) operational stress
e) occupational stress

6.23. If a police officer experiences stress because of constant schedule changes, this is an example of...
a) external stress
b) organizational stress
c) personal stress
d) operational stress
e) occupational stress

6.24. If a police officer experiences stress because of a high speed chase, this is an example of ...
a) external stress
b) organizational stress
c) personal stress
d) operational stress
e) occupational stress

6.25. If a police officer experiences stress because he/she is afraid of a lawsuit being filed, this is an example of...
a) external stress
b) organizational stress
c) personal stress
d) operational stress
e) occupational stress

## TRUE/FALSE QUESTIONS

6.1. Women are prohibited from being patrol officers "on the street."

6.2. Police often feel isolated from the public.

6.3. Before the 1970s, many police departments did not hire nonwhites.

6.4. Police officers are generally well-paid.

6.5. Policing is not a stressful job.

6.6. Lola Baldwin was the first female police officer.

6.7. Most police work generally is reactive.

6.8. Patrol officers account for two-thirds of all sworn officers.

6.9. Line functions are those that directly involve field operations.

6.10. Police training affects the attitudes of the recruits.

6.11. Police agencies are usually disorganized.

6.12. Police do not use proactive strategies.

6.13. Police assign priorities to calls for service.

6.14. Most police action is initiated by an officer in the field.

6.15. All police departments have vice squads.

6.16. There have not been any attempts made to quantify police work.

6.17. The clearance rate is the percentage of crimes solved through an arrest.

6.18. Arrests for drug selling has a 100 percent clearance rate.

6.19. Rapid response time is valuable for only a small fraction of police calls.

6.20. Most calls to police involve service and order maintenance, not law enforcement.

# ANSWER KEY

Key Terms
1.    problem-oriented policing
2.    line functions
3.    productivity
4.    reactive patrol
5.    response time
6.    directed patrol
7.    foot patrol
8.    preliminary investigation
9.    sworn officers
10.   vice unit
11.   forensic techniques
12.   proactive patrol
13.   clearance rate
14.   differential response
15.   detectives
16.   traffic unit
17.   community-oriented policing
18.   staff functions
19.   aggressive patrol or preventive patrol
20.   external job stress
21.   socialization
22.   operational job stress
23.   danger
24.   organizational job stress

Key People
1.    Lola Baldwin
2.    George W. Bush
3.    Cristina Murphy

General Practice Questions
1.    directed patrol
2.    proactive patrol
3.    problem-oriented policing
4.    foot patrol or community-oriented policing
5.    response time
6.    productivity
7.    working personality
8.    danger
9.    authority
10.   minority police officers
11.   prejudice

Multiple Choice
6.1.    a
6.2.    e
6.3.    e
6.4.    a
6.5.    a
6.6.    b
6.7.    c
6.8.    d

6.9. c
6.10. b
6.11. c
6.12. b
6.13. d
6.14. a
6.15. c
6.16. c
6.17. b
6.18. c
6.19. c
6.20. d
6.21. a
6.22. c
6.23. b
6.24. a
6.25. d

True/False
6.1. F
6.2. T
6.3. T
6.4. F
6.5. F
6.6. T
6.7. T
6.8. T
6.9. T
6.10. T
6.11. F
6.12. F
6.13. T
6.14. F
6.15. F
6.16. F
6.17. T
6.18. T
6.19. T
6.20. T

WORKSHEET 6.1: RECRUITMENT AND TRAINING OF POLICE OFFICERS

1. What qualifications would you require for someone to be hired as a police officer?  Why?

2. What salary and benefits would you offer in order to attract the police officer-candidates that you described?

3. What are the three most important subjects that should be taught to new police recruits?  Why?

4. Could you use training to combat any negative aspects of the police subculture and working personality?  If so, how?

WORKSHEET 6.2: DETECTIVES

A study has raised questions about whether or not your police department should keep a separate
investigation division containing detectives. There are questions about whether or not detectives solve
many crimes because most arrests result from the work of patrol officers or the assistance of citizens.
Pretend that you have to draft a report making recommendations about the future of the detective
bureau. How would you address the following questions?

1. What is the job of the detectives? (write a job description)

_____

_____

_____

_____

_____

2. How are investigations conducted and what is the role of the detectives in investigations?

_____

_____

_____

_____

3. What is the relationship between detectives and patrol officers?

_____

_____

_____

_____

_____

4. How would the police department be different if there were no detectives?

_____

_____

_____

_____

# CHAPTER 7

## POLICE AND CONSTITUTIONAL LAW

### LEARNING OBJECTIVES

After covering the material in this chapter, students should understand:

1. police officers' responsibility to control crime under the rule of law;

2. search and seizure issues

3. arrest and interrogation issues

4. circumstances justifying warrantless searches

5. the exclusionary rule, its application to the states, and exceptions to the rule.

### CHAPTER SUMMARY

The Supreme Court has defined rules for the circumstances and justifications for stops, searches, and arrests in light of the Fourth Amendment's prohibition on "unreasonable searches and seizures." Most stops must be supported by reasonable suspicion and arrests, like search warrants, must be supported by enough information to constitute probable cause. The plain view doctrine permits officers to visually examine and seize any contraband or criminal evidence that is in open sight when they are in a place that they are legally permitted to be. Searches are considered "reasonable" and may be conducted without warrants in a number of specific circumstances such as borders, airports, and other situations required by special needs beyond the normal purposes of law enforcement. Limited searches may be conducted without warrants when officers have reasonable suspicions to justify a stop-and-frisk for weapons on the streets; when officer make a lawful arrest; when exigent circumstances exist; when people voluntarily consent to searches of their persons or property; and in certain situations involving automobiles. The Fifth Amendment privilege against compelled self-incrimination helps to protect citizens against violence and coercion by police as well as to maintain the legitimacy and integrity of the legal system. The Supreme Court's decision in *Miranda v. Arizona (1966)* required officers to inform suspects of specific rights before custodial questioning, although officers have adapted their practices to accommodate this rule and several exceptions have been created. The exclusionary rule is a remedy designed to deter police from violating citizens' rights during criminal investigations by barring the use of illegally obtained evidence in court. The Supreme Court has created several exceptions to the exclusionary rule, including the inevitable discovery rule and the "good faith" exception in defective warrant situations.

### CHAPTER OUTLINE

I. INTRODUCTION
   The arrest of Dallas Cowboys football star, Michael Irvin, in November 2000 demonstrated the legal limits of police investigation. While Irvin was arrested and charged with possession of drugs, the judge ruled that the police had searched the apartment without a warrant. Therefore, the evidence against Irvin was thrown out of court. This high-profile case demonstrates that police must follow the law or risk losing evidence by way of the exclusionary rule.

II. LEGAL LIMITS OF POLICE INVESTIGATIONS

A.   In a democratic society, police are expected to control crime while complying with the rule of law as it protects the rights of citizens, including criminal suspects. Evidence used against suspects must be admissible evidence.

B.   Search and Seizure Concepts
   1.   The Fourth Amendment prohibits unreasonable searches and seizures. The Supreme Court defines searches as actions by law enforcement officials that intrude upon people's reasonable expectations of privacy. If people are not free to leave when officers' assert their authority to halt someone's movement, then a **seizure** has occurred and the Fourth Amendment requires that the seizure be reasonable

C.   The Concept of Arrest
   1.   Seizure of an individual by government official who takes suspect into custody. Courts prefer arrest warrants for felonies, but have not required them. The Fourth Amendment also speaks of seizures (e.g., arrests) being based on probable cause.
   2.   A Question of Ethics: Apartment search.

D.   Warrants and Probable Cause
   1.   Officer must show reliable information establishing *probable cause* to believe that a crime has been or is being committed. The particular premises and pieces of property to be seized must be identified and the officer must swear under oath that they are correct.

III.   PLAIN VIEW DOCTRINE: during a search, incident to arrest or with a warrant, officers can seize and examine items in plain view even if not listed on warrant, if those items may be evidence of illegal activity
   A.   Open Fields Doctrine: property owners have no reasonable expectation of privacy in open fields on and around their property.
   B.   Plain Feel and Other Senses: Police officers can justify a warrantless search based upon smell or odor and also based upon feel (Minnesota v. Dickerson 1993)

IV.   WARRANTLESS SEARCHES
   A.   Special Needs Beyond the Normal Purpose of Law Enforcement: Officers do not need any suspicion to justify a search in specific contexts, such as airline passengers or border searches.
      1.   U.S. Customs Service Policies for Personal Searches
      2.   Close Up State Supreme Courts and Constitutional Rights
   B.   Stop and Frisk on the Streets: brief questioning and pat down searches (stop and frisk) permitted based on reasonable judgment of police officers (*Terry v. Ohio*, 1968) that a crime as occurred or is about to occur, and that the stopped person may have a weapon.
   C.   Search Incident to Lawful Arrest: police can search person and areas in immediate vicinity for weapons when a lawful arrest is made (*Chimel v. California*, 1969).
   D.   Exigent Circumstances: officers might find themselves in the middle of an urgent situation where they must act swiftly and do not have time to go to court to seek a warrant.
   E.   Consent : citizen may waive Fourth Amendment and other rights and thereby allow police to conduct a search. Police may search an apartment based on the consent of someone whom police reasonably believe possesses the authority to consent even if the person does not actually possess such authority (*Illinois v. Rodriguez*, 1990).
   F.   Automobile Searches: automobiles distinguished from homes in terms of people's expectations of privacy and the risk that evidence may be contained in a mobile vehicle (*Carroll v. United States*, 1925; *United States v. Ross*, 1982). Officers may search automobiles and containers in such vehicles if they have probable cause to do so.

## V. QUESTIONING SUSPECTS

A. Miranda Rules

1. Upon arrest, suspects must be informed of their rights, based on Supreme Court decisions in *Escobedo v. Illinois* (1964) and *Miranda v. Arizona* (1966). *Miranda* warnings consist of police informing arrestee:

   a. Of the right to remain silent

   b. If they make a statement, it can and will be used against them in court

   c. Of right to have attorney present during interrogation, or have an opportunity to consult with an attorney.

   d. If they cannot afford an attorney, the state will provide one.

B. The Consequences of Miranda

1. Police officers have adapted their techniques in various ways to question suspects and get information despite Miranda limitations. *Miranda* rights must be provided *before questions are asked* during custodial interrogations. Miranda does not apply if a police officer simply comes up to a person and starts to ask questions. The Supreme has ruled that people know that they can walk away from a police officer.

2. Departments train officers to read the *Miranda* warnings to suspects as soon as an arrest is made. This is done in order to make sure the warnings are not omitted as the suspect in processed in the system. The warnings may be read off a standard "Miranda card" to make sure that the rights are provided consistently and correctly. However, the courts do not require that police inform suspects of their rights immediately after arrest.

3. Officers are also trained in interrogation techniques that are intended to encourage suspects to talk despite *Miranda* warnings suspects of their rights immediately after arrest.

C. New Directions in Criminal Justice Policy: The Suspension of Rights in a Time of Terrorism

## VI. EXCLUSIONARY RULE: illegally seized evidence must be excluded from court. The Supreme Court created the exclusionary rule in *Weeks v. United States (1914)* as a judicial remedy to guard against police corruption.

A. Application of the Exclusionary Rule to the States: The Supreme Court incorporated the Fourth Amendment upon the states in Wolf v. Colorado (1949) and later applied the exclusionary rule to the states in Mapp v. Ohio (1961) through the due process clause of the Fourteenth Amendment. Without the exclusionary rule, the Fourth Amendment has no meaning

B. Exceptions to the Exclusionary Rule: As composition of the Supreme Court became more conservative in the 1970s and 1980s, a number of decisions limited or created exceptions to the exclusionary rule. Among the modifications created:

1. Public safety exception (*New York v. Quarles*, 1984).

2. Inevitable discovery rule (*Nix v. Williams*, 1984).

3. Good faith exception (*United States v. Leon*, 1984).

## REVIEW OF KEY TERMS

Fill in the appropriate term for each statement

searc  incide :t to lawful arrest
right to counsel
public safety exception
search warrant
"plain view"

automobile search
search by consent
good faith exception
exclusionary rule
inevitable discovery exception
Terry v. Ohio
Chimel v. California
New York v. Class
Mapp v. Ohio
Arizona v. Hicks
Nix v. Williams
United States v. Leon
New York v. Quarles
Miranda v. Arizona

1. _____ established the public safety exception to the exclusionary rule.

2. _____ established the "stop and frisk" doctrine permitting pat-down searches during field interrogations.

3. _____ established the good faith exception to the exclusionary rule.

4. _____ established that a gun protruding from under seat is within the scope of the plain view doctrine.

5. _____ established the permissibility of searches incident to lawful arrests to ensure no weapons are on the arrestee or within reach of the arrestee.

6. _____ established that police must inform arrestees of their rights.

7. _____ applied the Fourth Amendment exclusionary rule to the states.

8. _____ maintained limits on the "plain view" doctrine by preventing officers from moving stereo to view serial numbers.

9. _____ established the inevitable discovery exception to the exclusionary rule.

10. _____ is justified as an exception to Fourth Amendment search warrant requirement because of diminished need to provide the same protection provided for house and persons.

11. _____ prevents police and prosecutors from using evidence that has been obtained through improper procedures.

12. _____ is one avenue to conduct a search without a warrant because of citizen cooperation.

13. _____ is based on the idea that evidence should not be excluded when police officers did everything that they thought they were supposed to do even though a mistake occurred.

14. _____ was announced by the Supreme Court for situations in which exclusion of evidence is not required because officers took necessary actions to protect citizens.

15. _____ is an exception to the warrant requirement because officers need to be sure there is no weapon on the person or within the person's reach.

16. _____ permits the use of improperly obtained evidence that would have been found by the police eventually through proper means.

17. _____ is a document issued by a judicial officer upon the sworn statement of a police officer.

18. _____ is a Sixth Amendment protection developed and expanded by the Supreme Court's interpretation of the Constitution.

19. _____ is an exception to the warrant requirement because officers need not ignore illegal objects that are clearly visible.

## REVIEW OF KEY PERSONS

Michael Irvin
Earl Warren
John Ashcroft
Warren Burger
O. J. Simpson

1. A warrantless search of football star _____'s house after his ex-wife was found murdered produced a bloody glove.

2. Under the direction of Attorney General _____, the government has jailed American citizens without charging them with any crimes, giving them access to court proceedings, or permitting them to meet with an attorney.

3. Dallas Cowboys football star, _____, was arrested for felony possession of cocaine but because of the exclusionary rule the evidence was thrown out of court.

4. The appointment of _____ as Chief Justice in 1953 ushered in an era in which the Supreme Court expanded the definitions of constitutional rights affecting a variety of issues, including criminal justice.

5. Chief Justice _____, who served from 1969 to 1986, criticized the exclusionary rule as ineffective and misguided.

## GENERAL PRACTICE QUESTIONS

The Supreme Court imposed the \_\_\_\_\_1\_\_\_\_ on all law enforcement, including state and local departments, in the case of \_\_\_\_2\_\_\_\_. However, after the Court's composition changed, police gained greater flexibility for honest mistakes through \_\_\_\_3\_\_\_\_, as established in the case of \_\_\_\_4\_\_\_\_.

## SELF-TEST SECTION

### MULTIPLE CHOICE QUESTIONS

7.1. How does the U. S. Supreme Court define a "search"?
a) an action by a law enforcement official that creates tension between the official and a citizen
b) an action by a law enforcement official that intrudes upon people's "reasonable expectations of privacy"
c) when a law enforcement official speaks to a person
d) when a law enforcement official informs a person that a search is taking place
e) when a law enforcement official looks at a person

7.2. Which of the following statements is TRUE regarding courts and warrants?
a) courts require arrest warrants for felonies, but do not prefer them
b) courts prefer arrest warrants for felonies, but do not require them
c) courts require arrest warrants for felonies and prefer them
d) courts prefer arrest warrants for felonies, and require them
e) courts require arrest warrants for felonies, but have no preference about them

7.3. All arrests must be supported by ...
a) reasonable suspicion
b) reasonable doubt
c) preponderance of the evidence
d) probable cause
e) real evidence

7.4. In what case did the U. S. Supreme Court decide that police officers can make a warrantless arrest for a minor traffic offense, such as a failure to wear a seatbelt?
a) Atwater v. City of Lago Vista (2001)
b) Maryland v. Wilson (1997)
c) Mapp v. Ohio (1961)
d) Terry v. Ohio (1968)
e) New York v. Quarles (1984)

7.5. What is a written statement confirmed by oath or affirmation?
a) warrant
b) perjury
c) interrogatory
d) booking
e) affidavit

7.6. If a judicial officer makes a generalized determination about whether the evidence is both sufficient and reliable enough to justify a warrant, this is called the standard of..
a) reasonable suspicion
b) reasonable doubt
c) preponderance of the evidence
d) the totality of the circumstances
e) real evidence

7.7. Which of the following search does not require a warrant?
a) stop and frisk
b) border searches
c) exigent circumstances
d) consent
e) all of the above

7.8. Which of the following would raise suspicion and justify a search of a person according to handbook of the U. S. Customs Service?
a) person has a beard
b) person has an earring
c) person shows signs of nervousness
d) person is alone
e) person is not smiling

7.9. In what case did the U. S. Supreme Court rule that an unverified anonymous tip is not adequate as basis for a stop and frisk search?
a) Maryland v. Wilson (1997)
b) Michigan v. Sitz (1991)
c) Minnesota v. Dickerson (1993)
d) New York v. Quarles (1984)
e) Florida v. J.L. (2000)

7.10. In what case did the U. S. Supreme Court that it would not permit thorough warrantless searches at crime scenes, even when a murder victim is discovered?
a) Maryland v. Wilson (1997)
b) Michigan v. Sitz (1990)
c) Minnesota v. Dickerson (1993)
d) Flippo v. West Virginia (1999)
e) Florida v. J.L. (2000)

7.11. In what cases did the U. S. Supreme Court rule that when officers are in hot pursuit of a fleeing suspected felon they need not stop to seek a warrant and thereby risk permitting the suspect to get away?
a) Minnesota v. Dickerson (1993)
b) Flippo v. West Virginia (1999)
c) Florida v. J.L. (2000)
d) Warden v. Hayden (1967)
e) New York v. Quarles (1984)

7.12. In what cases did the U. S. Supreme Court approve warrantless bloodtests?
a) Minnesota v. Dickerson (1993)
b) New York v. Quarles (1984)
c) Breihaupt v. Abram (1957)
d) Flippo v. West Virginia (1999)
e) Florida v. J.L. (2000)

7.13. In what cases did the U. S. Supreme Court approve a warrantless search of an automobile?
a) Atwater v. City of Lago Vista (2001)
b) Carroll v. United States (1925)
c) Mapp v. Ohio (1961)
d) Terry v. Ohio (1968)
e) Myers v. United States (1923)

7.14. In what cases did the U. S. Supreme Court expand officers' authority to search automobiles even when no formal arrest has yet occurred?
a) Michigan v. Long (1983)
b) Carroll v. United States (1925)
c) Weeks v. United States (1914)
d) Terry v. Ohio (1968)
e) Myers v. United States (1923)

7.15. Why does the Fifth Amendment contain the privilege against self-incrimination?
a) because suspects do not tell the truth and this infringes upon an investigation
b) because police officers often ask the wrong questions
c) because suspects can talk too much and this interferes with the investigation
d) to discourage police officers from using violent or coercive means to get suspects to confess
e) because police officers often fail to remember what suspects have to say

7.16. Which of the following movies is based on a true story in England in which police officers gain a confession from a bombing suspect whom they know to be innocent by placing a gun in the suspect's mouth and threatening to pull the trigger?
a) Minority Report
b) Clear and Present Danger
c) In the Name of the Father
d)The Sum of All Fears
e) Patriot Games

7.17. In what case did the U. S. Supreme Court rule that officers could forego Miranda warnings if there would be a threat to "public safety"?
a) Minnesota v. Dickerson (1993)
b) Flippo v. West Virginia (1999)
c) Florida v. J.L. (2000)
d) Warden v. Hayden (1967)
e) New York v. Quarles (1984)

7.18. In what case did the U. S. Supreme Court rule that the police could not use as evidence a statement made by a suspect in response to a question that was posed prior to the issuance of the Miranda warnings?
a) Pennsylvania v. Muniz (1990)
b) Minnesota v. Dickerson (1993)
c) Flippo v. West Virginia (1999)
d) Florida v. J.L. (2000)
e) Warden v. Hayden (1967)

7.19. Which of the following is FALSE regarding the Miranda warnings?
a) police must inform suspects of their rights immediately after arrest
b) the warnings do not have to be provided until the police begin to ask questions
c) the warnings involve the Fifth and Sixth Amendments to the Constitution
d) the warnings are designed to deter police misconduct
e) all of the above are TRUE

7.20. Who wrote the opinion in Mapp v. Ohio (1961) where the U. S. Supreme Court nationalized the exclusionary rule?
a) Chief Justice Earl Warren
b) Justice Hugo Black
c) Justice William Day
d) Justice Tom Clark
e) Justice Felix Frankfurter

7.21. Which of the following exceptions to the exclusionary rule means that the officers acted with the honest belief that they were following the proper rules?
a) inevitability of discovery exception
b) public safety exception
c) good faith exception
d) "Honest Abe" exception
e) mistaken identity exception

7.22 . In what case did the U. S. Supreme Court rule that improperly obtained evidence can be used at parole revocation proceedings?
a) Minnesota v. Dickerson (1993)
b) Pennsylvania Board of Pardons and Parole v. Scott (1998)
c) Flippo v. West Virginia (1999)
d) Florida v. J.L. (2000)
e) Warden v. Hayden (1967)

7.23. In what case did the U. S. Supreme Court rule that improperly obtained evidence can be used at deportation hearings?
a) Minnesota v. Dickerson (1993)
b) Pennsylvania Board of Pardons and Parole v. Scott (1998)
c) Flippo v. West Virginia (1999)
d) Florida v. J.L. (2000)
e) Immigration and Naturalization Service v. Lopez-Mendoza (1984)

7.24. In what case did the U. S. Supreme Court rule that improperly obtained statements can be used to impeach the credibility of defendants who take the witness stand and testify?
a) Harris v. New York (1971)
b) Pennsylvania Board of Pardons and Parole v. Scott (1998)
c) Flippo v. West Virginia (1999)
d) Florida v. J.L. (2000)
e) Immigration and Naturalization Service v. Lopez-Mendoza (1984)

7.25. Which of the following is TRUE about the exclusionary rule?
a) it is specifically mentioned in the Fourth Amendment
b) it currently applies only to the federal courts
c) the Rehnquist Court has expanded criminal defendants' rights by supporting the exclusionary rule
d) it was created by the judiciary to prevent police misconduct
e) all of the above are TRUE


## TRUE/FALSE QUESTIONS

7.1. The U.S. Border Patrol regularly makes warrantless stops and searches.

7.2. An officer may NOT enter a vehicle to see the Vehicle Identification Number when a car has been validly stopped.

7.3. A warrant must be signed by a judicial officer.

7.4. Border searches without a warrant are an automatic violation of the Fourth Amendment.

7.5. The exclusionary rule applies to federal and state courts.

7.6. The American Bar Association is NOT concerned about the rights of defendants who are tried before military commissions.

7.7. Police can stop and frisk a person without a warrant if reasonable suspicion exists.

7.8. Chief Justice Earl Warren was a supporter of the exclusionary rule.

7.9. The Rehnquist Court has created a number of exceptions to the exclusionary rule.

7.10. The Fourth Amendment does not contain the word "warrant."

7.11. The Fifth Amendment contains the right against unreasonable search and seizure.

7.12. The Sixth Amendment contains the right to counsel.

7.13. The privilege against self-incrimination is found in the Fourth Amendment.

7.14. Evidence that was obtained illegally will not be thrown out if a police officer acted in good faith.

7.15. Warrantless searches are justified if exigent circumstances exist.

7.16. The handbook for the U. S. Customs Service advises agents to conduct a search if a person avoids eye-contact.

7.17. Sobriety checkpoints violate the Fourth Amendment rights of citizens.

7.18. Dallas Cowboys' football star, Michael Irvin, was arrested for cocaine possession but the evidence was thrown out because of the exclusionary rule.

7.19. Chief Justice William Rehnquist wrote the majority opinion in Miranda v. Arizona (1966).

7.20. Blood tests without a warrant violate the right against unreasonable search and seizure.

# ANSWER KEY

### Key Terms
1. New York v. Quarles
2. Terry v. Ohio
3. United States v. Leon
4. New York v. Class
5. Chimel v. California
6. Miranda v. Arizona
7. Mapp v. Ohio
8. Arizona v. Hicks
9. Nix v. Williams
10. automobile search
11. exclusionary rule
12. search by consent
13. good faith exception
14. public safety exception
15. search incident to a lawful arrest
16. inevitable discovery exception
17. search warrant
18. right to counsel
19. plain view

### Key Persons
1. O. J. Simpson
2. John Ashcroft
3. Michael Irvin
4. Earl Warren
5. Warren Burger

### General Practice
1. exclusionary rule
2. Mapp v. Ohio
3. good faith exception
4. United States v. Leon

### Multiple Choice
7.1.   b
7.2.   b
7.3.   d
7.4.   a
7.5.   e
7.6.   d
7.7.   e
7.8.   c
7.9.   e
7.10.  d
7.11.  d
7.12.  c
7.13.  b
7.14.  a
7.15.  d
7.16.  c
7.17.  e
7.18.  a
7.19.  a

| | |
|---|---|
| 7.20. | d |
| 7.21. | c |
| 7.22. | b |
| 7.23. | e |
| 7.24. | a |
| 7.25. | d |

True/False

| | |
|---|---|
| 7.1. | T |
| 7.2. | F |
| 7.3. | T |
| 7.4. | F |
| 7.5. | T |
| 7.6. | F |
| 7.7. | T |
| 7.8. | T |
| 7.9. | T |
| 7.10. | F |
| 7.11. | F |
| 7.12. | T |
| 7.13. | F |
| 7.14. | T |
| 7.15. | T |
| 7.16. | T |
| 7.17. | F |
| 7.18. | T |
| 7.19. | F |
| 7.20. | F |

WORKSHEET 7.1. THE JUSTIFICATION FOR WARRANTLESS SEARCHES

Warrantless searches are important for police officers in regard to gathering evidence that might otherwise be lost or endanger the safety of others in society. In the following exercise, students should list the basis for justifying the warrantless searches listed below. What purpose(s) are served by allowing law enforcement officers to conduct a search without a warrant? Are these searches justified in violating a person's rights based upon the purposes that you listed?

Stop and Frisk on the Streets _____

_____

_____

_____

Warrantless Search of Hispanics five miles from the Mexican border _____

_____

_____

_____

Search Incident to a Lawful Arrest _____

_____

_____

_____

Automobile Searches _____

_____

_____

_____

Searching through someone's luggage at the airport _____

_____

_____

Consent searches_____

_____

# CHAPTER 8

## POLICING: ISSUES AND TRENDS

### LEARNING OBJECTIVES

After covering the material in this chapter, students should understand:

1. police patrol activities, including issues of preventive patrol, response time, foot versus motorized patrol, aggressive patrol, and community-oriented policing;

2. police use of new technology and weapons in the fight against crime

3. police abuse, including police brutality and corruption;

4. civic accountability, including internal affairs divisions, civilian review boards, standards and accreditation, and civil liability;

5. the issues and problems posed by the increase in private policing.

### CHAPTER SUMMARY

Police administrators must make decisions about possible patrol strategies, including directed patrol, foot patrol, and aggressive patrol. Community policing seeks to involve the citizens in identifying problems and working with police officers to prevent disorder and crime. The development of new technologies has assisted police investigations through the use of computers, databases, surveillance devices, and methods to detect deception. Police departments are seeking to identify non-lethal weapons that can incapacitate suspects and control unruly crowds without causing serious injuries and deaths. The problems of police misuse of force and corruption cause erosions of community support. Internal affairs units, civilian review boards, standards and accreditation, and civil liability suits are four approaches designed to increase police accountability to citizens. The expansion of security management and private policing reflects greater recognition of the need to protect private assets and plan for emergencies but it also produces new issues and problems concerning the recruitment, training, and activities of lower-level private security personnel.

### CHAPTER OUTLINE

I. INTRODUCTION
A. The Louima Case
   New York City police brutalize a Haitian immigrant leading to imprisonment for at least one officer.

II. ISSUES IN PATROLLING

A. Allocation of Patrol Personnel: Distribution of police often focused on "problem" neighborhoods.
B. Allocation decisions usually determined by:
   1. crime statistics
   2. degree of urbanization
   3. pressures from business and community groups
   4. ethnic composition of area
   5. socioeconomic conditions
C. Preventive Patrol: Kansas City study on proactive crime-prevention patrol indicates that such patrols make little difference on crime or fear of crime. Officers spent much of their time on administrative tasks and other matters unrelated to patrolling.

D.  Findings contributed to shift in emphasis toward order maintenance and service in some departments.

E.  Hot Spots:  Research indicates crime is not evenly distributed.  Certain kinds of predatory crimes may be reduced if police focus on places with motivated offenders, suitable targets, and an absence of capable guardians.

F.  Knowledge of hot spots can permit officers to be assigned to directed patrol focusing on hot spots and hot times (i.e., times during the day when activity most likely to occur at a location).

G.  Response Time:  Studies indicate police response time is not crucial factor in making arrests; instead it is citizen response time in reporting crime right away.

H.  Citizen delay is a major problem; citizens distracted by coping, lending assistance, interpreting ambiguous situation.  Many departments now classify calls to determine which ones actually need immediate response.

I.  Three major reasons for delay are not easily overcome by citizen education or other innovations:
    1.  Some people find situations to be *ambiguous* and they are not sure whether to call the police.
    2.  Other people are involved in *coping* activities (e.g., taking care of victim, directing traffic, otherwise helping out).
    3.  Other people experience conflict in making decision about whether to call. They may avoid making immediate decision or seek the advice of others.

J.  Elimination of citizen delay would only have partial impact on problem because many crimes, such as burglary, are not reported until after they are "discovered" -- long after perpetrator has left. In some other cases (robbery, rape, assault), the victim may know the perpetrator and therefore could call the police sooner.

K.  Foot Patrol versus Motorized Patrol:  Many contemporary arguments for putting police back on foot patrol beat:  better relationship with community, gain knowledge of neighborhoods, better able to detect criminal activity.  Leads to higher citizen satisfaction and some evidence of lower crime rates.

L.  Motorized patrol changed police from watching to prevent crime to waiting to respond to crime.

M.  One- versus Two-Person Patrol Units:  1991 study of large cities showed 70 percent of patrol cars staffed by one officer.  One-person more economical, permits more cars to be out on streets at one time, can increase response time throughout city.  One-person cars becoming more common.

N.  Despite being uneconomical, officers and union leaders believe it provides additional safety for the officers and the public.  Policies often developed through negotiations between police chiefs, unions, and local government.  By contrast, administrators believe that solo officers are less distracted with no partner for idle conversation.

O.  Aggressive Patrol:  Effort to maximize interventions and observations in the community.

P.  James Q. Wilson argues that aggressive stops should be used to cut down on the number of crime-prone people carrying guns.  New York has employed zero-tolerance policing to crack down on disorderly public behavior.  The city also uses proactive, plain clothes crime units that make a disproportionate number of arrests.  Kansas City used aggressive traffic enforcement to find handguns that people were carrying.

Q.  "Sting" operations and repeat offender programs are expensive because they take officers away from usual duties.

R.  Most cost-effective strategy seems to be to create incentives for officers to increase number of traffic stops and field interrogations.

S.  Aggressive patrol in minority neighborhoods can produce tension with the police if people believe they are being singled out because of their race.

III.  COMMUNITY POLICING
    A.  Most commonly associated with attempts by police to involve community in making their neighborhoods safe.
    B.  Approach has emerged due to perceived deficiencies in crime-fighter orientation. Four elements:
        1.  Community-based crime prevention.
        2.  Reorientation of patrol activities to focus on nonemergency services.

3.      Increased accountability of the police to the public.

4.      Decentralization of police decision making so as to include citizens.

C.      Problem-oriented policing (related approach): Attempts to ascertain what is causing citizens' calls for help. With knowledge of underlying problems, police can enlist help from community agencies and citizens to address the underlying problems. These problems may concern quality of life rather than crime.

D.      Baltimore County, MD and Newport News, VA have gained national attention for problem-oriented approach that goes beyond responding to incidents and instead seeks to understand and address crime, disorder, and fear. San Diego's Neighborhood Policing Philosophy emphasizes shared responsibility of police and citizens and the fact that law enforcement is just one tool for addressing crime. Emphasis on listening to the community. Use of volunteers, neighborhood watch, and strict building code enforcement.

E.      Community-oriented approach embraced by national police leadership but difficult to implement because it is difficult to change old ways. Also there are questions about the meaning and definition of "community."

IV.      THE FUTURE OF PATROL

A.      Police patrol by itself does little to control many kinds of crime. New strategies need to maintain community cooperation, develop sensitivity to demographic characteristics of communities and neighborhoods, and emphasize attention to service, order maintenance, and fear of crime.

V.      COMPARATIVE PERSPECTIVE: PATROL IN JAPAN

A.      Foot patrol officers work in pairs out of mini-police stations in urban neighborhoods.

B.      Patrolling primarily consists of watching and occasionally asking questions. Rarely discover genuine emergencies.

C.      Patrol demonstrates the existence of authority, corrects minor inconveniences (e.g., illegally parked cars), and generates trust through familiar personal relations with the neighborhood's inhabitants.

D.      In different neighborhoods, officers look for different kinds of signs of illegal activity (e.g., loitering males in parks, unescorted stylishly dressed women in neighborhoods with bars, etc.).

E.      Officers make it a point to engage citizens in conversations. National competitions held for rewarding outstanding skills in on-street interrogation. Treat each person individually.

VI.      POLICING AND NEW TECHNOLOGY

Questions exist about the accuracy of new technology as well as the dilemma posed by infringing upon the constitutional rights of citizens.

A.      <u>Investigative Tools</u>

1.      One of the most rapidly advancing tools used by law enforcement is the computer, specifically portable computers in patrol cars. Computers are especially helpful in investigating cybercrimes.

2.      Law enforcement are also employing a variety of surveillance and detection systems in public areas to apprehend criminals

3.      Scientists are looking to employ new technologies in questioning suspects because polygraph tests have been unreliable.

B.      <u>Weapons Technology</u>

1.      Police are trying to develop alternative nonlethal weapons because officers and departments have been sued for using force against suspects resulting in injuring or killing persons.

2.      Alternative weapons such as airguns or tasers can be used to incapacitate a person temporarily with minimum harm.

VII.      POLICE ABUSE OF POWER

A.    Use of Force
    1.    Issues and accusations of brutality more common in heightened racial conflict situations of major cities.
    2.    Citizens use the term police brutality to describe a wide range of practices, from the use of profane or abusive language to physical force and violence.
    3.    It is important to distinguish between police use of force and police use of excessive force.
    4.    Police have authority to use force if necessary. However, police use of deadly force often causes great emotional upheaval within a community. Typical victim is African-American male.
    5.    Shooting by police led to riot in St. Petersburg, Florida. Shooting of unarmed immigrant in New York City led to prosecution of police officers.
    6.    In 1985, Supreme Court ruled for first time that police use of deadly force to apprehend an unarmed, nonviolent, fleeing felony suspect violated the Fourth Amendment guarantee against unreasonable seizure (case of unarmed 15-year-old shot and killed by Memphis Police B

        *Tennessee v. Garner*). Previously, police in many states followed common law principle that allowed the use of any force necessary to arrest a fleeing felon.
    7.    In *Graham v. Conner* (1989) the Supreme Court established the "objective reasonableness" standard and said that the officer's use of
        force should be evaluated in terms of the "reasonableness of the moment."
    8.    The risk of significant lawsuits by victims of improper police shootings looms over contemporary police departments and creates incentives for administrators to set and enforce standards for the use of force.

B.    Corruption
    1.    Police corruption is a long-standing problem in American history.
    2.    Corruption is not easily defined. Some see it in things as simple as accepting a free cup of coffee.
    3.    A Question of Ethics: a free meal given to a police officer at a restaurant.

C.    "Grass Eaters" and "Meat Eaters"
    1.    "Grass eaters" are officers who accept payoffs that circumstances of police work bring their way. Most common form of corruption.
    2.    "Meat eaters" aggressively misuse their power for personal gain. Recent examples of officers getting actively involved in crimes related to illegal drug trafficking, either working with drug dealers or else robbing drug dealers.
    3.    Corruption has been so rampant in some departments that it can=t be attributed to "a few bad apples." Most police work is out of public view, so norms of police work and department policies may shield corrupt officers from detection.
    4.    1993 investigation in New York City found some officers seeking profits from drug trafficking and other crimes.
    5.    "Vice" and victimless crimes are so profitable and so unlikely to produce complaints that corruption is tempting and often easy.
    6.    Officers may suffer from role ambivalence. Officers responsible for protecting community but not given the necessary powers to do so. As a result, conscientious officers must often violate the law in order to perform their duties. Infractions by officers are overlooked. Eventually department's informal norms make types of illegal activity routinized.
    7.    Terms of the "blue coat code":
        a.    Mooching: accepting free coffee, cigarettes, etc.
        b.    Bribery: acceptance of cash or gift, distinguished from mooching" by higher value of gift.
        c.    Chiseling: demanding price discounts and free admission to places of entertainment.

<ol type="a" start="4">
<li>Extortion: demand that businesses or individuals purchase tickets to police functions or buy advertising space in police magazine; or forcing motorists to pay the officer for traffic tickets.</li>
<li>Shopping: picking up small items, such as candy bars and gum at a store when door has accidentally been left open after business hours.</li>
<li>Shakedown: appropriating expensive items for personal use during investigation of a break-in, burglary, or other event, and attributing loss to criminal activity.</li>
<li>Premeditated theft: planned burglary</li>
<li>Favoritism: issuing license tabs, window stickers, and courtesy cards that exempt officers, families, and friends from traffic citations or arrest.</li>
<li>Perjury: lying to provide an alibi for fellow officers.</li>
<li>Prejudice: substandard treatment of minority groups, especially people who lack political influence with City Hall.</li>
</ol>

<ol start="8">
<li>There are multiple effects from corruption:
<ol type="a">
<li>Criminals are left free to pursue their illegal activities.</li>
<li>Departmental morale and supervision drop.</li>
<li>The image of the police suffers.</li>
</ol>
</li>
<li>Some citizens do not equate police corruption with criminal activity.</li>
</ol>

D. <u>Controlling Corruption</u>
<ol>
<li>Public needs to be involved by filing complaints about improper actions.</li>
<li>To a great extent, the American political and legal systems have left it to police departments to keep their own houses in order.
<ol type="a">
<li>Police leadership must set the tone against corruption.</li>
</ol>
</li>
</ol>

VIII. CIVIC ACCOUNTABILITY

A. <u>Challenge of Maintaining Public Confidence in Police</u>
<ol>
<li>Challenge of making police accountable to civilian control in order to give public confidence that officers are behaving according to governing laws and rules.</li>
</ol>

B. <u>Internal Affairs</u>
<ol>
<li>Often lack formal mechanisms for public to register complaints effectively.</li>
<li>Risk that internal affairs investigators will view complaints by public as attacks on entire department.</li>
<li>Investigations by Internal Affairs units do not often fit Hollywood model: frequently investigating allegations of sexual harassment, substance abuse problems, or misuse of physical force rather than grand corruption</li>
<li>Internal affairs officers normally assigned only for set period (e.g., 8 years); work is stressful and makes it difficult to maintain relationships with other officers. Unit needs sufficient resources from department in order to be effective.</li>
<li>Often difficult to get officers to provide information about other officers.</li>
</ol>

C. <u>Civilian Review Boards</u>
<ol>
<li>Political battles over creation of such boards because police oppose civilians evaluating of their actions. Such boards exist in 36 of the 50 largest cities and in 13 of the next 50 largest cities.</li>
<li>Although officers believe such boards cannot understand and judge them fairly, the boards have not been harsh on police.</li>
<li>Because of the low visibility of actions that result in complaints, most complaints cannot be substantiated.</li>
</ol>

D. <u>Standards and Accreditation</u>
<ol>
<li>Communities can gain greater accountability if they require that operations be conducted by nationally recognized standards. Commission on Accreditation of Law Enforcement</li>
</ol>

Agencies (CALEA), for example, includes the creation of standards for the use of discretion.

    2.    Accreditation is voluntary. Certification may instill public confidence, provide management tool, and provide basis for educating officers about being accountable for their actions.

E.    <u>Civil Liability Suits</u>

    1.    Civil lawsuits against departments for misconduct are another avenue for civic accountability. Lawsuits for brutality, false arrest, and negligence are increasingly common. Such suits first approved by the Supreme Court in 1961.

    2.    *Monell v. Dept. of Social Services for the City of New York* in 1978 permitted suits against individual officials and agencies when person's civil rights violated by the "customs and usages" of the department.

    3.    Successful lawsuits and even the threat of lawsuits can affect the development of departmental policies.

    4.    Insurance companies that provide civil liability coverage for police departments now give discounts to departments that achieve accreditation.

IX.    SECURITY MANAGEMENT AND PRIVATE POLICING

A.    <u>Introduction</u>

    1.    Private policing has existed for a long time, including bounty hunters and strikebreakers in American history.

    2.    Private policing larger in terms of personnel and resources than federal, state, and local law enforcement combined.

    3.    The rise of private agencies occurred for a number of reasons:

        a.    An increase of crime in the workplace.

        b.    An increase in the fear of crime.

        c.    The fiscal crises of the states that have limited public protection.

        d.    Increased public and business awareness and use of more cost-effective private security services.

    4.    Some private officers are merely watchmen who stand ready to call the police but others are deputized and granted arrest authority when a felony is committed in their presence. Uncertain if legal restrictions on police that protect individuals' constitutional rights apply to actions by private police.

    5.    Some states have passed antishoplifting laws to give civil immunity to store personnel who reasonably but mistakenly detain people suspected of larceny.

    6.    A study indicated that many private agencies are ready to assume increased responsibility for minor criminal incidents and that some governments are willing to consider letting private agencies handle some responsibilities (e.g. security at public buildings).

B.    <u>Functions of Security Management and Private Police</u>

    1.    Top-level security managers have a range of responsibilities that call upon them to fulfill multiple roles that would be handled by a variety of separate individuals in the public sector.

    2.    Private sector corporations own and control security for vital facilities in the United States, including nuclear power plants, oil refineries, military manufacturing facilities, and other important sites. Fires, tornadoes, or earthquakes at such sites could release toxic materials into the air and water.

    3.    At lower levels, specific occupations in private security are more directly comparable to those of police officers. Many security personnel are the equivalent of private sector detectives.

    4.    Other activities are more directly comparable to those of police patrol officers, especially for lower level security officers who must guard specific buildings, apartments, or stores.

C.    <u>Private Employment of Public Police</u>

1.      Private employers are eager to hire police. An estimated 150,000 police officers moonlight for private security firms. Off-duty police retain their full authority and powers to arrest, stop and frisk, etc.

2.      Conflict of Interest: police officers banned from being process servers, bill collectors, repossessors, investigators for criminal defense attorneys and bail bondsmen, or employees at gambling establishments.

3.      Management Prerogatives: departments require officers to gain permission to accept outside work, and department may deny permission if work degrading to department, physically exhausting, dangerous, etc.

     a.      Some departments control through a *department contract model* in which department pays officer for off-duty work and then business reimburses department. Helps to maintain departmental control and protect departmental needs and interests.

     b.      *Officer contract model* lets officers contract independently with permission.

     c.      *Union brokerage model* lets union set pay scale and working conditions for outside employment.

4.      The more closely a department controls its officers' off-duty employment, the more liability it assumes for officers' actions when they work for private firms.

D.      <u>The Public-Private Interface</u>

1.      Private employers' interests may not always coincide with the goals and policies of the local police department. Lack of communication between public and private agencies can lead to botched investigations, loss of evidence, and overzealousness by private officers.

2.      Some cooperative efforts and investigations have occurred between security and police.

3.      Private agencies tend to report UCR index crimes, but do not report fraud, commercial bribery, employee theft, and other "white collar" type offenses within the companies for which they work. Tends to provide more lenient private justice for corporate employees caught in wrongdoing and never reported to law enforcement authorities. Internal punishment through payroll deduction restitution or firing is usually much quicker than turning evidence over to police and prosecutor.

E.      <u>Recruitment and Training</u>

1.      Serious concerns of law enforcement officials and civil libertarians about the recruitment and training of private officers. Relatively little training provided in most places. Fewer than half of the states have licensing requirements.

2.      Because pay is low and many private officers work only temporarily, work often done by the young or the retired, with few formal qualifications.

3.      Regulations that exist tend to be aimed at contractual private police (agencies that work for fees) rather than proprietary (officers hired by a company to provide security for that company).

## REVIEW OF KEY TERMS

<u>Fill in the appropriate term for each statement</u>

police brutality
*Tennessee v. Garner*
police corruption
"grass eaters"
"meat eaters"
Mollen Commission
mooching
bribery
chiseling
extortion

shopping
shakedown
premeditated theft
favoritism
perjury
prejudice
civic accountability
internal affairs units
civilian review boards
accreditation
civil liability suits
private policing
*Monell v. Dept. of Social Services*
department contract model
officer contract model
union brokerage model
contractual private police

1. _____ is the corrupt behavior that involves stealing small items from a place of business with an unlocked door after business hours.

2. _____ is the private policing practice of using police unions to find part-time jobs for their members.

3. _____ is the corrupt behavior that involves accepting cash or significant gifts in exchange for assisting the avoidance of prosecution.

4. _____ is the behavior involving treatment of minority groups is a manner less than impartial, neutral, and objective.

5. _____ is the growing phenomenon of hiring personnel to be paid by corporate and other entities for crime control and order maintenance activities.

6. _____ is the private policing practice that permits police departments to keep close control over the outside, part-time work of their officers.

7. _____ is the corrupt behavior that involves planning and undertaking a burglary of a locked building.

8. _____ was the forum for the investigation into police corruption in New York City.

9. _____ is the general term for reviewing police behavior to ensure that law enforcement personnel perform within the boundaries of the law.

10. _____ is the corrupt behavior that involves taking expensive items from a home while investigating a burglary by claiming that the items were taken by the burglar.

11. _____ is the corrupt behavior that involves demanding price discounts and free admission to places of entertainment.

12. _____ are the divisions within police department responsible for investigating officers' misconduct.

13. _____ is the Supreme Court case that found a Fourth Amendment violation in the shooting of an unarmed, nonviolent fleeing felony suspect.

14. _____ is the corrupt behavior that involves issuing courtesy cards to police relatives so that they can avoid traffic tickets.

15. _____ is the use of the courts for recovering money damages for harms caused by improper police behavior.

16. _____ are the supervisory entities opposed by police officers as an improper means to evaluate misconduct and discipline officers.

17. _____ is the private policing practice in which individual police officers are hired for part-time security work.

18. _____ is the corrupt behavior that involves lying to provide an alibi for fellow police officers who are apprehended undertaking unlawful activities.

19. _____ is the private policing context in which the government is most likely to apply regulations.

20. _____ is a voluntary program for certifying that police departments meet national standards.

21. _____ are officers who actively misuse their position and power in seeking illegal personal profit and other favors.

22. _____ is a general problem that is generated by officers' discretionary and low visibility opportunities to seek personal gain or mistreat the public through the use of their official positions.

23. _____ is the corrupt behavior that involves demanding money in exchange for withholding a parking ticket.

24. _____ is the U.S. Supreme Court decision that established rules for lawsuits against police officers and police departments for harms caused by misconduct.

25. _____ is the corrupt behavior that involves acceptance of small gifts of limited value.

26. _____ are officers who accept personal gifts and profits that are presented to them in the course of performing their duties.

27. _____ is a problem that may be reduced through better recruitment and training programs in conjunction with clear departmental standards for handling conflict situations.


## REVIEW OF KEY PEOPLE

Amadou Diallo
Jerry Sanders
Tom Cruise
Abner Louima
Mr. Walkabout.
James Q. Wilson and George L. Kelling
James Q. Wilson

1. In "Broken Windows: The Police and Neighborhood Safety," _____ and _____ argue that disorderly behavior that is unregulated and unchecked is a signal to residents that the area is unsafe

2. _____, a 32 year old Haitian immigrant, was arrested for disorderly conduct and brutally assaulted by New York City police officers.

3. _____ argues that the police should focus their gun-control efforts on guns being carried in high-risk places, by high-risk people, at high-risk times

4. Police chief_____ states that "community policing begins with a practical consideration, "Listen to the community and letting them tell us what their priorities are"

5. Japanese policemen are addressed by the public as _____.

6. Iris-recognition technology was employed throughout the fictional futuristic world in the Stephen Spielberg film, *Minority Report*, starring _____.

7. _____, an unarmed West African immigrant, died in a fuselage of 41 bullets fired by four members of New York City's Street Crime Unit.


## GENERAL PRACTICE QUESTIONS

Because of the power gained through the police union movement that has affected police departments in the past twenty years, police officers have greater input into policy decisions affecting law enforcement. In some cities, this power carries over into the organization of opportunities to gain extra income through _____1_____, because under the _____2_____, part-time jobs are secured by police unions.

Officers learn through on-the-job experience the informal practices of policing that constitute the _____3_____ process. Unfortunately, if a department has problems with _____4_____ or _____5_____, new officers may learn harmful values and practices. Even if these officers do not engage directly in these practices, they may participate in _____6_____ by creating alibis for fellow officers because there are such strong pressures to remain loyal to fellow officers.

**MULTIPLE CHOICE QUESTIONS**

8.1. Which of the following would NOT be considered a "hot time" in police work?
a) 8 PM
b) 10 PM
c) 8 AM
d) 2 AM
e) midnight

8.2. What "remains the most influential test of the general deterrent effects of patrol on crime"?
a) Uniform Crime Report
b) National Crime Victimization Survey
c) The Mollen Commission Study
d) Kansas City Preventive Patrol Experiment
e) Robert Peel's "Bobbies on Patrol Analysis"

8.3. When do rates of predatory crimes such as robbery and rape increase during the year?
a) fall months
b) spring months
c) summer months
d) winter months
e) rate is constant during the year

8.4. When does domestic violence increase during the year?
a) fall months
b) spring months
c) summer months
d) winter months
e) rate is constant during the year

8.5. In a study by William G. Spelman and Dale K. Brown, how often are police successful in using the rapid response approach?
a) 29 of 1,000 cases
b) 98 of 1,000 cases
c) 512 of 1,000 cases
d) 786 of 1,000 cases
e) 987 of 1,000 cases

8.6. According to a 1991 study of large cities, how many patrol cars are staffed by one officer?
a) 25 percent
b) 45 percent
c) 70 percent
d) 90 percent
e) 99.9 percent

8.7. What theory assert that disorderly behavior in public will frighten citizens and attract criminals, thus leading to more serious crime problems?
a) directed patrol
b) aggressive patrol
c) problem-oriented policing
d) private justice theory
e) broken windows theory

8.8. What is the term used to describe a police officer accepting free coffee, cigarettes, meals, liquor, groceries, or other items, which are thought of as compensation either for receiving a low salary?
a) perjury
b) premeditated theft
c) mooching
d) bribery
e) stealing

8.9. What is the term used to describe a police officer receiving cash or a "gift" in exchange for past or future help in avoiding a prosecution?
a) perjury
b) premeditated theft
c) mooching
d) bribery
e) stealing

8.10. What is the term used to describe a police officer demanding discounts to places of entertainment, whether on duty or not?
a) chiseling
b) premeditated theft
c) mooching
d) bribery
e) stealing

8.11. What is the term used to describe a police officer demanding payment for an ad in a police magazine?
a) chiseling
b) premeditated theft
c) mooching
d) extortion
e) stealing

8.12. What is the term used to describe a police officer picking up small items such as candy bars, gum, and cigarettes at a store where the door has been left unlocked at the close of business hours?
a) shopping
b) chiseling
c) premeditated theft
d) mooching
e) extortion

8.13. What usually happens if an officer reports that another officer has done something unethical or illegal?
a) the reporting officer is given a promotion
b) the reporting officer is considered a snitch and ostracized
c) the reporting officer serves as a counselor for the offending officer
d) the reporting officer is given a job with internal affairs
e) the reporting officer is fired

8.14. What is the term used to describe a police officer taking expensive items for personal use during an investigation of a break-in or burglary?
a) borrowing
b) chiseling
c) premeditated theft
d) mooching
e) shakedown

8.15. What is the term used to describe a police officer using tools, keys, or other devices to force entry and steal property?
a) borrowing
b) chiseling
c) premeditated theft
d) mooching
e) shakedown

8.16. What is the term used to describe a police officer issuing license tabs, window stickers, or courtesy cards that exempt users from arrest or citation for traffic offense?
a) favoritism
b) chiseling
c) premeditated theft
d) mooching
e) shakedown

8.17. What is the term used to describe a police officer lying in a court of law to provide an alibi for fellow officers engaged in unlawful activity?
a) perjury
b) premeditated theft
c) mooching
d) bribery
e) stealing

8.18. What is the term used to describe a police officer treating members of minority groups in a biased fashion?
a) perjury
b) premeditated theft
c) mooching
d) prejudice
e) stealing

8.19. Which of the following techniques are used to control the police?
a) internal affairs units
b) civilian review boards
c) standards and accreditation
d) civil liability lawsuits
e) all of the above

8.20. What is the size of an Internal Affairs Department?
a) ten officers
b) twenty officers
c) thirty officers
d) fifty officers
e) it may vary between one officer and an entire section of officers

8.21. In a study of crime in Minneapolis, how much crime was found on a small number of "hot spots" of streets and intersections?
a) 25 percent
b) 35 percent
c) 50 percent
d) 75 percent
e) 90 percent

8.22. In what ratio of crime are police "reactive," or responding to calls for assistance?
a) one-fourth
b) one-half
c) two-thirds
d) three-fourths
e) nine-tenths

8.23. In terms of costs and benefits, where are foot patrols most effective?
a) low density rural areas
b) high density urban neighborhoods
c) high density suburban areas
d) low density urban neighborhoods
e) foot patrols are not effective anywhere

8.24. In Kansas City, Missouri, aggressive traffic enforcement was used as a way to seize firearms. How many guns were seized per traffic stop?
a) one gun per two traffic stops
b) one gun per ten traffic stops
c) one gun per eighteen traffic stops
d) one gun per twenty-eight traffic stops
e) one gun per fifty traffic stops

8.25. The professional crime fighter role has dominated policing in America since the...
a) 1920s
b) 1940s
c) 1960s
d) 1980s
e) 1990s

## TRUE/FALSE QUESTIONS

8.1. Tasers can be used to incapacitate a person temporarily with minimum harm.

8.2. Police accreditation is voluntary.

8.3. Domestic violence crimes increase in the spring months.

8.4. Rape crimes increase in the summer months.

8.5. The service function is considered more important when police assume the crime fighting role.

8.6. Disorder, such as a broken window, creates fear in a community and increases crime problems.

8.7. The Violent Crime Control and Law Enforcement Act called for decreases in the numbers of officers assigned to community policing.

8.8. Japanese policemen usually patrol in vehicles.

8.9. "Crimemapping" databases provide updated information about crime trends.

8.10. Most police departments are using the iris-recognition technology made famous by the movie, Minority Report.

8.11. In *Kyllo v. United States (2001)*, the use of a thermal imaging device by law enforcement was ruled to be an illegal search.

8.12. Abuse of police power is a major issue on the public's agenda.

8.13. Police may use "legitimate" force to do their job.

8.14. Police scandals rarely have occurred in the last quarter-century.

8.15. The use of new technology does not raise issues related to privacy.

8.16. In regard to community policing, Rudolph Guliani argued that police officers engaged in too much social work and made too few arrests.

8.17. A problem with community policing is that it does not reduce costs.

8.18. The order maintenance function is considered less important when police assume the crime fighting role.

8.19. The demands on the police differ according to the time of day, day of the week, and even season of the year.

8.20. Internal Affairs officers usually have good relationships with officers outside of their department.

# ANSWER KEY

## Key Terms

1. shopping
2. union brokerage model
3. bribery
4. prejudice
5. private policing
6. department contract model
7. premeditated theft
8. Mollen Commission
9. civic accountability
10. shakedown
11. chiseling
12. internal affairs units
13. *Tennessee v. Garner*
14. favoritism
15. civil liability suits
16. civilian review boards
17. officer contract model
18. perjury
19. contractual private policing
20. accreditation
21. "meat eaters"
22. police corruption
23. extortion
24. *Monell v. Dept. of Social Services*
25. mooching
26. "grass eaters"
27. police brutality

## Key People
1. James Q. Wilson and George L. Kelling
2. Abner Louima
3. James Q. Wilson
4. Jerry Sanders
5. Mr. Walkabout.
6. Tom Cruise
7. Amadou Diallo

## General Practice Questions
1. private policing
2. union brokerage model
3. socialization
4. police brutality
5. police corruption
6. perjury

## Multiple Choice
8.1. c
8.2. d
8.3. c
8.4. d
8.5. a
8.6. c

8.7. e
8.8. c
8.9. d
8.10. a
8.11. d
8.12. a
8.13. b
8.14. e
8.15. c
8.16. a
8.17. a
8.18. d
8.19. e
8.20. e
8.21. c
8.22. d
8.23. b
8.24. d
8.25. a

True/False
8.1. T
8.2. T
8.3. F
8.4. T
8.5. F
8.6. T
8.7. F
8.8. F
8.9. T
8.10. F
8.11. T
8.12. T
8.13. T
8.14. F
8.15. F
8.16. T
8.17. T
8.18. T
8.19. T
8.20. F

# WORKSHEET 8.1: PATROL STRATEGIES

You are the police chief in medium-sized city. In one residential neighborhood, citizens are alarmed (and complaining to city hall) because there has been a rash of burglaries. In the downtown area, an increase in muggings has the merchants concerned about losing business. At a city council meeting, representatives from both groups ask you how you can adjust patrol strategies to address the problems in each area. Pretend that you are responding to their questions in explaining below how each patrol strategy might impact (or not impact) the two problems areas in the city.

1. Preventive
Patrol_____

_____

_____

_____

_____

_____

_____

2. Foot Patrol_____

_____

_____

_____

_____

_____

3. Aggressive Patrol_____

_____

_____

_____

_____

_____

Whether or not you would adopt any of the foregoing patrol strategies, describe how you would address the crime problems in each area in order to reduce the problem and/or make the citizens feel less concerned.

_____

_____

# CHAPTER 9

## COURTS AND PRE-TRIAL PROCESSES

### LEARNING OBJECTIVES

After covering the material in this chapter, students should understand:

1. the dual court system, the hierarchy of courts (general jurisdiction, appellate etc.) and the fragmented nature of the organization of courts in the United States;

2. the reform efforts to unify court systems and centralize court administration;

3. the judge's functions and roles in the criminal court;

4. the methods used for selecting judges and the results of those selection methods;

5. the central role of plea bargaining and prosecutor's discretion in determining the outcomes of 90 percent of criminal cases;

6. defense attorneys' use of pretrial motions;

7. the underlying purposes of bail;

8. the actors who influence the bail decision;

9. the consequences of being detained, especially for poor defendants, and the debate over preventive detention;

10. mechanisms utilized to reform the bail system or as alternatives to money bail.

### CHAPTER SUMMARY

The United States has a dual court system consisting of state and federal courts that are organized into separate hierarchies. Trial courts and appellate courts have different jurisdictions and functions. Despite resistance from local judges and political interests, reformers have sought to improve state court systems through centralized administration, state funding, and a separate personnel system. The judge is a key figure in the criminal justice process, who assumes the roles of adjudicator, negotiator, and administrator. State judges are selected through various methods, including partisan elections, nonpartisan elections, gubernatorial appointment, and merit selection. Merit selection methods for choosing judges have gradually spread to many states. Such methods normally use a screening committee to make recommendations of potential appointees who will, if placed on the bench by the governor, go before the voters for approval or disapproval of their performance in office. Pretrial processes determine the fates of nearly all defendants through case dismissals, decisions defining the charges, and plea bargains that affect more than 90 percent of cases. Defense attorneys use motions to their advantage to gain information and delay proceedings to benefit their clients. The bail process provides opportunities for many defendants to gain pretrial release, but poor defendants may be disadvantaged by their inability to come up with the money or property needed to secure release. Preventive detention statutes may permit judges to hold defendants considered dangerous or likely to flee. Bail bondsmen are private businesspeople who provide money for defendants' pretrial release for a fee. Their activities create risks of corruption and discrimination in the bail process, but they may help the system by reminding defendants about court dates and tracking down defendants who disappear. Although judges bear primary responsibility for setting bail, prosecutors are especially influential in recommending amounts and conditions for pretrial release.

Initiatives to reform the bail process include release on own recognizance (ROR), police-issued citations, and bail guidelines. Pretrial detainees, despite the presumption of innocence, are held in difficult conditions in jails containing mixed populations of convicted offenders, detainees, and troubled people. The shock of being jailed creates risks of suicide and depression.


**CHAPTER OUTLINE**

I.      THE STRUCTURE OF AMERICAN COURTS

A.      <u>American Courts</u>
"Dual court system" includes state and federal courts. Both have trial and appellate courts. American trial courts are strikingly decentralized. Except for a few states with centralized court systems, courts operate under the state penal code but are staffed and funded by county or city government. Leads to local political influence and community values shaping courts and their decisions.
There are also Native American tribal courts.
      1.      Doing Your Part: Court-Appointed Special Advocates-citizens volunteer to assist people in the court system.

B.      <u>Federal Courts</u>
      1.      94 U.S. District Courts: trial courts where cases are first filed and heard.
      2.      12 U.S. Courts of Appeals, 11 with jurisdiction over a geographic area and one for the District of Columbia, which hears cases involving federal agencies.
      3.      U.S. Supreme Court has original (trial) jurisdiction over only a few kinds of cases (e.g., lawsuits between states). Nine justices have great discretion to decide which cases they will hear that arrive from the lower federal and state court.
      4.      Federal judges and U.S. Supreme Court justices are appointed to the bench by the president and are confirmed by the Senate to serve life terms.

C.      <u>State Courts</u>
      1.      Basic structure reflects inheritance from English roots; in United States, efforts were made to make sure courts were responsive to the local community, so legislatures created court systems that were decentralized, linked to local political system, and dependent for resources on the non-judicial branches of government.
      2.      Growth of commerce and population in nineteenth century generated new types of disputes requiring judicial attention.
            a.      states and localities responded to these developments by creating courts with particular legal or geographical jurisdictions: small claims, juvenile, family, and other kinds of courts: created a confusing structure of multiple courts with varying jurisdictions, overlapping responsibilities, and intercounty differences.
      3.      States' courts organized into three tiers, although the number, variety, and names of courts differ from state to state:
            a.      Trial courts of limited jurisdiction: limited to hearing formal charges against accused persons, holding preliminary hearings, and perhaps trials for minor offenses.
What Americans Think: concerns about impact of politics and bias in courts.
            b.      Trial courts of general jurisdiction: trials in all cases, criminal and civil. Often referred to as felony courts.
            c.      Appellate courts (courts of last resort and (in most states) intermediate appellate courts: appeals from the lower courts. Intermediate appellate courts often lack discretion to decline to hear cases and usually sit in panels of three judges.

    d.     State Supreme Courts (courts of last resort) often have significant discretion to choose which cases they want to hear. Judges normally sit *en banc* (as a whole group).

II.    EFFECTIVE MANAGEMENT OF STATE COURTS

A.    Court Reform Issues
    1.    Scholars have claimed there were too many courts, waste of judicial power because of rigid jurisdictional boundaries, poor use of resources, and frequent granting of new trials.
    2.    Reformers often point to inefficient resources and questionable quality of politically appointed judges and the fragmented structure of most state courts.
    3.    Most common remedy prescribed: unified court system with four objectives:
        a.     elimination of overlapping and conflicting jurisdictional boundaries (of both subject matter and geography);
        b.     a hierarchical and centralized court structure, with administrative responsibility vested in a chief justice and court of last resort;
        c.     financing of courts by state government;
        d.     separate personnel system, centrally run by a state court administrator.
    4.    Dominant themes represented by reform movement: a structure;
        b.     centralization of administrative authority;
        c.     funding;
        d.     a separate personnel system.

B.    Court Structure
    1.    Structure and reform efforts essentially seek to consolidate and simplify court structure. Although this is attractive for the appearance of clarity and efficiency, judicial decentralization and autonomy make it possible for local courts to become integral parts of the local political system -- thus providing community interest groups with access to judicial decision makers.

C.    Centralization of Administration
    1.    Reformers argue that state supreme court or chief justice should take charge of functions that need to be centralized: assignment of judges, assignment of cases, record keeping, personnel, and financing. Local judges are not trained to be administrators.

D.    State Funding
    1.    Method of funding probably most influential element for bringing into being the centralized administration model. Control of the purse strings is essential to the power of any organization.
        a.     Reformers consistently propose that state fully fund the courts (rather than local funding) and a court administrator, under the direction of the chief justice, prepare for the legislature a budget covering the entire system.
        b.     Marcia Lim's study found the state share of funding varied from 13 percent to 100 percent but only twenty-one state court systems receive substantial or full support of their budget from the state.
        c.     In general, the larger a state's population, the lower its percentage of court funding from the state.
        d.     Recent movement toward more state funding; local leaders more willing to let state control funding as court costs increase burden on local governments.

E.    Separate Court Personnel System
    1.    Without a civil service system, courts are captured by local political interests. Sometimes reforms toward centralization produce separate rules for judicial personnel; in other states, judicial personnel are subject to the same rules as other state employees.

F.   Trend Toward Unified Court Systems
     1.   Recent criticisms that assumptions underlying reforms aimed at centralizing court
          administration wrongly assume that formal structures determine behavior.  However, a
          tidy organization chart is no guarantee of better or more efficient management.
III.  TO BE A JUDGE

A.   The Role of the Judge
     1.   Judges perceived to be most powerful actor [although prosecutor arguably really more
          powerful]; judges not just involved in trials, also a presence in a range of activities:
          signing warrants, setting bail, arraignments, accepting guilty pleas, scheduling cases.
     2.   Judge is the person in the system who is expected to *embody* justice;  specific
          expectations about judge's manner and demeanor; judges frequently function as lawgivers
          as other actors involved in fact-finding; judges are believed to be removed from the
          social context of the courtroom participants and to base their decisions on their own
          interpretation of the law after thoughtful consideration of the issues.
     3.   Discretion in disposition of summary offenses without constant supervision of a higher
          court; have wide latitude in fixing sentences; courtroom tasks actually relatively routine
          producing assembly-line processing of cases.
     4.   Image and role of judge shaped by the adversary system in which Judges passively rule
          on motions and evidence as opposing attorneys battle each other in court.
     5.   In Europe, many countries use inquisitorial system in which judge actively investigates
the

          case and questions witnesses in court.  But this system typically provides fewer rights
     and

          legal protections for defendants.

B.   Who Becomes a Judge?
     Judges enjoy high status and salaries well above the rates for most American workers, yet lower
     than pay for partners at large law firms.
     1.   Judges overwhelmingly white and male.
     2.   In many cities, political factors dictate that judges be drawn from specific racial,
          religious, and ethnic groups -- black and Hispanic still underrepresented:  affects
          symbolic aspect of justice when contrasted with demographic composition of defendants
          in urban centers.
     3.   Criminal court judges frequently have lowest status on judicial hierarchy; get less respect
          and prestige from public; many judges seek to move to civil or appellate judgeships.

C.  Functions of the Judge
     1.   Adjudicators: play role as neutral actor between prosecution and defense in making
          decisions on bail, pleas, sentencing, motions. Must avoid any appearance of bias.
     2.   Negotiators:  because most case dispositions determined by negotiation, judges spend
          much of their time talking to prosecutors, defense attorneys, etc. Judges may even
          provide informal advice to defense attorney or even defendant about what is likely to
          happen.  Court rules in some states forbid judicial participation in plea bargaining --
          although participate behind the scenes in many others.
     3.   Administrators:  seldom-recognized function is the administration of the courthouse.  In
          urban areas, there may be a professional court
          administrator. Judges, however, will still be responsible for administration of their
          courtroom and staff.  In rural areas,
          administrative burdens on judges may be more substantial.

).   11.  . to Become a Judge
     Quality of courts and justice depends on having judges with proper skills and qualities. Public
     confidence in courts diminished by poor or impolite performance.
     1.   CLOSE-UP: The Image of Justice

2.      Debates exist about whether higher quality judges would emerge from selection processes that de-emphasize politics or, alternatively, whether voters in a democracy should be able to choose their public officials, including their judges.

3.      Methods of Selection:
   a.      Gubernatorial selection
   b.      Legislative selection
   c.      Merit selection
   d.      Nonpartisan election
   e.      Partisan election

4.      Election Systems:
   a.      Campaigns for judgeships are generally low-key, low-visibility contests marked by little controversy; and usually only a small portion of the voters participate in the election. Candidates are constrained by ethical requirements from discussing issues. State supreme courts may produce highly visible campaigns.
   b.      In many cities, judgeships are fuel for the political machine as a means to reward party loyalists; in addition, the judgeships captured by a political party may permit the appointment of other loyalists to a variety of courthouse positions (clerks, bailiffs, etc.)
   c.      By contrast, in Europe many judges receive special training and work their way up through a civil service model court organization.
   d.      Partisan elections provide extra information for voters by giving the party identification for each candidate. In nonpartisan elections, people may not know anything about the candidates.

5.      Merit Selection
   First initiated in Missouri in 1940 and now has spread to other states.
   a.      When a vacancy occurs, a nominating commission of lawyers and citizens sends the governor a list of three recommended names and the governor chooses one of them be the new judge. After one year, the citizens vote in a retention election on whether to approve the judge's continued service.
   b.      Process still contains politics within the legal profession and selection process can favor elite lawyers with ties to corporations.

6.      Results of Selection Methods
   Selection method can produce differences in judges selected (e.g., legislative selection tends to favor former legislators), but no evidence that any selection method produces superior judges.

IV.      FROM ARREST TO TRIAL OR PLEA
Examples: Bail issues with a wealthy defendant and a poor defendant.

A.      <u>Pretrial Processes</u>
   1.      After arrest, the suspect is taken to the station for booking, including photographs and fingerprints. For warrantless arrests, a probable cause hearing must be held within forty-eight hours.
   2.      At the subsequent arraignment, the formal charges are read and the defendant enters a plea.
   3.      Prosecutors evaluate the evidence to make discretionary determinations about what charges to pursue or whether the charges should be dropped.
   4.      Decisions to drop charges may be influenced by the defendant's age, prior record, seriousness of offense, or jail overcrowding. Such decisions may also be influenced by bias based on race or some other factor.
   5.      Large numbers of cases are filtered out of the court system through prosecutor's discretionary decisions.
   6.      Approximately 90 percent of people arraigned on an indictment plead guilty and thus do not have a trial. Various factors influence how and when cases are filtered out of the

system before trial. Most cases pass through a process that operates somewhat like an assembly line.

B.  Pretrial Motions
    The defense attempts to use motions to its advantage by, for example, seeking to suppress evidence or to learn about the prosecutor's case. Filed in only about 10 percent of felony cases and 1 percent of misdemeanor cases.
    1.  Motion defined: a motion is an application to a court requesting an order be issued to bring about a specified action. A court hearing may be held on the motion with the opposing attorneys presenting arguments about the legality of the procedures used in police arrests and investigations, the sufficiency of the evidence, or the exclusion of evidence. Typical pretrial motions by defense include:
        a.  Motion to quash search warrant.
        b.  Motion to exclude evidence (e.g., confession).
        c.  Motion for severance (separate trials in cases with more than one defendant).
        d.  Motion to dismiss because of a delay in bringing the case to trial.
        e.  Motion to suppress evidence illegally obtained.
        f.  Motion for pretrial discovery of the evidence held by the prosecutor.
        g.  Motion for a change of venue (new location for trial) because a fair and impartial trial cannot be held in the original jurisdiction.
    2.  Motions are filed for a number of strategic reasons:
        a.  They force a partial disclosure of the prosecutor's evidence at an early date.
        b.  They put pressure on the prosecutor to consider plea bargaining early in the process.
        c.  They force exposure of the primary state witnesses at an inopportune time for the prosecution.
        d.  They raise before the trial judge early in the proceedings matters the defense may want to call to his or her attention.
        e.  They force the prosecutor to make decisions before final preparation of the case.
        f.  They allow the defendant to see the defense counsel in action, which affects the client-attorney relationship.
    3.  Additional function: motions can be used to pressure plea bargain since use of motions can convey the impression that defense is prepared to go to trial on the case if necessary.
    4.  New Directions in Criminal Justice Policy: Community Courts try to make courts more accessible to the public.

V.  BAIL: PRETRIAL RELEASE
    Bail is a sum of money or property specified by the judge that will be posted by the defendant as a condition of pretrial release and that will be forfeited if the defendant does not appear in court for scheduled hearings. Bail is a mechanism to permit presumptively innocent defendants to avoid loss of liberty pending the outcome of the case. The Eighth Amendment to the U.S. Constitution forbids excessive bail but does not establish a right to bail. Congress and some states have reformed bail's underlying purpose (i.e., return of the defendant) to allow preventive detention in order to permit holding some defendants in jail without bail, especially if they might pose a danger to the community upon release

A.  The Reality of the Bail System
    1.  Issue of bail may arise at the police station, during an initial court appearance (misdemeanor), or at the arraignment (felony).
    2.  Question of Ethics: police officers discussing setting bail too high for a suspect to gain release even though they know that they have inadequate evidence against him.
    3.  Amount of bail normally based on judge's perception of the seriousness of the crime and the defendant's record. Because bail is set within 24 to 48 hours after arrest, there is little time to seek background information about the defendant. Within particular localities, judges develop, in effect, standard rates for particular offenses.

4.      To post bail, prisoner must give the court some form of monetary surety, usually cash, property, or bond from a bonding company. For lesser offenses, may be released on their own recognizance (ROR).

5.      Bail system favors affluent defendants who have enough money for bail and disadvantages poor defendants who may end up stuck in jail.

6.      Study of urban courts showed that nearly two-thirds of felon defendants released prior to disposition of their cases and almost half were released on the day of their arrest or on the following day.

B.      Bail Bondsmen

1.      Bondsmen are central figures, available 24 hours per day to those who need to produce sufficient cash to gain release. Using their own assets or those of an insurance company, they will provide the surety for a fee ranging from 5 to 10 percent.

     a.      They are licensed by the state and choose their own clients, and may set their own collateral requirements.

     b.      They may track down and return bail jumpers without extradition and by force if necessary.

2.      Bondsmen exert influence on the court through their ability to cooperate with police officers who recommend their services rather than those of other bondsmen. In return, bondsmen may refuse to provide bail for defendants whom the police would like to keep in jail. Bondsmen are private, profit-seeking actors with no official connection to the court who can, in effect, nullify a judge's decision that a defendant is eligible for release on bail.

3.      Positive impact of bondsmen is to maintain social control over defendant during the pretrial period; remind clients about court dates; put pressure on defendant's friends and family to make sure defendant appears for court; bondsmen may help prepare defendants for ultimate outcome and may encourage and facilitate guilty pleas by using their experience to accurately predict how specific judges will sentence for particular crimes; help to relieve pressure on overcrowded jails by assisting with release of some defendants.

4.      Any potential benefits provided by bondsmen might be provided as well or better if courts had effective pretrial services offices.

5.      New Directions in Criminal Justice Policy Bail by Credit Card and ATM- Two counties in California experimented with techniques that bypass bail bondsmen by permitting the installation of an interactive kiosk as a means to make bail. Minutes after being booked, arrestees can slide their credit card through a device that looks like at ATM (automatic teller machine). The machine will charge the credit card the bail amount.

C.      Setting Bail

1.      For misdemeanors, bail generally set by a police officer according to a set schedule.

2.      For felonies, judges use discretion to set bail by taking account of severity of offense, defendant's characteristics, and concern for community protection. Also may consider pretrial detention if available under state or federal law, or set a high bail to prevent release.

3.      In addition to formal criteria, the judicial officer (judge or magistrate) is also influenced by expectations of prosecutor, police, defense attorney, and sometimes the bondsman.

4.      Study of Hispanic arrestees shows that those who could afford their own attorneys were seven times more likely to gain pretrial release than indigent defendants.

5.      The police may be particularly active in attempting to influence the bail decision if they do not want to see a particular defendant released.

6.      Frederic Suffet's study of New York courts found that acknowledged rules of the game emerged with seriousness of charge, prior record, and defendant's ties to the community

providing the recognized boundaries for bail amount and conditions within which the actors could negotiate with a minimum of conflict.

7. Prosecutor was shown to have more prestige and influence than defense attorney in suggesting bail amount. Prosecutor's request for higher bail granted in four out of five cases; judge and prosecutor hold similar conceptions of proper bail amount and tend to be mutually supportive.

8. Latent purpose of bail seems to be to spread responsibility for the release. By including the prosecutor and defense attorney in the process, the judge can buffer the court against an outraged public if an accused defendant commits a crime while out on bail.

9. In addition to interpersonal influences, local legal and political culture can be important factors. Roy Flemming's comparison of Detroit and Baltimore found more releases and lower bail amounts in Detroit, a city with limits on jail overcrowding and judges secure in their jobs. In Baltimore, lower status court officials or commissioners set bail; they had insecure tenure and therefore were more vulnerable to criticism by police and other public officials.

10. From a constitutional standpoint, it has been argued that bail should be set in accordance with six presumptions:
    a. Accused is entitled to release on his or her own recognizance.
    b. Nonfinancial alternatives for bail should be used whenever possible.
    c. Accused should receive a full and fair bail hearing.
    d. Reasons should be stated for the bail decision.
    e. Clear and convincing evidence should be offered to support a decision.
    f. There should be a prompt and automatic review of all bail determinations.

11. The foregoing criteria are at the center of a debate between those who believe the justice system needs discretion to deal with offenders and protect society and those who believe that personal freedom is so important that presumptively innocent defendants should be given full consideration for their pretrial release.

D. Reforming the Bail System

1. Concentrated efforts to reform bail system have existed for three decades in response to judicial discretion in setting bail amounts, poor defendants being deprived of their freedom while better-off citizens can afford bail, the perceived unsavory role of bondsmen, and bad jail conditions imposed on those detained while awaiting trial.

2. Alternatives to Bail:
    a. Citation: citation or summons issued by police officer; avoids booking, arrest, bail, and jailing; in some jurisdictions, fewer than five percent of those issued citations failed to appear; bailbondsmen have opposed this method as a threat to their livelihood.
    b. Release on Own Recognizance (ROR): pioneered by Vera Institute of Justice in New York City. Court personnel talk to defendants about their family ties and roots in the community (i.e., job, family, prior record, length of time in local area), then recommend ROR if sufficient contacts exist. In first three years, 3,500 of 10,000 defendants released on ROR, only 1.5 percent failed to appear -- a rate three times better than regular bail.
    c. Ten Percent Cash Bail: many judges are unwilling to use ROR, so some states have instituted policy in which defendants deposit a percent of bail as collateral -- when they return to court, they receive 90 percent of this back. Program assists release; does not enrich bondsmen.
    d. Bail Guidelines: guidelines developed to establish criteria that will produce more consistency in bail decisions.
    e. Preventive Detention: called a basic threat to liberties by civil libertarians, but approved by Congress for federal court in Bail Reform Act of 1984. Judges can consider whether defendant poses a danger to community and decide not to set bail. Decision is made at hearing at which prosecution contends there is risk of flight, risk that defendant will obstruct justice by threatening a witness or juror,

and defendant accused of crime of violence, or one punishable by life imprisonment or death. Supreme Court upheld preventive detention (e.g., *U.S. v. Salerno*).

    i.      Advocates of preventive detention point to studies indicating that seven to twenty percent of defendants commit crimes while out on bail.

    ii.     Detention most common for violence, drugs, and immigration offenses.

  f.     CLOSEUP: Preventive Detention: Two Sides of an Issue

  g.    One study suggested that the Bail Reform Act did not lead to more preventive detention, but simply permitted judges to be more honest by declining to set bail when they previously would have simply set an impossibly high bail.

## VI. PRETRIAL DETENTION

A.     <u>Jail</u>

    1.    About half of 600,000 people in jail at any given moment are in pretrial detention while the other half are serving short sentences; nearly all are poor.

    2.    Initial time after arrest often moments of panic and crisis: vulnerability, helplessness, fright, and ominous threat of loss of freedom produce high stress and most jail suicides occur within the first six to ten hours of detention, and most psychotic episodes occur during or just after intake.

    3.    Crisis can be exacerbated when arrested person is intoxicated or under the influence of drugs; for young offenders, the threat of victimization by violence can produce debilitating depression.

B.     <u>Impact of Pretrial Detention</u>

    1.    Conditions in jail for presumptively innocent defendants are deplorable -- creates pressures on defendants to waive their rights and plead guilty.

    2.    COMPARATIVE PERSPECTIVE: Pretrial Detention in Russia. Dangerous conditions during long periods of pretrial detention.

    3.    Ultimate outcome of case affected by whether or not defendant held in jail. Jailed defendant may look guiltier in eyes of judge and jury when escorted into court by guards rather than by friends and family (as is the case for released defendant). Some research shows greater likelihood of conviction and incarceration for those jailed prior to trial, but difficult to know if it is jailing that increases severity of outcome (as opposed to some other factor, such as prior record, etc.).

## REVIEW OF KEY TERMS

<u>Fill in the appropriate term for each statement</u>

jurisdiction
appellate court
trial court of general jurisdiction
nonpartisan election
trial court of limited jurisdiction
partisan election
merit selection
Roscoe Pound
unified court system
adjudicator
negotiator
administrator
legislative selection
gubernatorial selection

retention election
arraignment
motion
bail
citation
release on own recognizance (ROR)
preventive detention
Bail Reform Act of 1984
bail bondsman
ten percent cash bail
Eighth Amendment
bail guidelines

1. _____ is a judicial selection method in which the selection of candidates is controlled by the political parties.

2. _____ is the trial court that handles specific categories of less serious cases.

3. _____ is the judges' functional role that involves them in decisions about resource allocation and other matters within the courthouse.

4. A court's _____ defines the boundaries of its authority over people, places, and types of legal actions.

5. _____ is a method of selecting judges that attempts to remove partisan politics, but merely replaces those politics with the political conflicts within the legal profession.

6. _____ is the level of the judicial hierarchy that looks for errors by trial judges.

7. _____ is the final step of the Missouri plan that is designed to permit the public to participate democratically in the decision that holds a judge accountable for decisions and actions.

8. _____ often produces the appointment of former legislators as judges.

9. _____ is the ideal of reformers who want centralized administration and funding for state courts.

10. _____ is one of judges' functional roles that involves them in discussions with prosecutors and defense attorneys behind the closed doors of their judicial chambers.

11. _____ is a conglomeration of people that needs interaction, common goals, and other influences to develop into a workgroup.

12. _____ is the trial court that handles felony cases.

13. _____ is a method of selecting judges that attempts but fails to remove politics because, for example, so many judges initially gain their judgeships through gubernatorial mid-term appointments to fill vacancies created by deaths and retirements.

14. _____ is one of judges' functional roles that comes the closest to embodying the idealized conception of what judges are supposed to do with their time.

15. _____ is the stage in the criminal justice process in which formal charges are read in court and a plea is entered.

16. _____ is a tactical tool employed by defense attorneys to challenge and discover aspects of the prosecution's case.

17. _____ is to ensure that a defendant returns to court for subsequent proceedings.

18. _____ is a method of summoning defendants to return to court without using the system's resources for arrests and jailing.

19. _____ is a mechanism developed to reduce the opportunities for profit-seekers to benefit from the bail process.

20. _____ permits defendants to be freed from jail without paying bail and therefore reduces the harsh effects of bail upon the poor.

21. _____ changed procedures in the federal courts to permit preventive detention after a hearing concerning the defendant's risk of flight and danger to the community.

22. _____ can be viewed as a means to gain greater consistency in bail decisions.

23. _____ is a private actor whose interests and decisions affect the liberty of jailed defendants.

24. _____ results when bail is not set and a defendant remains in jail because he or she has been determined to be a danger to the community.

25. _____ prohibits excessive bail.


## REVIEW OF KEY PEOPLE

Hernando Williams
Ricardo Armstrong
John Rigas

1. _____, the 78-year-old founder of Adelphia Communiction Corporation, one of the nation's largest cable television systems, was arrested for improperly taking the company's money for personal use.
2. _____ was one of the first defendants held under the Bail Reform Act of 1984. The 28-year-old janitor, who had a prior burglary conviction, was denied bail after being charged with robbing two Ohio banks.

3. Prosecutors point to the release of _____ as the classic example of the need for preventive detention. As he drove to court to face charges of raping and beating a woman he abducted at a shopping mall, another woman lay trapped inside his car trunk.


## GENERAL PRACTICE QUESTIONS

Although reformers hoped that _____1_____ would remove the influence of politics from the selection judges, there is still political maneuvering in the formation of the selection committee and there is the potential for politics in campaigning against judges who must stand for _____2_____ during their terms on the bench.

After the _____3_____ permitted the federal courts to keep defendants in custody as a form of _____4_____, the Supreme Court approved the constitutionality of the practice in the case of _____5_____ despite widespread concerns that the practice developed by the statute was a constitutional violation of the _____6_____.

Because they have a financial interest in the maintenance of the current bail system, _____7_____ prefer not to see defendants freed without bail through _____8_____ and they especially object to reforms, such as _____9_____, which directly imitate their business practices and therefore cut them out of the system.

## MULTIPLE CHOICE QUESTIONS

9.1. What is CASA?
a) Court of Appeals for San Antonio
b) Court of Alabama State of Appeals
c) Court Appointed Special Advocates
d) Children Advocates Serving America
e) Counsel Appointed by Special Attorneys

9.2. Which of the following is a goal of a unified court system?
a) eliminating overlapping and conflicting jurisdictional boundaries
b) creating a hierarchical and centralized court structure
c) having the courts funded by state government instead of local counties and cities
d) creating a separate civil service personnel system run by a state court administrator
e) all of the above

9.3. Which of the following is NOT a reason to become a judge?
a) perform public service
b) gain political power
c) gain prestige
d) gain wealth
e) all of the above are reasons to become a judge

9.4. Which of the following is a seldom-recognized function of most judges?
a) negotiating
b) managing the courthouse
c) adjudicating
d) all of the above
e) none of the above

9.5. In Europe, how does a person become a judge?
a) special training in law school
b) elected to office
c) judicial lottery
d) appointed by the old boys network
e) inherit a judgeship

9.6. Which statement best describes U. S. election campaigns for lower court judgeships?
a) low-key contests with great controversy
b) high-profile contests with little controversy
c) high-profile contests with great controversy
d) low-key contests with little controversy
e) there are no elections for lower court judgeships in the United States

9.7. Which of the following U.S. Supreme Court decisions invalidated Minnesota's ethics rule that forbade judicial candidates from announcing their views on disputed legal or political issues?
a) Buckley v. Valeo (1976)
b) Republican Party of Minnesota v. White (2002)
c) Rutan v. Republican Party (1990)
d) FEC v. Ventura (2000)
e) Minnesota Republican Party v. Wellstone (2001)

9.8. How often do acquittals occur in urban felony cases?
a) frequently
b) sometimes
c) rare
d) never
e) almost always

9.9. How often do guilty pleas occur in urban felony cases?
a) frequently
b) sometimes
c) rare
d) never
e) almost always

9.10. How often are decisions made quickly about bail?
a) never
b) not very often
c) often
d) almost always
e) always

9.11. Which of the following is a TRUE statement about courts in the United States?
a) courts are under pressure to limit the number of cases going to trial
b) courts are under pressure to limit the number of plea bargains
c) courts are under pressure to limit the number of persons releases on bail
d) all of the above are TRUE
e) all of the above are FALSE

9.12. What was the name of the two wealthy young brothers in California who were convicted of murdering their parents?
a) Gonzalez
b) Menendez
c) Arias
d) Hernandez
e) Gomez

9.13. What is the rate of conviction for offenses that a prosecutor decides to pursue?
a) very low rate of conviction
b) average rate of conviction
c) low rate of conviction
d) high rate of conviction
e) 100% rate of conviction

9.14. Which of the following is NOT a purpose of bail?
a) to ensure that the defendant appears in court for trial
b) to protect the community from further crimes that some defendants may commit while out on bail
c) to punish the defendant
d) all of the above are purposes of bail
e) none of the above are purposes of bail

9.15. When does the question of bail arise?
a) at the police station
b) at the initial court appearance
c) at the arraignment
d) all of the above
e) none of the above

9.16. When does the question of bail arise in most misdemeanor cases?
a) at the police station
b) at the initial court appearance
c) at the arraignment
d) at the opening arguments of the trial
e) in chambers between the attorney and the judge

9.17. When does the question of bail arise in most felony cases?
a) at the police station
b) at the initial court appearance
c) at the arraignment
d) at the opening arguments of the trial
e) in chambers between the attorney and the judge

9.18. Who usually sets bail for serious offenses?
a) police officer
b) prosecutor
c) public defender
d) judge
e) jury

9.19. Who usually sets bail for minor offenses?
a) police officer
b) prosecutor
c) public defender
d) judge
e) jury

9.20. Where is the right to representation by an attorney at bail hearings found in the Bill of Rights?
a) Fifth Amendment
b) Sixth Amendment
c) Seventh Amendment
d) Eighth Amendment
e) there is no constitutional right to representation by an attorney at bail hearings

9.21. In 1998, how many felony suspects in the largest U. S. counties were unable to make bail or utilize the services of a bail bondsman to gain release?
a) none
b) 1,500
c) 9,000
d) 16,000
e) 27,000

9.22. What is the usual fee charged by a bail bondsperson?
a) 1 percent of the bail amount
b) 5 to 10 percent of the bail amount
c) 20 to 30 percent of the bail amount
d) 40 to 50 percent of the bail amount
e) 90 percent of the bail amount

9.23. What is the requirement for becoming a bail bondsperson?
a) high school education
b) college degree
c) state license
d) $100,000 cash as collateral
e) there are no formal requirements

9.24. Which of the following is NOT true about bail bondspersons?
a) they usually act in their own self-interest
b) they usually have close relationships with police and correctional officials
c) they slow the processing of cases
d) they are required to be licensed by the state
e) all of the above are TRUE

9.25. What determines the amount of bail set by the judge?
a) the interactions of the judge, prosecutor, and defense attorney
b) the interactions of the bailiff, jury, and defense attorney
c) the interactions of the judge, clerk, and defendant
d) the interactions of the judge, court reporter, and defense attorney
e) the interactions of the judge, probation officer, and bail bondsperson


## TRUE/FALSE QUESTIONS

9.1. Most criminal cases are heard at the state level.

9.2. Native Americans have their own court systems in the United States.

9.3. State court systems do not have appellate courts.

9.4. The United States Supreme Court has the power to decide which cases it wants to hear.

9.5. The American state court systems are centralized.

9.6. The larger a state's population, the lower the portion of court funds that come from the state government.

9.7. The American Bar Association has prohibited the control of court jobs by political parties and judges.

9.8. Under the adversary system of justice in the U. S., each side (prosecution and defense) is represented by an attorney.

9.9. Under the inquisitorial system, the judge takes a very passive role in deliberations.

9.10. The work of a judge is limited to presiding at trials.

9.11. Judges are given considerable discretion in performing their duties throughout the judicial process.

9.12. Some judges are responsible for managing the administrative affairs at their courthouses.

9.13. The selection process of judges is nonpolitical.

9.14. Judicial elections are characterized by high voter turnout.

9.15. The bail bondsperson does not profit from his position.

9.16. The Eighth Amendment created the bail bondsperson as a key actor within the criminal justice system.

9.17. A person cannot be denied bail.

9.18. The bail bondsperson is a private businessman.

9.19. Bail is always set by a judge.

9.20. A person cannot be deprived of their freedom until they are found guilty in a court of law.

# ANSWER KEY

## Key Terms
1.    partisan election
2.    trial court of limited jurisdiction
3.    administrator
4.    jurisdiction
5.    merit selection
6.    appellate court
7.    retention election
8.    legislative selection
9.    unified court system
10.    negotiator
11.    grouping
12.    trial court of general jurisdiction
13.    nonpartisan election
14.    adjudicator
15.    arraignment
16.    motion 6
17.    bail
18.    citation
19.    ten percent cash bail
20.    release on own recognizance (ROR)
21.    Bail Reform Act of 1984
22.    bail guidelines
23.    bail bondsman
24.    preventive detention
25.    Eighth Amendment

## Key People
1.    John Rigas
2.    Ricardo Armstrong
3.    Hernando Williams

## General Practice Questions
1.    merit selection
2.    retention election
3.    Bail Reform Act of 1984
4.    preventive detention
5.    Bail Reform Act of 1984
6.    Eighth Amendment
7.    bail bondsmen
8.    release on own recognizance
9.    ten percent cash bail

## Multiple Choice
9.1.    c
9.2.    e
9.3.    d
9.4.    b
9.5.    a
9.6.    d
9.7.    b
9.8.    c
9.9.    a

| 9.10. | c |
| 9.11. | a |
| 9.12. | b |
| 9.13. | d |
| 9.14. | c |
| 9.15. | d |
| 9.16 . | b |
| 9.17. | c |
| 9.18. | d |
| 9.19. | a |
| 9.20. | e |
| 9.21. | d |
| 9.22. | b |
| 9.23. | c |
| 9.24. | c |
| 9.25. | a |

True/False
| 9.1. | T |
| 9.2. | T |
| 9.3. | F |
| 9.4. | T |
| 9.5. | F |
| 9.6. | T |
| 9.7. | F |
| 9.8. | T |
| 9.9. | F |
| 9.10. | F |
| 9.11. | T |
| 9.12. | T |
| 9.13. | F |
| 9.14. | F |
| 9.15. | F |
| 9.16. | F |
| 9.17. | F |
| 9.18. | T |
| 9.19. | F |
| 9.20. | F |

## WORKSHEET 9.1: BAIL

Imagine that you are a judge responsible for setting bail. For each of the following cases, indicate whether you would order Release on Own Recognizance (ROR), set bail at some specific amount [state the amount], or deny bail and order preventive detention. Provide brief comments that explain each decision.

1. Jane Williams is a new assistant professor of literature at the local university. She is twenty-six years old. She has no relatives in the area and her family lives 500 miles away in the city where she went to college for the eight years it took to earn her undergraduate and graduate degrees. She is charged with fraud in obtaining $50,000 in student loans during the previous three years by lying about her income and assets on student loan application forms. Seven years earlier she pleaded guilty in her hometown to a misdemeanor charge of underage drinking.

_____

_____

_____

_____

_____

_____

2. Karl Schmidt is charged with attempted rape. He is accused of attacking a woman in his car while giving her a ride home from the bar where he met her. He is a twenty-two year old, rookie police officer [now suspended from the force] who has lived in the city for his entire life and has no prior record.

_____

_____

_____

_____

_____

3. Susan Claussen is charged with theft for ordering and eating dinner at an expensive restaurant, and then leaving without paying the bill. She has been charged with and entered guilty pleas to the offense on five previous occasions over the past three years. She has been placed on probation several times and served one thirty-day jail sentence. She is unemployed and a life-long resident of the city. She lives with her parents.

_____

_____

WORKSHEET 9.2: JUDICIAL SELECTION

Respond to the following questions in light of the text's discussion of the importance of judicial selection methods. Think about the implications and consequences of each selection methods (Gubernatorial Appointment, Legislative Appointment, Partisan Election, Nonpartisan Election, Merit Selection)

1. What are the four most important qualities that we should look for in the people we select to be judges?

_____

_____

_____

_____

2. How do we know which people possess these qualities?

_____

_____

_____

3. Which judicial selection method would provide the best means to identify and select the people who possess these qualities?

_____

_____

_____

_____

4. What are the drawbacks to this judicial selection method?

_____

_____

_____

_____

5. Which judicial selection method is used in the state where you live or go to school? Why do you think that this state uses this selection method instead of one of the other methods?

_____

_____

_____

# CHAPTER 10

## PROSECUTION AND DEFENSE

### LEARNING OBJECTIVES

After covering the material in this chapter, students should understand:

1.    the decentralized organization of prosecution in the United States;

2.    the significant discretionary power of prosecutors to make unsupervised, low visibility decisions that shape criminal justice outcomes;

3.    the exchange relations between prosecutors and other actors that affect prosecutors' decisions (e.g., police, victims, court, community, etc.);

4.    the prosecutor's dilemma of seeking to win cases for the state while also ensuring that justice is served;

5.    the role conceptions of prosecutors: trial counsel for police; house counsel for police; representative of the court; and elected official;

6.    the nature of the accusatory process and the models for prosecutorial decision making, Legal Sufficiency, System Efficiency, and Trial Sufficiency;

7.    the Supreme Court's requirement for the appointment of defense counsel for indigent defendants facing incarceration;

8.    the difference between the television of image of the defense trial attorney and the reality of defense attorneys engaged in plea bargaining and exchange relations;

9.    the role of the defense attorney as client-counselor and agent-mediator, and the environment of criminal defense work;

10.   the characteristics and weaknesses of the three systems for indigent defense: assigned counsel, contract counsel, and public defender; and comparison of effectiveness of private versus public defense;

11.   the issue of attorney competence and standards for assessing the ineffective assistance of counsel.

### CHAPTER SUMMARY

American prosecutors at all levels have considerable discretion to determine how to handle criminal cases. There is no higher authority over most prosecutors that can overrule a decision to decline to prosecute (*nolle prosequi*) or to pursue multiple counts against a defendant. The prosecutor can play a variety of roles, including trial counsel for the police, house counsel for the police, representative of the court, and elected official.

Prosecutors' decisions and actions are affected by their exchange relationships with many other important actors and groups, including police, judges, victims and witnesses, and the public. Three primary models of prosecutors' decision-making policies are legal sufficiency, system efficiency, and trial sufficiency. The image of defense attorneys portrayed in the media as courtroom advocates is often vastly different from the reality of pressured, busy negotiators constantly involved in bargaining with the prosecutor over guilty plea agreements. Relatively few private defense attorneys make significant incomes from criminal work, but larger numbers of private attorneys accept court appointments to handle indigent defendants' cases quickly for relatively low fees. Three primary methods for providing attorneys to represent indigent defendants are appointed counsel, contract counsel, and public defenders. Defense attorneys must often wrestle with difficult working conditions and uncooperative clients as they seek to provide representation, usually in the plea negotiation process. The quality of representation provided to criminal defendants is a matter of significant concern, but U.S. Supreme Court rulings have made it difficult for convicted offenders to prove that their attorneys did not provide a competent defense.

**CHAPTER OUTLINE**

I.  CASE EXAMPLE: Actress Winona Ryder attempted to leave a Saks Fifth Avenue store without paying for items. Her bag was allegedly found to contain nearly $5,000 worth of merchandise as well as unauthorized prescription painkillers. Ryder was charged with second-degree burglary, grand theft, and possession of a controlled substance, all felonies. She faced the possibility of three years in prison. Another actress, Rebecca Gayheart, plead guilty to the vehicular manslaughter of a nine-year old boy and only received probation. These two incidents occurred in the same county. The Los Angeles prosecutor determined the nature and number of charges filed against Ryder and Gayheart. This illustrates the discretion and disparity within the prosecutorial system.

II.  THE PROSECUTORIAL SYSTEM
     State laws govern most criminal cases.

A.   Introduction
     1.   U.S. Attorney: federal prosecutor, appointed by the President in each of 94 districts around the country; responsible for prosecuting federal crimes.
     2.   Attorney General: elected in most states; in Alaska, Delaware, and Rhode Island, they direct all local prosecutions as well as state prosecutions.
     3.   County Prosecutors: 2,341 offices in country; primary location of prosecutions; elected except in Connecticut and New Jersey and therefore heavily involved in local politics.
          a.   Number of assistant prosecutors will vary by size of office -- all the way up to 500 in Los Angeles; assistants usually young attorneys who use position to gain trial experience.

B.   Politics and Prosecution
     1.   Process and organization of prosecution inescapably political. For example:
          a.   Appointment of deputies may serve the political party's purposes
          b.   Decision about whether or not to prosecute may include consideration of prosecutor's or political party's electoral interests.
          c.   Historically, some groups (e.g., racial minorities) received harsher treatment when prosecutors used their discretion to pursue their cases while not pursuing others' cases.

C.   The Prosecutor's Influence
     1.   Low visibility of prosecutors' decisions increases their power in making discretionary decisions; voters cannot easily hold elected prosecutors accountable because they do not know the range and nature of prosecutors' decisions.
     2.   Prosecutors' discretion rarely recognized of controlled substances by statutes; statutes generally state that all crimes shall be prosecuted, but it is really up to the prosecutor to decide if and how that will really happen
     3.   Prosecutors may decline to prosecute crimes if they believe that the local community no longer considers such behavior worthy of punishment, even if the law is still on the books; because most prosecutors are in smaller counties, they can be highly influenced

by local public opinion -- especially with respect to the discretionary enforcement of such things as victimless crimes (gambling, drug use, etc.)

III. THE PROSECUTOR'S ROLES

A. "Prosecutor's Dilemma"
As lawyers for the state, they are expected to do everything in their power to win the public's case, but as officers of the court and members of the local legal profession, they are also obligated to see that justice is done.
  1. Environment can create "prosecutors' bias" or "prosecutors' complex": prosecutors can come to consider themselves instruments of law enforcement although they are supposed to represent all people, including the accused.
  Prosecutors sometimes make mistakes, but they are immune from lawsuits if they prosecute innocent people.

B. Role Concept
A person may hold a legally defined position yet hold a conception of the role -- the manner of action on a daily basis -- that differs from those of other persons in the same position.
  1. Complications of Role Definition: prosecutor has need to maintain relationships and cooperation with a variety of other actors: police, judges, defense attorneys, political party leaders, electorate, etc. Prosecutors' decisions affect the work and goal attainment of the other actors in the criminal justice system.
  2. Role Definition: defined by a variety of factors in addition to formal professional responsibilities -- individual prosecutor's personality, the political and social environment in which the prosecutor operates, the individual prosecutor's expectations concerning the attitudes of other actors.
  3. Four role conceptions found among prosecutors:
      a. Trial counsel for the police: crime-fighter stance and follow police department policies.
      b. House counsel for the police: give legal advice so that arrests will stand up in court.
      c. Representative of the court: enforce rules of due process to ensure that police act in accordance with law and respect rights of defendants.
      d. Elected official: make decisions that are responsive to local public opinion -- but this creates risks of partisan political influence on decision making.

IV. DISCRETION OF THE PROSECUTOR
Autonomy, lack of supervision, and low visibility of decisions give prosecutors broad discretionary authority to make decisions at each step of the criminal justice process.

A. Prosecutors May Decline to Prosecute
  1. Screening out cases may be based on office policies. For example, the U.S. Department of Justice provides guidelines for determining whether cases should be pursued or dropped.
      The relevant criteria are:
      a. federal law enforcement priorities
      b. nature and seriousness of the offense
      c. deterrent effect of prosecution
      d. person's culpability in connection with the offense
      e. person's history of criminal activity
      f. probable sentence or other consequences if the person is convicted

  2. Comparative Perspective : Prosecution in Germany. German prosecutors are civil servants who do not face the same public pressures as Americans in applying their discretion.

B.    A Question of Ethics
      Case of prosecutor determining robbery charges when the evidence is not crystal clear.

C.    Prosecutors Determine the Charges to Be Filed
      1.    Prosecutors determine number of *counts* to be pursued.
      2.    Discovery: Legal requirement that information be made available to the defense attorney, part of prosecutor's obligation to act impartially in seeking justice rather than in seeking only convictions on behalf of the state.
      3.    Prosecutor may reduce charge in exchange for a plea bargain.
      4.    Prosecutor may drop charge (*nolle prosequi* or nol. pros.) completely according to discretionary judgment without providing any reason to anyone.

V.    KEY RELATIONSHIPS OF THE PROSECUTOR
      The decisions made by the prosecuting attorney's office reflect the personal and organization clients with whom it interacts. Precise decisions and procedures will vary with each environment: e.g., prosecutors may make actual charging decisions or they may merely rubber stamp police decisions.

A.    Police
      1.    Prosecutors are dependent on the police to bring them the raw material with which they must achieve their goals -- solid cases.
      2.    Prosecutors depend on the police for investigations; prosecutors' success can depend on the quality of police investigations.
      3.    Prosecutors can affect police by returning cases for further investigation or by refusing to approve arrest warrants.
      4.    Police requests to prosecute a case may be turned down for a number of reasons:
            a.    Prosecutors seek to regulate caseloads in a criminal justice system of limited resources.
            b.    Prosecutors may not want to be in embarrassing position in courtroom by pursuing cases that interest the police but do not fit the prosecutors' goals.
            c.    Prosecutors may return cases as a means to check on the quality of police work.
      5.    Police-Prosecution Teams: cases may slip through the cracks without proper coordination between offices.
            a.    Formation of task forces can coordinate and obtain the evidence necessary for conviction, especially through use of prosecutorial discretion to decline to prosecute informers who cooperate with the police.

B.    Victims and Witnesses
      1.    Victims generally play a passive role in the criminal justice system. They assist the police and provide evidence.
      2.    The relationship of the victim to the accused can create problems for prosecutors: complaining witnesses may refuse to cooperate because they know or have a continuing relationship with the perpetrator. Studies show significantly higher conviction rates in stranger crimes than in nonstranger crimes in which the victim may decide not to cooperate with the prosecution. May lead prosecutor to dismiss cases.
      3.    Prosecutors may also drop cases when they think the victims will be unreliable or will not be believed as witnesses: prostitutes who claim they were raped; drug users who are assaulted by pushers; child victims who may be unable to withstand the courtroom pressure and thereby testify effectively at trial.
      4.    Victims' rights movement has produced proposals, including a proposed constitutional amendment that would give victims the opportunity to comment on plea bargains, sentences, and parole decisions.

C.    Judges and Courts

171

Sentencing history of each judge may influence prosecutors' decisions about which charges to file and whether or not to prosecute.

    1.      Sentencing behavior of judges must be predictable in order for plea bargaining to run smoothly.

    2.      Prosecutors can often control the timing and flow of cases; they can seek delays if it suits their interests (e.g., so that public attention to the case dies down).

    D.      The Community

Like other elected officials, prosecutors cannot remain unresponsive to public opinion. Otherwise they may risk losing their jobs.

    1.      Public especially influential in "gray areas" of law in which full enforcement is not expected (e.g., does community want prostitution, gambling, and pornography to be fully prosecuted, or is there public toleration for many activities that are ostensibly illegal?).

    2.      In general, however, public attention to the criminal justice system in low. Prosecutors often concerned with avoiding decisions that will generate public reactions.

    3.      Prosecutors' decisions are also affected by relationships with news media, state and federal officials, legislators, and political party officials.

VI.     DECISION-MAKING POLICIES

A.     Pretrial Phase

    1.      Pretrial phase involved with screening cases
to remove those that do not meet legal standard for probable cause, to divert eligible cases to other agencies, and to prepare appropriate charges for remaining cases.

        a.      Patterns vary among offices: screening emphasized by some prosecutors, generating quickly negotiated guilty pleas emphasized by others, and delaying pleas to build pressure on defendant up to trial date used by others.

B.     Implementing Prosecution Policy

    1.      Joan Jacoby found three policy models. Each model requires prosecutors to use strategies for allocating time and skills of assistant prosecutors:

        a.      Legal Sufficiency Model: cases initially screened for evidentiary defects before being sent to preliminary hearing. Many cases accepted for prosecution, places high reliance on plea bargaining, high numbers of eventual acquittals and dismissals because assistant prosecutors cannot prepare for each case.

        b.      System Efficiency Model: speedy and early disposition of cases -- based on continuing question "What charges should be made in view of the caseload pressures on the system?"; charges reduced in exchange for quick guilty pleas.

        c.      Trial Sufficiency Model: based on continuing question "Will this case result in conviction?" When facts are present to sustain a conviction, every effort is made to obtain that conviction. Requires good police work, prosecution staff experienced in trial work, and court capacity. Reduced emphasis on plea bargaining.

C.     Case Evaluation

The accusatory process consists of the series of activities that take place from the moment of arrest and booking through the formal charging (either information or indictment). This process involves activities of police, grand jury, bail agency, and court linked with the activities of the prosecuting attorney.

    1.      Prosecutor must make sure there is evidence to fulfill all of the elements of the crime. Prosecutor concerned with whether the reported crime will appear credible and meet legal criteria in the eyes of judge and jury.

    2.      Formal charges filed with the court through an indictment, if issued by a grand jury, or an information if the prosecutor files the charges directly.

3.      The prosecutor's decision may be influenced by the office's charging policies as well as the prosecutor's sense of individualized justice in a particular case.

VII.    DEFENSE ATTORNEY: IMAGE AND REALITY

A.    Image
1.      Television shows have made defense lawyers familiar figures in the minds of the public as outspoken courtroom advocates.
2.      In reality, defense attorneys are involved in interactions outside of public view that lead to plea bargains and dismissals.

B.    Role of the Defense Attorney
1.      Criminal defense lawyers are essential advocates on behalf of defendants through the application of pretrial investigative skills, verbal skills in plea negotiations and courtroom proceedings, and ability to creatively question prosecution witnesses.
2.      The defense attorney plays an important role in protecting the defendant's constitutional rights.
3.      In addition to advocacy functions, defense counsel provide psychological support to the defendant and the defendant's family.
4.      An effective defense requires respect, openness, and trust between attorney and client.

C.    The Realities of the Defense Attorney
1.      If defense attorneys are inexperienced or uncaring, they may not present an effective defense.
2.      The provision of defense counsel does not automatically create the adversarialness assumed by the due process model. Defense attorneys' actual behavior will depend on exchange relations and organizational setting of the court.
3.      Defense attorneys may, in fact, act as mediators between the defendant, judge, and prosecutor. By facilitating the smooth processing of cases, the defense counsel may be able to bargain for a better deal for his client.
4.      Effective defense attorneys seek to understand the facts of the case and the nature of the prosecution's evidence before deciding on the best course of action for the client, whether it is a plea bargain or a trial.
5.      Neither the public nor defendants understand the defense attorney's responsibilities for protecting people's rights and working, often in a cooperative fashion with the prosecution, to secure the most favorable outcome for the client.

D.    Environment of Criminal Practice
1.      Much of the service provided by defense counsel involves preparing clients for possible negative outcomes of cases.
2.      Defense counsel's "guilty knowledge" may be psychological burden; defense counsel is only judicial actor to view the defendant in the context of social environment and family ties.
3.      Defense counsel interact continuously with lower class clients and with police, social workers, and minor political appointees. They may be required to visit jails at all hours of day or night. Even if they prevail in the case, they may be unable to collect their fees from their clients.
4.      The low pay for such work is a key factor in the environment: defense attorneys must make every effort to obtain payment ahead of time, including trying to get payment from defendant's relatives if defendant does not pay. Leads to handling a multitude of cases for very modest fees. Creates incentives to negotiate quick pleas, since they may pay the same as a three-day trial.

5.	Defense counsel must adjust to burden of losing most of their cases. May risk censure by the community for using legal "technicalities" to the advantage of people who are guilty of serious crimes. The pressures create risks that attorneys will become "burned out" and leave criminal practice.

VIII.	COUNSEL FOR INDIGENTS
A.	Legal Requirements
1.	Supreme Court requirement that counsel be appointed early in criminal process for all defendants facing incarceration has drastically raised the percentage of defendants relying on publicly supported criminal defense lawyers. In some jurisdictions, 90 percent of accused must be provided with counsel.
2.	Major Supreme Court Rulings on Right to Counsel.
3.	The quality of representation for the poor is often questioned. Appointed counsel and public defenders have few incentives to fight each case vigorously.
4.	Frequently the image of the zealous defense lawyer is contradicted by the reality of a lawyer appointed in the courtroom who speaks briefly with the client before entering a quick guilty plea.

B.	Methods of Providing Indigents With Counsel
1.	Assigned Counsel: court appoints a private practice attorney to represent indigent. Widely used in small cities and rural areas, but also used in some urban areas, including those that use public defenders for most cases.
	a.	Ad Hoc System: judge selects lawyers at random from a prepared list or appoints lawyers who are present in the courtroom.
	b.	Coordinated System: court administrator oversees the appointment of counsel.
	c.	Attorney competence is sometimes questionable. Lawyers seeking appointments may be recent law school grads who need income or else attorneys who were not successful in more lucrative areas of legal practice.
	d.	Fee schedules may be so low as to lead assigned counsel to encourage their clients to plead guilty; spares attorney from prospect of working hard on a case for very little money. Profitability comes from doing a large number of cases as quickly as possible.
	e.	A Question of Ethics: Attorneys sometimes need to build a relationship with a judge in order to get court appointments.
2.	Contract System: currently in use in about 200 counties, the government enters into a contract with a law firm, individual attorney, or non-profit organization that will provide representation for all indigent defendants.
	a.	Terms of contract may vary, but commonly a block grant/set amount that a law firm receives under the contract. Also common to have fixed-price contracts that pay a certain amount for each case. Also may be cost-plus contracts that provide an estimated cost per case until a certain amount is expended and then a new contract is negotiated.
3.	Public Defender: Started in Los Angeles in 1914 and now in 1,144 counties, covering 70 percent of the nation's population, public defenders are salaried government employees who handle indigents' criminal cases. Public defender systems predominate in large cities.
	a.	Public defenders often viewed as superior to assigned counsel because attorneys are full-time specialists in criminal law. Public defenders also regarded as more efficient because they are less inclined to create delays.
	b.	Public defenders may tend to routinize decision making in the face of overwhelming caseloads. They may have little time to investigate cases or to interview clients. They may negotiate with prosecutors concerning pleas in groups of cases simultaneously.
	c.	Public defenders often assigned to a "zone" or stage in the criminal process rather than assigned to one-on-one representation. One public defender may handle preliminary hearings, another may handle arraignments, and another may

handle trials (if there is a trial).  The dispersion of responsibility may create a routinization of defense work and lose the special elements of individualized representation.

C.   Close-Up:  Counsel for Indigents in Four Locales
   1.   Study to compare indigent defense systems.
      a.   Denver, Colorado:  State-wide public defender system.  Attorneys paid less than prosecutors, usually work six or seven years, and are assisted by investigators.
      b.   Detroit, Michigan:  Assigned counsel and non-profit organization similar to a public defender agency.  Attorneys must apply and be approved by committee of judges before sharing in any of the 75 percent of cases directed to appointed counsel.
      c.   Oxford, Maine:  Private counsel assigned to represent indigents at forty dollars per hour which is paid by the state.
      d.   Gila County, Arizona:  Large geographic area with sparse population relies on four contract attorneys.

D.   Private Versus Public Defense
   1.   Recent studies have cast doubt on previous assumptions that public defenders enter more guilty pleas than did privately retained and assigned counsel.  Difficult to compare with retained counsel because they may serve only upper-income clients charged with white-collar crime, drug dealing, or involvement in organized crime.
      a.   Peter Nardulli found no different results by attorney types in pleas negotiated in study of nine counties in Illinois, Michigan, and Pennsylvania.
      b.   Study by National Center for State Courts in nine courts found little difference with regard to case disposition and length of sentences when comparing public defenders, assigned counsel, contract counsel, and privately retained attorneys.

IX.  DEFENSE COUNSEL IN THE SYSTEM
A.   Defense Attorney Behavior
   1.   Defense attorneys work very hard in unpleasant environment to earn small fees.
   2.   It is essential for their professional survival and for the interests of their clients that they develop good exchange relations with other courthouse actors.  They are dependent on the decisions of others at every stage in the process.  They need cooperation from others, so that even seemingly minor matters go smoothly, such as visiting the defendant in jail, learning about the prosecutor's case against the defendant, and setting bail.
   3.   Defense attorneys are not entirely at the mercy of others, because they can invoke the adversary model and prepare a formal battle with the prosecutor -- although that is expensive and time-consuming.  However, the tactic of asking for a trial may give them a means of pressuring a prosecutor to gain a favorable plea bargain.
   4.   Clients may expect to see that they are getting their money's worth, so lawyer will put on a verbal show in the courtroom even though the lawyer knows that the outcome has already been determined through plea negotiations.  Sometimes described as "slow plea of guilty."
   5.   Some scholars have labeled defense attorneys as "agent-mediators" who serve the system by facilitating and preparing the client for the eventual guilty plea.  Others call defense attorneys "beleaguered dealers" who cut deals for defendants within a pressurized environment.

B.   Close-Up:  The Public Defender:  Lawyer, Social Worker, Parent

C.   Attorney Competence

1. Right to counsel is of little value if attorneys are not competent and effective.
2. It is difficult to define inadequate representation, especially when many defense attorneys struggle with high caseloads or make tactical decisions which turn out to be unsuccessful.
3. *United States v. Cronic* (1984): inexperienced attorney had 25 days to prepare case in which prosecution had spent 4 1/2 years preparing. Conviction upheld by Supreme Court: although the lawyer made errors, there was no showing that the trial had not been a "meaningful" test of the prosecution's case or that the conviction had not been reliable.
4. *Strickland v. Washington* (1984): Against his attorney's advice, murder defendant confessed, pleaded guilty, and waived right to be sentenced by an advisory jury. Feeling that the situation was hopeless, the defense attorney did not prepare for sentencing hearing (i.e., no psychiatric evidence, no witnesses, no cross-examination of medical experts, etc). Client then alleged ineffective assistance of counsel. Supreme Court rejected the claim.
5. *Cronic* and *Strickland* create a standard of "reasonable competence" when issue of inadequate representation arise. Performance legally defective only if a reasonably competent attorney would not have acted as the trial counsel did and specific errors resulted in an unfair proceeding and an unreliable result.


**REVIEW OF KEY TERMS**

Fill in the appropriate term for each statement

prosecuting attorney
attorney general
United States Attorney
necessarily included offenses
count
discovery
*nolle prosequi*
Legal Sufficiency Model
System Efficiency Model
Trial Sufficiency Model
accusatory process
large caseload
diversion
discretionary power
prosecutor's dilemma
trial counsel for police
house counsel for police
representative of the court
elected official
prosecution complex
evaluating guilt
client control
exchange relations
investigative resources
police-prosecutor teams
community values
evidential considerations
pragmatic considerations
organizational considerations

*United States v. Cronic*
defense attorney
assigned counsel
public defender
contract counsel
exchange relations
"double agent"
private defense attorney
low pay
adversary system
charging agency
indigents
*Gideon v. Wainwright*
*Strickland v. Washington*
Denver, Colorado criminal defense
Detroit, Michigan criminal defense
Oxford, Maine criminal defense
Gila County, Arizona criminal defense

1. _____ is the factor which hinders even dedicated public defenders in some cities from effectively and zealously representing their clients in every case.

2. _____ is a salaried government employee who represents indigent criminal defendants in most large cities.

3. _____ is the idealized version of the criminal defense system that is often absent in the actual practice of representing defendants.

4. _____ set the standard for attorney competence in capital cases.

5. _____ relies on a system that combines public defenders from non-profit agencies and assigned counsel approved by a panel of judges.

6. _____ are the defendants eligible for free representation provided by the state.

7. _____ is the role played by defense attorneys in "cooling out" defendants, educating them about the justice process, and preparing them to plead guilty.

8. _____ is a problem that challenges private defense attorneys, assigned counsel, and public defenders in attempting to proceed on cases according to their own preferred strategies.

9. _____ is the lawyer who represents the accused in the criminal justice process.

10. The prosecutor's office in Germany is called the _____ .

11. _____ relies on assigned counsel.

12. _____ relies on a state-wide public defender system.

13. _____ established that the Sixth Amendment right to counsel entitled all defendants to representation when they faced the possibility of incarceration for felony charges.

14. _____ is a factor which encourages high personnel turnover in some public defender offices and discourages assigned counsel from spending much time on each case.

15. _____ relies on contract counsel.

16. _____ set the standard for reasonable attorney competence by effectively discouraging courts from second-guessing attorneys.

17. _____ is a private attorney among a list of attorneys appointed to represent an indigent defendant for a relatively small fee.

18. _____ is a private attorney who successfully submits a bid to represent all indigent defendants in a county for one year.

19. _____ may be among the relatively small number of attorneys who make comfortable profits representing white-collar defendants.

20. _____ is an essential element of the success of defense attorneys in gaining favorable plea bargains for clients.

21. _____ is the prosecutor responsible for federal crimes in each federal district court.

22. _____ is the series of activities from arrest through the filing formal charges.

23. _____ is a prosecutor's role that involves providing advice for law enforcement personnel.

24. _____ is an individual charge filed against a defendant.

25. _____ is the assessment by German prosecutors under the supervision of other prosecutors in the system's hierarchy.

26. _____ involves the pursuit of charges in any cases for which there is the minimum legal evidence against a defendant.

27. _____ is the removal of a defendant from the criminal justice process and into some alternative treatment or public service program.

28. _____ provide a basis for complex criminal investigations and the use of informants.

29. _____ is a prosecutor's role that involves taking a crime-fighter stance and supporting policies of the police department.

30. _____ involves considerations of whether the prosecutor can win the case in front of a judge and jury.

31. _____ make the prosecutor dependent on the police in order to successfully pursue cases.

32. _____ may change and lead a prosecutor to alter decisions about which crimes to pursue.

33. _____ is the discretionary decision to decline to initiate a prosecution.

34. _____ include the assessment of the defendant's characteristics in order to consider whether someone should be diverted from the criminal justice system.

35. _____ is an elected official who is responsible for the legal duties of a state.

36. _____ is the process that permits defense attorneys to gain access to information possessed by the prosecutor.

37. _____ is the factor that makes prosecutors exceptionally influential in the criminal justice system.

38. _____ serve as a useful tool for prosecutors who wish to add additional charges against a defendant.

39. _____ involves the tension between serving as an advocate for the government and bearing responsibility for seeing that justice is done.

40. _____ is the prosecutor's role in which he or she emphasizes concerns for appropriate procedures and defendants' rights.

41. _____ is a biased orientation that may detract from a prosecutor's responsibilities as an officer of the court.

42. _____ is regarded as the most powerful figure in the criminal justice system.

43. _____ shape decisions about filing charges against defendants based on assessments of interests and resources within the criminal justice system.

44. _____ involve an assessment of the strength of testimony and other elements of proof that may be presented in court.

45. _____ serve as a primary influence over a prosecutor's decisions, including organizational considerations in determining charges.

46. _____ is a prosecutor's role that involves responsiveness to community opinion.

47. _____ involves case screening and other decision making that emphasizes the limited resources possessed by the prosecutor and the criminal justice system generally.


**REVIEW OF KEY PEOPLE**

Rebecca Gayheart
Winona Ryder
F. Lee Bailey
Wilton Davis

1. _____, an experienced criminal defense lawyer, stated that the best way to attract clients is to start seeking assignments to represent indigent defendants.

2. _____ was arrested for stealing items from a Saks Fifth Avenue in Los Angeles.

3. _____, an actress and model from the television show "Beverly Hills 90210," was charged with vehicular manslaughter in the death of a 9-year old boy.

4. _____ reinforces the image of the defense attorney that is portrayed in the news media because he takes high profile, sensational cases that result in jury trials.

## GENERAL PRACTICE QUESTIONS

In many counties and cities that use the ____1____ system for representing ____2____ defendants, virtually any attorney can have the opportunity to participate. By contrast, in some other countries, attorneys are carefully selected because of the emphasis on quality. Within the United States, there is quality control in some locations such as in ____3____, where a panel of judges approves only a select list of applicants to participate in the 75 percent of cases handled in this manner.

Larger cities tend to use the ____4____ system, and some places, such as ___5___, even have a state-wide system in place to use this mechanism. Although many observers believe this approach provides the highest quality representation because of the attorneys' interest and expertise, ____6____ can lead to personnel turnover and ____7____ can prevent careful attention to individual cases.

When defense attorneys' self-interest encourages them to facilitate a speedy plea bargain, they can best serve in the role as ____8____ when they have conquered the problem of ____9____ by gaining their clients' trust and even obedience.

Because prosecutors depend on the police for ____10____, prosecutors must maintain positive relationships with the police and therefore use ____11____ considerations when making decisions about charging defendants.

Prosecutors who are sensitive to ____12____ may decide not to pursue some kinds of crimes because their role as ____13____ leads them to seek to please the voters.

Prosecutors who adopt the role of ____14____ run the greatest risk of having a ____15____ or a prosecutor's bias that leads them to ignore their obligation to see that justice is done in each case.

Prosecutors who apply ____16____ considerations can use their ____17____ in order to move defendants out of the criminal justice system through ____18____.

Because ____19____ influence a prosecutor's decisions about charging and plea bargaining, victims who refuse to cooperate in providing testimony against defendants can lead prosecutors to end the case by entering a notation of ____20____.

Prosecutors have adopted the ____21____ when their decisions are based on whether or not they can win the case in front of a judge or jury. They are unlikely to use this decision-making model if they view their role as ____22____ by primarily reflecting law enforcement views in the courtroom and therefore being less discriminating about which cases to push forward.

# SELF-TEST SECTION

## MULTIPLE CHOICE QUESTIONS

10.1. Which actress was arrested for stealing $5,000 worth of items from a Saks Fifth Avenue store?
a) Rebecca Gayheart
b) Winona Ryder
c) Courtney Love
d) Neve Campbell
e) Halle Berry

10.2. Which actress entered a guilty plea to the charge of misdemeanor vehicular manslaughter?
a) Rebecca Gayheart
b) Winona Ryder
c) Courtney Love
d) Neve Campbell
e) Halle Berry

10.3. The vast majority of criminal cases are handled in...
a) city level offices of the prosecuting attorney
b) state level offices of the prosecuting attorney
c) township level offices of the prosecuting attorney
d) county level offices of the prosecuting attorney
e) federal offices of the prosecuting attorney

10.4. How does each state obtain an attorney general?
a) gubernatorial appointment
b) state legislative appointment
c) state bar appointment
d) state supreme court appointment
e) election by the voters

10.5. Which of the following best describes the role of prosecutors within the criminal justice system?
a) prosecutors are involved in every aspect of the criminal justice system
b) prosecutors are only involved with adjudication
c) prosecutors are concerned with pre-trial processes and adjudication
d) prosecutors define their own roles for themselves
e) state law defines the role of a prosecutor

10.6. Which of the following is TRUE concerning prosecutors in Germany?
a) they always act against a criminal suspect
b) they are immune from public opinion
c) they are elected
d) all of the above are TRUE
e) all of the above are FALSE

10.7. When are prosecutors less inclined to drop charges?
a) if the damage (monetary value or physical injuries) was considerable
b) if the suspect had previously been convicted
c) if the evidence is strong
d) all of the above
e) none of the above

10.8. What type of relationship exists between the prosecutor and police?
a) conflictual relationship
b) informal relationship
c) exchange relationship
d) no relationship at all
e) unethical relationship

10.9. Which of the following traits of a victim will affect whether a prosecutor pursues charges?
a) criminal record of the victim
b) victim's role in his or her own victimization
c) credibility of the victim
d) all of the above
e) none of the above

10.10. What percent of arrests for robberies by strangers led to conviction?
a) 15 percent
b) 24 percent
c) 37 percent
d) 58 percent
e) 88 percent

10.11. What percent of arrests for robberies by acquaintances led to conviction?
a) 15 percent
b) 24 percent
c) 37 percent
d) 58 percent
e) 88 percent

10.12. What is the name given to the proposed constitutional amendment that would require prosecutors to keep victims informed on the progress of criminal cases?
a) Informed Progress Amendment
b) Victims' Rights Amendment
c) Victims' Due Process Amendment
d) Anti-Defendants' Rights Amendment
e) Criminal Rights for Victims Amendment

10.13. In most jurisdictions, a person arrested on felony charges must be given a preliminary hearing within...
a) 24 hours
b) 48 hours
c) five days
d) ten days
e) one month

10.14. According to studies, what is the public's level of attention on the criminal justice system?
a) extremely high
b) high
c) moderate
d) low
e) the public does not pay attention at all

10.15. Which of the following is TRUE about most defense attorneys?
a) defense attorneys usually earn high fees from wealthy clients
b) defense attorneys work in a pleasant environment
c) defense attorneys work very hard
d) all of the above are TRUE
e) all of the above are FALSE

10.16. What model involves prosecutors aiming at speedy and early disposition of a case?
a) legal sufficiency model
b) system efficiency
c) trial sufficiency
d) due control model
e) crime process model

10.17. How many assistant prosecutors serve in a prosecutor's office?
a) two
b) five
c) ten
d) twenty
e) it varies based upon the size of the office

10.18. At what stage is evidence presented to a grand jury made up of citizens who determine whether to issue a formal charge?
a) arrest
b) booking
c)sentencing
d) appeal
e) indictment

10.19. What is the main reason for declining to prosecute a case?
a) lack of resources
b) insufficient evidence
c) politics
d) lack of prison space
e) defendant's lack of a criminal record

10.20. Based upon a study in Los Angeles County, which of the following is most likely to be prosecuted?
a) white female
b) African American female
c) Hispanic male
d) white male
e) Hispanic female

10.21.Which of the followings is NOT a basic duty of the defense attorney?
a) to save criminals from punishment
b) to protect constitutional rights
c) keep the prosecution honest in preparing and presenting cases
d) prevent innocent people from being convicted
e) all of the above are basic duties

10.22. Most criminal defense attorneys interact with...
a) upper class clients
b) middle class clients
c) lower class clients
d) upper and middle class clients
e) upper and lower class clients

10.23. The right to an attorney is found in the _____ Amendment.
a) First
b) Second
c) Fourth
d) Fifth
e) Sixth

10.24. When does the U. S. Supreme Court require that attorneys be appointed to defend suspects?
a) early in the criminal justice process
b) immediately prior to jury selection
c) immediately prior to a trial
d) immediately prior to sentencing
e) the Court has no such requirement

10.25. In the past three decades, the portion of defendants who are provided with counsel because they are indigent has...
a) remained constant
b) increased greatly
c) increased slightly
d) decreased slightly
e) decreased greatly

## TRUE/FALSE QUESTIONS

10.1. Prosecutors in America have very little discretion.

10.2. Prosecutors in America are active only at the adjudication stage of the criminal justice process.

10.3. Most prosecutors in America are elected officials.

10.4. Prosecutors might not file charges if a victim is dressed shabbily.

10.5. German prosecutors are civil servants who do not face the same public pressures as Americans.

10.6. Most charges are filed by county prosecutors in the United States.

10.7. The Fifth Amendment contains the right to counsel.

10.8. Most criminal defense attorneys have wealthy clients.

10.9. The public defender system started in Los Angeles in 1914.

10.10. Studies show significantly higher conviction rates in stranger crimes than in non-stranger crimes.

10.11. The main reason that charges are dropped by prosecutors is insufficient evidence.

10.12. It is easy for convicted offenders to prove that their attorneys did not provide a competent defense.

10.13. The system efficiency model emphasizes the speedy and early disposition of cases.

10.14. Defense attorneys rarely have to visit jails.

10.15. The sentencing history of a judge may influence prosecutors' decisions about which charges to file.

10.16. Prosecutors are immune from lawsuits if they prosecute innocent people.

10.17. The service provided by defense counsel usually involves preparing clients for positive outcomes of cases.

10.18. Federal law enforcement maintains priority in prosecuting cases.

10.19. Prosecutors may reduce charges in exchange for a plea bargain.

10.20. If a person is too poor to pay for legal counsel, the state will not provide an attorney.

Key Terms
1. large caseload
2. public defender
3. adversary system
4. *Strickland v. Washington*
5. Detroit, Michigan criminal defense
6. indigents
7. "double agent"
8. client control
9. defense attorney
10. charging agency
11. Oxford, Maine
12. Denver, Colorado criminal defense
13. *Gideon v. Wainwright*
14. low pay
15. Gila County, Arizona
16. *United States v. Cronic*
17. assigned counsel
18. contract counsel
19. private defense attorney
20. exchange relations
21. United States Attorney
22. accusatory process
23. house counsel for police
24. count
25. evaluating guilt
26. Legal Sufficiency Model
27. diversion
28. police-prosecutor teams
29. trial counsel for police
30. Trial Sufficiency Model
31. investigative resources
32. community values
33. *nolle prosequi*
34. pragmatic considerations
35. attorney general
36. discovery
37. discretionary power
38. necessarily included offenses
39. prosecutor's dilemma
40. representative of the court
41. prosecution complex
42. prosecuting attorney
43. organizational considerations
44. evidential considerations
45. exchange relations
46. elected official
47. System Efficiency Model

Key People
1. Wilton Davis
2. Winona Ryder

3.      Rebecca Gayheart
4.      F. Lee Bailey

General Practice Questions
1.      assigned counsel
2.      indigent
3.      Detroit, Michigan criminal defense
4.      public defender
5.      Denver, Colorado
6.      low pay
7.      large caseloads
8.      "double agent"
9.      client control
10.     investigative resources
11.     organizational
12.     community values
13.     elected officials
14.     trial counsel for police
15.     prosecution complex
16.     pragmatic
17.     discretionary power
18.     diversion
19.     exchange relations
20.     *nolle prosequi*
21.     Trial Sufficiency Model
22.     trial counsel for police

Multiple Choice
10.1.    b
10.2.    a
10.3.    d
10.4.    e
10.5.    a
10.6.    c
10.7.    d
10.8.    c
10.9.    d
10.10.  e
10.11.  c
10.12.  b
10.13.  d
10.14.  d
10.15.  c
10.16.  b
10.17.  e
10.18.  e
10.19.  b
10.20.  c
10.21.  a
10.22.  c
10.23.  e
10.24.  a
10.25.  b

True/False

| | |
|---|---|
| 10.1. | F |
| 10.2. | F |
| 10.3. | T |
| 10.4. | T |
| 10.5. | T |
| 10.6. | T |
| 10.7. | F |
| 10.8. | F |
| 10.9. | T |
| 10.10. | T |
| 10.11. | T |
| 10.12. | F |
| 10.13. | T |
| 10.14. | F |
| 10.15. | T |
| 10.16. | T |
| 10.17. | F |
| 10.18. | T |
| 10.19. | T |
| 10.20. | F |

WORKSHEET 10.1: PROSECUTION POLICIES

A man and a woman were brutally murdered with a knife. A bloody glove was found near the bodies. A second bloody glove with blood samples matching those of the victims was found two miles away outside the home of the woman's ex-husband. The ex-husband claims that he was at home preparing to leave for the airport at the time of the killings, but testimony from his driver indicates that he may not have been at his house until after the time that the killings occurred. The husband behaved erratically when he came under suspicion for the killing by disappearing for a day and then threatening to kill himself before surrendering to the police. He claims that he is innocent. The trial court in Los Angeles is backlogged with thousands of cases awaiting disposition.

Imagine that you are the prosecutor. Tell whether or not (and why) you would decide to prosecute based on the following prosecution policies. How would the facts of the case fit with each model?

LEGAL SUFFICIENCY

_____

_____

_____

_____

_____

_____

SYSTEM EFFICIENCY

_____

_____

_____

_____

_____

_____

TRIAL SUFFICIENCY_____

_____

_____

_____

_____

_____

WORKSHEET 10.2:  COUNSEL FOR INDIGENTS

If you were given the responsibility for selecting the method of providing counsel for indigent defendants within your local courthouse, which method would you choose?  For each method listed below, state whether you would select that method and explain why or why not?

ASSIGNED COUNSEL _____

_____

_____

_____

_____

_____

CONTRACT COUNSEL _____

_____

_____

_____

_____

_____

PUBLIC DEFENDER _____

_____

_____

_____

_____

_____

Is there some other feasible alternative? _____

_____

_____

_____

_____

_____

# CHAPTER 11

## DETERMINATION OF GUILT: PLEA BARGAINING AND TRIALS

### LEARNING OBJECTIVES

After covering the material in this chapter, students should understand:

1.  the impact of local legal culture on the courts;

2.  the development and impact of courtroom workgroups.

3.  the central role of plea bargaining and prosecutor' discretion in determining the outcomes of 90 percent of criminal cases;

4.  the difference between implicit and explicit plea bargaining;

5.  the role of exchange relationships in plea bargaining, the actors who influence plea negotiations, and the tactics used by those actors;

6.  the justifications for and criticisms of plea bargaining.

7.  the stages of the trial process;

8.  the nature and prevalence of jury trials;

9.  the functions of the jury;

10. the selection of juries and the experience of being a juror.

### CHAPTER SUMMARY

The outcomes in criminal cases are largely influenced by a court's local legal culture, which defines the "going rates" of punishment for various offenses. Courtroom workgroups composed of judges, prosecutors, and defense attorneys who work together to handle cases through cooperative plea bargaining processes. Most convictions are obtained through plea bargains, a process that exists because it fulfills the self-interest of prosecutors, judges, defense attorneys, and defendants. Plea bargaining is facilitated by exchange relations between prosecutors and defense attorneys. In many courthouses, there is little actual bargaining, as outcomes are determined through the implicit bargaining process of settling the facts and assessing the "going rate" of punishment according to the standards of the local legal culture.

The U.S. Supreme Court has endorsed plea bargaining and addressed legal issues concerning the voluntariness of pleas and the obligation of prosecutors and defendants to uphold agreements. Plea bargaining has been criticized for pressuring defendants to surrender their rights and reducing the sentences imposed on offenders. Through the dramatic courtroom battle of prosecutors and defense attorneys, trials are presumed to provide the best way to discover the truth about a criminal case. Less than 10 percent of cases go to trial, and half of those are typically bench trials in front of a judge, not jury trials. Cases typically go to trial because they involve defendants who are wealthy enough to pay attorneys to fight to the very end, they involve charges that are too serious to create incentives for plea bargaining. The U.S. Supreme Court has ruled that juries need not be made up of twelve members, and twelve-member juries can, if permitted by state law, convict defendants by a majority vote instead of a unanimous vote. Juries serve vital functions for society by preventing arbitrary action by prosecutors and judges, educating citizens about the justice system, symbolizing the rule of law, and involving citizens from diverse segments of the community in judicial decision making.

The jury selection process, especially in the formation of the jury pool and the exercise of peremptory challenges, often creates juries that do not fully represent all segments of a community. The trial process consists of a series of steps: jury selection, opening statements, presentation of prosecution's evidence, presentation of defense evidence, presentation of rebuttal witnesses, closing arguments, judge's jury instructions, and the jury's decision. Rules of evidence dictate what kinds of information may be presented in court for consideration by the jury. Types of evidence include are real evidence, demonstrative evidence, testimony, direct evidence, and circumstantial evidence.

Convicted offenders have the opportunity to appeal, although defendants who plead guilty--unlike those convicted through a trial--often have few grounds for an appeal.

Appeals focus on claimed errors of law or procedure in the investigation by police and prosecutors or the decisions by trial judges. Relatively few offenders win their appeals, and most of those simply gain an opportunity for a new trial, not release from jail or prison. After convicted offenders have used all of their appeals, they may file a habeas corpus petition to seek federal judicial review of claimed constitutional rights violations in their cases. Very few petitions are successful.


**CHAPTER OUTLINE**

I.  INTRODUCTION:
    Example: New York Subway Attacker
    Issues involved with mentally ill man pushing a woman into the path of a subway train.

II. THE COURTROOM: HOW IT FUNCTIONS
    Guilt or innocence determined in pretty much the same fashion in every state although the definitions of crimes and practices in setting punishments may vary significantly. Differences are most pronounced in results of the judicial process rather than in the formal processes themselves.

A.  Local Legal Culture
    The shared beliefs, attitudes, and norms of a court community – great influence over what happens. Can be used to explain why courts operate differently even though they have the same formal rules and procedures. Shared norms serve to:
    1.  Help participants distinguish between "our" court and other jurisdictions (e.g., judges and prosecutors talk about how "we" do a better job than neighboring courts).
    2.  Stipulate how members should treat one another. For example, strongly adversarial defense actions may not be in keeping with expected local behavior -- attorneys expected to not "rock the boat" by challenging local customary practices.
    3.  Describe how cases *should* be processed. Most importantly, affect the "going rate" -- the local view of the appropriate sentence given the offense and defendant's prior record and other characteristics. Also affects attitudes about proper plea negotiations, motions, continuances, and eligibility for appointed counsel or public defender.

B.  The Courtroom Workgroup
    Cases processed and decisions made through interactions and reciprocal relationships of prosecutor, defense attorney, judge, and perhaps others (bailiff, court clerk, etc.). Workgroup concept seems especially important in urban courts.
    1.  There must be interaction of the members of the group.
    2.  The members have the same attitudes about one or more motives or goals that determine the direction in which the group will move.
    3.  The members develop a set of norms that determine the boundaries within which interpersonal relations may be established and activity carried out.
    4.  If interaction continues, a set of roles becomes stabilized and the group differentiates itself from other groups.
    5.  A network of interpersonal relationships develops on the basis of the members' likes and dislikes for one another.
    6.  The degree to which the foregoing conditions (1-5) are met distinguishes a workgroup from a grouping.

a.  A rotation of judges among courtrooms may limit the opportunity to develop workgroup norms and roles -- even though same prosecutor and public defender may work together on cases everyday. Without workgroup development, cases proceed more formally and with less reliance on agreed-upon routines.

b.  When a workgroup develops, the defendant -- an outsider to the group -- will confront an organized network of relationships among actors making decisions by interacting with and anticipating the reactions of other actors with whom they are very well-acquainted.

c.  Each member of the workgroup has a set role and therefore can develop stable expectations among the other group members.

d.  Each actor from a different sponsoring organization: judge (court), prosecutor (prosecutor's office), public defender (public defender's office). Policies of these sponsoring organizations may stipulate conditions for plea bargaining and thereby inhibit or encourage development of the workgroup.

e.  Courthouse staff has access to vast amounts of confidential information. They may use this and their access to the judge to enhance their power within the group. Probation officers, for example, may be influential by regularly supplying pre-sentence reports for use by judge and other members of workgroup.

f.  Workgroup members have other relationships and external constituencies (media, sponsoring organizations, etc.). There may be cooperation within the group for providing a public "show" of their processing of cases although the workgroup already has actually worked out a disposition for each case.

g.  The workgroup operates in an environment in which the local legal culture, recruitment and selection processes, cases, and the socioeconomic, political, and legal structures of the broader community are conceived as having an impact on decision making.

7.  Physical Setting: The work site of the courtroom workgroup strengthens the interaction patterns of the members and separates them from clientele groups.

a.  Low visibility of courtroom interactions to outside world. Elevated judge's bench facing the attorneys' tables frequently permits discussion among workgroup members that others in the courtroom, including the defendant, cannot hear.

b.  Although privately-retained counsel sit in defense chair for some cases, the high percentage of indigent cases, especially in urban areas, can lead public defender to consider a particular courtroom as his or her workplace.

8.  The Role of the Judge: Judges, especially those who are aggressive, can be leaders of courtroom workgroup although it may appear to defendants that judges are not involved. Judges can provide cues to other actors, threaten, persuade, and other actions in an effort to get the workgroup's goals accomplished.

a.  Close-Up: Miami's Drug Court

9.  Roles in the Workgroup: in part, actors teach defendants how to help the proceedings move smoothly.

a.  Outcomes based on role performance may be affected by the agent-mediator (or double agent) actions of defense attorney; the dress of the defendant and the other actors in the courtroom. Defendants may learn from agent-mediators (esp. defense lawyers) how to act out their role in the processing experience (i.e., contrite demeanor). Defendants who do not plead guilty or who otherwise give inappropriate performances may incur significant sanctions. In most cases, defendants' courtroom behavior conforms to norms and expectations.

b.  Harsh reactions by judges may not be linked to seriousness of offense charged, but instead to the defendant's actions and attitudes in conforming to norms and expectations of the guilty plea "ceremony."

C.   The Impact of Courtroom Workgroups
    1.   Eisenstein and Jacob studied felony disposition processes in courtrooms in Baltimore, Chicago, and Detroit and provided insights on the courtroom workgroup. Same type of felony case handled differently in each court, but dispositions remarkably similar for defendants who reached the trial court.
        a.   Outcomes were determined by structure of courtroom workgroups, influence of sponsoring organizations, and sociopolitical environment of each city rather than by law, rules of procedure, and crime rates.
        b.   Fewer than half of felony arrestees convicted because many were filtered out through dismissals, reduced charges, or diversion.
        c.   Baltimore: three-fifths of cases at preliminary hearing moved ahead to trial courtroom; half of defendants remained in jail without making bail; 21 percent released on ROR but the remainder had high money bail. Unstable courtroom workgroups because members frequently rotated and sponsoring organizations exercised little supervisory control: produced fewer guilty pleas and more cases going to trial.
        d.   Chicago: two-thirds of cases dismissed at preliminary hearing; 40 percent of defendants do not make bail; almost no defendants let out ROR but money bail kept low. Stable courtroom workgroups developed informal procedures for screening out cases.
        e.   Detroit: four-fifths of cases moved to trial court because preliminary hearings usually found probable cause; 40 percent did not make bail; almost half released ROR and money bail kept low. Prosecutors had already screened cases before they reached the courtroom; also had stable workgroups. Operated at pace three times faster than the other cities.
    2.   Stability of courtroom workgroups can be upset by variety of factors: new docket system; shift by public defender's office from a zone to a person-to-person strategy; or a decision by a prosecutor to institute new policies about which cases to move forward.

III.   PLEA BARGAINING
A.   Dominant Means of Case Disposition
    1.   The most crucial stage in the criminal justice process: generally 90 percent of felony defendants plead guilty.
    2.   Supreme Court has ruled that plea bargaining is legal; prosecutors and judges call it necessary; defense attorneys call it advantageous to their clients.
    3.   Supreme Court in *Blackledge v. Allison* (1976) acknowledged the mutuality of advantage to defendants and prosecutors from the process.
    4.   Plea bargaining defined: defendant's agreement to plead guilty to a criminal charge with the reasonable expectation of receiving some consideration from the state for doing so.
        a.   Implicit plea bargaining: defendants plead guilty without entering into negotiations, but expect to receive some benefit nonetheless.
        b.   Explicit plea bargaining: arrangement made between prosecutor and defense attorney, sometimes with the participation of the judge, whereby a plea of guilty is made in exchange for pressing less serious charge and perhaps recommendation to judge of more lenient sentence.
    5.   Defendant seeks to avoid maximum sentence or charges with legislatively mandated sentence, or to avoid label as "rapist" or "child molester."
    6.   Prosecutor seeks to avoid courtroom combat and gains certainty of conviction; prosecutor still determines the charges and influences the sentence.
    7.   When plea bargaining was barred in one state's felony court, it did not disappear. It simply moved to the arraignment stage in the lower court.

8. Close-Up: Banning Plea Bargaining in Tennessee. Effort by Memphis District Attorney to ban plea bargaining for specific serious murder, rape, and robbery charges.

B. Exchange Relationships in Plea Bargaining
    1. Defense attorney, prosecutor, defendant, and sometimes judge participate. All have particular objectives and all can gain from the process (defense attorney gets fee quicker for less work; prosecutor gets sure conviction; defendant gets less than maximum possible sentence; judge gets quick disposition of case without time-consuming trial)
    2. Tactics: ritual in which friendliness and joking may mask antagonistic views. Each side tries to impress the other with confidence in the strength of its case; little effort to conceal information because standard practice seems to be that confidences shared in negotiations will not be used in court -- defense attorneys who violate this norm may not receive favorable bargains in future cases; defense attorneys seek to "humanize" the defendant so prosecutor will not treat as just another case.
        a. Prosecutors' tactic is the multi-count indictment -- even when cannot prove all charges; puts greater pressure on defendant to plead guilty; gives prosecutor more items to negotiate away.
        b. Defense attorneys may threaten to move ahead with jury trial; defense attorneys may threaten delays, during which witnesses' memories may fade -- but other defense attorneys feel more effective bargaining on friendly basis rather than trying to pin down or threaten the prosecutor.
        c. Negotiations may run by unwritten code words ("I think I can sell this deal to the boss") rather than explicit promises.
        d. Both prosecutor and defense attorney dependent on cooperation from defendant and judge.
        e. Judges may be reluctant to interfere with plea agreements to avoid jeopardizing future exchange relationships; prosecutors and defense attorneys often consult with judge to be sure about what sentence will result from guilty plea; judge possesses power to go against recommended sentence.
    3. Pleas Without Bargaining
        a. Guilty pleas may not result from formal negotiations. In some courthouses, prosecutor, defense attorney, and sometimes judge talk simply to settle the facts in the case. (i.e., was it really an assault or just a pushing and shoving match?); when they agree on what kind of crime it was, then the local "going rate" punishment for such crimes is clear to all actors and the defense attorney can know what the punishment will be upon entering a guilty plea.
        b. Both prosecutor and defense attorney may be members of the same local legal culture with shared values and under-
standings about the punishments for particular offenses.
        c. Implicit plea bargaining may be less likely to occur when there is personnel turnover in a court community that inhibits recognition of shared values.
        d. Process may differ from courthouse to courthouse; some courts may use "slow plea of guilty" as defendant pleads to lesser charge as case progresses through trial; prosecutors may use diversion or dropping cases to reduce caseload in other courts.

C. Legal Issues in Plea Bargaining
    1. Questions exist concerning the voluntariness and sanctity of plea bargains. Many judges now more open about admitting in court that they are aware of plea bargains struck in particular cases.
    2. *Boykin v. Alabama* (1969): defendant must make affirmative statement that plea was voluntary before judge accepts the plea. Thus courts have created standardized list of questions for judges to read to defendants when entering guilty pleas to ensure no coercion was used against defendant.

3.     *Alford v. North Carolina* (1970): court can accept guilty plea entered by a defendant who still maintains he was innocent but is willing to accept punishment for lesser charge to avoid risk of maximum penalty.

4.     *Santobello v. New York* (1971): prosecutor's promises of leniency must be kept.

5.     *Ricketts v. Adamson* (1987): defendants must keep their part of the bargain if they agree to testify against others as part of the plea bargain.

6.     *Bordenkircher v. Hayes* (1978): prosecutors can threaten defendants with additional charges if they do not agree to plead guilty. Supreme Court regards this as part of the "give and take" of plea bargaining but critics regard it as coercion.

7.     A QUESTION OF ETHICS: Guilty plea ceremony reveals that defendant believes that promises have been made.

D.     Criticisms of Plea Bargaining

Practice has been deplored by a number of scholars as well as by the American Bar Association

1.     Due process considerations: plea bargaining does not provide procedural fairness because defendants forfeit the constitutional rights designed to protect them -- argument by civil libertarians

2.     Sentencing policy: society's interest in applying appropriate punishments for crimes is diminished by plea bargaining; in overcrowded urban courts, harried prosecutors and judges make concessions for the sake of administrative expediency -- argument by law and order advocates.

3.     Low Visibility: plea bargaining hidden from judicial scrutiny; judge has little information about the crime or defendant when decisions primarily made by prosecutor and defense attorney; judge cannot check on how much pressure applied to the defendant; result is "bargain justice" in which the judge, public, and even defendant cannot know for sure who got what from whom in exchange for what -- because prosecutor and defense attorney's self-interest and exchange relationship is not visible to others in the process.

4.     Inconsistent with the espoused values of the adversarial system; makes the criminal justice process look like a "game" in the eyes of the criminal offenders and therefore no different than the other forms of unprincipled deal making occurring elsewhere in society, including deals among criminals.

5.     Unjust to penalize people for asserting their right to have a trial; based on findings that more people go to prison when they demand a trial than when they plea bargain.

6.     Concern that innocent people will be pressured to plead guilty out of fear of what might happen to them if they happened to be convicted at trial. Innocent people who lack faith in the justice system may plead guilty because they do not want to take the chance of being convicted of something more serious.

IV.     TRIAL: THE EXCEPTIONAL CASE

A.     Symbolic Combat Between Prosecution and Defense

Because trials are public, they are a kind of stylized drama -- with news media, publicity, and political careers at stake.

1.     Trial by jury composed of members of the community is one of the greatest safeguards against arbitrary and unlawful actions by criminal justice officials.

2.     The rules of evidence, the quality of the attorneys' performances, unequal resources, jurors' biases and other factors may prevent trials from revealing the truth.

3.     Only four percent of criminal cases have jury trials and only five percent have bench trials (presided over by a judge alone).

4.     Despite their relatively infrequent usage, jury trials are important because anticipated jury verdicts serve to guide plea bargaining and other decisions (e.g., police may ask themselves before making an arrest, "Would a jury convict on the evidence available?"). The decision to prosecute, plea bargain, and sentence are also affected.

5.   Trials are very costly in terms of time and resources. Wealthy defendants are better able to afford the costs necessary to prepare a strong, vigorous trial defense.

B. Deciding to Go to Trial
    1.    Why do cases go to trial?
        a.    The fact-finding function of the jury serves to resolve cases when prosecutor and defense cannot agree on the facts in order to form the basis for a plea bargain.
        b.    If the evidence against a repeat offender is weak, the prosecutor may prefer to have a jury find the accused innocent rather than strike a bargain that would produce only a minimal sanction -- sends message to the defendant that "we are after you."
        c.    The seriousness of the charge is probably the most important factor influencing the decision to go to trial. When the potential penalty is harsh, defendants are more willing to take the risk of going to trial.
    2.    Trials are based on the idea that the adversarial process and laws of criminal procedure and evidence will produce the truth.
        a.    The judge must make sure that rules are followed, and the jury must impartially evaluate the evidence and reflect the community's interests. The jury is the sole evaluator of the facts in the case.
    3.    Only common law countries (e.g., U.S., Great Britain, Australia, Canada, etc.) leave it entirely to a group of lay people to decide guilt or innocence. In civil law countries, this function is usually performed by a judge or judges often assisted by lay assessors. Eighty percent of all jury trials in the world take place in the United States.
    4.    Juries perform six vital functions in the criminal justice system:
        a.    Prevent government oppression by safeguarding citizens against arbitrary law enforcement.
        a.    Determine whether the accused is guilty on the basis of the evidence present.
        b.    Represent diverse community interests so that no one set of values or biases dominates decision making.
        d.    Serves as a buffer between the accused and the accuser.
        e.    Educates citizens selected for jury duty about the criminal justice system.
        f.    Symbolizes the rule of law and the community foundation that supports the criminal justice system.
    5.    Juries provide the element of direct democracy in the judicial process through citizens' participation in decision making in a branch of government controlled by lawyers and judges.
    6.    In the United States, a jury in a criminal trial traditionally consists of twelve citizens but some states now allow as few as six persons. This reform was recommended as a way to modernize court procedures and reduce expenses.
        a.    Smaller jury size was upheld by the Supreme Court in *Williams v. Florida* (1970). For a jury of six, a unanimous vote is required (*Burch v. Louisiana*, 1979) but with larger verdicts a majority vote is enough for conviction.
        b.    Twelve-person juries are generally used for capital cases.
COMPARATIVE PERSPECTIVE: Comparing Trial Processes in France and the United States. Example of fugitive murder suspect living in France who was not returned to the United States because of American law permitting trials in the absence of a fugitive defendant.

C.    The Trial Process
    1.    After jury selection, the trial proceeds through stages of attorneys' statements, presentation of witnesses and evidence, closing arguments, and decisions.

D.    Jury Selection
    1.    Juries should be made up of a cross-section of the community, but until the mid-twentieth century many states excluded women and members of minority groups.
        a.    The jury's function is to represent diverse community interests. A cross-section is necessary to counter-balance biases and minimize the likelihood that a jury

will convict on minimal evidence. The reality of jury selection, however, is that a cross-section of the community is not likely to be represented.

b. Jury Pool: when jurors are drawn from registered voters, then nonwhites, the poor, and young people are underrepresented.

c. Underrepresentation of people from different backgrounds can affect decisions because it limits the presence of alternative experiences and values among the decision makers.

d. A Question of Ethics: Person called for jury duty decides to claim dishonestly that he is a student in order to avoid serving as a juror.

e. Jury unrepresentativeness can best be attacked by the use of comprehensive list from which citizens are randomly selected for duty. Supplementary pools: drivers' license lists, utility customers, taxpayers--would add names to the roster.

f. Depending on local rules and practices, potential jurors may be excused because of their occupation (e.g., doctor, firefighter, etc.), economic hardship, or disability. Thus only about 15 percent of the American adult population have ever served on juries.

g. As a result, retired people, housewives with grown children and the unemployed tend to be overrepresented on juries.

h. *Voir dire* is the process of examining (i.e., questioning) potential jurors to ensure a fair trial. Attorneys for both sides and the judge may question each juror about background, knowledge of the case, or acquaintance with people involved in the case.

i. If a juror says something to indicate that he or she may be unable to make a fair decision, then he or she may be *challenged for cause*. The judge must rule on the challenge and whether or not the juror will be excluded from the pool. There is usually no limit on the number of challenges for cause.

j. *Peremptory challenge* is the attorneys' power to exclude a juror without giving use hunches to exclude potential jurors whom they believe may be sympathetic to the opposing side. Some attorneys hire "jury experts" -- social scientists who can advise on how to use peremptory challenges in order to gain sympathetic demographic groups of jurors.

k. Although the Supreme Court has said that peremptory challenges cannot be based on the race or gender of potential jurors, the Court also permits trial judges to accept flimsy excuses when it appears that race or gender is being improperly applied.

l. Close-Up: The Peremptory Challenge Controversy. The U.S. Supreme Court permits lawyers to use excuses for excluding people when it appears that the exclusion may really be based on race.

2. Opening Statements: statements by attorneys are not evidence, so judges try to keep each side from making inflammatory or prejudicial remarks. Lawyers use this opportunity to establish themselves with the jurors and to emphasize points they intend to make during the trial.

3. Presentation of the Prosecution's Evidence: the prosecution bears the burden of providing proof beyond a reasonable doubt because the American system has a formal presumption of innocence that the prosecutor must overcome.

a. Real evidence: objects, weapons, records, fingerprints, or stolen property.

b. Demonstrative evidence: maps, x-rays, photographs, and diagrams. These are things that the jurors can see for themselves. Real evidence is one kind of demonstrative evidence.

c. Testimony: witnesses must be legally competent: have the intelligence and memory capacity to remember events and tell the truth; witnesses may be cross-examined by opposing counsel.

d. Direct evidence: eyewitness accounts.

        e.      Circumstantial evidence: requires that the jury infer a fact from witness observation.

        f.      Rules of evidence govern what judge will either exclude from presentation or permit the attorneys to put into evidence.

   4.    Presentation of Defense's Evidence: evidence usually presented for one or more of the following purposes:

        a.      Rebut or cast doubt on state's case.

        b.      Offer an alibi.

        c.      Affirmative defense is presented (e.g., self-defense, insanity, etc.) to claim that defendant cannot be held responsible under the law.

        d.      Defense also must consider whether or not the defendant will take the stand and thereby be subject to impeachment and cross-examination.

        e.      New Directions in Criminal Justice Policy Computer Simulations in the Courtroom-In recent years, attorneys have attempted to use computer technology to present clearer images of events. Just as computer programmers have developed realistic games for computers, similar realism has now been developed in computer-generated recreations of crime scenes.

   5.    Presentation of Rebuttal Witnesses: prosecution witnesses to rebut the defense's case.

   6.    Closing Arguments by Each Side: opportunity to tie case together and to make impassioned, persuasive presentation to the judge or jury.

   7.    Judge's Instructions to the Jury: judge determines the law and instructs jury on the manner in which the law bears on their decision.

        a.      Judge may discuss standard of proof (beyond a *reasonable doubt*), the necessity of the prosecution proving all of the elements of a crime, and the rights of the defendant (e.g., not required to testify and no inference should be drawn regarding the defendant's silence).

        b.      Judge will explain the charges and the possible verdicts. Instructions may be an ordeal for jurors and it may be difficult for them to understand and retain instructions since instructions may last more than an hour or two.

   8.    Decision by the Jury: jurors deliberate in private room; may request that judge reread to them portions of the instructions, or they may ask for additional instructions, or for portions of the trial transcript.

        a.      Verdict must be unanimous except in Louisiana, Montana, Oregon, Oklahoma, and Texas which permit majority verdicts.

        b.      If the jury becomes deadlocked and cannot reach a verdict, the trial may end with a hung jury -- and the prosecution can choose to retry the case with a different jury.

        c.      When the jury reaches a verdict, the prosecutor, defense attorney, and judge assemble in the courtroom to hear it; the prosecutor or defense lawyer can request that the jury be polled: each member of the jury must state their decision in open court. This procedure presumably ensures that there is no pressure on a juror by other members of the jury.

        d.      If it is a guilty verdict, the judge may continue bail or incarcerate the defendant while awaiting the presentence report: a report prepared by a probation officer on the defendant's background and record which will be used by the judge in determining the sentence.

E.    Evaluating the Jury System

   1.    Social scientists are hampered in studying the jury decision making process because of the secrecy of actual juries. Scholars can attempt to interview jurors after cases or make use of experimental juries in mock cases.

   2.    Studies indicate that juries' behavior is consistent with theories of group behavior; participation and influence in the process are related to social status: men were found to be more active than women; whites more than minority members; better educated more than less well educated.

3.　Much of jurors' discussion does not concern the testimony and evidence, but instead the court procedures, opinions about witnesses, and personal reminiscences.

4.　30 percent of cases, a vote taken soon after sequestration was the only one necessary to reach a verdict; in the rest of cases, the majority on the first ballot eventually won out 90 percent of the time. Because of group pressures, only rarely did a lone juror produce a hung jury; recent research has reconfirmed the importance of group pressures on decision making.

V.　APPEALS

A.　<u>Basis for Appeals</u>

Appeals are based on the contention that one or more errors were made during the criminal justice process.

1.　Unlike most other Western countries, the United States does not allow appeals concerning the terms of the sentence, unless the punishment was not within the law or in violation of due process or equal protection.

2.　A case originating in state court is usually appealed through the state appellate courts. there is a federal constitutional question, then the case may subsequently enter the federal court system and perhaps ultimately be considered by the U.S. Supreme Court.

3.　Study by Chapper and Hanson looked at appeals in five states. Found an increase in appeals, and:

a.　Majority of appeals occur after trial conviction but about a quarter result from nontrial proceedings such as guilty pleas and probation revocations.

b.　Homicides and other serious crimes against persons make up over fifty percent of appeals.

c.　Most appeals come from cases in which the sentence is five years or longer.

d.　The issues raised on appeal tend to concern the introduction of evidence, the sufficiency of evidence, and jury instructions.

4.　Study found that eighty percent of appeals unsuccessful because the appellate court affirmed the trial court decision.

5.　The right of appeal performs an important function not only of righting wrongs but its presence is a constant influence on the daily operations of the criminal justice system.

B.　<u>Habeas Corpus</u>

1.　The "great writ" is a command by a court to a person holding a prisoner in custody requiring that the prisoner be brought before the judge. This procedure permits the judge to determine whether the person is legally held. Federal courts can review whether or not there are any constitutional violations affecting the convictions of federal *and* state prisoners.

2.　There has been a tremendous increase in habeas corpus petitions although only about one percent are successful; this causes an increase in caseloads for federal judges; many federal courts cope with caseload burdens by assigning such cases to law clerks or to U.S. magistrate judges.

3.　There is no right to counsel for habeas corpus petitions, so most prisoners must attempt to present their own cases. They generally lack sufficient knowledge to identify and raise constitutional issues effectively.

4.　Since the 1980s, the Supreme Court has made decisions imposing more difficult procedural requirements on prisoners seeking to file habeas corpus petitions. In 1996, Congress created further restrictions on petitions by passing a new statute affecting habeas corpus procedures.

C.　<u>Evaluating the Appellate Process</u>

1.　Some conservatives argue that appeals should be limited; appeals are regarded as a burden on the system and an impediment to swift punishment of convicted offenders. However, since 90 percent of accused persons plead guilty and relatively few of these people have any basis for appeal, the actual number of appeals (as a percentage of total cases) seems less significant.

2. Appeals can serve the function of correcting errors. Even if a defendant wins an appeal, there is no automatic release from prison. A successful appeal may simply lead to a new trial or provide the basis for a new plea bargain.

## REVIEW OF KEY TERMS

Fill in the appropriate term for each statement

jury
bench trial
*voir dire*
real evidence
challenge for cause
testimony
peremptory challenge
direct evidence
individualized justice
administrative necessity
circumstantial evidence
*habeas corpus*
appeal
*Williams v. Florida*
continuance
unanimous verdict
jury functions
jury instructions
cross-section of the community
voter lists
reasonable doubt
courtroom workgroup
local legal culture

1. _____ are requested by attorneys and granted (or denied) by the trial judge.

2. _____ permits defense attorneys and prosecutors to exclude jurors without providing a reason.

3. _____ requires the jurors to draw inferences.

4. _____ is the most common source of the jury pool.

5. _____ stands for the requirement that the jury be representative.

6. _____ creates the opportunity for reviews to determine whether trial judges made errors or constitutional rights were violated.

7. _____ is when a judge presides over a trial without a jury.

8. _____ is not constitutionally required except for cases involving six-member juries.

9. _____ is the process of questioning and selecting jurors.

10. _____ provides the basis for incarcerated people to challenge the legal basis for their detention.

11. _____ is evidence presented by witnesses.

12. _____ permits, with the judge's approval, the exclusion of jurors who demonstrate a particular bias.

13. _____ is the representative of the community in the criminal trial that finds facts and decides whether the defendant is guilty.

14. _____ is the standard of proof in criminal cases.

15. _____ stands for the proposition that juries can have fewer than twelve members.

16. _____ is presented by the prosecutor and includes concrete objects, such as fingerprints and stolen property.

17. _____ includes the prevention of government oppression and the education of citizens about the criminal justice system.

18. _____ includes eye witness accounts of what happened.

19. _____ are the final words considered by the jury before they begin their secret deliberations.

20. _____ is the organizational entity that can process cases quickly, efficiently, and consistently in a particular courthouse if the relevant actors remain in their positions for a sufficient length of time.

21. _____ is the shared norms and values within a court community that helps to shape the speed and content of case processing.

22. _____ is a justification for plea bargaining that emphasizes the values and judgments of prosecutors and defense attorneys.

23. _____ is a justification for plea bargaining that assumes that courts will be overburdened without negotiated pleas.


## REVIEW OF KEY PEOPLE

John Walker Lindh
Kendra Webdale
Helen "Holly" Maddux
Ira Einhorn
Bill Clinton
Andrew Goldstein
Joy Chapper and Roger Hanson


1. In their study of appeals, _____ and _____ found that the decision of the trial courts was affirmed in almost 80 percent of the cases
2. In 1977, _____, a 30-year-old woman from a wealthy Texas family, disappeared. She had been living in Philadelphia with her boyfriend, _____, a former hippie leader was charged with her murder.

3. _____ was killed by a mentally ill person who pushed her in front of a subway train on January 3, 1999.

4. _____ a mental patient, who stopped taking his medication killed a person on the New York subway system.

5. President _____ signed the Antiterrorism and Effective Death Penalty Act, which placed additional restrictions on habeas corpus petitions, because prisoners' cases were a burden on the courts.

6. _____ was a twenty-one-year-old American captured while fighting with the Taliban in Afghanistan in 2002.

## GENERAL PRACTICE QUESTIONS

In order to obtain a jury containing _____1_____, many reformers have advocated the use of drivers' license lists and other lists in addition to the usual _____2_____ that have traditionally been used to create the jury pool.

During the process of _____3_____, attorneys can use _____4_____ to seek exclusion of potential jurors who make prejudicial statements before deciding strategically which remaining potential jurors to remove through the use of _____5_____.

The _____6_____ court examines arguments concerning errors that occurred during the trial. It may also consider _____7_____ petitions from prisoners challenging the basis for their incarceration.

## MULTIPLE CHOICE QUESTIONS

11.1. What did the Supreme Court hold concerning six person juries in *Burch v. Louisiana (1979)?*
a) six person juries are unconstitutional
b) six person juries must deliver at least a five to one vote to convict a defendant
c) six person juries must deliver at least a four to two vote to convict a defendant
d) six person juries must deliver at least a unanimous vote to convict a defendant
e) six person juries must contain at least one minority juror in cases with a minority defendant.

11.2. Which of the following is true about the trial process?
a) the selection of the jury occurs after the opening statements by the prosecution and the defense
b) the defense presents evidence and witnesses before the prosecution
c) the judge offers instructions to the jury after a decision is reached in a case
d) the selection of jurors is never bias toward the defendant
e) retired persons and homemakers are overrepresented on juries

11.3. The courtroom process of questioning prospective jurors in order to screen out those who might be incapable of being fair is called...
a) mala in se
b) habeas corpus
c) voir dire
d) ex post facto
e) demonstrative evidence

11.4. In the elimination of jurors from the jury pool, what is the difference between a peremptory challenge and challenge for cause?
a) peremptory challenges cannot be used in felony cases
b) challenge for cause cannot be used in felony cases
c) a judge must rule on a peremptory challenge, but attorneys control a challenge for cause
d) a judge must rule on a challenge for cause, but attorneys generally control a peremptory challenge
e) peremptory challenges and challenge for cause are the same

11.5. The prosecution must prove that a defendant is guilty beyond...
a) probable cause
b) all doubt
c) reasonable doubt
d) a preponderance of the evidence
e) reasonable suspicion

11.6. In a trial, fingerprints submitted as evidence would be considered...
a) circumstantial evidence
b) reasonable evidence
c) real evidence
d) direct evidence
e) probable evidence

11.7 In a trial, eyewitness accounts submitted as evidence would be considered...
a) circumstantial evidence
b) reasonable evidence
c) real evidence
d) direct evidence
e) probable evidence

11.8. In a trial, what type of evidence requires the jury to infer a fact from what a witness observed?
a) circumstantial evidence
b) reasonable evidence
c) real evidence
d) direct evidence
e) probable evidence

11.9. Which of the following is true concerning Fifth Amendment rights?
a) defendants must take the stand and face cross examination
b) defendants do not have to testify against themselves, but a prosecutor can criticize a defendant for this strategy
c) defendants do not have to testify against themselves and a prosecutor cannot criticize a defendant for this strategy
d) defendants must take the stand, but the Fifth Amendment prevents cross-examination by the prosecution
e) all of the above are TRUE

11.10. In criminal cases, the majority of states require that a twelve person jury reach ...
a) at least a seven to five vote to convict
b) at least an eight to four vote to convict
c) at least a nine to three vote to convict
d) at least a ten to two vote to convict
e) a unanimous vote to convict

11.11. Who is absent if a trial is conducted "in absentia"?
a) judge
b) jury
c) defense attorney
d) defendant
e) prosecutor

11.12. Social scientists who wish to study jury deliberations...
a) can observe or film after getting permission from the judge
b) can ask to become a member of the jury
c) are barred because jury deliberations are secret
d) must stay behind a two-way mirror
e) can watch the videos that the courts takes of all jury meetings

11.13. According to social scientists, who is more likely to be active and influential during jury deliberations?
a) white women who are less educated
b) minority women who are less educated
c) white men who are less educated
d) minority men who are better educated
e) white men who are better educated

11.14. Who are the key participants in a plea bargain?
a) bailiff and clerk
b) probation officer and bail bondsperson
c) prosecutor and defense attorney
d) jury and the judge
e) all of the above are key participants

11.15. Which of the following is NOT a function of a jury?
a) safeguarding citizens against arbitrary law enforcement
b) determining whether the accused is guilty
c) representing the interests of the prosecutor
d) educating citizens selected for jury duty about the criminal justice system
e) symbolizing the rule of law

11.16. Who was the American citizen who was captured in 2002 fighting with the Taliban in Afghanistan?
a) John Walker Lindh
b) Andrew Goldstein
c) Ira Einhorn
d) Roger Hanson
e) Bill Clinton

11.17. What is the strategy called when police file charges for selling a drug when they know they can probably convict only for possession?
a) voir dire
b) multiple-offense indictment
c) intimidation
d) habeas corpus
e) peremptory challenge

11.18. Who is the former hippie leader who had developed a network of friends among prominent people that allowed him to flee the U. S. after being charged with murder in the 1970s?
a) John Walker Lindh
b) Roger Hanson
c) Ira Einhorn
d) Andrew Goldstein
e) Michael Irvin

11.19. What is it called when the judge, the public, and sometimes even the defendant do not know for sure who got what from whom in exchange for what?
a) bargain justice
b) multiple-offense indictment
c) implicit plea bargaining
d) voir dire
e) challenged for cause

11.20. In a study of the nation's seventy-five largest counties, how many murder cases went to trial?
a) 10 percent
b) 17 percent
c) 26 percent
d) 37 percent
e) 50 percent

11.21. How many felony cases go to trial?
a) fewer than two percent
b) fewer than five percent
c) fewer than 10 percent
d) more than 20 percent
e) more than 40 percent

11.22. How many constitutional amendments mention the right to a trial?
a) one
b) two
c) three
d) four
e) none

11.23. How many percent of jury trials worldwide take place in the United States?
a) 20
b) 40
c) 60
d) 80
e) 90

11.24. Which of the following is a function of a jury?
a) to prevent government oppression
b) to determine whether the accused is guilty on the basis of the evidence presented.
c) to represent diverse community interests
d) to serve as a buffer between the accused and the accuser
e) all of the above

11.25. How many percent of adult Americans have ever been called to jury duty?
a) 5 percent
b) 15 percent
c) 25 percent
d) 40 percent
e) 75 percent

## TRUE/FALSE QUESTIONS

11.1. Juries serve as a buffer between the accused and the accuser.

11.2. Juries in the United States must always be comprised of twelve members.

11.3. The prosecution presents evidence and witnesses before the defense presents its case.

11.4. Among all occupational groups, lawyers are mostly likely to be chosen to serve on juries because of their knowledge about law.

11.5. A judge has a final ruling on all peremptory challenges made by attorneys.

11.6. Racial discrimination has been a problem in lawyers' use of peremptory challenges.

11.7. Circumstantial evidence is always sufficient to convict a defendant.

11.8. Juries decide the facts of case, but judges determine the law.

11.9. Judges in France handle only civil cases.

11.10. Research indicates that jurors' deliberations often include their perceptions of the trial process rather than just the facts of the case.

11.11. Jury duty rarely involves personal and financial hardship.

11.12. A defendant who wins an appeal must be set free and cannot be tried again.

11.13. The vast majority of jury trials worldwide take place in Europe.

11.14. Courts apply rules and procedures in exactly the same way across the nation.

11.15. The going rate is the view of the proper sentence for a crime.

11.16. Television shows, such as *Law and Order*, provide a realistic view of the courtroom.

11.17. In a workgroup, each participant has a specified role.

11.18. Plea bargaining has always been discussed publicly

11.19. Plea bargaining reduces the time that people must spend in jail.

11.20. Plea bargaining always occurs in a single meeting between prosecutor and defense attorney.

# ANSWER KEY

## Key Terms
1. continuances
2. peremptory challenge
3. circumstantial evidence
4. voter list
5. cross-section of the community
6. appeals
7. bench trials
8. unanimous verdict
9. *voir dire*
10. *habeas corpus*
11. testimony
12. challenge for cause
13. jury
14. reasonable doubt
15. *Williams v. Florida*
16. real evidence
17. jury functions
18. direct evidence
19. jury instructions
20. courtroom workgroup
21. local legal culture
22. individualized justice
23. administrative necessity

## Key People
1. Joy Chapper and Roger Hanson
2. Helen "Holly" Maddux and Ira Einhorn
3. Kendra Webdale
4. Andrew Goldstein
5. Bill Clinton

## General Practice Questions
1. cross-section of the community
2. voter registration lists
3. *voir dire*
4. challenges for cause
5. peremptory challenges
6. appeals
7. *habeas corpus*

## Multiple Choice
11.1. d
11.2. e
11.3. c
11.4. d
11.5. c
11.6. c
11.7. d
11.8. a
11.9. c
11.10. e
11.11. d
11.12. c.

11.13.  e
11.14.  c
11.15.  c
11.16.  a
11.17.  b
11.18.  c
11.19.  a
11.20.  c
11.21.  c
11.22.  c
11.23.  d
11.24.  e
11.25.  b

True/False
11.1.   T
11.2.   F
11.3.   T
11.4.   F
11.5.   F
11.6.   T
11.7.   F
11.8.   T
11.9.   F
11.10.  T
11.11.  F
11.12.  F
11.13.  F
11.14.  F
11.15.  T
11.16.  F
11.17.  T
11.18.  F
11.19.  T
11.20.  F

WORKSHEET 11.1. COURTROOM WORKGROUP

A newly elected prosecutor has hired you as a consultant. She wants to know whether she should assign assistant prosecutors to single courtrooms to handle all cases before a specific judge or, alternatively, rotate assistant prosecutors to different courtrooms and other assignments every week. She says, "I've heard that these 'courtroom workgroups,' whatever they are, form if you keep assistant prosecutors in one courtroom. What should I do?"

1. Define the concept of "courtroom workgroup."

_____

_____

_____

2. Describe how courtrooms will work if an assistant prosecutor is permanently assigned to one courtroom. What are the consequences?

_____

_____

_____

_____

_____

_____

3. How will courtrooms work if assistant prosecutors are rotated? What are the consequences?

_____

_____

_____

_____

_____

_____

4. Which approach do you recommend? Why?

_____

_____

_____

_____

_____

## WORKSHEET 11.2: PLEA BARGAINING

Imagine that you are the prosecutor who has been responsible for investigating and prosecuting the case of a suspected serial killer. Over the span of a few years, eight hunters, fishermen, and joggers have been found dead in isolated areas of a three-county rural area. Each one had been shot by a sniper from a great distance. Two bits of evidence led you to arrest a suspect. First, among the many tips you received about possible suspects, one informant described the employee of a nearby city water department who owned many guns and frequently drove out into the country to shoot at random animals he encountered, including farmers' cows and pet dogs. Second, you knew that one of the victims was shot with a rifle that was made in Sweden and was not commonly available in local gun stores. You learned from a second informant that the city employee sold one of these unusual Swedish rifles to another gun enthusiast shortly after the time that a hunter was killed by a shot from such a rifle. You located the gun and ballistics tests indicated a high probability that it was the weapon used in that particular murder. You charged the suspect with five of the eight murders and you scrambled to find evidence to link him with these and the remaining three murders. You have spoken publicly about seeking the death penalty. Now, after months of heavy publicity about the case, you announce that the defendant will plead guilty to one count of murder and be sentenced to life in prison. (Based on a real case in Canton, Ohio).

When giving a guest lecture in a criminal justice course at a nearby university, a student asks you to explain how the plea bargain in this case can be viewed as a "good" or "fair" result in light of the number of victims and the fact that you could have pursued the death penalty. Whether or not you personally agree with the plea bargain, in your role as the prosecutor, how would you explain the benefits of the plea bargain with respect to various interested actors and constituents listed below.

BRIEFLY EXPLAIN IF AND HOW THE PLEA BARGAIN BENEFITS THE:

PROSECUTOR_____

_____

JUDGE_____

_____

COURT SYSTEM_____

_____

DEFENSE ATTORNEY_____

_____

DEFENDANT_____

_____

SOCIETY_____

VICTIMS' FAMILIES_____

WORKSHEET 11.3: JURY SELECTION

Imagine that a thirty-year-old African-American woman is facing trial for the murder of her Hispanic husband. He was shot while standing in the doorway of the house soon after he returned home from work. There are no eyewitnesses. The murder weapon had the wife's fingerprints on it. On the advice of her lawyer, she never answered any questions from the police. Several defense witnesses will testify that the deceased husband used to beat his wife frequently.

1. If you are the prosecutor in this case, what is the demographic profile of your ideal juror? (e.g., age, race, education, occupation, gender, political party affiliation, religion, etc.) Why?

_____

_____

_____

_____

_____

2. If you are the defense attorney in this case, what is the demographic profile of your ideal juror? Why?

_____

_____

_____

_____

_____

3. If you were the prosecutor, what questions would you want to ask the potential jurors during *voir dire*? Why?

_____

_____

_____

_____

_____

_____

4. If you were the defense attorney, what questions would you want to ask the potential jurors during *voir dire*?

_____

_____

_____

WORKSHEET 11.4: JURY PROCESSES

There are many debates about changing the jury system  How would you address the following issues?

1. Should peremptory challenges be abolished?  What would be the consequences of excluding potential jurors only for cause and not through attorneys' discretionary decisions?

_____

_____

_____

_____

_____

_____

_____

2. Should juries have twelve members or should we use six-member juries for criminal cases?  What are the consequences of using small juries?

_____

_____

_____

_____

_____

_____

_____

3. Should guilty verdicts be unanimous?  What would be the consequences of permitting people to be convicted of crimes by nonunanimous jury decisions?

_____

_____

_____

_____

_____

_____

_____

# CHAPTER 12

## PUNISHMENT AND SENTENCING

---

## LEARNING OBJECTIVES

After completing the material in this chapter, students should understand:

1. the philosophical basis for criminal punishment;

2. the goals and weaknesses of retribution;

3. the goals and weaknesses of deterrence;

4. the goals and weaknesses of incapacitation;

5. the goals and weaknesses of rehabilitation;

6. the nature and extent of the various forms of criminal sanctions, including incarceration, intermediate sanctions, probation, and death;

7. the constitutional and policy debates concerning the application of capital punishment;

8. the influences on sentencing, including administrative context, attitudes and values of judges, presentence report, and sentencing guidelines;

9. the debates about who receives the harshest punishment.

## CHAPTER SUMMARY

The four goals of the criminal punishment in the United States are 1) retribution, 2) deterrence, 3) incapacitation, and 4) rehabilitation. The U. S. system is experimenting with restoration is a new approach to punishment. These goals are carried out through a variety of punishments such as incarceration, intermediate sanctions, probation, and death. Penal codes vary as to whether the permitted sentences are indeterminate, determinate, or mandatory. Each type of sentence makes certain assumptions about the goals of the criminal sanction. Good time allows correctional administrators to reduce the sentence of prisoners who live according to the rules and participate in various vocational, educational, and treatment programs. The death penalty is allowed as a form of punishment by the U.S. Supreme Court if the judge and jury are allowed to take into consideration mitigating and aggravating circumstances. The death penalty can be used by the states against juveniles, but not against the mentally retarded or the mentally insane. The U. S. Supreme Court led by Chief Justice William Rehnquist (1986-present) is attempting to limit the number of appeals for defendants on death row in multiple courts within the United States criminal justice system. Judges have considerable discretion in handing down sentences. Judges consider such factors as the seriousness of the crime, the offender's prior record, and mitigating and aggravating circumstances. The sentencing process is influenced by the administrative context of the courts, the attitudes and values of the judges, and the presentence report. Since the 1980s, sentencing guidelines have been formulated in federal courts and seventeen states as a way of reducing disparity among the sentences given offenders in similar situations. Severe or unjust punishments may result from racial discrimination or wrongful convictions.

**CHAPTER OUTLINE**

I.     EXAMPLE:  Sentencing of Marjorie Knoller for involuntary manslaughter in the fatal dog mauling of her neighbor, Diane Whipple.

II.    THE GOALS OF PUNISHMENT

A.     <u>Philosophical Underpinnings of Punishment</u>
       1.     Punishment has always been shaped by philosophical and moral orientations.  Although the ultimate purpose of the criminal sanction is assumed to be the maintenance of social order, different justifications have emerged in different eras to legitimize the punishment imposed by the states.
       2.     Over time, Western countries have moved away from the imposition of physical pain as a form of retribution and toward greater reliance on restrictions of freedom and the use of social and psychological efforts to change behavior.
       3.     In the twentieth century, four goals of the criminal sanction are acknowledged in the United States:
              a.     Retribution (deserved punishment).
              b.     Deterrence.
              c.     Incapacitation.
              d.     Rehabilitation.

B.     <u>Retribution or Deserved Punishment</u>
       1.     Idea that those who do wrong should be punished alike, in proportion to the gravity of the offense or to the extent to which others have been made to suffer ("an eye for an eye").
       2.     Some claim that retribution is a basic human emotion and that the community may express its revulsion at offensive acts by taking the law into their own hands if the state does not impose retribution on offenders:  Retribution is thus an expression of the community's disapproval of crime.
       3.     Risk of chaos may not exist for failure to punish all crimes, such as an adult smoking marijuana.
       4.     Resurgence of interest in retribution among scholars and observers of criminal justice in recent years.  Andrew von Hirsch and others argue that punishment should be applied only for the wrong inflicted and not primarily to achieve utilitarian benefits (deterrence, incapacitation, rehabilitation).  Offenders should be penalized for their wrongful acts because fairness and justice dictate that they deserve punishment.

C.     <u>Deterrence</u>
       1.     Jeremy Bentham, leader of the 18th and 19th century utilitarians, found retribution to be pointless.  Benthamites saw human behavior as governed by individual calculations about the degree of pleasure over pain to be derived from an act.  Advocated seeking "good" results from punishment:  namely deter potential criminals by the example of sanctions laid on the guilty.
       2.     General deterrence:  idea that the general population will be dissuaded from criminal behavior by observing that punishment will necessarily follow commission of a crime and that the pain will be greater than the benefits that may stem from the illegal act.  The punishment must be severe enough so that all will be impressed by the consequences.
              a.     For general deterrence to be effective, the public must be informed of the equation and continually reminded of it by the punishments of the convicted (e.g., public hanging thought to be a general deterrent).
       3.     Special deterrence (often called specific or individual deterrence):  concerned with changes in the behavior of the convicted.  It is individualized in that the amount and kind of punishment are calculated to deter the criminal from repeating the offense.
       4.     Problems with deterrence

<ol type="a">
<li style="list-style-type: none;">a. Deterrence presumes that people act rationally, but many people commit crimes while under the influence of alcohol and drugs.</li>
<li style="list-style-type: none;">b. Problem of obtaining proof of the effectiveness of deterrence. General deterrence suffers because social science is unable to measure its effects; only those who are *not* deterred come to the attention of criminal justice researchers.</li>
<li style="list-style-type: none;">c. Not clear how the criminal justice system influences the effect of deterrence through the speed, certainty, and severity of the allocated punishment. Low probability of being caught for some crimes defeats the goal of deterrence.</li>
</ol>

D.    <u>Incapacitation</u>

1. The assumption of incapacitation is that a crime may be prevented if criminals are physically restrained.

2. Prison is the typical mode of incapacitation, since offenders can be kept under control so that they cannot violate the rules of society. Capital punishment is the ultimate method of incapacitation.

3. Incapacitative sanction is different from these other goals in that it is future-oriented (unlike retribution); is based on personal characteristics of the offender, not on characteristics of the crime (unlike general deterrence); and is not intended to reform the criminal.

4. Problems of incapacitation:

    a. Undue severity. Offenders are not released until the state is reasonably sure that they will no longer commit crimes; length of sentence not necessarily dependent on seriousness of offense. Under incapacitation theory, a one-time impulse killer could get

    less punishment than a habitual shoplifter.

    b. Flawed predictions: not able to predict accurately which offenders will commit future offenses.

5. Selective incapacitation of great interest in recent years because of research suggesting that a relatively small number of offenders are responsible for a large number of violent and property crimes (e.g., burglars tend to commit many offenses before they are caught).

    a. Such policies can impose significant costs because the costs of incarceration are so high.

E.    <u>Rehabilitation</u>

1. The most appealing modern justification for use of the criminal sanction: the offender should be treated and resocialized while under the care of the state.

2. Assumes that techniques are available to identify and treat the causes of the offender's behavior.

3. Because rehabilitation is oriented solely toward the offender, no relationship can be maintained between the severity of the punishment and the gravity of the crime.

4. According to the concept of rehabilitation, offenders are not being punished, they are being treated and will return to society when they are well.

    a. Leads to indeterminate sentences with maximum and minimum terms, as well as discretion for the parole board to decide when the offender is ready for release.

5. Until the 1970s the rehabilitative ideal was so widely shared that it was almost assumed that matters of treatment and reform of the offender were the only questions worthy of serious attention in the whole field of criminal justice and corrections. Since then, however, the model has come under closer scrutiny and in some quarters has been discredited. Some social scientists have wondered whether the causes of crime can be diagnosed and treated.

6. There is still support for the idea of rehabilitation in public opinion polls and among prison wardens.

F.    <u>New Approaches to Punishment</u>

Restorative Justice: Crime violates sense of community as well as the individual victim. Use mediation to devise ways to restore victim and community.

Close-Up: Restorative Justice in Vermont. Community sentencing boards instead of judges to tailor penalties to lesser crimes. Sanctions are often more severe than probation but there are questions about whether penalties are applied equally and fairly.

III. FORMS OF THE CRIMINAL SANCTION

A. Images of Punishment
   1. Less than one third of adults under correctional supervision are in prison or jail, but incarceration is viewed by the public as the primary form of punishment so that people who receive probation and other sanctions are regarded as getting off easy.
   2. COMPARATIVE PERSPECTIVE: Corporal Punishment in Singapore.

B. Incarceration
   1. Most visible penalty imposed by U.S. courts although less than 30 percent of persons under correctional supervision are in prisons and jails.
   2. Believed to have high deterrent value, but expensive and may hamper offender's reintegration into society.
   3. Indeterminate Sentences: in accord with the goal of rehabilitation, state legislatures also adopted indeterminate (often termed indefinite) sentences. Based on idea that correctional personnel must be given the discretion to make a release decision on the grounds of successful treatment, penal codes with indeterminate sentences stipulate a minimum and maximum amount of time to be served in prison.
      a. "Good time" may be subtracted from either the minimum or maximum; "good time" is earned through good behavior in prison.
   4. Determinate Sentences: Growing dissatisfaction with the rehabilitative goal led to efforts in support of determinate sentences based on the assumption of deserved punishment. A convicted offender is given a specific length of time to be served and at the end of this term (minus credited "good time") the prisoner is automatically freed (there is no parole board).
      a. Release is not tied to participation in any treatment program or the judgement of the parole board about the future recidivism of the offender.
      b. Many states have moved toward setting a specific term in prison for each crime category; tends to reduce judges' discretion ("presumptive sentence").
   5. Mandatory Sentences: criticisms of excessive leniency and early releases have led legislatures to adopt mandatory sentences, stipulating some minimum period of incarceration that must be served by persons convicted of selected crimes. No regard may be given to the circumstances of the offense or the background of the individual; the judge has no discretion and is not allowed to suspend the sentence.
      a. Examples include "three strikes and you're out" life sentences.
      b. Mandatory prison terms are most often specified for violent crimes, drug violations, habitual offenders, or crimes where a firearm was used. Plea bargaining can undercut the intentions of the legislature by negotiating for a different charge. For example, such actions have undercut the Massachusetts law mandating one-year sentences for possessing an unregistered firearm.
   6. Three Strikes Law: impact on nonviolent crimes and increase in imprisonment costs.
   7. Sentence versus Actual Time Served: in all but four states, days are subtracted from prisoners' minimum or maximum term for good behavior or for participation in various types of vocational, educational, and treatment programs ("good time"). Service also shortened by release to the community on parole.
      a. Correctional officials consider these sentence-reduction policies necessary for the maintenance of institutional order and as a mechanism to reduce overcrowding.

            b.       Good time is also taken into consideration by prosecutors and defense attorneys during plea bargaining.

      8.     Felony offenders spend an average of less than three years in prison.

"Truth in Sentencing": requirement that offenders serve a substantial portion of their sentences before release on parole usually must serve 85 percent of sentence for a violent crime. Policy can increase imprisonment costs.

Todd Clear argues that current offenders are actually serving sentences about as severe as in past even if they serve a smaller proportion of the sentence.

C.     Intermediate Sanctions

    1.     Punishments such as fines, home confinement, intensive probation supervision, restitution and community service, boot camp, and forfeiture are among the sentencing forms that fit this category that is expanding in response to the expense and overcrowding of prisons.

    2.     Morris and Tonry stipulate that these sanctions not be used in isolation from each other but that they be combined to reflect the severity of the offense, the characteristics of the offender, and the needs of the community.

    3.     For effective use of intermediate punishments it is recommended that they be enforced by mechanisms that take seriously any breach of the conditions of the sentence. Too often criminal justice agencies have put few resources into the enforcement of non-incarcerative sentences.

D.     Probation

    1.     Nearly 60 percent of adults under correctional supervision are on probation; designed as a means of simultaneously maintaining control and assisting offenders while permitting them to live in the community under supervision; if conditions violated, probation may be revoked and the sentence may be served in prison.

    2.     The sanction is often tied to incarceration. Judges may set a prison term but suspend it upon successful completion of a period of probation.

    3.     In some jurisdictions the court is authorized to modify an offender's prison sentence after a portion is served by changing it to probation. This is often referred to as "shock probation" (called "split probation" in California).

    4.     Probation is generally advocated as a way of rehabilitating offenders with less serious offenses or clean prior records. It is less expensive than prison and may avoid prison's embittering effects on young offenders.

E.     Death

    1.     Other Western democracies have abolished the death penalty but the United States continues to use it.

    2.     History: Prior to the 1960s, capital punishment was used regularly in the U. S.; in recent years critics have questioned how capital punishment fits with the Eighth Amendment's prohibition against cruel and unusual punishment.

            a.       The number of persons under sentence of death has increased dramatically in the past decade. About 3,700 incarcerated persons were awaiting execution in thirty-seven death penalty states in 2002; two-thirds of those on death row were in the South, with the greatest number in that area concentrated in Florida, Georgia, Alabama, and Texas.

            b.       About 250 people are added to death row each year.

            c.       African-Americans are overrepresented on death row.

    3.     The Death Penalty and the Constitution: capital cases conducted according to higher standards of fairness and due process

            a.       *Furman v. Georgia* (1972): the Supreme Court ruled that the death penalty, as administered, constituted cruel and unusual punishment, thereby voiding the laws of thirty-nine states and the District of Columbia. Only two of the justices argued that capital punishment per se was cruel and unusual, in violation of the Eighth Amendment.

b. *Gregg v. Georgia* (1976): thirty-five states had enacted new legislation designed to eliminate the faults cited in *Furman v. Georgia*. The Court upheld those laws that required the sentencing judge or jury to take into account specific aggravating and mitigating factors in deciding which convicted murderers should be sentenced to death. Capital cases two-part process: first trial to determine guilt and second hearing focused solely on punishment.

c. *McCleskey v. Kemp* (1987): McCleskey's attorneys cited research that showed a disparity in the imposition of the death sentence in Georgia based on the race of the murder victim and, to a lesser extent, the race of the defendant. By a 5-4 vote the justices rejected McCleskey's assertion. Justice Lewis Powell, for the majority, said that the appeal challenged the discretionary aspects of the criminal justice system, especially with regard to prosecutors, judges, and juries. McCleskey would have to prove that the decision makers in his case had acted with a discriminatory purpose by producing evidence specific to the case and not the generalized statistical study.

d. Execution of the Retarded: In *Atkins v. Virginia (2002),* Justice John Paul Stevens wrote for the majority in ruling that it was unconstitutional for states to execute the mentally retarded.

4. Continuing Legal Issues:

Legal issues related to the death penalty occupied the attention of jurists and activists during recent years.

a. Execution of the Insane: U. S. Supreme Court said in *Ford v. Wainwright* that states cannot execute the insane. However, there are problems with defining and identifying insanity.

b. Execution of Minors: twenty-three of the thirty-eight death penalty states allow for the execution of juveniles.

   i. *Thompson v. Oklahoma* (1988): the court narrowly decided offender who was fifteen years old when he committed murder should not be executed.

   ii. *Stanford v. Kentucky* (1989) and *Wilkins v. Missouri* (1989): the justices upheld the convictions and death sentences of offenders who were 16 and 17 years old at the time of their crime.

c. Effective Counsel: Issues about the adequacy of defense lawyers' efforts.

d. Death-Qualified Juries: Should people who are opposed to the death penalty be excluded from juries in capital cases?

e. Appeals: the average length of time between imposition of the sentence by a trial court to the date that the sentence is carried out is between seven and eight years. During this time sentences are reviewed by the state courts and through the writ of habeas corpus by the federal courts.

   i. Chief Justice Rehnquist has been particularly active in pushing to allow only one habeas corpus appeal to the federal courts in death penalty cases. This position was upheld by the Supreme Court in April 1991 when it said that only in exceptional circumstances should a prisoner be allowed to use the writ more than once. In 1996 President Clinton signed a new law setting new limits on habeas corpus review.

   ii. Appellate review is time-consuming and expensive process, but it also has an impact. Dozens of death row inmates have been released when their innocence was later discovered.

5. Death: A Continuing Controversy

More than 250 new death sentences are now being given out each year yet the number of executions remains low. Is this situation the result of a complicated appeals process or of lack of will on the part of both political leaders and a society that is perhaps uncertain about the taking of human life?  Maybe the death penalty has more significance as a political symbol than as a deterrent to crime.  Also, death sentences are expensive.

IV.    THE POLICY DEBATE: Should the death penalty to be abolished?  The moratorium imposed by Governor George Ryan of Illinois in 2000 renewed debate about the death penalty.

A.    Arguments for the death penalty include social retribution, deterrence, and less expensive that allowing offenders to live in prison.

B.    Arguments against the death penalty include the idea that it violates the human dignity in the U. S. Constitution, it is not a deterrent, innocent persons are executed, it is a financial burden of the legal system because it involves millions of dollars in legal fees, and it is applied largely to the poor and minorities.

V.    THE SENTENCING PROCESS
Judges have responsibility for sentencing after conviction, whether the conviction was by judge, jury, or plea bargain.  Initial definitions of punishments are defined by legislatures.  There may be room under the law for judges to use discretion in shaping individuals sentences.

A.    The Administrative Context of the Courts
       1.    Misdemeanor Courts:  Assembly Line Justice-limited jurisdiction courts have limits on the punishments that can be meted out for specific offenses, usually maximum of one year in jail. These courts handle over 90 percent of criminal cases for arraignment and preliminary hearing before referring case to a general jurisdiction trial court or for completion through dismissal or sentence.
              a.    Most lower courts are overloaded and the time allotted for each case is minimal. Judicial decisions are mass produced because the actors in the system work together on the basis of three assumptions:
                     i.    There is a high probability that anyone brought to court is guilty and doubtful cases will be filtered out beforehand by the prosecutor and police.
                     ii.    The vast majority of defendants will plead guilty.
                     iii.    Those charged with minor offenses will be processed    in volume: normally a guilty plea is entered and a sentence is pronounced immediately after the charges are read.
              b.    Some researchers argue that informality, availability, and diversity of lower courts are their most valuable qualities: these courts (through judges' discretion) can be oriented toward individualized justice that is responsive to the community's values.
              c.    Even those who are not convicted, experience punishment from being drawn into the system.  People who are arrested and detained suffer psychic and social costs that range from losing jobs to being stigmatized.
                     i.    These costs can also encourage rapid, perfunctory practices in the courtroom and guilty pleas.  This helps to explain why so many people waive their right to a jury trial and plead guilty.  Better to take the punishment (probably probation) than to remain in jail, incurring more personal costs, and risking that a more serious punishment may ultimately be applied.
       2.    Felony Court: in courts of general jurisdiction, sentencing influenced by organizational considerations and community norms, including interactions and relationships between judges, prosecutors, and defense attorneys.

B.    Attitudes and Values of Judges
       1.    Sentencing differences among judges can be ascribed to a number of factors:
              a.    Conflicting goals of criminal justice.

221

b. The fact that judges are the products of different backgrounds and have different social values.
c. The administrative pressures on the judge.
d. The influence of community values on the system.
e. The particular judge's attitude toward law, toward a particular crime, and toward a particular type of offender.

C. The Presentence Report
1. An important ingredient in sentencing; the report is based on the investigation of the probation officer. In some states, the probation officer makes an actual recommendation; in others, the probation officer merely provides information. Report can be based on hearsay.
2. CLOSE-UP: New Mexico Presentence Report
3. The language of the report is crucial in conveying an impression. It may be written in a neutral style or it may suggest something negative about the offender's attitude.
4. A Question of Ethics: Sentencing of two co-defendants. Should there be a different sentence for an offender convicted at trial as compared to one who enters a guilty plea?
5. The presentence report helps judges to ease the strain of decision making; helps to shift responsibility to the probation department.
   a. a study found a high correlation between a recommendation for probation in the presentence report and the court's disposition of individual cases. When the probation officer recommended incarceration, there was a slight weakening of the relationship, an indication that probation officers were more punitive than judges.

D. Sentencing Guidelines
Guidelines have emerged in the federal system and some state systems as a means to limit the discretion of judges and to reduce sentencing disparities for offenders convicted of the same offense. Sentencing ranges in the guidelines are based on seriousness of offense and criminal history of the offender.
1. Guidelines appear in a grid constructed on the basis of two scores, seriousness of offense and offender's history/prior record or other offender characteristics. The grid provides an offender score which indicates the sentencing range for the particular offender who commits a specific offense. Judges are expected to provide a written explanation if they depart from the guidelines/grid.
New Directions in Criminal Justice Policy-Sentencing By Computer: In Michigan, private computer companies have developed software that will do sentencing calculations quickly for judges and for the probation officers who write presentence reports.

E. Who Gets the Harshest Punishment?
1. The evidence is inconclusive. Some studies have shown that members of racial minorities and the poor are treated more harshly by the system. Other studies show no clear link between harshness of sentence and the offender's race or social status.
2. The Wrongly Convicted: While much public concern is expressed over those who "beat the system" and go free, comparatively little attention is paid to those who are innocent, yet convicted. Each year several such cases of persons convicted but innocent come to national attention.

**REVIEW OF KEY TERMS**

Fill in the appropriate term for each statement.

aggravating factors

administrative context
sentencing
retribution
general deterrence
special deterrence
incapacitation
rehabilitation
selective incapacitation
indeterminate sentence
intermediate sanctions
incarceration
good time
shock probation
corporal punishment
determinate sentence
mandatory sentence
presentence report
*Furman v. Georgia*
*McCleskey v. Kemp*
*Gregg v. Georgia*
*Stanford v. Kentucky*
sentencing guidelines
probation

1. _____ is the careful choosing of offenders who will receive long prison sentences that will prevent them from committing additional crimes.

2. _____ is a term of incarceration based on a minimum and maximum amount of time; the actual amount to be served will be based on the judgment of the parole board.

3. _____ is punishment inflicted on criminals with the intent to discourage them from committing any future crimes.

4. _____ is a sentence in which the offender is released after a short incarceration and placed in the community under supervision.

5. _____ is the specification of the sanction to be applied to the offender after he or she is convicted of a crime.

6. _____ is the detaining of an offender as a form of punishment.

7. _____ is a type of sentence determined by statutes which require that a certain penalty shall be imposed and executed upon certain convicted offenders.

8. _____ is the Supreme Court case which reactivated capital punishment after states revised their death penalty decision-making procedures.

9. _____ is generally associated with the infliction of physical pain as a form of punishment.

10. _____ is a variety of punishments that are more restrictive than traditional probation but less stringent and costly than incarceration.

11. _____ is a punishment involving conditional release under supervision.

12. _____ is the underlying goal of punishment in which the offender is considered deserving of punishment and the punishment fits the seriousness of the crime.

13. _____ is the Supreme Court case that approved the execution of offenders who committed capital offenses at age sixteen.

14. _____ is the deprivation of the ability to commit crimes against society, usually through means of detention in prison.

15. _____ is a case in which the Supreme Court rejected a claim that systematic racial discrimination made the death penalty unconstitutional.

16. _____ is a sentence that fixes the term of imprisonment at a specified period of time.

17. _____ are a reform designed to reduce the disparities in sentences for people who have committed the same or similar crimes.

18. _____ is the goal of restoring a convicted offender to a constructive place in society.

19. _____ is the credit awarded to prisoners in most states which permits them to earn days off of their sentences through proper behavior.

20. _____ is the Supreme Court case that temporarily halted executions in the United States.

21. _____ is the punishment of criminals that is intended to serve as an example to the public and discourage others from committing crimes.

22. _____ is submitted by the probation officer to the judge.

23. _____ must be taken into consideration in capital punishment sentencing.

24. _____ of the courts affects sentencing, especially in misdemeanor courts.

## REVIEW OF KEY PEOPLE

Andrew von Hirsch
Jeremy Bentham
Robert Satter
Michael Fay
George Ryan
Michael L. Radelet
William Rehnquist
John Paul Stevens

1. Chief Justice _____ has been particularly active in pushing to allow only one habeas corpus appeal to the federal courts in death penalty cases.

2. In 2000, Governor _____ of Illinois called for a moratorium on the death penalty in his state.

3. In Atkins v. Virginia (2002), Justice _____ wrote for the majority in ruling that it was unconstitutional to execute the mentally retarded.

4. The deterrence approach has its roots in eighteenth-century England and the social philosopher_____.

5. _____ believed that basic morality demands that wrongdoers be punished.

6. A Singapore court sentenced _____, an American teenager, to receive a flogging for vandalizing cars with spray paint.

7. Judge _____ states that sentencing requires balancing the scales of justice between society, violated by a crime, and the defendant, fallible, but nonetheless human.

8. _____examined the cases of sixty-eight death row inmates later released because of doubts about their guilt.

## GENERAL PRACTICE QUESTIONS

Among the purposes of punishment, ____1____ and ____2____ focus on the specific offender by, respectively, focusing the seriousness of the offense committed and seeking to turn the offender into a productive citizen. By contrast, ____3____ and ____4____ focus on society by, respectively, seeking to discourage others from crime and protecting society from acts by repeat offenders.

The underlying purpose of ____5____ is to identify sentencing options that will save money while giving the offender a punishment more harsh than ____6____, in which the restrictions and supervision may not drastically change the offender's behavior while living in the community.

The ____7____ of misdemeanor courts includes the assumption that police and prosecutors have filtered out the innocent people. This assumption contrasts sharply with capital punishment cases in which jurors must carefully way mitigating and ____8____ in deciding whether to impose the death penalty.

SELF-TEST SECTION

## MULTIPLE CHOICE QUESTIONS

12.1. The U. S. Supreme Court declared that the death penalty did not violate the Constitution through imposition in a racially discriminatory manner in the case of...
a) Furman v. Georgia (1972)
b) Gregg v. Georgia (1976)
c) McClesky v. Kemp (1987)
d) Payne v. Tennessee (1991)
e) Ford v. Wainwright (1986)

12.2. Which of the following is true concerning the current majority on the Rehnquist Court and the appeal process for death penalty cases?
a) the Rehnquist Court majority is satisfied with the appeals process
b) the Rehnquist Court majority wants to provide more appeals across multiple courts for death row inmates
c) the Rehnquist Court majority wants to limit the opportunities for capital punishment defendants to have their appeals heard by multiple courts
d) the Rehnquist Court majority wants to abolish the death penalty so it won't have to deal with the issue of appeals
e) the Rehnquist Court majority wants to end all state and federal appeals for capital punishment defendants

12.3. Punishments that are less severe and costly than prison, but more restrictive than traditional probation, are called...
a) indeterminate sentences
b) mandatory sentences
c) "good time" sentences
d) presumptive sentences
e) intermediate sanctions

12.4. Which is the most frequently applied criminal sanction?
a) probation
b) the death penalty
c) life in prison
d) indeterminate sentences
e) presumptive sentences

12.5. The U. S. Supreme Court declared that the death penalty is illegal in the case of the mentally retarded in the case of...
a) Payne v. Tennessee (1991)
b) Ring v. Arizona (2002)
c) McClesky v. Kemp (1987)
d) Stanford v. Kentucky (1989)
e) Atkins v. Virginia (2002)

12.6. In what case did the U. S. Supreme Court rule that juries, rather than judges, must make the crucial factual decisions as to whether a convicted murderer should receive the death penalty?
a) Payne v. Tennessee (1991)
b) Ring v. Arizona (2002)
c) McClesky v. Kemp (1987)
d) Stanford v. Kentucky (1989)
e) Atkins v. Virginia (2002)

12.7. In what case did the U. S. Supreme Court rule that under a hate crime statute a higher sentence may be imposed if the judge found that a crime was committed with a biased motive?

226

a) Payne v. Tennessee (1991)
b) Ring v. Arizona (2002)
c) McClesky v. Kemp (1987)
d) Apprendi v. New Jersey (2000)
e) Atkins v. Virginia (2002)

12.8. In what case did the Supreme Court rule that the Eighth Amendment prohibited the state from executing the insane?
a) Furman v. Georgia (1972)
b) Gregg v. Georgia (1976)
c) McClesky v. Kemp (1987)
d) Payne v. Tennessee (1991)
e) Ford v. Wainwright (1986)

12.9. Which of the following justices supports the use of the death penalty?
a) William Rehnquist
b) Antonin Scalia
c) Clarence Thomas
d) all of the above
e) none of the above

12.10. Which of the following justices opposed the use of the death penalty?
a) Sandra Day O'Connor
b) Antonin Scalia
c) Clarence Thomas
d) Thurgood Marshall
e) Warren Burger

12.11. Which of the following countries allows for the execution of juveniles?
a) United States
b) Nigeria
c) Iran
d) Yemen
e) all of the above

12.12. The U. S. Supreme Court declared that the death penalty did not violate the Constitution in the case of juveniles in the case of...
a) Furman v. Georgia (1972)
b) Gregg v. Georgia (1976)
c) Stanford v. Kentucky (1989)
d) Payne v. Tennessee (1991)
e) Ford v. Wainwright (1986)

12.13. The U. S. Supreme Court ruled that defendants in capital cases had the right to representation that meets an "objective standard of reasonableness" in the case of...
a) Furman v. Georgia (1972)
b) Gregg v. Georgia (1976)
c) Stanford v. Kentucky (1989)
d) Payne v. Tennessee (1991)
e) Strickland v. Washington (1984)

12.14. In what case did the U. S. Supreme Court hold that potential jurors who have general objections to the death penalty cannot be automatically excluded from jury service in capital cases?
a) Witherspoon v. Illinois (1968)

b) Ring v. Arizona (2002)
c) McClesky v. Kemp (1987)
d) Apprendi v. New Jersey (2000)
e) Atkins v. Virginia (2002)

12.15. What is the average amount of time that a death row inmate is under the sentence of the death before the execution?
a) one year
b) six years
c) eleven years
d) twenty-one years
e) six months

12.16. Which chief justice has actively sought to reduce the opportunities for capital punishment defendants to have their appeals heard by multiple courts?
a) Earl Warren
b) Warren Burger
c) Earl Burger
d) William Rehnquist
e) John Paul Stevens

12.17. Which of the following factors influence the sentencing process?
a) the administrative context of the courts
b) the attitudes and values of judges
c) the presentence report
d) sentencing guidelines
e) all of the above

12.18. What type of jurisdiction do misdemeanor, or lower courts, maintain in the American system?
a) general
b) limited
c) intermediate
d) all of the above
e) none of the above

12.19. What type of jurisdiction do felony courts, maintain in the American system?
a) general
b) limited
c) intermediate
d) all of the above
e) none of the above

12.20. Which goal of punishment is based upon the biblical expression, "An eye for an eye, a tooth for a tooth?"
a) retribution
b) deterrence
c) incapacitation
d) rehabilitation
e) all of the above

12.21. Who is responsible for the presentence report?
a) bailiff
b) police
c) clerk

d) judge

e) prosecutor

12.22. Which of the following is TRUE about presentence reports?

a) they are scientific

b) they are not stereotypical

c) they are largely determined by the present offense and the prior criminal record

d) all of the above are true

e) none of the above are true

12.23. If a person believes that techniques are available to identify and treat the causes of criminal behavior, then which goal of punishment would that person support?

a) retribution

b) deterrence

c) incapacitation

d) rehabilitation

e) all of the above

12.24. Legislatures construct sentencing guidelines as a grid of two scores. What are the two scores?

a) seriousness of the offense and likelihood of recidivism

b) race and age

c) judges' attitudes and values

d) age and status of employment

e) community ties and family history

12.25. Which of the following is a goal of punishment in the American system of criminal justice?

a) retribution

b) deterrence

c) incapacitation

d) rehabilitation

e) all of the above

## TRUE/FALSE QUESTIONS

12.1. Virtually all states and the federal government have some types of mandatory sentences.

12.2. It is legal for states to execute the mentally retarded.

12.3. "Good time" refers to the amount of a time that a judge allows a jury to deliberate a decision.

12.4. The majority of industrialized democracies in the world use the death penalty as a form of punishment.

12.5. Intermediate sanctions are punishments that are less severe and financially burdensome than prison.

12.6. The most frequently employed criminal sanction is probation.

12.7. Jeremy Bentham supported the deterrence approach toward punishment.

12.8. In recent years less attention has been paid to the concept of selective incapacitation, whereby offenders who repeat certain kinds of crimes are sentenced to long prison terms.

12.9. At sentencing, judges rarely give reasons for the punishments imposed.

12.10. Rehabilitation is focused upon the victim of a crime.

12.11. The country of Singapore offers harsh punishment for a wide range of crimes.

12.12. Less than 30 percent of persons under correctional supervision are in prisons and jails.

12.13. Truth-in-sentencing refers to laws that require offenders to serve a large proportion of their prison sentence before being released on parole.

12.14. Most states do not use the death penalty as punishment in the United States.

12.15. It is illegal to execute the mentally insane.

12.16. Offenders can have their prison sentence increased by earning good time for bad behavior.

12.17. Felony cases are processed and offenders are sentenced in courts of limited jurisdiction.

12.18. Presentence reports are not scientific and can reflect stereotypes.

12.19. Since the 1980s sentencing guidelines have been established in the federal courts and in all fifty states.

12.20. Sentencing guidelines are constructed on the basis of past sentences.

**ANSWER KEY**

Key Terms
1.     selective incapacitation
2.     indeterminate sentence
3.     special deterrence
4.     shock probation
5.     sentencing
6.     incarceration
7.     mandatory sentence
8.     *Gregg v. Georgia*
9.     corporal punishment
10.    intermediate sanctions
11.    probation
12.    retribution
13.    *Stanford v. Kentucky*
14.    incapacitation
15.    *McCleskey v. Kemp*
16.    determinate sentence
17.    sentencing guidelines
18.    rehabilitation
19.    good time
20.    *Furman v. Georgia*
21.    general deterrence
22.    presentence report
23.    aggravating factors
24.    administrative context

Key People
1.     William Rehnquist
2.     George Ryan
3.     John Paul Stevens
4.     Jeremy Bentham
5.     Andrew von Hirsch
6.     Michael Fay
7.     Robert Satter
8.     Michael L. Radelet

General Practice Questions
1.     retribution
2.     rehabilitation
3.     general deterrence
4.     incapacitation
5.     intermediate sanctions
6.     probation
7.     administrative context
8.     aggravating factors

Multiple Choice Questions
12.1.    c
12.2.    c
12.3.    e
12.4.    a
12.5.    e
12.6.    b
12.7.    d

| 12.8. | e |
|---|---|
| 12.9. | d |
| 12.10. | d |
| 12.11. | e |
| 12.12. | c |
| 12.13. | e |
| 12.14. | a |
| 12.15. | c |
| 12.16. | d |
| 12.17. | e |
| 12.18. | b |
| 12.19. | a |
| 12.20. | c |
| 12.21. | a |
| 12.22. | c |
| 12.23. | d |
| 12.24. | a |
| 12.25. | e |

True/False

| 12.1. | T |
|---|---|
| 12.2. | F |
| 12.3. | F |
| 12.4. | F |
| 12.5. | T |
| 12.6. | T |
| 12.7. | T |
| 12.8. | F |
| 12.9. | F |
| 12.10. | F |
| 12.11. | T |
| 12.12. | T |
| 12.13. | T |
| 12.14. | F |
| 12.15. | T |
| 12.16. | F |
| 12.17. | F |
| 12.18. | T |
| 12.19. | F |
| 12.20. | T |

WORKSHEET 12.1   FORMS OF THE CRIMINAL SANCTION

Discuss whether and how the underlying purposes of the criminal sanction fit with various forms of punishment.  Ask yourself:  Does this form of punishment effectively advance any or all of the underlying purposes?  For each punishment, comment on the pros and cons of all of the following:  rehabilitation, deterrence, incapacitation, retribution.

1. INCARCERATION:_____

_____

_____

_____

_____

_____

_____

2. PROBATION:

_____

_____

_____

_____

_____

3. FINES: _____

_____

_____

_____

_____

4. CAPITAL PUNISHMENT:_____

_____

_____

_____

_____

5. COMMUNITY SERVICE:_____

_____

WORKSHEET 12.2    SENTENCING

Imagine that you are a judge deciding on sentences for individuals who have entered guilty pleas in the following situations. What sentence would you impose?

1. A nineteen-year-old high school dropout pleads guilty to burglary. He broke into a home and was caught carrying a VCR out the window when the homeowners awoke from the noise of someone in their living room. He has one previous felony conviction for burglary.

SENTENCE:_____

2. A college senior who was caught copying copyrighted computer software from a university computer system onto his own diskette without permission. The value of the software was $700. The student entered a guilty plea to a simple theft charge with an agreement that the prosecutor would recommend leniency. The student has been suspended from college for one year by the school's disciplinary board.

SENTENCE:_____

3. A man who recently completed a prison sentence for armed robbery killed a man during an argument at a bar. The defendant claimed that the victim owed him money so he went to the bar with a knife in order to scare the victim. A confrontation between the two developed into a fight and the victim was stabbed to death. The defendant entered a guilty plea to the charge of second-degree murder. He has served prior prison terms for two armed robbery convictions.

SENTENCE:_____

Now look at the Minnesota sentencing guidelines in the chapter. What would be the sentence for each offender under the guidelines?

1. _____

2. _____

3. _____

Do you think the guidelines are too harsh, too lenient, or just right? Explain.

_____

_____

_____

_____

_____

_____

# CHAPTER 13

## CORRECTIONS

## LEARNING OBJECTIVES

After covering the material in this chapter, students should understand:

1.  the history of corrections, from the development of the penitentiary to reformatories to the rise and fall of rehabilitation, including the Pennsylvania and New York systems and community corrections;

2.  the nature of prisons by classification and the fragmented organization of corrections nationally;

3.  the nature of and problems facing local jails;

4.  institutions for women and private prisons;

5.  hypotheses that purport to explain increases in prison populations.


## CHAPTER SUMMARY

From the colonial days to the present, the methods of criminal punishments that are considered appropriate have variety. The development of the penitentiary ended corporal punishment. The Pennsylvania and New York systems competed with different ideas about the penitentiary. In 1870, the Declaration of Principles was written in Cincinnati and it contained critical ideas about reform and rehabilitation for prisoners. The administration of corrections in the U. S. is decentralized and scattered across all levels of government. Jails are distinct from prisons and usually to hold persons awaiting trial and persons who have been sentenced for misdemeanors to terms of less than one year. Prison populations have increased dramatically during the last ten years and there has also been a great increase in facilities and staff to administer them.


## CHAPTER OUTLINE

I.    INTRODUCTION

   A.   Corrections includes prisons, probation, parole, work camps, Salvation Army facilities, medical facilities, and other contexts.
   B.   More than 6.5 million adults and juveniles are given correctional supervision by more than 700,000 administrators, psychologists, officers, counselors, social workers, and others. One of every 20 men and one out of every 100 women in America either is being supervised in the community (on probation or parole) or is incarcerated.
   C.   One of every six African-American adult males and one of three African-American young males.
   D.   Corrections is a system authorized by all levels of government, administered by both public and private organizations, and with a total cost of over $50 billion yearly.

II. DEVELOPMENT OF CORRECTIONS

   A.   The Invention of the Penitentiary
        1.      18th century scholars and social reformers in Europe and America engaged in an almost complete rethinking of the nature of society and the place of the individual in it.

The Enlightenment, as the philosophical movement was called, challenged traditional assumptions by emphasizing the individual, the limitations on government, and rationalism.

2. At a time of overcrowded, tough jails, brutal corporal punishment, and rising levels of crime in Europe and the United States, the great period of correctional reform was launched.

3. According to Michel Foucault, the period following the French Revolution led to the elimination of torture as a public spectacle and the adoption of "modern" penal codes that emphasized selecting and modifying punishment to fit the individual offender.

4. Punishment moved away from the infliction of pain; instead, correctional intervention was to change the individual and set him or her on the right path.

5. John Howard (1726-1790), sheriff of Bedfordshire, England, wrote *The State of Prisons in England and Wales* (1777) which led to the development of the *penitentiary*.

   a. Howard described horrible prison conditions; led to creation by Parliament of house of hard labor. The institution would be based on four principles:
      i. a secure and sanitary building;
      ii. systematic inspection;
      iii. the abolition of fees; and
      iv. a reformatory regime.

   b. Prisoners were to be confined to solitary cells during the night, and to labor silently in common rooms during the day. The regimen was to be strict and ordered.

   c. Howard believed that the new institution (penitentiary) was to give criminals an opportunity for penitence (sorrow and shame for their wrongs) and repentance (willingness to change their ways), its purpose was to punish and reform.

   d. Howard's conception of the penitentiary was borrowed and implemented in Pennsylvania and New York.

B. Reform in the United States

   1. In the fifty years following 1776, emphasis shifted from the assumption that deviance was part of human nature to a belief that crime was a result of forces operating in the environment. If the humane and optimistic ideals of the new nation were to be realized, it must be possible to reform the criminal element of society.

   2. In the first decades of the nineteenth century, the creation of penitentiaries in Pennsylvania and New York attracted the attention of legislators in other states and also investigators from Europe.

   3. Visitors from abroad made it a point to include a penitentiary visit on their itinerary.

C. The Pennsylvania System

   1. The Philadelphia Society for Alleviating the Miseries of Public Prisons, formed in 1787 under the leadership of Dr. Benjamin Rush included a large number of Quakers. It urged replacement of capital and corporal (bodily) punishment by incarceration. The Quakers believed that criminals could best be reformed if they were placed in solitary confinement so that, alone in their cells, they could consider their deviant acts, repent, and reform themselves.

   2. Walnut Street Jail in Philadelphia (1790): provided for solitary confinement; each cell held one inmate and was small and dark (only six feet by eight feet, and nine feet high). No communications of any kind were allowed. It was from this limited beginning that the Pennsylvania system of *separate confinement* evolved based on premise of rehabilitation.

   3. Eastern Penitentiary near Philadelphia (1829) isolated inmates not only from the community but also from one another. In each cell was a fold-up steel bedstead, a simple toilet, a wooden stool, a workbench, and eating utensils. Light came from an eight-inch window in the ceiling. Solitary labor, Bible reading, and reflection were regarded as the keys to the moral rehabilitation.

        a.       The only human voice the prisoner heard would be that of a clergyman who would visit on Sundays.

    4.       However, the system soon proved unworkable. The Walnut Street Jail became overcrowded and a virtual warehouse of humanity. The Western Penitentiary (near Pittsburgh) also soon became overcrowded and was soon declared outmoded because isolation was not complete and the cells were too small for solitary labor. It was recommended for demolition in 1833.

D.    The New York System

    1.       Auburn penitentiary (1819): Under the Auburn system, prisoners were kept in individual cells at night but congregated in workshops during the day. In this *congregate system*, however, inmates were forbidden to talk to one another or even to exchange glances while on the job or at meals.

        a.       Cheaper because one guard could supervise an entire group of prisoners.

        b.       Reflected some of the growing emphases of the Industrial Revolution. The men were to have the benefits of labor as well as meditation. They were to work to pay for a portion of their keep.

    2.       American reformers saw the New York approach as a great advance in penology, and it was copied throughout the Northeast

    3        Advocates of both systems agreed that the prisoner must be isolated from society and placed on a disciplined routine. They believed that deviancy was a result of corruption pervading the community.

    4.       By the middle of the nineteenth century, reformers had become disillusioned with the results of the penitentiary movement. Deterrence and rehabilitation had been achieved in neither the New York nor the Pennsylvania systems nor in their copies.

        a.       It was seen as a problem of poor administration rather than as an indictment of the concept of incarcerative penalties.

E.    Prisons in the South and the West

    1.       Scholars neglect the development of the prisons in the South and the West.

    2.       In the South, the *lease system* was developed. This allowed businesses in need of workers to negotiate with the state for the labor and care of prisoners. Prisoners were leased to firms that used them in milling, logging, cotton picking, mining, and railroad construction.

    3.       Except in California, the prison ideologies of the East did not greatly influence penology in the West. Prior to statehood, prisoners were held in territorial facilities or federal military posts and prisons.

F.    The Reformatory Movement

    1.       Prisons had become overcrowded and understaffed. Discipline, brutality, and corruption were common as, for example, in Sing Sing Prison in New York.

    2.       In 1870 the newly formed National Prison Association (predecessor of today's American Correctional Association) met in Cincinnati and issued a Declaration of Principles, which sounded the trumpet for a new round of penal reform. Progressive penologists advocated a new design for *penology*.

        a.       The goal should be the treatment of criminals through their moral regeneration: the reformation of criminals, "not the infliction of vindictive suffering."

    3.       The Declaration of Principles asserted that prisons should be operated in accordance with a philosophy of inmate change that would reward reformation with release. Fixed sentences should be replaced by sentences of indeterminate length, and proof of reformation should replace the "mere lapse of time" in bringing about the prisoner's freedom.

4.     Elmira Reformatory (1876) under Zebulon Brockway, the superintendent, regarded education the key to reform and rehabilitation.
        a.     Brockway's approach at Elmira Reformatory was supported by legislation passed by New York providing for indeterminate sentences, permitting the reformatory to release inmates on parole when their reform had been assured.
        b.     Elmira used the "mark" system of classification in which prisoners earned their way up (or down) by following rules.
5.     Difficulties with reformatory movement: institutions frequently emphasized punishment rather than education and rehabilitation, and difficult to judge whether or not a prisoner had been reformed.

G.     <u>Improving Prison Conditions for Women</u>
    1.     Until the beginning of the nineteenth century, women offenders in North America and Europe were treated no differently than men. Both men and women were incarcerated together.
    2.     An English Quaker, Elizabeth Fry, led reform efforts in England after visiting London's Newgate Prison in 1813.
    3.     Women's Prison Association formed in New York in 1944. Elizabeth Farnham, head matron at Sing Sing Prison's women's wing sought to implement Fry's ideas in the United States. Her efforts were blocked by male supervisors and legislators.
    4.     The National Prison Association's Cincinnati meeting did not address the issue of women offenders.
    5.     Although the House of Shelter, a women's reformatory, was founded in Detroit after the Civil War, it was not until 1873 that the first independent female-run prison opened in Indiana. Within fifty years, thirteen other states had followed this lead.
    6.     Three principles guided female prison reform during this period:
        a.     the separation of women prisoners from men;
        b.     the provision of care in keeping with the needs of women;
        c.     the management of women's prisons by female staff.
    7.     Shortly after the establishment of the first federal prison for women (Alderson, West Virginia with Mary Belle Harris as warden), the reform movement had run its course and largely achieved its objective of establishing separate prisons.

H.     <u>Reforms of the Progressives</u>
    1.     Early twentieth century belief in state action to deal with the social problems of slums, vice, and crime. The Progressives believed that with the concepts of the social and behavioral sciences, rather than religious or moral precepts, they could rehabilitate criminals.
    2.     The new activists relied on the developments of modern criminology associated with a scientific approach to crime and human behavior known as the positivist school, which focused on the behavior of the offender.
    3.     Progressives emphasized two strategies:
        a.     The need to improve conditions in the environments they believed to be breeding grounds of crime.
        b.     Emphasize ways to rehabilitate the individual offender.
    4.     Progressives instituted the presentence report, with its extensive personal history, as a means to enable judges and correctional officials to analyze the individual's problem and to take action toward rehabilitation.
    5.     By the 1920s, probation, indeterminate sentence and parole, and treatment programs were being espoused by reform penologists as the instruments of this more scientific approach to criminality.

I.     <u>Rehabilitation Model</u>

1.    In 1930s, attempts were made to implement fully what became known as the rehabilitation model of corrections. Penologists using the newly prestigious social and behavioral sciences helped shift the emphasis of the postconviction sanction to treatment of criminals, whose social, intellectual, or biological deficiencies were seen as the causes of their illegal activities.

2.    The essential structural elements of parole, probation, and the indeterminate sentence were already in place in most states. Therefore, incorporating the rehabilitation model required only the addition of classification systems to diagnose offenders and treatment programs that would rehabilitate them.

3.    Because they compared their correctional methods to those used by physicians in hospitals, this approach was often referred to as the *medical model*. Under this approach, correctional institutions were to be staffed with persons who could diagnose the causes of an individual's criminal behavior, prescribe a treatment program, and determine when a cure had been affected so that the offender could be released to the community.

4.    After World War II, group therapy, behavior modification, counseling, and numerous other approaches all became part of the "new penology" emphasizing rehabilitation.

5.    Allocation of state budgets maintained a gap between the rhetoric of the rehabilitation model and the reality that institutions were still being run with custody as an overriding goal.

6.    The failure of these new techniques to stem crime, the changes in the characteristics of the prison population, and the misuse of the discretion required by the model prompted another cycle of correctional reform, so that by 1970s rehabilitation as a goal had become discredited.

J.    Community Model

1.    *Community corrections* was based on the assumption that the goal of the criminal justice system should be to reintegrate the offender into the community. Arose from sense of social disorder in turbulent 1960s and 1970s.

2.    It was argued that corrections should turn away from an emphasis upon psychological treatment to programs that would increase the opportunities for offenders to be successful citizens, e.g., vocational and educational programs.

3.    Programs attempted to help offenders find jobs and remain connected to their families. Correctional workers served as advocates for offenders.

4.    This swing trend was brief. By the middle of the 1970s the reform movement seemed so dispirited that many penologists threw up their hands in despair.

K.    Crime Control Model

1.    Legislators, judges and corrections officials responded in the 1980s and 1990s with a renewed emphasis upon incarceration as a way to solve the crime problem.

2.    Policy attacks were mounted against certain structures of rehabilitation including indeterminate sentences, treatment programs, and discretionary release on parole.

3.    States created "supermax" prisons and limited prisoners' activities. Some states banned weightlifting and college courses. Other places reinstituted chain gangs.

4.    The doubling of the probation and prison populations during the 1980s put such great pressure on correctional approaches that most states found they were only able to provide minimal services.

III.    ORGANIZATION OF CORRECTIONS IN THE UNITED STATES

A.    Fragmented Administration

1.    Each level of government has some responsibility for corrections, and often one level exercises little supervision over another. The federal government, the fifty states, the District of Columbia, the 3,047 counties, and most cities each have at least one facility

and many programs. State and local governments pay about 95 percent of the cost of all correctional activities in the nation.

    2.    Only about 200,000 adults are under federal correctional supervision because fewer activities constitute federal crimes.

    3.    In most areas, maintaining prisons and parole is the responsibility of the state, while counties have some misdemeanant jails but no authority over the short-term jails operated by towns and cities. Jails are operated mainly by local governments (usually sheriff's departments), but in six states they are integrated within the state prison system.

    4.    Most correctional activities are part of the executive branch of government, but most probation offices are attached to the judiciary and are paid for by county government. In addition, there is a division between juvenile and adult corrections.

B.    The Federal Corrections System

    1.    The U.S. Bureau of Prisons was created by Congress in 1930. Facilities and inmates are classified in a security-level system ranging from Level l (the least secure, camp-type settings such as the Federal Prison Camp at Tyndall, Florida) through Level 6 (the most secure, such as the U.S. Penitentiary, Florence, Colorado).

    2.    The federal prison population contains many inmates who have been convicted of white-collar crimes, although drug offenders are increasing. There are fewer offenders who have committed crimes of violence than are found in most state institutions.

    3.    Probation and parole supervision for federal offenders are provided by the Division of Probation, a branch of the Administrative Office of the United States Courts. Officers are appointed by the federal judiciary and serve at the pleasure of the court.

    4.    The Pretrial Services Act of 1982 required pretrial services to be established in each judicial district. Pretrial services officers must collect, verify, and report to the judge concerning information relevant to the pretrial release of defendants.

C.    The State Corrections System

    1.    Every state has a centralized department of the executive branch that administers corrections, but the extent of these departments' responsibility for programs varies.

    2.    Wide variation exists in the way correctional responsibilities are divided between the state and local governments.

D.    Community Corrections

    1.    Probation, intermediate sanctions, and parole are the three major ways that offenders are punished in the community.

    2.    In many states probation and intermediate sanctions are administered by the judiciary, often by county and municipal governments.

    3.    By contrast, parole is handled by state government. Parole boards are either part of the department of corrections or an independent agency. Parole supervision is handled by a state agency in each community.

    4.    Community corrections emphasizes the "least restrictive alternative," the idea that the criminal sanction should be applied only to the minimum extent necessary to meet the community's need for protection, the seriousness of the offense, and society's need for offenders to get their deserved punishment. To this end, probation and parole are geared to assist and reintegrate the offender into the community.

E.    State Prison Systems

    1.    State correctional institutions for adult felons include a great range of facilities and programs, including prisons, reformatories, industrial institutions, prison farms, conservation camps, forestry camps, and halfway houses. This variety does not exist for women.

2.  Most state prisons are generally old and large. Over half of the nation's inmates are in institutions with average daily populations of more than 1,000, and about 35 percent are in prisons built more than fifty years ago. Most inmates are in very large "megaprisons" that are antiquated and often in need of repair.

3.  State correctional institutions are classified according to the level of security.

a.  The maximum security prison (where 26 percent of state inmates are confined) is built like a fortress, surrounded by stone walls with guard towers and designed to prevent escape.

b.  The medium security prison (holding 49 percent of state inmates) resembles the maximum security prison in appearance, but is less rigid and tense. Prisoners have more privileges, and contact with the outside world through visitors, mail, and freer access to radio and television. Greater emphasis on rehabilitative programs.

c.  The minimum security prison (with 25 percent of state inmates) houses least violent offenders, principally white-collar criminals. The minimum security prison does not have the guard towers and walls usually associated with correctional institutions. Prisoners may live dormitory style or even in small private rooms rather than barred cells. There is a relatively high level of personal freedom: inmates may have television sets, choose their own clothes, and move about casually within the buildings.

i.  May be greater emphasis on treatment programs, work release, and opportunities for education.

F.  State Institutions for Women

1.  Only 6.6 percent of the incarcerated population are women. Thus there are relatively few institutions for women.

2.  A higher proportion of women defendants are sentenced to probation and intermediate punishments, partly as a result of males' more frequent commission of violent crimes.

3.  Female offenders are incarcerated in 141 institutions for women and 162 coed facilities.

4.  Institutions for women are often more pleasant that similar institutions for men.

5.  Because there may only be one prison in a state, women are often isolated from their families and communities.

G.  Private Prisons

1.  Idea that private businesses can run prisons effectively and inexpensively. Has long been used for specific services but only recently for entire prisons.

2.  The first privately operated correctional institution was juvenile facility in Pennsylvania in 1975. First adult facility for felons was in Kentucky in 1985. By 1994, eighty-eight private prisons for adults were in operation with a total capacity of 49,000 inmates in the eighteen states that allow them.

3.  The $1 billion per year private prison business is dominated by Corrections Corporation of America and Wackenhut.

4.  Cost comparisons between public and private facilities often do not include true costs, such as fringe benefits. In regard to flexibility, it is argued that because correctional space requirements rise and fall, private entrepreneurs can provide additional space when it is needed, and their contracts can go unrenewed when space is in oversupply. The daily cost for the Corrections Corporation of America reported for holding an inmate ($40) was less than the costs in most state prisons.

5.  Several private prisons have had highly-publicized problems with violence and poor conditions.

6.  Political, fiscal, and administrative issues remain:

a.  Ethical questions of the propriety of delegating social-control functions to persons other than the state--may be the most difficult to overcome.

         b.      Contractors might use their political influence to continue programs not in the public interest.

         c.      Labor unions have pointed out that the salaries, benefits, and pensions of workers in private prisons are lower than those of their public counterparts.

         d.      Questions remain about quality of services, accountability of service providers to corrections officials, and problems related to contract supervision.

    7.     Competition from private sector might be beneficial during era of financial constraints on government units that need new prison space.

## IV. JAILS: DETENTION AND SHORT-TERM INCARCERATION

Most people do not distinguish between jails and prisons. Prisons are at the federal or state level and house inmates with sentences of one year or more. Jails are local facilities for person awaiting trial.

A.     Origins and Evolution
1. Jails in the United States derived from feudal practices in twelfth-century England. The colonists brought the idea of the jail to America.

B.     The Contemporary Jail
1. There are 3,365 locally administered jails in the United States with the authority to detain individuals for more than forty-eight hours. The ten largest hold 20 percent of the nation's jailed inmates. The Los Angeles County Men's Central Jail holds more than six thousand inmates. Most jails, are much smaller: 67 percent hold fewer than fifty persons.
2. The U.S. jail has been called the "poorhouse of the twentieth century;" part detention center for people awaiting trial, part penal institution for sentenced misdemeanants, and part holding facility for social misfits of one kind or another taken off the street.
3. Local jails and short-term institutions in the United States are generally regarded as poorly managed custodial institutions.
      a.      Small jails are becoming less numerous because of new construction and new regional, multicounty facilities.

C.     Who Is in Jail?
1. There are an estimated 11 million jail admissions every year. Nationally, about 600,000 people are in any given day. Many people are held for less than twenty-four hours, others may reside in jail as sentenced inmates for up to one year, a few may await their trials for more than a year.
2. Ninety percent of jail inmates are men and under thirty years old. More than half are of color and most are low income with little education.

D.     Managing Jails
1. Jails are usually locally administered by elected officials (sheriffs or county administrators).
2. Traditionally jails have been run by law enforcement agencies. Sheriffs think of jail as merely an extension of law enforcement activities, but many serve corrections functions because half of jail inmates are sentenced offenders under correctional authority.
3. Function: primary function of jails is to hold persons awaiting trial and persons who have been sentenced as misdemeanants to terms of no more than one year.
      a.      Increasingly jails are housing sentenced felony offenders for whom space is lacking at the state prison. Others held in jail are persons awaiting transportation to prison, and persons convicted of parole or probation violations.
      b.      This backup in the flow has caused difficulties for judges and jail administrators who must often put misdemeanants on probation because there is no jail space available.

4.      The deinstitutionalization of mental patients in particular has shifted a new population to jails.  Many such people are unable to cope with urban living and come to the attention of the police upon reports that they are acting in a deviant manner that, although not illegal, is upsetting to the citizenry (urinating in public, appearing disoriented, shouting obscenities, and so on). The police must handle such situations, and temporary confinement in the lockup or jail may be necessary if no appropriate social service facilities are immediately available.

5.      Because of the great turnover and because local control provides an incentive to keep costs down, correctional services (i.e., recreation, medical, education, vocational) are usually absent or minimal.  Idleness may contribute to high levels of violence and suicides.

6.      The mixture of offenders of widely diverse ages and criminal histories is another often cited problem in U.S. jails. Because most inmates are viewed as temporary residents, little attempt is made to classify them for either security or treatment purposes. Horror stories of the mistreatment of young offenders by older, stronger, and more violent inmates occasionally come to public attention.

V.      CORRECTIONAL POLICY TRENDS

A.      General Demographic Development
1.      Since the mid 1970s, the size of the prison population has risen dramatically. This has meant a 500 percent increase in budgets, more than 3.8 million persons on probation, 750,000 under parole supervision and 2 million persons in prison and jails.

B.      Community Corrections
1.      Escalating prison grown has captured the public's attention, yet the number of person's on probation and parole has grown dramatically. Why? Because of more arrests, successful prosecutions and the lower costs of probation compared to incarceration.
2.      POLICY DEBATE: Is there a Prison-Commercial Complex? Are corporations expanding their domain by working with legislators who are getting "tough on crime?" or is prison expansion simply related to the need for increased space to house more serious offenders?

C.      Probation
1.      People on probation make up over seventy percent of the correctional population but resources such as money and staff have not risen accordingly.

D.      Parole
1.      The number of persons on parole has also grown rapidly. Over one-half million felons are released from prison each year and allowed to live within a community under supervision.

E.      Incarceration
1.      Since 1973, the incarceration rate has quadrupled but crime levels have stayed the same. In 2001, the nation's prison population rose only one percent which is the lowest since 1979. It is difficult to predict if this trend will continue.

F.      Comparative Perspective: Behind Bars in North America and Europe
1.      The incarceration rate in the United States is higher than that in any other  developed country. Even though crime rates are roughly the same in the U. S. and Europe, the incarceration in the U. S. is much higher.
2.      Courts in a number of states demanded that changes be made, because they viewed overcrowding as a violation of the equal protection and cruel and unusual punishment portions of the Bill of Rights.

3.	In most states prison construction has become a growth industry with massive public expenditures for new facilities that immediately become filled when they open.
4.	There are some regional differences in increases in prison populations.
5.	Five reasons often given to account for the growth of the American prison population:
    a.	Increased Arrests and More Likely Incarceration
    b.	Tougher Sentences: hypothesis is a hardening of public attitudes toward criminals during the past decade reflected in longer sentences, in a smaller proportion of those convicted being granted probation, and in fewer being released at the time of the first parole hearing.  Move toward determinate sentencing in many states means that many offenders are now spending more time in prison.
    c.	Prison Construction: the increased rate of incarceration may be related to the creation of additional space in the nation's prisons. Again, public attitudes in favor of more punitive sentencing policies may have influenced legislators to build more prisons.  If serious offenses are less common, judges will be inclined to use prison space for less harmful offenders.
    CLOSE-UP: Connecticut: Trying to Build Its Way Out
    d.	War on Drugs:  Crusades against illegal narcotics have produced stiff mandatory sentences by federal government and states.
    e.	State Politics: Election of "law and Order" governors associated with increases in prison populations even in states with lower crime rates than neighboring states.
    f.	Because of public attitudes, crime rates, and the expansion of prison space, incarceration rates are likely to remain high.  A policy shift may occur if taxpayers begin to object to the high costs.


## REVIEW OF KEY TERMS

Fill in the appropriate term for each statement

penitentiary
separate confinement
congregate system
penology
community corrections
minimum security
medium security
maximum security
women's prisons
Quakers
the Enlightenment
the Progressives
corporal punishment
Walnut Street Jail
Auburn penitentiary
Pennsylvania system
New York system
Elmira Reformatory
presentence report
rehabilitation model
medical model
reintegration
U.S. Bureau of Prisons

probation departments
jails
misdemeanants
pretrial detainees
private prisons
tougher sentencing
state politics
prison construction
increased arrests and more likely incarceration

1. _____ are frequently more pleasant than other institutions yet are often located in a single isolated, rural location.

2. _____ is the prison classification in which institutions permit some personal freedom and may look like college campuses.

3. _____ is the federal agency responsible for administering prisons.

4. _____ are offenders serving sentences of one year or less in jails.

5. _____ was a philosophical movement that emphasized the individual, limitations on government, and rationalism.

6. _____ was the analogy for the rehabilitation model which sought to hold offenders until they were cured.

7. _____ is a growing phenomenon in corrections as states seek ways to spend less money in administering correctional institutions.

8. _____ is the hypothesis which explains prison growth in terms of patterns of law enforcement and sentencing.

9. _____ is a penitentiary system developed in New York in which prisoners worked together silently during the day before being held in isolation at night.

10. _____ is an institution intended to isolate prisoners from society and from one another so that they could reflect on their misdeeds and repent.

11. _____ was an innovation from the Progressive era which permitted judges to learn more about individual offenders.

12. _____ is the hypothesis about prison population growth that acknowledges that legislatures have responded to the citizenry's fears by mandating stiffer punishments.

13. _____ constitute half of the people held in jails who are awaiting processing to determine whether they will be prosecuted or convicted of crimes.

14. _____ is a penitentiary system developed in Pennsylvania by the Quakers involving isolation in individual cells.

15. _____ is a branch of criminology dealing with the management of prisons and the treatment of offenders.

16. _____ was the first institution to establish the New York system for the penitentiary.

17. _____ is the hypothesis about prison population growth that posits that available cells will be used to house offenders no matter how serious the crime is (or is not) at any given moment.

18. _____ is the prison classification with fortress--like structures and an emphasis on security.

19. _____ is any of a series of punitive measures directed at the human body.

20. _____ is the underlying goal of Swedish corrections and community corrections in the United States.

21. _____ are frequently under the administration of the judiciary rather than corrections departments.

22. _____ is the hypothesis concerning prison population growth which attributes national growth figures to the political culture and elected officials in different locales.

23. _____ provided Zebulon Brockway's opportunity to demonstrate his ideas in action.

24. _____ is a model of corrections based on the assumption that the reintegration of the offender into society should be the goal of the criminal justice system.

25. _____ is a model based on behavioral and social sciences that emphasized treatment of criminals' deficiencies which caused them to commit crimes.

26. _____ are usually under the administration of local, elected law enforcement officials rather than corrections specialists.

27. _____ were primary reformers who helped to develop the Pennsylvania model of the penitentiary.

28. _____ is the prison classification that permits privileges and contact with the outside world yet contains prisoners who have committed serious crimes.

29. _____ comprised a twentieth-century reform movement that expressed faith in the government's ability to address social problems.

30. _____ is the first penitentiary model institution established in Philadelphia.

31. _____ is the penitentiary model that emphasized isolation in cells and the opportunity to repent.

32. _____ is the penitentiary model that emphasized silent work in large workrooms.

## REVIEW OF KEY PEOPLE

Michel Foucault
Zebulon Brockway
Benjamin Rush
Elizabeth Fry
John Howard

1. _____ was the English reformer who is associated with sparking reform for women offenders.

2. _____ was a French philosopher who analyzed the shift in criminal punishment away from a focus on inflicting pain on the body of the offender.

3. _____ was the prominent physician who spearheaded reform of criminal punishment, including opposition to capital punishment and corporal punishment.

4. _____ was the English reformer whose investigation of prison conditions led Parliament to enact reforms and sparked reform movements in England and the United States.

5. _____ was the American corrections specialist who advanced his ideas about reformatories while serving many decades as a corrections administrator.

## GENERAL PRACTICE QUESTIONS

The ____1____ led the reform movement which led to the establishment of ____2____, the first institution to implement the ____3____ of ____4____ as a means to encourage offenders to repent.

____5____ served as the warden of ____6____ in which he tried to put into practice his ideas for gearing the length and nature of incarceration to the reform of prisoners. Because of the emphasis on indeterminate sentences, these nineteenth century practices shared a similarity with the so-called ____7____ of the ____8____ which relied on science to determine when a prisoner had been cured.

____9____ are short-term holding facilities that contain both ____10____ serving short sentences and ____11____ awaiting completion of their cases.

# SELF-TEST SECTION

## MULTIPLE CHOICE QUESTIONS

13.1. How many adults are under some form of correctional control in The United States?
a) 1 million
b) 3.5 million
c) 6.5 million
d) 10.9 million
e) 20 million

13.2. What is the ratio of men under correctional control to the entire population of men ?
a) 1 out of every 5
b) 1 out of every 10
c) 1 out of every 20
d) 1 out of every 50
e) 1 out of every 100

13.3. What is the ratio of women under correctional control to the entire population of women ?
a) 1 out of every 5
b) 1 out of every 10
c) 1 out of every 20
d) 1 out of every 50
e) 1 out of every 100

13.4. What is the ratio of adult African-American men under correctional supervision to the entire population of African-American men?
a) 1 out of every 3
b) 1 out of every 6
c) 1 out of every 25
d) 1 out of every 75
e) 1 out of every 100

13.5. What is the ratio of African-American men in their 20s under correctional supervision to the entire population of African-American men in their 20s?
a) 1 out of every 3
b) 1 out of every 6
c) 1 out of every 25
d) 1 out of every 75
e) 1 out of every 100

13.6. How much money is spent on corrections annually?
a) $1 billion
b) $3 billion
c) $10 billion
d) $50 billion
e) $100 billion

13.7. Which countries spawned a movement in the eighteenth century known as the Enlightenment?
a) U. S. and Canada
b) England and France
c) Spain and Italy
d) Sweden and Denmark
e) Japan and China

13.8. Prior to 1800, who did Americans copy in using physical punishment as the main criminal sanction?
a) Europeans
b) Japanese
c) Africans
d) Mexicans
e) Chinese

13.9. As sheriff of Bedfordshire, England, who was especially influential in promoting the reform of corrections?
a) John Howard
b) Michel Foucault
c) Zebulon Brockway
d) Benjamin Rush
e) Elizabeth Fry

13.10. What law passed by Parliament called for the creation of a house of hard labor where offenders would be imprisoned for up to two years?
a) English Prison Association Act of 1870
b) Penitentiary Act of 1779
c) English Bureau of Prisons Act of 1930
d) London Newgate Prison Act of 1813
e) Walnut Street Jail Act of 1790

13.11. Who inspired the Philadelphia Society for Alleviating the Miseries of Public Prisons which formed in 1787?
a) John Howard
b) Michel Foucault
c) Zebulon Brockway
d) Benjamin Rush
e) Elizabeth Fry

13.12. What was the first penitentiary created by the Pennsylvania legislature in 1790?
a) Philadelphia Jail Institute
b) Pittsburgh Prison House
c) Auburn House
d) Walnut Street Jail
e) Sing Sing Prison

13.13. Who was the warden at the Auburn Penitentiary who was convinced that convicts were incorrigible and that industrial efficiency should be the overriding purpose of the prison?
a) John Williams
b) John Howard
c) Elizabeth Fry
d) Benjamin Rush
e) Elam Llynds

13.14. Which system rented prisoners to firms that used them in milling, logging, cotton picking, mining and railroad construction?
a) New York system
b) Pennsylvania system
c) lease system
d) Auburn system
e) loan system

13.15. The prison ideologies of the East did not greatly influence penology in the West, except for the state of...
a) Arizona
b) California
c) New Mexico
d) Oregon
e) Nevada

13.16. Which law passed by Congress restricted the employment of federal prisoners?
a) Federal Bureau of Prisons Act of 1930
b) Anticontract Law of 1887
c) Hatch Act of 1940
d) Pendleton Act of 1883
e) The Prisoners Services Act of 1982

13.17. What system based prisoner release on performance through voluntary labor, participation in educational and religious programs, and good behavior?
a) enlightenment system
b) congregate system
c) lease system
d) mark system
e) Walnut Jail system

13.18. What is a release under supervision which could be revoked if the offender did not live up to the conditions of his release?
a) mere lapse of time
b) corporal punishment
c) mark system
d) ticket-of-leave
e) lease system

13.19. When did the reformatory system start to decline?
a) around the Civil War
b) around World War I
c) around World War II
d) around the Korean conflict
e) around the Vietnam conflict

13.20. When and where was the Women's Prison Association was formed?
a) 1804 in Boston
b) 1844 in New York
c) 1903 in Cleveland
d) 1925 in Kansas City
e) 1987 in Las Vegas

13.21. Who was the head matron of the women's wing at Sing Sing (1844 to 1848), sought to implement Elizabeth's Fry's ideas but was thwarted by the male overseers and legislators and was forced to resign?
a) John Williams
b) John Howard
c) Elizabeth Farnham
d) Benjamin Rush
e) Zebulon Brockway

13.22. What was NOT addressed in the Cincinnati Declaration of Principles?
a) rewarding reformed prisoners with release
b) fixed sentences should be replaced with indeterminate sentences
c) the treatment of criminals through moral regeneration
d) the problems of female offenders
e) all of the above were addressed

13.23. When and where was the first independent female-run prison opened?
a) 1809 in Massachusetts
b) 1824 in New Jersey
c) 1873 in Indiana
d) 1953 in Missouri
e) 1976 in California

13.24. In the late nineteenth century, which of the following principles guided female prison reform?
a) the separation of women prisoners from men
b) the provision of care in keeping with the needs of women
c) the management of women's prisons by female staff
d) all of the above
e) none of the above

13.25. Who was the warden of the first federal prison for women which opened in Alderson, West Virginia in 1927?
a) Mary Belle Harris
b) John Howard
c) Elizabeth Farnham
d) Benjamin Rush
e) Elizabeth Fry


## TRUE/FALSE QUESTIONS

13.1. The Quakers played a large role in developing the Pennsylvania system.

13.2. The Declaration of Principles did NOT deal with the problems of female offenders.

13.3. Since the 1700s, Women and men have been treated differently in prison.

13.4. Group therapy became part of rehabilitation after World War II.

13.5. John Howard was the first prisoner executed at Sing Sing prison.

13.6. From 1776-1826, the emphasis shifted to a belief that crime was a result of forces operating in the environment.

13.7. Corrections cost less than one billion dollars a year.

13.8. The Enlightenment focused upon increasing the powers of government, group behavior, and irrationalism.

13.9. The Crime Control Model emphasized incarceration as a way to solve the crime problem.

13.10. The U. S. Bureau of Prisons was created by executive order in 1990.

13.11. Community corrections focuses on reintegrating the offender into society.

13.12. There are fewer adults under federal correctional supervision because fewer activities constitute federal crimes.

13.13. Women comprise roughly 35 percent of the incarcerated population.

13.14. Private run prisons do not exist anymore in the U. S.

13.15. Private prisons provide better security than government-operated prisons.

13.16. Private prisons are more expensive than government-operated prisons.

13.17. There is a difference between prisons and jails within the U. S. system.

13.18. Jails in the United States descend from feudal practices in twelfth-century England.

13.19. The primary function of jails is to hold persons awaiting trial and persons who have been sentenced for misdemeanors to terms of less than one year.

13.20. Most jails are at the county level.

# ANSWER KEY

<u>Key Terms</u>
1.    women's prisons
2.    minimum security
3.    U.S. Bureau of Prisons
4.    misdemeanants
5.    the Enlightenment
6.    medical model
7.    private prisons
8.    increased arrests and more likely incarceration
9.    congregate system
10.   penitentiary
11.   presentence report
12.   tougher sentencing
13.   pretrial detainees
14.   separate confinement
15.   penology
16.   Auburn
17.   prison construction
18.   maximum security
19.   corporal punishment
20.   reintegration
21.   probation departments
22.   state politics
23.   Elmira Reformatory
24.   community corrections
25.   rehabilitation model
26.   jails
27.   Quakers
28.   medium security
29.   the Progressives
30.   Walnut Street Jail
31.   Pennsylvania system
32.   New York system

<u>Key People</u>
1.    Elizabeth Fry
2.    Michel Foucault
3.    Benjamin Rush
4.    John Howard
5.    Zebulon Brockway

<u>General Practice Questions</u>
1.    Quakers
2.    Walnut Street Jail
3.    Pennsylvania system
4.    separate confinement
5.    Zebulon Brockway
6.    Elmira Reformatory
7.    medical model
8.    rehabilitation model
9.    jails
10.   misdemeanants

11.     pretrial detainees

<u>Multiple Choice</u>
13.1.     c
13.2.     c
13.3.     e
13.4.     b
13.5.     a
13.6.     d
13.7.     b
13.8.     a
13.9.     a
13.10.    b
13.11.    a
13.12.    d
13.13.    e
13.14.    c
13.15.    b
13.16.    b
13.17.    d
13.18.    d
13.19.    b
13.20.    b
13.21.    c
13.22.    d
13.23.    c
13.24.    d
13.25.    a

<u>True/False</u>
13.1.     T
13.2.     T
13.3.     F
13.4.     T
13.5.     F
13.6.     T
13.7.     F
13.8.     F
13.9.     T
13.10.    F
13.11.    T
13.12.    T
13.13.    F
13.14.    F
13.15.    F
13.16.    F
13.17.    T
13.18.    T
13.19.    T
13.20.    T

WORKSHEET 13.1: HISTORY OF CORRECTIONS

Imagine that you are the head of a state department of corrections during several eras of American history. Describe each of the following approaches to corrections as you would implement them to make them work as well as they could. Then describe the drawbacks of each approach.

Separate Confinement (Pennsylvania)

_____

_____

_____

_____

Drawbacks:_____

_____

_____

Congregate System (New York)_____

_____

_____

_____

Drawbacks:_____

_____

_____

Rehabilitation Model_____

_____

_____

_____

Drawbacks:_____

_____

_____

Community Model_____

_____

_____

Drawbacks:_____

_____

# WORKSHEET 13.2: CAUSES OF RISING PRISON POPULATIONS

Describe each of the theories used to explain the increase in imprisonment of offenders.

Tougher Sentencing_____

_____

_____

_____

Increased Arrests and More Likely Incarceration_____

_____

_____

_____

State Politics_____

_____

_____

_____

Construction_____

_____

_____

_____

War on Drugs_____

_____

_____

_____

Which theory do you believe provides the best explanation?  Explain why.

_____

_____

_____

_____

# CHAPTER 14

## PROBATION, INTERMEDIATE SANCTIONS, AND PAROLE

### LEARNING OBJECTIVES

After covering the material in this chapter, students should understand:

1. the assumptions underlying community corrections;

2. the evolution of probation, the nature of probation services, and probation revocation;

3. intermediate sanctions including fines, restitution, forfeiture, home confinement, community service, intensive probation, and boot camps;

4. the day-fine system in Germany;

5. the difficulties in implementing intermediate sanctions;

6. community programs following release;

7. the role of the parole officer;

8. problems facing parolees;

9. revocation of parole.

### CHAPTER SUMMARY

Community supervision through probation, intermediate sanctions, and parole are a growing part of the criminal justice system. Probation is imposed on more than half of offenders. Persons with this sentence live in the community according to conditions set by the judge and under the supervision of a probation officer.

Intermediate sanctions are designed as punishments that are more restrictive than probation and less restrictive than prison. The range of intermediate sanctions allows judges to design sentences that incorporate one or more of the punishments. Some intermediate sanctions are implemented by courts (fines, restitution, forfeiture), others in the community (home confinement, community service, day reporting centers, intensive supervision probation) and in institutions and the community (boot camps). Parolees are released from prison on the condition that they do not violate the law and they live according to rules designed to help them adjust to society. Parole officers are assigned to assist ex-inmates make the transition to society, and to ensure that they follow the conditions of their release. The problem of reentry has become a major policy issue.

### CHAPTER OUTLINE

I. COMMUNITY CORRECTIONS: ASSUMPTIONS

A. Background
   1. Tough sentences of incarceration imposed during the 1980s produced high costs for state governments. Helps to lead to questioning of whether all offenders need to be imprisoned.
   2. Even during the nineteenth-century reform period it was recognized that supervision in the community was a more appropriate means to bring about the

desired change in some offenders. The development of probation in the 1840s and the transplantation of parole from England in the 1880s best exemplify this approach.

3. Until the 1950s, however, many states still relied more on incarceration than on probation and parole, and it was not until the 1960s that a variety of community alternatives was developed.

4. In the late 1980s with prison crowding becoming a major national problem, there was new interest in creating a set of intermediate sanctions--intensive probation supervision, home confinement, and electronic monitoring.

5. *Community corrections* aims at building ties that can reintegrate the offender into the community: assumes that the offender must change, but it also recognizes that factors within the community that might encourage criminal behavior (unemployment, for example) must change, too. Four factors are usually cited in support of community corrections:

   a. Some offenders' background characteristics or crimes are not serious enough to warrant incarceration.

   b. Community supervision is cheaper than incarceration.

   c. If rehabilitation is measured by recidivism rates, prison is no more effective than community supervision. In fact, some studies show that just being in prison raises the offender's potential for recidivism.

   d. Incarceration is more destructive to both the offender and society. In addition to the pains of imprisonment and the harmful effects of prison life, there is the suffering of family members, particularly the children of women offenders.

6. Central to the community corrections approach is a belief in the "least restrictive alternative," the notion that the criminal sanction should be applied only to the minimum extent necessary to meet the community's need for protection, the gravity of the offense, and society's need for deserved punishment.

II. PROBATION: CORRECTION WITHOUT INCARCERATION

A    Overview

1. Probation denotes the conditional release of the offender into the community under supervision. It imposes conditions and retains the authority of the sentencing court to modify the conditions of sentence or to re-sentence the offender. Conditions may include drug tests, curfews, and orders to stay away from certain people or parts of town.

2. Judges may impose a prison term but then suspend execution of that sentence and instead place the offender on probation.

3. Shock probation or split sentence involves brief incarceration followed by probation.

4. Probation may be combined with other sanctions, such as fines, restitution, or community service.

5. The probationer who violates these terms or is arrested for another offense may have probation revoked and be sent to prison.

6. The number of probationers is at a record level and is still rising. Prison overcrowding forces judges to place more offenders convicted of serious crimes, especially drug crimes, on probation. This means that probation will be dealing with an increasing number of clients whose risk of recidivating is high.

7. The public frequently views probation as merely a "slap on the wrist."

8. Probation officers frequently have high case-loads that make it difficult to provide adequate supervision.

B.    Origins and Evolution of Probation

1. Historical antecedents for probation can be found in the procedures of reprieves and pardons of early English courts.
2. John Augustus, a prosperous Bostonian, has become known as the world's first probation officer. By persuading a judge in the Boston Police Court to place a convicted offender in his custody for a brief period, Augustus was able to assist his probationer so that the man appeared to be rehabilitated when he returned for sentencing.
3. Massachusetts developed the first statewide probation system in 1880, and by 1920 twenty-one other states had followed suit. The federal courts were authorized to hire probation officers in 1925, and by the beginning of World War II forty-four states had implemented the concept.
4. Probation officers began with a casework model to be actively involved in the family, employment, free time, and religion of first-time and minor offenders.
5. With the rising influence of psychology in the 1920s, the probation officer continued as a caseworker, but the emphasis moved to therapeutic counseling in the office rather than on assistance in the field. This shift in emphasis brought a number of important changes.
   a. The officer was no longer primarily a community supervisor charged with enforcing a particular morality.
   b. The officer became more of a clinical social worker whose goal was to help the offender solve psychological and social problems.
   c. The offender was expected to become actively involved in the treatment program.
   d. In keeping with the goals of the Rehabilitation Model, the probation officer had extensive discretion to diagnose the problem and treat it.
6. During the 1960s, perhaps reflecting the emphasis of the war on poverty, a third shift occurred: rather than counseling offenders in their offices, probation officers provided them with concrete social services, such as assistance with employment, housing, finances, and education.
   a. Instead of being a counselor or therapist, the probation officer was to be an advocate, dealing with the private and public institutions on the offender's behalf.
7. In the late 1970s the orientation of probation again changed. The goals of rehabilitation and reintegration gave way to an orientation widely referred to as risk control. This approach, dominant today, tries to minimize the probability that an offender will commit a new crime.
   a. The amount and type of supervision provided are a function of estimates of risk that the probationer will return to criminal behavior.

C. Organization of Probation
   1. Probation may be viewed as a form of corrections, but in many states it is administered by the judiciary, usually with local control.
   2. Locally based probation accounts for about two thirds of all persons under probation supervision.
   3. Frequently the locally elected county judges are really in charge. However, judges usually know little about corrections and probation administration.
   4. Perhaps the strongest argument in favor of judicial control is that probation works best when there is a close relationship between the judge and the supervising officer.
   5. Some states have combined probation and parole in the same department, even though parolees are quite different than probationers. Parolees need greater supervision and have significant adjustment problems when they come out of prison.

D. Probation Services

1.        Probation officers have come to be expected to act as both police personnel and social workers. They prepare presentence reports for the courts and they supervise clients in order to keep them out of trouble and to assist them in the community.

        a.     Individual officers may emphasize one role over the other, and the potential for conflict is great.

        b.     Studies have shown that most probation officers have backgrounds in social service and are partial to that role.

2.        The 50-unit caseload established in the 1930s by the National Probation Association was reduced to 35 by the President's Commission in 1967; yet the national average is currently about 150, and in extreme cases it reaches more than 300.

3.        However, recent evidence indicates that the size of the caseload is less significant than the nature of the supervision experience, the classification of offenders, the professionalism of the officer, and the services available from the agencies of correction.

4.        During the past decade probation officials have developed methods of classifying clients according to their service needs, the element of risk that they pose to the community and the chance of recidivism.

        a.     Probationers may be granted less supervision as they continue to live without violation of the conditions of their sentence.

5.        In dangerous urban neighborhoods, direct supervision can be a dangerous task for the probation officer. In some urban areas, probationers are merely required to telephone or mail reports of their current residence and employment. It such cases, which justification for the criminal sanction--deserved punishment, rehabilitation, deterrence, or incapacitation-- is being realized? If none is being realized, the offender is getting off free.

E.      Revocation and Termination of Probation

      1.     Revocation of probation can result from a new arrest or conviction or from failure to comply with a condition of probation. Since probation is usually granted in conjunction with a suspended jail or prison sentence, incarceration may follow revocation. In 1998 a national survey of probationers found that 59 percent of adults released from probation successfully completed their sentences, while only 17 percent had been reincarcerated.

      2.     Probation officers and judges have widely varying notions of what constitutes grounds for revoking probation. Once the officer has decided to call a violation to the attention of the court, the probationer may be arrested or summoned for a revocation hearing. Common reasons for revocation include failing a drug urinalysis test, failure to participate

in treatment, fleeing, arrest for a new crime, and failure to report to probation officer.

      3.     The current emphasis is on avoiding incarceration except for flagrant and continual violation of the conditions of probation, thus most revocations occur because of a new arrest or conviction. Some studies show that even serious misconduct will not necessarily lead to revocation.

Question of Ethics: Revocation

      4.     In *Mempa v. Rhay* (1967), the Supreme Court determined that a state probationer had the right to counsel at a revocation proceeding, but nowhere in the opinion did the Court refer to any requirement for a hearing.

      5.     In *Gagnon v. Scarpelli* (1973), the Supreme Court ruled that revocation of probation and parole requires a preliminary and a final hearing.

        a.   At these hearings the probationer has the right to cross-examine witnesses and to be given notice of the alleged violations and a written report of the proceedings.

        b.   The Supreme Court ruled that although there is no automatic right. to counsel this decision is to be made on a case-by-case basis. It is then that the judge decides upon incarceration and its length. If the violation has been minor, the judge may simply continue probation, but with greater restrictions.

F.  Assessing Probation
    1.    Critics argue that, especially in urban areas, probation does nothing. Because of huge caseloads and indifferent officers, offenders can easily avoid supervision and check in only perfunctorily with their probation officers. In such cases, probation has little effect on crime control.
    2.    Probation does produce less recidivism than incarceration, but researchers now wonder if this effect is a direct result of supervision or an indirect result of the maturation process.
        a.    Most offenders placed on probation do not become career criminals, their criminal activity is short-lived, and they become stable citizens as they get jobs and marry.
    3.    What rallies support for probation is its relatively low cost: keeping an offender on probation rather than behind bars costs roughly $1,000 a year, resulting in a savings to the criminal justice system of more than $20,000 yearly.
    4.    Due to prison overcrowding, today almost one-half of the nation's probationers have been convicted on felony charges.  In addition, upwards of 75 percent of probationers are addicted to drugs or alcohol.
        a.    Officers can no longer assume that their clients pose little threat to society and that they are capable of living productive lives in the community.
    5.    The new demands upon probation have given rise to calls for increased electronic monitoring and for risk management systems that will differentiate the levels of supervision required for different offenders.

III.  INTERMEDIATE SANCTIONS IN THE COMMUNITY

A.  Overview
    1.    Dissatisfaction with the traditional means of probation supervision and the crowding of American prisons has resulted in a call for intermediate sanctions that will allow serious offenders to be punished in the community.
    2.    Intermediate sanctions may be viewed as a continuum--a range of punishments that vary in terms of level of intrusiveness and control.
        a.    Probation plus a fine or community service may be appropriate for minor offenses while six weeks of boot camp followed by intensive probation supervision may be the deserved punishment for someone who has been convicted of a more serious crime.
        b.    Each individual intermediate sanction may be imposed singly or in tandem with others.

B.  Sanctions Administered Primarily by the Judiciary
    1.    All involve the transfer of money or property from the offender to the government, the judiciary is deemed as the proper branch to not only impose the sanction but also to collect that which is due.
    2.    *Fines* are routinely imposed today for offenses ranging from traffic violations to felonies. Recent studies have shown that the fine is used very widely as a criminal sanction and that probably well over $1 billion in fines are collected annually by courts across the country.
    3.    Fines are rarely used as the *sole* punishment for crimes more serious than motor vehicle violations.  In European countries, fines are much more commonly used as the sole punishment.
    4.    Judges cite the difficulty of collecting and enforcing fines as the reason that they do not make greater use of this punishment.  Judges report that fine enforcement, which is the judiciary's responsibility, receives a low priority.
    5.    Since offenders tend to be poor, the judges are concerned that fines would be paid from the proceeds of additional illegal acts.

a. Reliance on fines as an alternative to incarceration might mean that the affluent would be able to "buy" their way out of jail and that the poor would have to serve time.

6. Fines are used extensively in Europe, and they are enforced. They are normally the sole sanction for a wide range of crimes. The amounts are geared to the severity of the offense and the resources of the offender.

a. Sweden and West Germany have developed the "day fine:" fines levied are adjusted to take into account the differing economic circumstances of offenders who have committed the same crime.

b. Experiments with the day fine concept are now taking place in several states.

7. Fines are gaining increased attention from judges and criminal justice planners as they struggle with overcrowded jails and prisons and overwhelming probation caseloads.

8. Comparative Perspective: Day Fines in Germany: Could the Concept Work Here?

a. Achieve greater fairness by imposing different level of burden on offenders with different levels of affluence who have committed the same offense.

b. Eighty percent of those convicted in Germany receive a fine alone as punishment. One fine unit is the offender's net income for one day and the number of units depends on the seriousness of the offense.

c. There has been an increase in the use of fines with a decrease in the amount of short term incarceration.

9. *Restitution* is repayment to a victim who has suffered some form of financial loss as a result of the offender's crime.

a. It is only since the late 1970s that it has been institutionalized in many areas. It is usually carried out as one of the conditions of probation.

10. *Forfeiture*: With passage of the Racketeer Influence and Corrupt Organizations Act (RICO) and the Continuing Criminal Enterprise Act (CCE) in 1970, Congress resurrected forfeiture, a criminal sanction that received little use since the American Revolution.

a. Similar laws are now found in most states, particularly with respect to controlled substances and organized crime.

11. Forfeiture is seizure by the government of property derived from or used in criminal activity. Forfeiture proceedings can take both a civil and a criminal form. Using the civil law, property utilized in criminal activity (contraband, equipment to manufacture illegal drugs, automobiles) can be seized without a finding of guilt. Criminal forfeiture is a punishment imposed as a result of conviction at the time of sentencing. It requires that the offender relinquish various assets related to the crime.

a. An estimated one billion dollar's worth of assets was confiscated from drug dealers by state and federal officials during 1990.

b. In a 1993 opinion, the Supreme Court ruled that the Eighth Amendment's ban on excessive fines requires that there be a relationship between the seriousness of the offense and the property that is taken.

c. In a 1996 opinion, the Supreme Court permitted innocent property owners to lose their property if it was used by others for criminal purposes.

12. Concerns have been raised about law enforcement self-interest in forfeiture because the forfeited assets are often directed into the budget of the law enforcement agency initiating the action.

C. Sanctions Administered in the Community

1. With electronic monitoring, *home confinement*, a sentence imposed by a court requiring convicted offenders to spend all or part of the time in their own residence, has gained new attention from criminal justice planners.

a. Conditions are placed on permissible actions; some offenders are allowed to go to a place of employment, education, or treatment during the day, but must return to their residence by a specific hour.

b. Can be used as a sole sanction or in combination with other penalties and can be imposed at almost any point in the criminal justice process: during the pretrial period, after a short term in jail or prison, or as a condition of probation or parole.

c. There are estimates that 100,000 offenders are being monitored at any given time.

2. Two basic types of electronic devices are now in use.

   a. A continuously signaling device has a transmitter that is attached to the probationer. A receiver-dialer is attached to the probationer's home telephone. It reports to a central computer at the monitoring agency when the signal stops, indicating that the offender is not in the house, alerting correctional officials of the unauthorized absence.

   b. A second device uses a computer programmed to telephone the probationer randomly or at specific times. The offender has a certain number of minutes to answer the phone and to verify that he or she is indeed the person under supervision.

   c. The devices are both expensive and not fool-proof, although this punishment is much less expensive than incarceration. Offenders are often charged weekly fees to cover the costs of home monitoring.

3. Problems:

   a. Some criminal justice scholars have questioned the constitutionality of the sanction, saying that it may violate the Fourth Amendment's protection against unreasonable searches and seizures.

   b. Technical problems with the monitoring devices have dogged many experiments.

   c. Failure rates among those under house arrest may prove to be high. Being one's own warden is a difficult task and visits by friends and enticements of the community may become too great for many offenders.

   d. Some observers believe that four months of full-time monitoring is about the limit before a violation will occur.

4. *Community Service* is unpaid service to the public to overcome or compensate society for some of the harm caused by the crime; it may take a variety of forms, including work in a social service agency, cleaning parks, or assisting the poor.

   a. The sentence specifies the number of hours to be worked and usually requires supervision by a probation officer.

   b. Labor unions and workers criticize it, saying that offenders are taking jobs from crime-free citizens.

   c. Some experts believe that if community service is used as the sole sanction, the result will be that certain courts may allow affluent offenders to purchase relatively mild punishments.

5. *Day reporting centers* incorporate a potpourri of common correctional methods. For example, in some centers, offenders are required to be in the facility for eight hours, or to report into the center for urine checks before going to work. In others, the treatment regime is comparable to that of a halfway house—but without the offender living in a residential facility. Drug and alcohol treatment, literacy programs, and job searches may be carried out in the center.

   a. If only specially selected offenders are chosen for these centers, it is difficult to assess the centers' effectiveness.

6. *Intensive probation supervision* is a way of using probation as an intermediate punishment. It is thought that daily contact between the probationer and officer may cut rearrests and may permit offenders who might otherwise go to prison to be released into the community.

   a. Probation diversion places offenders deemed too risky for routine supervision under intensive monitoring.

   b. Institutional diversion selects low-risk offenders sentenced to prison and provides supervision for them in the community.

264

c.      Each officer has only twenty clients, and frequent face-to-face contacts are required. Because the intention is to place high-risk offenders who would normally be incarcerated in the community instead, it is expected that resources will be saved.

d.      Judges and prosecutors may like ISP because it gives the appearance of being "tough" on offenders by setting many specific conditions.

e.      ISP programs have higher failure rates, in part because officers can detect more violations through close contact.

f.      In several states, offenders have expressed a preference for serving a prison term rather than being placed under the demanding conditions of ISP.

D.      <u>Sanctions Administered in Institutions and Community</u>

     1.      *Boot camps* now operate in thirty states. They are all based on the belief that young offenders can be "shocked" out of their criminal ways if they undergo a physically rigorous, disciplined, and demanding regimen for a short period, usually three or four months, before being returned to the community for supervision. Programs sometimes referred to as "shock incarceration."

         a.      Like the Marine Corps, most programs emphasize a spit-and-polish environment and keep the offenders in a disciplined routine constantly to help build self-esteem.

         b.      On successful completion of the program, offenders are released to the community and remain under supervision. At this point probation officers take over, and the conditions of the sentence are imposed.

         c.      Critics believe that the emphasis on physical training does not get to the bottom of the real problems affecting young offenders.

         d.      Other critics note that shock incarceration builds esprit de corp and solidarity, characteristics that have the potential for improving the leadership qualities of the young offender and that when taken back to the streets may actually enhance a criminal career.

         e.      The director of Arizona's prisons asked for the elimination of boot camps because of the program's ineffectiveness.

     2.      Close-Up: After Boot Camp a Harder Discipline

E.      <u>Implementing Intermediate Sanctions</u>

     1.      In many states there is competition as to which agency will receive additional funding to run the intermediate sanctions programs. Probation organizations argue that they know the field, have the experienced staff, and --given the additional resources--could do an excellent job.

         a.      Critics of probation argue that the traditional agencies are hide-bound and not receptive to the innovations of intermediate sanctions.

     2.      A second issue concerns the type of offender given an intermediate sanction. One school of thought emphasizes the seriousness of the offense, the other concentrates on the problems of the offender.

         a.      Some agencies want to accept into their intermediate sanctions program only those offenders who *will* succeed. The agencies are concerned about their success ratio, especially as this factor might jeopardize future funding.

         b.      Critics point out that this strategy leads to "creaming" (i.e., taking the cream of the crop), taking the most promising offenders and leaving those with problems to traditional sanctions.

     3.      "Net widening" is the term used to describe a process in which the new sanction increases, rather than reduces the control over offender's lives. This can occur when a judge imposes a *more* intrusive sanction than usual, rather than the *less* intrusive option. For example, rather than merely giving an offender probation, the judge might also require that

the offender perform community service.

4.   Critics of intermediate sanctions argue that they have created:
    a.   Wider nets: Reforms increase the proportion of individuals in society whose behavior is regulated or controlled by the state.
    b.   Stronger nets: Reforms augment the state's capacity to control individuals through intensification of the state's intervention powers.
    c.   Different nets:  Reforms transfer or create jurisdictional authority from one agency or control system to another.

III.   PAROLE SUPERVISION IN THE COMMUNITY

A.   Conditions, Expectations, and Problems
    1.   Parolees are released from prison on condition that they do not further violate the law and that they live according to rules designed both to help them readjust to society and to control their movements.
        a.   These rules may require them to abstain from alcoholic beverages, to keep away from bad associates, to maintain good work habits, and not to leave the state without permission.
        b.   Question:  Should parolees be subject to restrictions that are not placed on law-abiding citizens?
    2.   When they first come out of prison, parolees lack jobs, money, clothes, etc.  In most states they are given only clothes, a token amount of money, the list of rules governing their conditional release, and the name and address of the parole supervisor to whom they must report within twenty-four hours.
    3.   Parolees often lack job skills, cannot move to areas where jobs may be located, and face discrimination because of their criminal record -- are even barred from some jobs by state laws against employing "ex-cons" in certain positions.
        a.   Many parolees just do not have the social, psychological, and material resources to adequately cope with the temptations and complications of modern life.
        b.   Many face difficulties in leaving the highly structured environment of prison.
    4.   CLOSE-UP:  Returning to America. Prisoner's description of being free in New York City after sixteen years in a maximum-security prison.

B.   Community Programs Following Release
    1.   Some programs provide employment and housing assistance in the community following release. Other programs are designed to prepare the prisoner prior to release for life in the community through evaluation and testing so that the individual can steadily move toward reintegration into the community.
    2.   In pursuit of pre-release assistance, programs of partial confinement are used to test the readiness of the offender for full release.
    3.   Work and Educational Release:  By 1972 most states and the federal government had release programs that allowed inmates to go into the community to work or to attend school during the day and return at night to an institution.
        a.   Although most of the programs are justifiable in terms of rehabilitation, many correctional administrators and legislators like them because they cost little.
        b.   In some states, a portion of the inmate's employment earnings may even be deducted for room and board.
        c.   One of the problems of administering the programs is that the person on release is often viewed by other inmates as being privileged, and such perceptions can lead to social troubles within the prison.
        d.   Another problem is that in some states organized labor complains that jobs are being taken from free citizens.
        e.   The releasee's contact with the community increases the chances of contraband being brought into the institution. To deal with such bootlegging

and to assist in the reintegration process, some states and counties have built special work and educational release units in urban areas.

4.   Furloughs: Consistent with the focus of community corrections, brief home furloughs have come into increasing use in the United States. In some states an effort is made to ensure that all eligible inmates are able to use the furlough privilege on Thanksgiving and Christmas.

 a.   In other states, however, the program has been much more restrictive, and often only those about to be released are given furloughs.

 b.   Furloughs are thought to offer an excellent means of testing an inmate's ability to cope with the larger society. Through home visits, family ties can be renewed, the tensions of confinement lessened, and prisoners' morale lifted.

 c.   There are serious risks involved because of the inevitable public outrage if a prisoner on furlough commits a crime or disappears.

5.   Residential Programs: Community correctional centers are designed to reduce the inmate's isolation from community services, resources, and support.

 a.   Often these facilities are established in former private homes or small hotels, which permit a less institutional atmosphere. Individual rooms, group dining rooms, and other homelike features are maintained whenever possible.

 b.   "Halfway houses" range from secure institutions in the community with programs designed to assist inmates preparing for release on parole to shelters where parolees, probationers, or persons diverted from the system are able to live with minimal supervision and direction.

  i.   Some halfway houses are organized to deliver special treatment services, such as programs designed to deal with alcohol, drug, or mental problems.

  ii.   In the early 1980s it was estimated that there were about eight hundred halfway houses, most operated under contract by private organizations. Their average capacity was twenty-five residents, who stayed eight to sixteen weeks on average.

 c.   Problems of Residential Programs: Resistance from neighborhoods can produce major political issue.

 d.   It is difficult and expensive to provide high-quality, effective programs and services. Thus far the data on recidivism have been discouraging.

C.   Parole Officer: Cop or Social Worker?

1.   Parole officer is responsible for seeing that the conditions imposed by the parole board are followed.

2.   The conditions imposed by Connecticut's Board of Parole are quite substantial, and not atypical.

 a.   Must follow instructions of the Parole Officer.

 b.   Must report to your Parole Officer when instructed to do so and must permit your Parole Officer to visit you at your home and place of employment at any time.

 c.   Must work steadily, and you must secure the permission of your Parole Officer before changing your residence or your employment.

 d.   Must submit written reports as instructed by your Parole Officer.

 e.   Must not leave the State of Connecticut without first obtaining permission from your Parole Officer.

 f.   Must not apply for a Motor Vehicle Operator's License, or own, purchase, or operate any motor vehicle without first obtaining permission from your Parole Officer.

 g.   Must not marry without first obtaining written permission from your Parole Officer.

f.      Must not own, possess, use, sell, or have under your control at any time, any deadly weapons or firearms.

g.      Must not possess, use, or traffic in any narcotic, hallucinatory, or other harmful drugs in violation of the law.

h.      Must support your dependents, if any, and assume toward them all moral and legal obligations.

i.      Must not consume alcoholic beverages (or alternatively, must not consume them to excess).

j.      Must comply with all laws and conduct yourself as a good citizen. You must show by your attitude, cooperation, choice of associates, and places of amusement and recreation that you are a proper person to remain on parole.

3       COMPARATIVE PERSPECTIVE: Community Corrections in Japan: Probation, parole, and after-care services in Japan are characterized by the extensive participation of community volunteers.

4.      Huge caseloads make effective supervision practically impossible in some states. A national survey has shown that parole caseloads range from fifty to seventy; this is smaller than probation caseloads, but former inmates require more extensive services.

5.      Parole officers are asked to play two different roles: cop and social worker.

a.      As police officers, they are given the power to restrict many aspects of the parolee's life, to enforce the conditions of release, and to initiate revocation proceedings if violations occur.

b.      Like other officials in the criminal justice system, the parole officer has extensive discretion in low-visibility situations.

c.      The parole officer's broad authority can produce a sense of insecurity in the ex-offender and hamper the development of mutual trust, which is important to the parole officer's other roles in assisting the parolee's readjustment to the community.

d.      Parole officers must act as social workers by helping the parolee to find a job and restore family ties.

e.      Parole officers must be prepared to serve as agent-mediators between parolees and the organizations with which they deal and to channel them to social agencies, such as psychiatric clinics.

f.      Some researchers have suggested that parole officers' conflicting responsibilities of cop and social worker should be separated.

6.      Parole officers work in a bureaucratic environment. Due to limitations on resources and expertise, officers often spend more time with the recently released offenders and check only periodically on parolees who have proven themselves to be reliable.

D.      Adjustment to Life Outside Prison

1.      With little preparation, the ex-offender moves from the highly structured, authoritarian life of the institution into a world that is filled with temptations, that presents complicated problems requiring immediate solution, and that expects him to assume responsibilities to which he has long been unaccustomed.

2.      The "Dangerous" Parolee. Due to extensive news coverage of crimes committed by parolees, there has been public hostility and even physical attacks on parolees, especially released sex offenders. Many states have enacted notification statutes which require sex offenders to register their addresses on lists with the police that are made available to the public.

3.      It is perhaps not too surprising that the recidivism rate is high in light of the fact that the average felon who has served time in today's prisons has been convicted of serious crimes, has a criminal record of multiple arrests and prior incarcerations.

4.      The numbers indicate that a large percentage of today's inmates are career criminals who will resort to their old habits upon release.

E.  Revocation of Parole
   1.   Parole may be revoked for either committing a new crime or for violating the conditions of parole.
   2.   In some states, liberal parole policies have been justified to the public on the ground that revocation is swift and can be imposed before a crime is committed.
   3.   If the parole officer alleges that a technical (noncriminal) violation of the parole contract has occurred, a revocation proceeding will be held.
      a.   The U.S. Supreme Court, in the case of *Morrissey v. Brewer* (1972), distinguished the requirements of such a proceeding from the normal requirements of the criminal trial but held that many of the due process rights must be accorded the parolee.
      b.   The Court has required a two-step hearing process whereby the parole board determines whether the contract has been violated. Parolees have the right to be notified of the charges against them, to know the evidence against them, to be heard, to present witnesses, and to confront the witnesses against them.
      c.   Under the new requirements for prompt and fair hearings, parole boards are discouraging the issuance of violation warrants following infractions of parole rules without evidence of serious new crimes.
   4.   Data do not always distinguish between parolees returned to prison for technical violations and those sent back for new criminal offenses. One study found that 22 percent of state inmates were on parole at the time of their commitment. Eighty percent were returned to prison for a new criminal offense. The others violated parole conditions.
Parole violators represent an increasing portion of people committed to prison. There are differences among states in the percentage of parolees returned to prison for violations.

F.  The Future of Parole
   1.   In some places, an increased emphasis on parole supervision inevitably leads to detection of more violations. There is increased use of electronic monitoring and home confinement in some jurisdictions.
   2.   As prison populations rise, demands that felons be allowed to serve part of their time in the community will undoubtedly mount. These demands will come from legislators and corrections officers rather than from the public.
   3.   In states with discretionary release, parole provides one of the few mechanisms available to correctional officials to relieve institutional pressures.

V.  THE FUTURE OF COMMUNITY CORRECTIONS

A.  Growth and Questions
   1.   There were 1.4 million Americans under community supervision in 1980; by 1999 this figure had grown to 3.9 million, an increase of more than 250 percent.
   2.   Yet, despite its wide usage, community corrections often lacks public support, in part because it suffers from an image of being "soft on crime."
   3.   Offenders today require greater supervision based on their crimes, prior records, and drug problems when compared to those placed on probation in previous eras.
   4.   Probation needs an infusion of resources to fulfill its responsibilities during an era of prison overcrowding.
   5.   To garner support for community corrections, citizens must believe that these sanctions are meaningful.

# REVIEW OF KEY TERMS

Fill in the appropriate term for each statement

community corrections
*Morrissey v. Brewer*
halfway house
furlough probation
fines
restitution
parole in Japan
work and education release
forfeiture
home confinement
community service
day reporting centers
halfway house
revocation of parole
intensive probation supervision
boot camp
shock incarceration
*Mempa v. Rhay*
*Gagnon v. Scarpelli*

1. _____ is a sentence that uses electronic monitoring devices and restrictions on activities within the community.

2. _____ is a punishment involving supervision and restrictions while living in the community.

3. _____ is compensation for an injury one has inflicted that must be paid to the victim.

4. _____ was the decision requiring hearings before probation could be revoked.

5. _____ is a sentence requiring the offender to work on projects that benefit the town or city.

6. _____ is a short period of imprisonment before being placed on probation and other intermediate sanctions.

7. _____ is a place that probationers may be ordered to report to every day.

8. _____ is designed to rehabilitate offenders through probation, diversion, halfway houses, and parole.

9. _____ are sums of money to be paid to the state by a convicted person as a punishment for an offense.

10. _____ uses a military model to build discipline and self-esteem for young offenders.

11. _____ is the seizure by the government of property and other assets derived from or used in criminal activity.

12. _____ was the decision granting a right to counsel at some probation revocation hearings.

13. _____ relies on very few professionals who supervise a large number of volunteers within the community.

14. _____ provides for release during the day in order for prisoners to work or attend school.

15. _____ provides the U.S. Supreme Court's decision on required proceedings for parole revocation.

16. _____ is a supervised home for parolees within the community.

17. _____ provides a mechanism for temporary release for a few days in order to visit family and prepare for release on parole.

18. _____ is an institution, usually located in an urban area, housing inmates soon to be released and designed to help reintegration into society.

19. _____ can be the result of violations of parole conditions.

## REVIEW OF KEY PEOPLE

Michael Tonry and Mary Lynch
Franklin Zimring
Norval Morris and Michael Tonry
John Augustus

1._____ was the originator of probation as a volunteer, community activist in nineteenth century Boston.
2. _____ and _____ have urged that punishments be created that are more restrictive than probation yet match the severity of the offense and the characteristics of the offender, and that can be carried out while still protecting the community.
3. Criminal justice expert, _____, has said, "Boot camps are rapidly becoming yesterday's enthusiasm"
4. _____ and _____ have written the discouraging news that "Few such programs have diverted large numbers of offenders from prison, saved public monies or prison beds, or reduced recidivism rates"

## GENERAL PRACTICE QUESTIONS

Many intermediate sanctions can be applied in the context of ____1____ because offenders who must provide labor under a sentence of ____2____ or are subject to electronic monitoring under a sentence of ____3____ are not sent away to prison. Although the officers who supervise ____4____ may make some efforts to fulfill the ideal of rehabilitation, many intermediate sanctions actually stem from prison overcrowding rather than from other underlying purposes.

With young offenders, judges may apply either or both ____5____ involving military discipline or ____6____ to provide a taste of deprivation of freedom. Like other forms of sanctions, these two do not necessarily prevent young offenders from becoming repeat offenders as adults.

When ____7____ first established the idea of ____8____ by volunteering his own time and money, he never could have imagined how the practice would eventually evolve with such developments as Supreme Court decisions mandating due process rights including hearings before revocation, as demonstrated in the ____9____ decision.

# SELF-TEST SECTION

## MULTIPLE CHOICE QUESTIONS

14.1. When was probation developed in the American criminal justice
system?
a) 1790s
b) 1840s
c) 1870s
d) 1920s
e) 1980s

14.2. When was parole developed in the American criminal justice system?
a) 1790s
b) 1840s
c) 1870s
d) 1920s
e) 1980s

14.3. When were intermediate sanctions developed in the American criminal justice system?
a) 1790s
b) 1840s
c) 1870s
d) 1920s
e) 1980s

14.4. Which of the following factors is cited in support of community corrections?
a) Many offenders' criminal records are not serious enough to warrant incarceration
b) Community supervision is cheaper than incarceration
c) Rates of those returning to crime for those under community supervision are no higher than for those who go to prison
d) Ex-inmates require both support and supervision as they try to remake their lives in the community
e) all of the above

14.5. How many offenders are on probation in the American criminal justice system?
a) 100,000
b) 500,000
c) 2.3 million
d) 3.8 million
e) 6.5 million

14.6. Which state developed the first statewide probation system in 1880?
a) Delaware
b) New Jersey
c) Pennsylvania
d) Massachusetts
e) New York

14.7. According to the Bureau of Justice Statistics, how many adults released from probation successfully completed their sentences?
a) 17 percent
b) 28 percent
c) 59 percent
d) 76 percent
e) 96 percent

14.8. According to the Bureau of Justice Statistics, how many adults released from probation had been reincarcerated?
a) 17 percent
b) 28 percent
c) 59 percent
d) 76 percent
e) 96 percent

14.9. Which of the following would most likely cause a revocation of parole?
a) credit problems
b) parking ticket
c) marital problems
d) failing a drug test
e) all of the above would cause a revocation of parole

14.10. Which of the following would least likely cause a revocation of parole?
a) violating curfew
b) failing a drug test
c) using alcohol
d) rearrest
e) credit problems

14.11. How much does it cost to keep an offender on parole?
a) $1,000 a year
b) $5,000 a year
c) $20,000 a year
d) $40,000 a year
e) there is no cost

14.12. How much money is saved by keeping an offender on parole instead of in prison?
a) $1,000 a year
b) $5,000 a year
c) $20,000 a year
d) $40,000 a year
e) there is no savings

14.13. How many percent of probationers are addicted to drugs or alcohol?
a) 25 percent
b) 50 percent
c) 75 percent
d) 90 percent
e) 95 percent

14.14. Which of the following can be combined with probation?
a) fines
b) restitution
c) community service
d) all of the above
e) none of the above

14.15. Which country created the day-fine system in 1921?
a) Denmark

b) Sweden
c) United States
d) Germany
e) Finland

14.16. In what case did the U. S. Supreme Court rule that the Eighth Amendment's ban on excessive fines requires that the seriousness of the offense be related to the property that is taken?
a) Austin v. United States (1993)
b) Atkins v. Virginia (2002)
c) Ring v. United States (2002)
d) McClesky v. Kemp (1985)
e) Gregg v. Georgia (1976)

14.17. Which constitutional right might be violated by electronic monitoring and home confinement?
a) double jeopardy clause
b) cruel and unusual punishment clause
c) quartering of troops clause
d) unreasonable search and seizure clause
e) reserved powers clause

14.18. What law passed by the Wisconsin legislature established the model for work and educational release programs?
a) Walnut Hill Act
b) Release Program and Probation Act
c) Labor and Education Act
d) Intermediate Sanction and Rewards Act
e) Huber Act

14.19. During the 1960s, what shift occurred in probation?
a) offenders were given less probation
b) offenders began to refuse probation and select incarceration
c) offenders began to abuse probation
d) offenders were given assistance with employment, housing, finances, and education
e) offenders were given more counseling

14.20. In the late 1970s, how did the orientation of probation change?
a) emphasis was placed upon rehabilitation
b) efforts were made to minimize the probability that an offender would commit a new offense
c) emphasis was placed upon reintegration into society
d) efforts were made to eliminate probation
e) probation did not change during the late 1970s

14.21. Probation seems to work best when the...
a) judge and the victim of the offender have a close relationship
b) judge and the offender have a close relationship
c) judge and the supervising officer have a close relationship
d) judge and the community are in agreement on probation issues
e) judge and the defense attorney have a close relationship

14.22. Which of the following is an example of an intermediate sanction administered primarily by the judiciary?
a) home confinement

b) day reporting centers
c) forfeiture
d) all of the above
e) none of the above

14.23. Which of the following is an example of an intermediate sanction administered primarily inside institutions and followed by community
supervision?
a) boot camp
b) day reporting centers
c) forfeiture
d) all of the above
e) none of the above

14.24. Which of the following is an example of an intermediate sanction administered primarily in the community with a supervision component?
a) home confinement
b) fines
c) forfeiture
d) all of the above
e) none of the above

14.25. Why don't American judges prefer to impose fines on offenders?
a) judges do not have time to factor fines into the budget of the court
b) money and justice should not become intertwined
c) fines are usually embezzled by court officials
d) fines are too light of a punishment for even minor offenses
e) fines are difficult to collect from offenders who are predominately poor

**TRUE/FALSE QUESTIONS**

14.1. The day fine has never been used in the United States.

14.2. Before probation can be revoked, the offender is entitled to a preliminary hearing.

14.3. Before parole is revoked, the offender is NOT entitled to a preliminary hearing

14.4. Fines are used extensively in Europe as punishment.

14.5. In regard to forfeiture laws, owners' property cannot be seized if they can demonstrate their innocence by a preponderance of evidence.

14.6. Forfeited assets often go into the budget of the law enforcement agency taking the action.

14.7. Because incarceration rates and probation caseloads are decreasing, intermediate sanctions probably will not play a major role in corrections during the first decade of the new century.

14.8. In most states, laws prevent former prisoners from working in certain types of establishments.

14.9. Most work and educational release programs cost relatively little.

14.10. Parole officers are given little power to restrict the parolee's life.

14.11. Parole officers are granted law enforcement powers.

14.12. In Japan, citizen volunteers are involved in helping newly released offenders adjust to the community.

14.13. Conjugal visits have been used in most U.S. correctional systems.

14.14. Few released prisoners are subject to conditional community supervision release.

14.15. The size of a probation officer's caseload is often less important for preventing recidivism than the quality of supervision and assistance provided to probationers.

14.16. Many judges order community service when an offender cannot pay a fine.

14.17. There are few technical problems with electronic monitoring devices.

14.18. The legislative branch is largely responsible for administering intermediate sanctions.

14.19. Probation costs more than keeping an offender behind bars.

14.20. A state probationer has a right to counsel at a revocation and sentencing hearing.

Key Terms
1.  home confinement
2.  probation
3.  restitution
4.  *Gagnon v. Scarpelli*
5.  community service
6.  shock incarceration
7.  day reporting centers
8.  community corrections
9.  fines
10. boot camp
11. forfeiture
12. *Mempa v. Rhay*
13. parole in Japan
14. work and education release
15. *Morrissey v. Brewer*
16. halfway house
17. furlough
18. halfway house
19. revocation of parole


Key People
1.  John Augustus
2.  Norval Morris and Michael Tonry
3.  Michael Tonry and Mary Lynch
4.  Franklin Zimring

General Practice Questions
1.  community corrections
2.  community service
3.  home detention
4.  probation
5.  boot camp
6.  shock incarceration
7.  John Augustus
8.  probation
9.  *Gagnon v. Scarpelli*

Multiple Choice
14.1.  b
14.2.  c
14.3.  e
14.4.  e
14.5.  d
14.6.  d
14.7.  c
14.8.  a
14.9.  d
11.10. e
4.11.  a
4.12.  c
4.13.  
4.14.  d
14.15. e

14.16.　a
14.17.　d
14.18.　e
14.19.　d
14.20.　b
14.21.　c
14.22.　c
14.23.　a
14.24.　a
14.25.　e

True/False
14.1.　F
14.2.　T
14.3.　F
14.4.　T
14.5.　T
14.6.　T
14.7.　F
14.8.　T
14.9.　T
14.10.　F
14.11.　T
14.12.　T
14.13.　F
14.14.　F
14.15.　T
14.16.　T
14.17.　F
14.18.　F
14.19.　F
14.20.　T

WORKSHEET 14.1: PROBATION

If you were a judge, what kinds of offenders would you put on probation? What kinds of offenders would you *not* place on probation?

_____

_____

_____

_____

_____

_____

_____

If you were a probation officer. hich aspect of your job would receive your strongest emphasis: surveillance/rule enforcement or social services/counseling to help reintegration? Why?

_____

_____

_____

_____

_____

_____

_____

If you were a judge, what conditions/restrictions would you impose on probationers? Why?

_____

_____

_____

_____

_____

_____

_____

WORKSHEET 14.2: INTERMEDIATE SANCTIONS

Take the following intermediate sanctions and list them in order of the sanctions that you believe are most effective (1 for most effective and 8 for least effective). For each one, describe its strengths and weaknesses with respect to the goals that should be accomplished: fines, restitution, boot camps, intensive probation supervision, forfeiture, day reporting centers, community service, home confinement.

1. _____ : _____

_____

_____

2. _____ : _____

_____

_____

3. _____ : _____

_____

_____

4. _____ : _____

_____

_____

5. _____ : _____

_____

_____

6. _____ : _____

_____

_____

7. _____ : _____

_____

_____

8. _____ : _____

_____

# CHAPTER 15

## PRISONS:  THEIR GOALS AND MANAGEMENT

---

**LEARNING OBJECTIVES**

After covering the material in this chapter, students should understand:

1. the goals of incarceration, including the custodial model, rehabilitation model, and reintegration model;

2. prison management and organization;

3. the "defects of total power" and the co-optation of corrections officers;

4. correctional officers' role;

5. violence in prison, including contributing causes, and the role of age, attitudes, race, and gangs;

6. the development of prisoners' rights;

7. constitutional protections for prisoners from the First, Eighth, and Fourteenth Amendments.

**CHAPTER SUMMARY**

Since the 1940s, three models of incarceration have been prominent: 1) the custodial model which emphasizes the maintenance of security, 2) the rehabilitation model which views security and housekeeping activities as mainly a framework for treatment efforts, and 3) the reintegration model which recognizes that prisoners must be prepared for their return to society. Popular belief that the warden and officers have total power over the inmates is outdated. Good management through effective leadership can maintain the quality of prison life as measured by levels of order, amenities, and service. Because they are constantly in close contact with the prisoners, correctional officers are the real linchpins in the prison system. The effectiveness of the institution lies heavily on their shoulders. Since the 1960s, the prisoners' rights movement, through lawsuits in the federal courts, has brought many changes to the administration and conditions of American prisons.

**CHAPTER OUTLINE**

I. INTRODUCTION
Maximum security prison in Lucasville, Ohio erupted into a full-scale riot. Prisoners and correctional officers were killed in the process. This type of prison violence is infrequent but gains considerable attention from the public. It demonstrates the need to manage prisons effectively.

II. THE MODERN PRISON:  LEGACY OF THE PAST

A. Overview

1.  Although "big houses" predominated in much of the country during the first this century, some prisons, especially in the South, did not conform to this r There, racial segregation was maintained, prisoners were involved in farm l and the massive walled structures were not so dominant a form.

2.  The typical big house of the 1940s and 1950s was a walled prison made up of large, tiered cell blocks, a yard, shops, and industries. The prisoners, averaging about 2,500, came from both urban and rural areas, were poor, and, outside the South, were predominantly white.

3.  The prison society was essentially isolated; access to visitors, mail, and other kinds of communication was restricted. Prisoners' days were strictly structured, with rules enforced by the guards: custody was the primary goal.

4.  During the 1960s and early 1970s most penologists accepted the Rehabilitation Model of corrections. Many states built new facilities and converted others into "correctional institutions" that included treatment programs.

5.  During the past thirty years, as the population of the United States changed, so did that of the inmate population. The proportion of     African-American and Hispanic inmates increased, and inmates from urban areas became more numerous, as did inmates convicted of drug-related and violent offenses. The average age decreased.

6.  Former street gangs regrouped inside prisons, disrupting the existing inmate society, raising the levels of violence in many institutions.

7.  Finally, with the rise of public employees' unions, correctional officers were no longer willing to accept the paramilitary work rules of the warden.

8.  A great increase in the number of persons being held in prisons made most overcrowded and under increased tension. Humane incarceration seems to have become the contemporary goal of correctional administrators.

III.  GOALS OF INCARCERATION

A.  Three Models
1.  The plan for a particular model may have little relation to the ongoing process of corrections and the experience of the inmates. New terms may be adopted to reflect changes in day-to-day practices, yet actual conditions may differ dramatically from these descriptions.

2.  The *custodial model* is based on the assumption that prisoners have been incarcerated for the protection of society and for the purpose of incapacitation, deterrence, or retribution.
    a.  Emphasis on maintenance of security and order through the subordination of the prisoner to the authority of the warden.
    b.  Discipline is strict, and most aspects of behavior are regulated. This model was prevalent within corrections prior to World War II, and it dominates most maximum security institutions today.

3.  The *rehabilitation model* of institutional organization developed in 1950s.
    a.  Security and housekeeping activities are viewed primarily as a framework for rehabilitative efforts.
    b.  Professional treatment specialists enjoy a higher status than that accorded other employees, in line with the idea that all aspects of the organization should be directed toward rehabilitation.
    c.  Since 1970s, the number of institutions geared toward this end has declined. Treatment programs still exist in most institutions, but very few prisons can be said to conform to this model.

4.  The *reintegration model* is linked to the structures and goals of community corrections.

a. Prisons that have adopted the reintegration model gradually give inmates greater freedom and responsibility during their confinement and move them to a halfway house, work release program, or community correctional center before their being released under supervision.

b. The reintegration model is based on the assumption that it is important for the offender to maintain or develop ties with the free community.

5. Most prisons for men fall much closer to the custodial than to the rehabilitation or reintegration models. Treatment programs do exist in prisons but they generally take second place to the requirements of custody. In many correctional systems, regardless of the basic model, inmates spend the last portion of their sentence in a prerelease facility.

6. Prisons are expected to pursue many different and often incompatible goals; hence as institutions they are almost doomed to failure.

a. Charles Logan believes that the mission of prisons should focus on confinement. He argues that the essential purpose of imprisonment is to punish offenders fairly and justly through lengths of confinement proportionate to the gravity of their crimes.

IV. PRISON ORGANIZATION

A. Characteristics of Prison
   1. Unlike in other governmental agencies, prison managers:
      a. Cannot select their clients.
      b. Have little or no control over the release of their clients.
      c. Must deal with clients who are there against their will.
      d. Rely on clients to do most of the work in the day-to-day operation of the institution and to do so by coercion and without fair compensation for their work.
      e. Must depend on the maintenance of satisfactory relationships between clients and staff.

B. Three Lines of Command
   1. Because individual staff members are not equipped to perform all functions, there are separate organizational lines of command for the groups of employees that fulfill these different tasks of custody, prisoners' work assignments, and treatment.
   2. The custodial employees are normally organized along military lines, from warden to captain to officer, with accompanying pay differentials and job titles that follow the chain of command.
   3. The professional personnel associated with the using and serving functions, such as clinicians and teachers, are not part of the regular custodial organizational structure, and they have little in common with the others. All employees are responsible to the warden, but the treatment personnel and the civilian supervisors of the workshops have their own salary scales and titles.
   4. As a result of multiple goals and separate employee lines of command, the administration of correctional institutions is often filled with conflict and ambiguity.

V. GOVERNING A SOCIETY OF CAPTIVES

A. Authority: Perception and Reality
   1. Much of the public believes that prisons are operated in an authoritarian manner. Corrections officers presumably possess the power to give orders and have those orders obeyed.
   2. John DiIulio says that a good prison is one that "provides as much order, amenity, and service as possible given the human and financial resources."

284

     a.  *Order* is the absence of individual or group misconduct that threatens the security of others with, for example, assaults and rape.

     b.  *Amenity* is anything that enhances the comfort of the inmates such as good food, clean cells, recreational opportunities and the like.

     c.  *Service* includes programs to improve the life prospects of inmates: vocational training, remedial education, and work opportunities.

  3.  Four factors that make the governing of prisons different from the administration of other public institutions:

     a.  The defects of total power.

     b.  The limited rewards and punishments that can be used by officials.

     c.  The cooptation of correctional officers

     d.  The strength of inmate leadership.

B.  The Defects of Total Power

     Enforcing commands is an inefficient method of making them carry out complex tasks. Efficiency is further diminished by the realities of the usual 1:40 officer-to-inmate ratio and the potential danger of the situation. Thus correctional officers' ability to threaten the use of physical force is limited in practice.

  1.  Rewards and Punishments:  Since prisoners receive most privileges at the outset, there is little that can be offered for exceptional behavior.

  2.  Rewards may be in the form of privileges offered for obedience: *good time* allowances, choice job assignments, and favorable parole reports.

     a.  Problems:

       i.  Because prisoners are already deprived of many freedoms and valued goods--heterosexual relations, money, choice of clothing, and so on--there is little left to take away.

       ii.  The system is often defective because the authorized privileges are given to the inmate at the start of the sentence and are taken away only if rules are broken.

       iii.  Few additional authorized rewards can be granted for progress or exceptional behavior, although a desired work assignment or transfer to the honor cell block will induce some prisoners to maintain good behavior.

       iv.  Wardens are undoubtedly aware of the fact that their actions may be subject to legal action or censure by groups outside the prison.

  3.  Gaining Cooperation: Exchange Relationships
     Correctional officers obtain inmates' cooperation through the types of exchange relationships described in earlier chapters.

     a.  The housing unit officer is the key official in the exchanges within the custodial bureaucracy.  Handles roll call, searches, passes, etc.

     b.  The officers need the cooperation of the prisoners so that they will look good to their superiors, and the inmates depend on the guards to relax the rules or occasionally look the other way. Thus, guards exchange or "buy" compliance or obedience in some areas by tolerating violation of the rules elsewhere.

     c.  Secret relationships that turn into manipulation of the guards by the prisoners may result in the smuggling of contraband or other illegal acts.

     d.  Question of Ethics: Risk of officer being used by developing too much of a friendly relationship with a prisoner.

  4.  Inmate Leadership

     a.  These leaders may serve as the essential communications link between the staff and inmates.

b.      Inmate leaders distribute benefits to other prisoners and thereby bolster their own influence within the prison.

c.      However, today's prison population is divided along racial, ethnic, offense, and hometown lines so that there are multiple centers of power and no single set of leaders.

5.      The Challenge of Governing Prisons: Successful wardens have made their prisons "work" by the application of management principles within the context of a their own style of leadership.

6.      Close-Up: A Model Prison. Effort by warden to build a culture of respect with a prison.

VI.      CORRECTIONAL OFFICERS: THE LINCHPIN OF MANAGEMENT

A.      The Officer's Role

1.      The officer functions as a member of a complex bureaucratic organization and thus is expected to deal with clients impersonally and to follow formally prescribed procedures, yet must also face and cope with individual prisoners' personal problems. It is difficult to fulfill the varied and contradictory role expectations.

2.      Contemporary officers are crucial to the management of prison since they are in closest contact with the prisoners and are expected to perform a variety of tasks, including counseling, supervising, protecting, and processing the inmates under their care.

3.      Many correctional officers look back with nostalgia to the days when their purpose was clear, their authority was unchallenged, and they were respected by the inmates.

B.      Recruitment of Officers

1.      Studies have shown that one of the primary incentives for becoming involved in correctional work is the security that civil service status provides.

2.      In addition, prisons offer better employment options than most other jobs available in the rural areas where most correctional facilities are located. Because correctional officers are recruited locally, most of them are rural and white, in contrast to the majority of prisoners who come from urban areas and are either black or Hispanic.

3.      Salaries have been increased so that now the yearly average entry level pay runs between $16,000 in some southern and rural states to $30,000 in places such as New Jersey and Massachusetts.

4.      Special efforts have been made to recruit women and minorities. Women are no longer restricted to working with female offenders, and the number of correctional officers from minority groups has increased dramatically.

4.      For most correctional workers a position as a custody officer is a dead-end job. Though officers who perform well may be promoted to higher ranks within the custodial staff, very few ever move into administrative positions.

a.      Increasingly it is possible for college educated people to achieve administrative positions without having to advance up through the ranks of the custodial force.

C.      Use of Force

1.      Corrections officers can use force in five specified situations:

1.      Self-defense

2.      Defense of third persons

3.      Upholding prison rules

4.      Prevention of a crime

5.      Prevention of escape

VII.    VIOLENCE IN PRISON

A.      Assaultive Behavior and Inmate Characteristics
        1.      Crowded conditions; an angry, frustrated population, many with psychological problems and histories of violence; also ethnic conflict, etc.
        2.      Many well-known violent riots produced in such conditions: Attica (1971), Santa Fe, New Mexico (1980), Atlanta (1987), etc.
        3.      About 150 prisoners commit suicide each year. About 90 are killed by others and 400 die of undetermined causes, which likely includes some homicides. Annually, about 27,000 assaults by other inmates and 15,000 assaults against staff take place.
        4.      Great numbers of prisoners live in a state of constant uneasiness, always on the lookout for persons who might subject them to homosexual demands, steal their few possessions, or make their time more painful.
                Close-Up: On Prison Rape
        5.      *Age*:   Studies have shown that young people, both inside and outside prison, are more prone to violence than their elders. Not only do young prisoners have greater physical strength, they lack those commitments to career and family that are thought to restrict antisocial behavior.
                a.      Many young men have difficulty defining their position in society; thus many of their interactions with others are interpreted as challenges to their status. To be macho is, for one thing, to have a reputation for physically retaliating against those who make slurs on one's honor.
        6.      *Attitudes*: One of the sociological theories advanced to explain crime is that there is a subculture of violence among certain economic, racial, and ethnic groups. Arguments are settled and decisions made by the fist rather than by verbal persuasion. These attitudes are brought into the prison as part of an inmate's heritage.
        7.      *Race*:  Race has become the major factor that divides the contemporary prison population, reflecting tensions in the larger society. Racist attitudes seem to be acceptable in most institutions and have become part of the convict code. Violence against members of another race may be the way that some inmates deal with the frustrations of their lives both inside and outside of prison. Also prison gangs often organized along racial lines and this contributes to violence in prison.

B.      Prisoner-Prisoner Violence
        1.      Most of the violence in prison is inmate to inmate. Leads many prisoners to avoid contact with other prisoners, request isolation, etc.
        2.      Race and ethnic gangs are now linked to acts of violence in many prison systems. In essence the gang wars of the streets are often continued in prison.
                a.      Contributing to prison violence is the fact that gang membership is often on a "blood-in, blood-out" basis: A would-be member must stab a gang's enemy to be admitted, and once in cannot drop out without putting his own life in danger.
        3.      The only national survey to date concerning prison gangs found that they existed in the institutions of forty states and in the federal system.
                a.      Although the gangs are small, they are tightly organized and have even been able to arrange the killing of opposition gang leaders housed in other institutions.
                b.      Administrators say that the prison gangs, like organized crime groups, tend to pursue their "business" interests, yet they are also a major source of inmate-inmate violence as they discipline members, enforce orders, and retaliate against other gangs.

C.      Prisoner-Officer Violence

1.      Annually, more than 14,000 prison staff members were injured by inmate assaults.
2.      Violence against officers is situational and individual. Correctional officers do not carry weapons within the walls of the institution because a prisoner may seize them. Prisoners do manage to obtain lethal weapons and can use the element of surprise to inflict injury on an officer.
3.      In the course of a workday an officer may encounter situations that require the use of physical force against an inmate--for instance, breaking up a fight or moving a prisoner to segregation. Officers know that such situations are especially dangerous and may enlist the assistance of others to minimize the risk of violence.

D.    Officer-Prisoner Violence
1.      Unauthorized physical violence against inmates by officers to enforce rules, uphold the officer-prisoner relationship, and maintain order is a fact of life in many institutions.
     a.      In some institutions, authorized "goon squads" made up of physically powerful correctional officers use their muscle to maintain order and the status quo.
2.      Prisoner complaints about officer brutality are often given little credence until an individual officer gains a reputation for harshness. Wardens may feel that they must uphold the actions of their officers if they are going to maintain their support.
3.      Questions as to what is *excessive* force for the handling of particular situations are usually unclear.

E.    Decreasing Prison Violence
1.      Lee Bowker lists five factors contributing to prison violence:
     a.      inadequate supervision by staff members;
     b.      architectural design that promotes rather than inhibits victimization;
     c.      the easy availability of deadly weapons;
     d.      the housing of violence-prone prisoners near relatively defenseless prisoners;
     e.      a general high level of tension produced by close quarters.
2.      The social and physical environment of the institution also plays a part. Such variables as the physical size and condition of the prison, and the relations between inmates and staff all have a bearing on violence.
     a.      The massive scale of some institutions provides opportunities for aggressive inmates to hide weapons, carry out private justice, and engage in other illicit activities free from supervision.
     b.      As the prison population rises and the personal space of each inmate is decreased, we may expect an increase in antisocial behavior.
3.      The degree to which inmate leaders are allowed to take matters into their own hands may have an impact on the amount of violence among inmates.
4.      Corrections officials must be careful or they may be sued by prisoners who allege that the officials failed to create a safe environment.
5.      Effective prison management that provides few opportunities for attacks may decrease the level of assaultive behavior.

VIII.   PRISONERS' RIGHTS

A.    Historical Background
1.      Until the 1960s, the courts, with few exceptions, took the position that the internal administration of prisons was an executive, not a judicial, function. Judges maintained a *hands-off policy.*
     a.      Judges accepted the view that they were not penologists and that their intervention would be disruptive of prison discipline.
     b.      This was a continuation of a position taken in *Ruffin v. Commonwealth* (1871). In that case, a Virginia court said that

the prisoner "has, as a consequence of his crime, not only forfeited his liberty, but all his personal rights except those which the law in its humanity accords to him. He is for the
time being the slave of the state."

2.      The courts have become a new factor in the prison management equation. Prisoners now have access to the courts to contest decisions made by officers and aspects of their incarceration that they believe violate basic rights.

3.      In 1964, the Supreme Court ruled in *Cooper v. Pate* that prisoners may sue state officials over the conditions of their confinement such as brutality by guards, inadequate nutritional and medical care, theft of personal property, and the denial of basic rights. These changes had the effect of decreasing the custodian's power and the prisoners' isolation from the larger society. This case activated the use by prisoners of civil rights lawsuits under Title 42, Section 1983 of the U.S. Code.

4.      The first successful cases concerning prisoner rights involved the most excessive of prison abuses: brutality and inhuman physical conditions. Gradually, however, prison litigation has focused more directly on the daily activities of the institution, especially on the administrative rules that regulate inmates' conduct.

B.     First Amendment

1.      Prisoner litigation has been most successful with respect to many of the restrictions of prison life--access to reading materials, censorship of mail, and some religious practices--have been successfully challenged by prisoners in the courts.

2.      For example, in 1974 the Court said that censorship of mail could be allowed only when there is a substantial governmental interest in maintaining security. The result has been a notable increase in communication between inmates and the outside world.

3.      However, in 1987 (*Turner v. Safley*), the Court upheld a Missouri ban on correspondence between inmates by saying that such regulation was reasonably related to legitimate penological interests.

4.      Challenges concerning the free exercise of religion have caused the judiciary some problems, especially when the practice may interfere with prison routine.

5.      The arrival in the 1960s of the Black Muslim religion in prisons holding large numbers of urban blacks set the stage for litigation demanding that this group be granted the same privileges as other faiths (special diets, access to clergy and religious publications, opportunities for group worship). Many prison administrators believed that the Muslims were primarily a radical political group posing as a religion, and they did not grant them the benefits accorded to persons who practiced accepted religions.

     a.      *Fulwood v. Clemmer* (1962), the U.S. District Court of the District of Columbia ruled that correctional officials must recognize the Muslim faith as a religion and not restrict members from holding services.

     b.      In *Cruz v. Beto* (1972), the Supreme Court declared that it was discriminatory and a violation of the Constitution for a Buddhist prisoner to be denied opportunities to practice his faith comparable to those accorded fellow prisoners who belonged to conventional religions.

6.      However, in *O'Lone v. Estate of Shabazz* (1987), the Court ruled that a Muslim's rights were not violated when officials would not change his work schedule to permit him to attend Muslim religious services.

C.     Fourth Amendment

1.      The Fourth Amendment prohibits "unreasonable" searches and seizures and the courts have not been active in extending these protections to prisoners. Thus regulations viewed as reasonable in light of the institutions' needs for security and order may be justified.

     a.      *Hudson v. Palmer* (1984) upheld the right of officials to search cells and confiscate any materials found.

2.      Decisions strike a fine balance between the right to privacy and institutional goals. Body searches have been harder for administrators to justify than cell searches, for example, but they have been upheld when they are part of a clear policy demonstrably related to an identifiable legitimate institutional need and when they are not intended to humiliate or degrade.

3.      The introduction of female officers in men's prisons has raised new issues because of concerns that prohibitions on women guards undertaking body searches will deprive these officers of equal employment opportunities.

D.     Eighth Amendment

1.      Eighth Amendment's prohibition of cruel and unusual punishments leads to claims involving the failure of prison administrators to provide minimal conditions necessary for health, to furnish reasonable levels of medical care, and to protect inmates from assault by other prisoners.

2.      Three principal tests were initially applied by courts to determine whether conditions violate the protection of the Eighth Amendment:
       a.      Whether the punishment shocks the general conscience of a civilized society.
       b.      Whether the punishment is unnecessarily cruel.
       c.      Whether the punishment goes beyond legitimate penal aims.

3.      Subsequently the Court gave greater emphasis to examining whether prison officials showed "deliberate indifference" in inhuman conditions and practices (*Wilson v. Seiter*, 1991).

4.      The "*totality of conditions*" may be such that life in the institution may constitute cruel and unusual punishment. Specific institutions in some states and the entire prison system in other states have been declared to violate the Constitution.

5.      In several dramatic cases, prison conditions were shown to be so bad that judges have demanded change.
       a.      In 1980, *Ruiz v. Estelle* established judicial supervision of the Texas prison system that lasted for a decade.

6.      Many conditions that violate the rights of prisoners may be corrected by administrative action, training programs, or a minimal expenditure of funds, but overcrowding requires an expansion of facilities or a dropping of the intake rate. Prison officials have no control over the capacities of their institutions or over the number of offenders that are sent to them by the courts.

E.     Fourteenth Amendment

1.      Two clauses of the Fourteenth Amendment are relevant to the question of prisoners' rights-- those requiring (*procedural*) *due process* and *equal protection*--and have produced a great amount of litigation in the 1970s.

2.      The statutes of many states provide inmates with certain protections with regard to parole release, intraprison transfers, transfers to administrative segregation, and disciplinary hearings.

3.      Due Process in Prison Discipline: Administrative discretion in determining disciplinary procedures can usually be exercised within the prison walls without challenge.

4.      Yet in a series of decisions in the 1970s the Supreme Court began to insist that procedural fairness be included in the most sensitive of institutional decisions: the process by which inmates are sent to solitary confinement and the method by which "good time" credit may be lost because of misconduct.
       a.      *Wolff v. McDonnell* (1974) extended certain procedural rights to inmates: to receive notice of the complaint, to have a fair hearing, to confront witnesses, to be assisted in preparing for the hearing, and to be given a written statement of the decision. Yet the Court also said that there is no right to counsel at a disciplinary hearing.

b. The courts have emphasized the need to balance the rights of the prisoner against the interest of the state.

c. Most prisons have established rules that provide some elements of due process in disciplinary proceedings. In many institutions, a disciplinary committee receives the charges, conducts hearings, and decides guilt and punishment.

5. Equal Protection: Institutional practices or conditions that discriminate against prisoners on the basis of race or religion have been held unconstitutional. In 1968 the Supreme Court firmly established that racial discrimination may not be official policy within prison walls. Racial segregation is justified only as a temporary expedient during periods when violence between the races is demonstrably imminent.

a. Equal protection claims have also been upheld in relation to religious freedoms and access to reading materials.

F. Redress of Grievances

1. State prisoners file thousands of lawsuits annually in the lower federal courts under the Civil Rights Act of 1871 (42 U.S. C. 1983); they contest aspects of the conditions by which they are being confined.

a. For example, claims that the conditions of their confinement violate their rights, that they are not receiving proper medical care, that the state has lost items of their personal property, that they are not being protected from violent inmates, or that crowding limits their freedom.

2. Few of these suits are successful. Most petitions to the court are written without the assistance of counsel and are often filed in error because of misinterpretations of the law.

3. Courts have developed screening processes so that clerks evaluate the complaints. Most complaints are returned to the prisoner because of errors and have not been seen by the judge.

4. Some prisoners have prevailed. Some have received monetary compensation for neglect; others have been given the medical attention they desired; still others have elicited judicial orders that end certain correctional practices.

5. As a result of the increase in conditions-of-confinement cases, correctional authorities have taken steps to ensure that fair procedures are followed and that unconstitutional practices are eliminated.
Publication of institutional rules, obligations, and procedures is one of the first and most important steps required to meet this goal.

6. Most states have developed grievance procedures to address prisoners' complaints before they result in lawsuits.

G. A Change in Judicial Direction?

1. 1980s and 1990s Supreme Court decisions have slowed expansion of prisoners' rights and moved a few steps in the direction of a return to "hands off."

2. Under Chief Justice William Rehnquist, the Supreme Court is less sympathetic to such civil rights claims.

a. Court ruled in 1986 that prisoners could sue for damages in federal court only if officials had inflicted injury intentionally or deliberately.

b. *Wilson v. Seiter* (1991): the Court ruled that a prison's conditions of confinement are not unconstitutional unless it can be shown that prison administrators had acted with "deliberate indifference" to basic human needs.

c. Even with regard to First Amendment rights (inmate to inmate correspondence and attendance at Muslim religious services) the Court upheld policies.

3. Actions that will limit prison cases:

a. Congress enacted the Prison Litigation Reform Act which reduces both prisoners' access to the courts and judges' authority to issue remedial orders.

b.     *Lewis v. Casey* (1996) limited federal judges' power to make sure prisoners have adequate access to law libraries and legal assistance.

H.    Impact of the Prisoners' Rights Movement

1.    The prisoners' rights movement led to concrete improvements in institutional living conditions and administrative practices. Law libraries and legal assistance are now generally available; communication with the outside is easier; religious practices are protected; inmate complaint procedures have been developed; and due process requirements are emphasized.

2.    The prisoners' rights movement has clearly had an impact on correctional officials. The threat of suit and public exposure has placed many in the correctional bureaucracy on guard.

    a.    This wariness may merely lead to the increased bureaucratization of corrections, with staff now required to prepare extensive and time-consuming documentation of their actions as a means of protecting themselves from suits.

    b.    On the other hand, judicial intervention has forced corrections to rethink many of the existing procedures and organizational structures.

3.    After one hundred years of judicial neglect of the conditions under which prisoners were held, courts acted during the past thirty years to improve living conditions and fair procedures.

## REVIEW OF KEY TERMS

Fill in the appropriate term for each statement

good time
deliberate indifference
conditions of confinement
"big house"
Custodial Model
hands-off policy
Rehabilitation Model
Reintegration Model
totality of conditions
42 U.S.C. 1983
inmate leaders
Prison Litigation Reform Act
prison violence
gangs
equal protection
Ruffin v. Commonwealth
Cooper v. Pate
Fulwood v. Clemmer
Cruz v. Beto
Hudson v. Palmer
Wolff v. McDonnell
Lewis v. Casey
Turner v. Safley
Wilson v. Seiter
O'Lone v. Estate of Shabazz
Estelle v. Ruiz

1. _____ is the model of correctional institutions that emphasizes maintenance of the offender's ties to family and the community as a method of reform.

2. _____ represents the stereotypical picture of the prison as a walled fortress with tiered cell blocks.

3. _____ are often used by prison officials as a communication source between officials and the inmate population.

4. _____ is the federal statute used by prisoners to file civil rights lawsuits against prison officials.

5. _____ is the circumstance examined by the Supreme Court in prior decades to determine whether or not conditions inside a prison constitute unconstitutional cruel and unusual punishment.

6. _____ is the model of corrections that emphasizes security, discipline, and order.

7. _____ is a reduction of a convict's prison sentence at the discretion of correctional administrators as a reward for good behavior.

8. _____ is the key factor that the contemporary Supreme Court says must exist in the minds of prison officials in order to find unconstitutional conditions of confinement.

9. _____ is the right within the Fourteenth Amendment that prevents prison officials from engaging in racial discrimination.

10. _____ is the orientation that judges had toward prisoners' rights prior to the 1960s.

11. _____ is the model of corrections that emphasizes a treatment program designed to reform the offender.

12. _____ is the basis for Eighth Amendment claims that lead federal judges to issue orders that involve detailed aspects of prison administration.

13. _____ was an action by Congress to limit prisoners civil rights lawsuits.

14. _____ declared that prison officials' conduct would be viewed according to a subjective "deliberate indifference" standard.

15. _____ declared that prison officials did not have to rearrange a prisoner's work schedule in order to permit him to attend religious services.

16. _____ declared that a prisoner is a slave of the state and thereby lacks rights.

17. _____ declared that prisoners have no right to send correspondence to another prisoner.

18. _____ declared that officials may search cells without a warrant and seize materials found there.

19. _____ declared that prisoners are entitled to file civil rights lawsuits against government officials.

20. _____ declared that the Muslim faith must be recognized as a religion by prison officials.

21. _____ declared that the basic elements of procedural due process must be present when decisions are made concerning the discipline of an inmate.

22. _____ declared that prisoners who adhere to other than conventional beliefs may not be denied the opportunity to practice their religion.

23. _____ declared that conditions of confinement in the Texas prison system were unconstitutional.

24. _____ made it more difficult for federal judges to make sure prisoners have enough access to law libraries and other legal resources.

25. In male prisons, _____ is associated with youthful prisoners, specific attitudes, and racial conflicts.

26. _____ are prisoner organizations that are usually formed on a racial or ethnic basis.

## REVIEW OF KEY PEOPLE

Charles Logan
John Hepburn
Dennis Luther
Paul Knepper
Denise Jenne
Robert Kersting
John DiIulio

1. _____ is the scholar who focused on the role of correctional administrators in running prisons effectively.
2. _____ and _____ found that officers who played a human services role rather than a purely custody role had greater job satisfaction
3. _____ argues that the mission of prisons is confinement.
4. _____ argues that prison time should be spent preparing offenders for their return to the community.
5. _____ and _____ found that women officers tended to respond to violent situations as aggressively as their male co-workers.

## GENERAL PRACTICE QUESTIONS

In examining whether _____1_____ in prisons violate the Eighth Amendment prohibition on cruel and unusual punishments, courts previously focused on the _____2_____ in those prisons until the Supreme Court used its decision in _____3_____ to refocus judges' attention on the thoughts of corrections officials, especially the question whether they showed _____4_____ toward inhuman conditions.

Although many of its elements remain, the _____5_____ have created and enforced additional rules for their own members which also serve as guidelines for prison life. These additional rules may involve _____6_____ as a form of initiation or as a means of dealing with rivals.

## MULTIPLE CHOICE QUESTIONS

15.1. Prison organizations are expected to fulfill goals related to…
a) keeping custody of the inmates
b) using and working the inmates
c) treating inmates
d) all of the above
e) none of the above

15.2. Who studied the management of selected prisons in various states and found differences in leadership philosophy, political environment, and administrative style of individual wardens?
a) Dennis Luther
b) Paul Knepper
c) Denise Jenne
d) Robert Kersting
e) John DiIulio

15.3. Who is listed at the top of the formal organization of a prison?
a) warden
b) deputy warden
c) counselors
d) physicians
e) accountants

15.4. What is a sub-rosa relationship?
a) a homosexual relationship between prisoners
b) a secret relationship between a correctional officer and a prisoner
c) a violent relationship between a correctional officer and a prisoner
d) a violent relationship between prisoners
e) a friendly and open relationship between correctional officer and prisoner

15.5. Which of the following is TRUE about prisons?
a) prisons have multiple goals and separate lines of command
b) prison goals are characterized by simplicity and consensus
c) individual staff members are equipped to perform all functions
d) all of the above are TRUE
e) all of the above are FALSE

15.6. Which of the following is a situation when a correctional officer CANNOT use force?
a) self-defense
b) to defend a third person
c) when he/she has a right to be angry at an inmate
d) to prevent a crime
e) to prevent an escape

15.7. Correctional officers have been unionized since the…
a) 1960s
b) 1970s
c) 1980s
d) 1990s
e) they presently are not unionized

15.8. Which of the following restrictions has been successfully challenged in court by prisoners?
a) access to reading materials
b) censorship of mail
c) freedom of speech
d) rules affecting religious practices
e) all of the above

15.9. What is the concept of male honor and sacredness of one's reputation as a man?
a) good time
b) machismo
c) inmate code
d) in the life
e) gleaning

15.10. What law limited the authority of federal judges to intervene in the operations of correctional institutions?
a) Omnibus Crime Control Act of 1968
b) Prison Reform Litigation Act of 1996
c) Civil Rights Act of 1991
d) Prisoner Violation Act of 1999
e) there is no such law

15.11. Which of the following is a factor in prison violence?
a) age
b) race
c) attitudes
d) ethnicity
e) all of the above

15.12. On average, how many prisoners commit suicide every year?
a) 10
b) 50
c) 150
d) 1,000
e) 5,000

15.13. A program designed to educate members and eventually encourage them to renounce their gang membership is called...
a) deprogramming
b) deganging
c) in the life
d) machismo
e) gleaning

15.14. Which of the following is TRUE about prison gangs?
a) they are often large
b) they are loosely organized
c) they pursue business interests
d) they are not a source of inmate-inmate violence
e) none of the above are TRUE

15.15. In what state were the major prison gangs founded in the 1960s and 1970s?
a) Idaho
b) New York
c) California
d) Ohio
e) Arizona

15.16. How many state prisoners are in protective custody?
a) 1000
b) 5000
c) 10,000
d) 20,000
e) 50,000

15.17. Which of the following does NOT contribute to prison violence?
a) inadequate supervision by staff
b) boredom among prisoners
c) availability of deadly weapons
d) architectural design that promotes victimization
e) housing of violence-prone prisoners

15.18. How many inmates can be held in a megaprison?
a) up to 500
b) up to 1000
c) up to 3000
d) up to 10,000
e) up to 50,000

15.19. The U. S. Supreme Court ruled that prisoners do not have rights in…
a) Cooper v. Pate (1964)
b) Ruffin v. Commonwealth (1871)
c) Turney v. Safley (1987)
d) Fulwood v. Clemmer (1962)
e) Weeks v. U. S. (1914)

15.20. In what case did a federal court rule that officials must recognize the Black Muslims as a religion and allow them to hold worship services as do inmates of other faiths.
a) Fulwood v. Clemmer (1962)
b) Ruffin v. Commonwealth (1871)
c) Turney v. Safley (1987)
d) Wesberry v. Sanders (1964)
e) Weeks v. U. S. (1914)

15.21. The U. S. Supreme Court declared that a Buddhist prisoner must be given reasonable opportunities to practice his faith, like those given fellow prisoners belonging to religions more commonly practiced in the case of...
a) Fulwood v. Clemmer (1962)
b) Ruffin v. Commonwealth (1871)
c) Turney v. Safley (1987)
d) Baker v. Carr (1962)
e) Cruz v. Beto (1972)

15.22. The U. S. Supreme Court upheld the right of officials to search cells and confiscate any materials found in the case of .
a) Hudson v. Palmer (1984)
b) Ruffin v. Commonwealth (1871)
c) Turney v. Safley (1987)
d) Baker v. Carr (1962)
e) Cruz v. Beto (1972)

15.23. The U. S. Supreme Court ordered the Texas prison system to address a series of unconstitutional conditions in the case of...
a) Hudson v. Palmer (1984)
b) Ruffin v. Commonwealth (1871)
c) Turney v. Safley (1987)
d) Ruiz v. Estelle (1980)
e) Cruz v. Beto (1972)

15.24. The Supreme Court firmly established that racial discrimination may not be official policy within prison walls in the case of...
a) Lee v. Washington (1968)
b) Hudson v. Palmer (1984)
c) Ruffin v. Commonwealth (1871)
d) Turney v. Safley (1987)
e) Ruiz v. Estelle (1980)

15.25. The U. S. Supreme Court ruled that because of differences and needs, identical treatment is not required for men and women in the case of...
a) Lee v. Washington (1968)
b) Hudson v. Palmer (1984)
c) Ruffin v. Commonwealth (1871)
d) Pargo v. Elliot (1995)
e) Ruiz v. Estelle (1980

## TRUE/FALSE QUESTIONS

15.1. The custodial model emphasizes security and order.

15.2. Prison managers can select their own clients.

15.3. Prison managers must rely on clients to do most of the work in the daily operation of the institution.

15.4. The most numerous employees in prisons are the custodial workers.

15.5. The goals and lines of command often bring about clarity and consensus in the administration of prisons.

15.6. The use of force by correctional officers is a controversial issue.

15.7. Correctional officers are NOT allowed to rely on rewards and punishment to gain cooperation from prisoners.

15.8. Officers and prisoners are independent of each other.

15.9. In most of today's institutions, prisoners are divided by race, ethnicity, age, and gang affiliation, so that no single leadership structure exists.

15.10. Correctional workers are not responsible for returning inmates to the community no more angry or hostile than when they were committed.

15.11. Over the past twenty five years, the correctional officer's role has changed greatly.

15.12. Employment as a correctional officer is a glamorous and sought-after occupation.

15.13. Correctional officers who are women are NOT allowed to work with female offenders.

15.14. Few states have training programs for correctional officers.

15.15. A correctional officer may use force to protect an inmate or another officer.

15.16. The problem of sexual assault in prison gets too much attention from policy makers and the public.

15.17. Violent behavior in prisons is related to the age of the inmates.

15.18. Race has become a major divisive factor in today's prisons.

15.19. Prisoners have no right against cruel and unusual punishment.

15.20. Prisoners have freedom of religion.

# ANSWER KEY

<u>Key Terms</u>
1.    Reintegration Model
2.    "big house"
3.    inmate leaders
4.    42 U.S.C. 1983
5.    totality of conditions
6.    Custodial Model
7.    good time
8.    deliberate indifference
9.    equal protection
10.   hands off policy
11.   Rehabilitation Model
12.   conditions of confinement
13.   Prison Litigation Reform Act
14.   Wilson v. Seiter
15.   O'Lone v. Estate of Shabazz
16.   Ruffin v. Commonwealth
17.   Turner v. Safley
18.   Hudson v. Palmer
19.   Cooper v. Pate
20.   Fulwood v. Clemmer
21.   Wolff v. McDonnell
22.   Cruz v. Beto
23.   Estelle v. Ruiz
24.   Lewis v. Casey
25.   prison violence
26.   gangs

<u>Key People</u>
1.    John DiIulio
2.    John Hepburn and Paul Knepper
3.    Charles Logan
4.    Dennis Luther
5.    Denise Jenne and Robert Kersting

<u>General Practice Questions</u>
1.    conditions of confinement
2.    totality of conditions
3.    Wilson v. Seiter
4.    deliberate indifference
5.    gangs
6.    prison violence

<u>Multiple Choice</u>
15.1.    d
15.2.    e
15.3.    a
15.4.    b
15.5.    a
15.6.    c
15.7.    b
15.8.    e

| | |
|---|---|
| 15.9. | b |
| 15.10. | b |
| 15.11. | e |
| 15.12. | c |
| 15.13. | b |
| 15.14. | c |
| 15.15. | c |
| 15.16. | b |
| 15.17. | b |
| 15.18. | c |
| 15.19. | b |
| 15.20. | a |
| 15.21. | e |
| 15.22. | a |
| 15.23. | d |
| 15.24. | a |
| 15.25. | d |

True/False

| | |
|---|---|
| 15.1. | T |
| 15.2. | F |
| 15.3. | T |
| 15.4. | T |
| 15.5. | F |
| 15.6. | T |
| 15.7. | F |
| 15.8. | F |
| 15.9. | T |
| 15.10. | F |
| 15.11. | T |
| 15.12. | F |
| 15.13. | F |
| 15.14. | F |
| 15.15. | T |
| 15.16. | F |
| 15.17. | T |
| 15.18. | T |
| 15.19. | F |
| 15.20. | T |

WORKSHEET 15.1    PRISONS AND THEIR PURPOSES

If you were in charge of a state corrections department, how would you design your prisons?  For each
question, assume that the prisons have one primary purpose (listed below) and describe the physical
design, policies, and programs that you would implement to help the institution advance the overriding
goal.

1. CUSTODIAL MODEL_____

_____

_____

_____

_____

_____

_____

2. REHABILITATION MODEL_____

_____

_____

_____

_____

_____

_____

3. REINTEGRATION MODEL_____

_____

_____

_____

_____

_____

_____

_____

# WORKSHEET 15.2 : PRISONERS' RIGHTS: YOU ARE THE JUDGE

Corrections officers at the main gate receive a report that a fight involving twelve prisoners has broken out in Cellblock C and that the corrections officers in Cellblock C are unable to break up the fight. Seven corrections officers run down the corridor from the main gate toward Cellblock C. As they round a corner, they practically run into inmate Joe Cottrell who is mopping and waxing the corridor floor. One officer grabs Cottrell by the shoulders and throws him aside while saying, "Get out of the way!" Cottrell falls into a wall, dislocates his shoulder, and later files a lawsuit against the officer by claiming that the rough treatment and resulting injury violated his Eighth Amendment right against cruel and unusual punishment. Were his Eighth Amendment rights violated? Explain.

_____

_____

_____

_____

_____

_____

_____

_____

A prison chapel is used every Sunday for Christian services. A small group of prisoners reserve the chapel for each Tuesday evening where they meet to study an ancient religion from Asia that they claim to follow. For two years, they use the chapel every Tuesday to meditate and discuss books about their religion, and they do not cause any trouble. Then, one year Christmas falls on a Wednesday, and the Asian religion group is told that they cannot have their meeting because the chapel is needed for a Christian Christmas eve service. They file a lawsuit claiming that their First Amendment right to free exercise of religion is being violated because they cannot use the chapel on Christmas eve. Are their rights being violated? Explain.

_____

_____

_____

_____

_____

_____

_____

_____

# CHAPTER 16

## PRISON SOCIETY AND RELEASE

---

## LEARNING OBJECTIVES

After covering the material in this chapter, students should understand:

1. pecial populations, including the elderly, prisoners wit HIV/AIDS, and long-term inmates;

2. rison society, including adaptive roles, inmate code, and the prison economy;

3. omen in prison, including social relationships and differences between men's and women's prisons;

4. rison classification and programs;

5. elease mechanisms and their impact

6. roblems facing parolees;

7. evocation of parole;

8. ardons and civil disabilities of convicts.


## CHAPTER SUMMARY

In the United States, state and federal prisoners do not serve their time in isolation but are members of a subculture with their own traditions, norms, and leadership structure. Inmates deal with the pain of incarceration by assuming an adaptive role and lifestyle. Today, major problems in prison society consist of AIDS, an increase in elderly and the mentally ill inmates and inmates serving long terms. The state provides housing, food, and clothes for all inmates. To meet the needs of prisoners for goods and services not provided by the state, an underground economy exists in the society of captives. Most prisoners are young men with little education and disproportionately from minority groups. Only a small portion of the inmate population is female. This is cited as the reason for the limited programs and services available to women prisoners. Social relationships among female inmates differ from those of their male counterparts. Women tend to form pseudo-families in prison. Many women experience the added stress of being responsible for their children on the outside. Educational, vocational, industrial, and treatment programs are available in prisons. Educational programs reduce the risk of an inmate committing a crime upon release from prison. Administrators also believe these programs are important for maintaining order. Prison violence is a major problem confronting administrators. The characteristics of the inmates and the rise of gangs contribute to this problem. Most inmates will receive parole, but they face a multitude of problems such as finding employment and avoiding a return to the criminal life. In addition, parolees who committed felonies cannot vote or hold office. The executive branch of government at the state (governors) and federal (President) levels can issue pardons to inmates to remove the stigma of a conviction or remedy a miscarriage of justice.


## CHAPTER OUTLINE

I. WHO IS IN PRISON?

A. Inmate Characteristics

1.	Prison inmates are primarily repeat offenders convicted of violent crimes. Most prisoners are in their late twenties to early thirties, have less than a high school education, and are disproportionately members of minority groups.
2.	Close-Up: One Man's Walk Through Atlanta's Jungle Michael G. Santos

B.	Elderly Prisoners
1.	Longer sentences produce increasing numbers of elderly prisoners who have special security and medical needs.
2.	The average annual cost to the institution of caring for elderly prisoners is double or triple the cost for the average prisoner.
3.	Many elderly prisoners receive better medical care and nutrition than they would in the outside world because, if released, they would return to poor neighborhoods.
New Directions in Criminal Justice Policy: Release of the Elderly. Many states are considering releasing elderly prisoners because they are less dangerous and problems exist regarding overcrowding.

C.	Prisoners with HIV/AIDS
1.	The rate of HIV/AIDS among prisoners is five times higher than the general U.S. population.
2.	Prisoners who test positive create many challenges for preventing transmission of disease, housing infected prisoners, and medical care.

D.	Mentally Ill Prisoners
Mass closings of mental hospitals has increased arrests and incarceration of mentally ill people. High percentages of inmates in some facilities are classified as mentally ill. Correctional facilities and workers are often poorly prepared to deal with mentally ill prisoners.

E.	Long-Term Inmates
1.	More prisoners serve long sentences in the U.S. than in any other Western country.
2.	The average first-time offender serves about twenty-two months, but an estimated eleven to fifteen percent of all prisoners will serve more than seven years--this amounts to more than 100,000 people.
3.	Long-term prisoners are less likely to cause disciplinary infractions, but they present administrators with challenges for maintaining livable conditions.
4.	Timothy Flanagan says administrators adhere to three principles for long-term inmates:
a.	Maximize opportunities for choice in living arrangements.
b.	Create opportunities for meaningful living.
c.	Help inmates maintain contact with the outside world.

II.	THE CONVICT WORLD

A.	Prison Society
1.	Inmates in today's prisons do not serve their terms in internal isolation. They form a society with traditions, norms, and a leadership structure.
2.	Membership in a group affords mutual protection from theft and physical assault, serves as the basis of wheeling and dealing activities, and provides a source of cultural identity.
3.	The *Inmate Code*: the values and norms that emerge within the prison social system and help to define the inmate's image of the model prisoner. The code also helps to emphasize the solidarity of all inmates against the staff.
a.	For example: never rat on a con, be nosy, have a loose lip, or put another con on the spot.
b.	Guards are "hacks or screws", and the officials are wrong and the prisoners are right.

4. Some sociologists believe that the code emerges from within the institution as a way to lessen the pain of imprisonment.
5. Others believe that it is part of the criminal culture that prisoners bring with them.
6. Inmates who violate the code will probably spend their prison life at the bottom of the convict social structure, alienated from the rest of the population and preyed upon by other inmates.
7. A single overriding inmate code may not exist in some institutions. Instead, race has become a key variable dividing convict society.
8. In the absence of a single code accepted by the entire population, administrators find their task more difficult.
   a. They must be aware of the variations that exist among the groups, recognize the norms and rules that members hold, and deal with the leaders of many cliques rather than with a few inmates who have risen to top positions in the inmate society.

B. Adaptive Roles
   1. Newcomers entering prison must decide how to serve their time: isolate themselves from others or become full participants in the convict social system.
      a. This choice of identity is influenced by prisoners' values. Are they interested primarily in achieving prestige according to the norms of the prison culture, or do they try to maintain or realize the values of the free world?
   2. Four categories have been used to describe the lifestyles of male inmates as they adapt to prison:
      a. "Doing time" is the choice of those who try to maintain their links with and the perspective of the free world. They avoid trouble and         form friendships with small groups of inmates.
      b. "Gleaning" is taking advantage of prison programs. Usually inmates not committed to a life of crime.
      c. "Jailing" is the style used by those who cut themselves off from the outside and try to construct a life within the prison. Often "state-raised youth" who grew up in foster homes and juvenile detention centers.
      d. The "disorganized criminal" includes those who are unable to develop role orientations to prison life; often afflicted with low intelligence or psychological problems.
   3. Prisoners are not members of an undifferentiated mass; individual members choose to play specific roles in the convict society.

C. The Prison Economy
   1. In prison, as in the outside world, individuals desire goods and services that are not freely provided.
   2. Although in some institutions inmates may own television sets, civilian clothing, hot plates, etc., the prison community generally has been deliberately designated as an island of poverty in the midst of a society of relative abundance.
      a. Prisoners are limited as to what they may have in their cells, restrictions are placed on what gifts may come into the institution, and money may not be in the inmate's possession.
   3. Officials have created a formal economic system in the form of a commissary or "store" in which inmates may, on a scheduled basis, purchase a limited number of items--toilet articles, tobacco, snacks, and other food items--in exchange for credits drawn upon their "bank accounts" -- composed of money deposited on the inmate's entrance, gifts sent by relatives, and amounts earned in the low-paying prison industries.
   4. An informal, underground economy exists as a major element in the society of captives. Many items taken for granted on the outside are inordinately valued on the inside.
      a. For example, talcum power and deodorant take on added importance because of the limited bathing facilities.

5.  David Kalinich has documented the prison economy at the State Prison of Southern Michigan in Jackson. He learned that a complete market economy provided the goods and services not available to prisoners through legitimate sources.

    a.  This informal economy reinforces the norms and roles of the social system, influences the nature of interpersonal relationships, and is thus one of the principal features of the culture.

    b.  The extent of the economy and its ability to produce desired goods and services -- food, drugs, alcohol, sex, preferred living conditions--vary according to the extent of official surveillance, the demands of the consumers, and the opportunities for entrepreneurship.

6.  The standard medium of exchange in the prison economy is cigarettes. Because possession of coins or currency is prohibited and a barter system is somewhat restrictive, "cigarette money" is a useful substitute. Prison currency may change in the future as more prisons consider banning smoking.

7.  Almost every job offers possibilities for "swagging" (stealing from the state): e.g., kitchen workers steal food for trading.

8.  Economic transactions may lead to violence when goods are stolen, debts are not paid, or agreements are violated.

## III. WOMEN IN PRISON

A.  Research on Women in Corrections

1.  Women constitute only six percent (about 92,000) of the entire U.S. prison population. But the rate of growth of incarcerated women has been greater than that of men since 1981, primarily due to drug offenses. Since 1990, the number of men behind bars rose 77 percent; the number of women 108 percent.

2.  Women's prisons are smaller; security is less tight; the relationships between inmates and staff are less structured; physical aggression seems less common; the underground economy is less well developed; and female prisoners appear to be even less committed to the convict code than men now are. Women serve shorter sentences, and there is perhaps more fluidity in the prison society as new members join and others leave.

3.  Problems of remoteness and heterogeneity: Because only three states (Florida, Oklahoma and Texas) operate more than one prison for women and some operate none, inmates are generally far removed from their families, friends, and attorneys. In addition, because the number of inmates is small, there is less pressure to design programs to meet an individual offender's security and treatment needs. Dangerous inmates are not segregated from those who have committed minor offenses.

4.  Women prisoners are typically young, poorly educated, are members of a minority group, and incarcerated for a serious offense.

B.  The Subculture of Women's Prisons

1.  Female inmates tend to form pseudofamilies in which they adopt various roles--father, mother, daughter, sister--and interact as a unit.

    a.  Esther Heffernan views these "play" families as a "direct, conscious substitution for the family relationships broken by imprisonment, or. . . the development of roles that perhaps were not fulfilled in the actual home environment."

2.  Close-Up: Surviving in Prison

C.  Male versus Female Subcultures Compared

1.  Male versus Female Subcultures: concepts of adaptive roles, the inmate code, indigenous and imported values, the prison economy, and so on, have explanatory value in both types of institution.

2.  A principal difference between male and female prison subcultures is in interpersonal relations.

a. Male prisoners act as individuals and their behavior is evaluated by the yardstick of the prison culture; autonomy, self-sufficiency, and the ability to cope with one's problems.
b. In prisons for women, close ties seem to exist among small groups of inmates. These extended families may essentially provide emotional support and emphasize the sharing of resources.
c. There are debates among researchers about whether these differences reflect distinctive female qualities (e.g., nurturing, etc.).

D. Issues in the Incarceration of Women
Under pressures for equal opportunity, states seem to believe that they should run women's prisons as they do prisons for men, with the same policies and procedures. Joycelyn Pollock believes that when prisons emphasize parity, then use a male standard, women lose.

E. Sexual Misconduct: As the number of women prisoners has increased, cases of sexual misconduct by male correctional officers have escalated.

F. Programs and the Female Role
1. Major criticisms:
a. Women's prisons do not have the variety of vocational and educational programs available in male institutions.
b. Existing programs for women tend to conform to sexual stereotypes of "feminine" occupational roles: cosmetology, food service, housekeeping, sewing.
2. Vocational and educational opportunities during incarceration are crucial; both for speeding time in prison and improving life after prison. Upon release most women have to support themselves, and many are financially responsible for children as well; education and training are vital.
3. By the 1980s, increases had occurred in the availability of programs for women, including vocational programs such as business, computers, auto repair, etc.
4. Women's prisons also suffer from a relative lack of medical, nutritional, and recreational services.
5. Medical services: Women often have special or more serious medical problems. Pregnancies raise important issues because surveys show about 25 percent of incarcerated women were pregnant upon admission to prison or had given birth within the prior year.

G. Mothers and Children
1. The greatest concern to incarcerated women is the fate of their children. About 65 percent of women inmates are mothers and on average they have two dependent children; estimated total of 167,000 children in the United States--two-thirds of whom are under ten years of age--have mothers who are in jail or prison.
2. One recent study found that roughly half of these children do not see their mothers while they are in prison. Children were most often taken care of by their maternal grandmothers.
a. When an inmate had no relative who would care for the children, they were often put up for adoption or placed in state-funded foster care.
3. Enforced separation from children is bad for the children and bad for the mothers; source of significant stress and anxiety.
a. Mothers have difficulty maintaining contact: distance from prison, restrictive visiting hours, may be restrictions against physical contact during visits, etc.
b. Increasingly, programs are being developed to deal with the problems of mothers and their children (e.g. nurseries, playrooms, transportation arranged, etc.).

      c.      Some states permit overnight visits; may include husband in mobile home on prison grounds.

    4.      In most states a baby born in prison must be placed with a family member or social agency within three weeks, to the detriment of the early mother-child bonding thought to be important for the development of a baby. Some innovative programs make longer periods possible.

## IV.   PRISON PROGRAMS

### A.   Institutional Programs

1. Because the public has called for harsher treatment of criminals, legislators have reduced education and other programs in many states.
2. Administrators must use institutional programs to manage the problem of time. They know that the more programs they are able to offer, the less likely it is that inmates' idleness and boredom will turn to hostility. Activity is the administrator's tool for controlling and stabilizing prison operations.
3. Contemporary programs include educational, vocational, and treatment.

### B.   Classification of Prisoners

1. Determining the appropriate program for an individual prisoner is usually made through a classification process.
2. Most states now have diagnostic and reception centers that are physically separated from the main prison facility.
3. A classification committee usually consists of the deputy warden and the heads of departments for security, treatment, education, industry, and the like.
4. Unfortunately, classification decisions are often made on the basis of administrative needs rather than inmate needs. Prison housekeeping, for example, requires inmate labor to cook and mop floors.
    a.      Inmates from the city may be assigned to farm work because that is where they are needed.
    b.      What is most upsetting to some prisoners is that release on parole often depends on a good record of participation in treatment or educational programs, some of which may have been unavailable.

### C.   Educational Programs

1. Education programs are the most popular programs in prison. In many prisons, inmates who have not completed eighth grade are assigned full-time to a prison school. Many programs permit inmates to earn a high school equivalency diploma (GED).
2. In some facilities, college-level courses are offered through an association with a local community college. Federal law and the laws of many states are increasingly banning any educational programs beyond high school.
3. Studies have shown that inmates who were assigned to the prison school are good candidates to achieve a conviction-free record after release. Evidence has also suggested, however, that this outcome may be due largely to the type of inmate selected for schooling rather than the schooling itself.

### D.   Vocational Education

1. Programs in modern facilities are designed to teach a variety of skills: plumbing, automobile mechanics, printing, computer programming. Unfortunately, most such programs are unable to keep abreast of technological advances and needs of the free market.
2. Too many programs are designed to train inmates for trades that already have an adequate labor supply or in which new methods have made the skills taught obsolete.
3. Some vocational programs are even designed to prepare inmates for careers on the outside that are closed to former felons. The restaurant industry, for example, would seem to be a place

where former felons might find employment, yet in many states they are prohibited from working where alcohol is sold.

E.    Prison Industries
  1.    Some scholars now point to the early industries established at Auburn as a reflection of the industrialization of the United States and the need for prison to instill good work habits and discipline in potential members of the labor force.
  2.    Traditionally, prisoners have been required to work at tasks that are necessary to maintain and run their own and other state facilities: food service, laundry, and building maintenance jobs. Also prison farms produce food for the institution in some states.
  3.    Industry shops make furniture, repair office equipment, and fabricate items. Prisoners receive a nominal fee (perhaps 50 cents an hour) for such work.
  4.    During the nineteenth century, factories were set up inside many prisons and inmates manufactured items that were sold on the open market. With the rise of the labor movement, however, state legislatures and Congress passed laws restricting the sale of prison-made goods so that they would not compete with those made by free workers.
  5.    The 1980s saw initiatives promoted by the federal government efforts to encourage private-sector companies to set up "factories within fences" so as to use prison labor effectively.
  6.    A survey showed that the number of inmates employed within prisons ranges from more than 20 percent in states such as Utah and North Carolina to less than 5 percent in most states.
  7.    Prison industries are often inefficient due to turnover of prisoners, low education levels, and poor work habits. Also need good security to keep materials from being stolen by prisoners.

F.    Rehabilitative Programs
  1.    There is much dispute about the degree of emphasis that should be given to these programs and the types that should be offered.
  2.    Reports in the mid-1970s cast doubt on the ability of treatment programs to stem recidivism and raised questions about the ethics of requiring inmates to participate in such programs in exchange for the promise of parole.
  3.    In most correctional systems a range of psychological, behavioral, and social services is available to inmates. Nationally very little money is spent for treatment services and these programs reach only 5 percent of the inmate population.

G.    Medical Services
  1.    Most prisons offer medical services through a full-time staff of nurses, augmented by part-time physicians under contract to the correctional system.

V.    RELEASE TO THE COMMUNITY
Except for the small number that die in prison, all inmates will eventually be released to the community. Currently about 80 percent of felons will be released on parole and will remain under correctional supervision for a specific period of time.

A.    Parole is the *conditional* release of an offender from incarceration but not from the legal custody of the state. Parole rests on three concepts:
  1.    Grace of privilege: The prisoner could be kept incarcerated but the government extends the privilege of release.
  2.    Contract of consent: The government enters into an agreement with the prisoner whereby the prisoner promises to abide by certain conditions in exchange for being released.
  3.    Custody: Even though the offender is released from prison, he or she is still a responsibility of the government. Parole is an extension of correctional programs into the community.

Release Mechanisms

There are four basic mechanisms for persons to be released from prison:

1. In states retaining indeterminate sentences, *discretionary release* by the parole board is the manner by which most felons leave prison. In the context of discretionary release it is underscored that the offender's past, the nature of the offense committed, the inmate's behavior and participation in rehabilitative programs, and the prognosis for a crime-free future should guide the decision.

2. The use of determinate sentences and parole guidelines to fix the end of a prisoner's incarceration is referred to as *mandatory release*, because the correctional authority has little leeway in considering whether the offender is ready to return to society. Many states have devised ways to get around the rigidity of mandatory release through the use of furlough, home supervision, halfway houses, emergency release, and other programs.

3. Because of the growth of prison populations, many states have devised ways to get around the rigidity of mandatory release by placing inmates in the community through furloughs, home supervision, halfway houses, emergency release, and other programs. These other conditional releases also avoid the appearance of the politically sensitive label, discretionary parole.

4. An increasing percentage of prisoners receive an expiration release. These inmates are released from any further correctional supervision and cannot be returned to prison for their current offense. Such offenders have served the maximum court sentence, minus good time--they have "maxed out."

C. Comparative Perspective: Parole Release in Japan

1. More than any other developed country, Japan has resolved to "just say no" to crime. Japanese society ostracizes offenders and demands that they not just be caught but that they also confess and show remorse. But as in the United States, few Japanese offenders die in prison; almost all are released on parole to live under supervision in the community.

2. Aftercare programs have been available for Japanese offenders since the 1880s. But not until the 1950s were all elements of community treatment for ex-offenders' probation, parole, and aftercare brought together on a national basis.

3. Today, decisions to release offenders from prison and place them under supervision in the community are made by eight regional parole boards (RPBs). Sitting in panels of three, the members review applications for parole from prisons and training schools. They also have the authority to revoke an individual's parole on the recommendation of a local office

4. Japanese probation, parole, and aftercare focus on community. Unpaid volunteers do the supervision; private organizations administer aftercare, paid only partly by governmental subsidies. The Japanese public largely believes that people can correct themselves. Repentant offenders tend to get out; others end up in prison. "Rehabilitation" is a way to earn the right to be reincluded in society.

D. Close-Up : A Roomful of Strangers: Armed Robber Ben Brooks goes before a parole review board

E. The Impact of Release Mechanisms

1. There is considerable variation among the states but, on a national basis it is estimated that felony inmates serve on the average less than two years before release -- based on good time, credit for time served in jail, and parole release.

2. Supporters of discretion for the paroling authority argue that the courts do not adequately dispense justice and that the possibility of parole has invaluable benefits for the system.

    a. Discretionary release mitigates the harshness of the penal code, it equalizes disparities inevitable in sentencing behavior, and it is necessary to assist prison administrators in maintaining order.

311

b.      Supporters also contend that the postponement of sentence determination to the parole stage offers the opportunity for a more detached evaluation than is possible in the atmosphere of a trial and that early release is economically sensible because the cost of incarceration is considerable.

3.      A major criticism of the effect of parole is that it has shifted responsibility for many of the primary decisions of criminal justice from a judge, who holds legal procedures uppermost, to an administrative board, where discretion rules.

     a.      In most states that allow discretion, states' parole decisions are made in secret hearings, with only the board members, the inmate, and correctional officers present. Often there are no published criteria to guide decisions, and the prisoners are given no reason for either the denial or granting of their release.

F.      Problems Facing Parolees

1.      Parolees face many problems when they are released from prison. Most states, they are given only clothes, a small amount of money, a list of rules governing their conditional release, and the name and address of the parole officer to whom they must report within twenty-four hours. A promised job is often a condition for release, but an actual job may be difficult to secure. Most former convicts are unskilled or semiskilled, and the conditions of release may prevent them from moving to areas where they could find work. If the parolee is African American, male, and under 30, they join the largest group of unemployed in the country.

VI.      CIVIL DISABILITIES OF EX-FELONS

A.      Overview

1.      In most states, certain civil rights are forever forfeited, some fields of employment may never be entered, and some insurance or pension benefits may be foreclosed to those who have served time in prison.

2.      The right to vote and to hold public office are two civil rights that are generally limited upon conviction. Three-fourths of the states return the right to vote after varying lengths of time, while the remainder keep felons off of the voting lists unless they are pardoned or apply for the restoration of full citizenship.

3.      Restrictions on voting and jury service have especially strong impacts on African-Americans and others overrepresented in the criminal justice system who are notable to participate in and serve their communities even if they have turned their lives around.

4.      Although most former felons may not believe that restrictions on their civil rights will make it difficult for them to lead normal lives, limitations on entry into certain fields of employment are a problem.

     a.      Occupations that currently restrict the entry of former offenders include nurse, beautician, barber, real estate salesperson, chauffeur, employee of a place where alcoholic beverages are served, cashier, stenographer, and insurance agent.

     b.      Many observers assert that the restrictions force offenders into menial jobs at low pay and may indirectly lead them back to crime.

     c.      Some states provide procedures for the restoration of rights.

5.      Critics of civil disabilities contend that such restrictions are counterproductive by impeding reintegration of the ex-offender into society.

VII.      PARDON

A.      Background

1.      References to *pardon* are found in ancient Hebrew law, and in medieval Europe the church and the monarch had the power of clemency. Later, pardon became known as the "royal prerogative of mercy" in England.

2.    Pardons are acts of the executive. In the United States, the president or governors of the states may grant such clemency in individual cases.
      a.    In each state the executive receives recommendations from the state's board of pardons (often combined with the board of parole) in regard to individuals who are thought to be deserving of the act.
3.    In contemporary times, pardons serve three main purposes:
      a.    To remedy a miscarriage of justice;
      b.    To remove the stigma of a conviction; and
      c.    To mitigate a penalty.
4.    The most typical activity of pardons boards is to expunge the criminal records of first-time offenders--often young people--so that they may enter the professions (whose licensing procedures bar former felons), obtain certain types of employment, and in general not have to bear the stigma of a single indiscretion.

## REVIEW OF KEY TERMS

Fill in the appropriate term for each statement

classification
discretionary release
expiration release
inmate code
mandatory release
other conditional release
expiration release
pardon
parole
inmate code
furlough
halfway house
pardon
civil disabilities
parole in Japan
Project for Older Prisoners
parole officer's roles
parole boards

1.    The _____ was organized at Tulane Law School in 1989 to cull low-risk geriatrics from overcrowded prisons so that they can live in the community.

2.    _____ relies on very few professionals who supervise a large number of volunteers within the community.

3.    _____ provides for release according to a time frame stipulated by a determinate sentence and/or parole guidelines.

4.    _____ is a supervised home for parolees within the community.

5.    _____ provides a mechanism for temporary release for a few days in order to visit family and prepare for release on parole.

6.    _____ include limitations on ex-convicts' ability to run for public office in many states.

7.    _____ is an action under the authority of executive branch officials.

8. _____ provides for release according to a decision by a parole board.

9. _____ is the conditional release of an offender from incarceration but not from the legal custody of the state.

10. _____ is an institution, usually located in an urban area, housing inmates soon to be released and designed to help reintegration into society.

11. _____ create a tension between enforcing rules and providing social services.

12. _____ is comprised of political appointees or corrections professionals.

13. _____ is the norms and values that develop within the prison social system and help to define the inmate's image of the model prisoner.

14. _____ is the choice of those who try to maintain their links with and the perspective of the free world.

15. _____ is taking advantage of prison programs.

16. _____ is the style used by those who cut themselves off from the outside and try to construct a life within the prison.

17. The _____ includes those who are unable to develop role orientations to prison life;

## REVIEW OF KEY PEOPLE

Esther Hefferman
David Kalinich
Mark Fleisher
Timothy Flanagan
Robert Johnson
Joseph Fishman

1. In 1934 a book entitled <u>Sex in Prison</u> by _____ marked the beginning of the scientific study of inmate subcultures in maximum-security prisons.

2. In women's prisons, _____ found that women develop "play" families as a "direct, conscious substitution for the family relationships broken by imprisonment .

3. _____ studied the State Prison of Southern Michigan in Jackson and found that a market economy provides the goods and services not available or not allowed by prison authorities.

4. A leading authority on long-term inmates, _____ found that administrators maximize opportunities for the inmate to exercise choice in living circumstances, create opportunities for meaningful living, and help the inmate maintain contact with the outside world.

5. _____ found that the public culture of the prison has norms that dictate behavior toward a masculine toughness.

6. _____ found an inmate running a "store" in most every cell block in the U.S. Penitentiary at Lompoc, California.

## GENERAL PRACTICE QUESTIONS

Whether a prisoner receives _____1_____, through a determinate sentence and parole guidelines, or a _____2_____, through a decision by the _____3_____, he or she immediately comes under the responsibility of the _____4_____, who tries to watch for improper behavior and also provide social assistance.

# SELF-TEST SECTION

## MULTIPLE CHOICE QUESTIONS

16.1. The Bureau of Justice statistics reports that most prisoners are...
a) 40 years or older
b) college graduates
c) females
d) recidivist offenders
e) none of the above

16.2. What percent of inmates have been either incarcerated or on probation at least twice?
a) 60%
b) 45%
c) 30%
d) 20%
e) 10%

16.3. What percent of inmates have been either incarcerated or on probation three times or more times?
a) 60%
b) 45%
c) 30%
d) 20%
e) 10%

16.4. What percent of inmates have been either incarcerated or on probation six or more times?
a) 60%
b) 45%
c) 30%
d) 20%
e) 10%

16.5. What fraction of inmates were serving a sentence for a violent crime or had previously been convicted of a violent crime?
a) one-half
b) one-third
c) one-fourth
d) two-thirds
e) three-fifths

16.6. Which of the following factors affect correctional operations?
a) the increased number of elderly prisoners
b) the many prisoners with HIV/AIDS
c) the thousands of prisoners who are mentally ill
d) the increase in long-term prisoners.
e) all of the above

16.7. From 1996-1999, what has been the increase of the elderly population within U. S. prisons?
a) 0%
b) 10%
c) 30%
d) 50%
e) 75%

16.8. What percent of serious crime is committed by people over 60?
a) 1%
b) 5%
c) 10%
d) 17%
e) 25%

16.9. In 1999, how many HIV-positive inmates occupied U. S. prisons?
a) none
b) under 10,000
c) more than 25,000
d) more than 100,000
e) more than 250,000

16.10. How much higher is the rate of AIDS cases in U. S. prisons compared to the U. S. general population?
a) twice as high
b) three times as high
c) four times as high
d) five times as high
e) ten times as high

16.11. Why is AIDS a problem in U. S. prisons?
a) unprotected homosexual activity in prison
b) inmates often were intravenous drug users
c) lack of education about AIDS
d) all of the above
e) none of the above

16.12. Which branch of government is checked by the pardon power?
a) executive
b) judicial
c) legislative
d) bureaucracy
e) executive and legislative

16.13. The most public sign of the lack of programs for the mentally ill is (are) ...
a) homelessness
b) murders caused by insanity
c) stalking laws
d) pornography
e) hate speech

16.14. Which state is the exception because it has mental health units in each of its prison facilities and one of its prisons has been set aside to house only the mentally ill?
a) Texas
b) New York
c) Ohio
d) Hawaii
e) Florida

16.15. The average first-time offender in the U. S. serves...
a) six months
b) nine months
c) thirteen months
d) twenty two months
e) forty months

16.16. Which of the following is a main principle followed by administrators according to Timothy Flanagan?
a) minimize opportunities for the inmate to exercise choice in living circumstances
b) create opportunities for meaningful living
c) prevent the inmate maintain from keeping contact with the outside world
d) all of the above
e) none of the above

16.17. What are the norms and values that develop within the prison social system and help to define the inmate's image of the model prisoner?
a) inmate code
b) jailer's code
c) prisoner's law
d) pardon code
e) parole law

16.18. Which of the following is NOT a survival tip for an inmate ?
a) don't snitch on other inmates
b) pick friends carefully
c) make eye contact at all times
d) fight dirty
e) mind your own business

16.19. Which of the following is a survival tip for an inmate ?
a) snitch on other inmates
b) don't talk to the guards
c) make eye contact at all times
d) fight fair
e) meddle in other inmate's business

16.20. Why has prison society become more unstable?
a) presence of gangs
b) changes in the type of inmate in prison
c) changes in prison policy
d) all of the above
e) prison society has not become more unstable

16.21. What is another name for a newcomer in prison society?
a) dog
b) fish
c) gleaner
d) jailer
e) woman

16.22. Which of the following is NOT provided by the state prison system?
a) housing
b) food
c) clothing
d) cigarettes
e) all of the above are provided by the state

16.23. Who found an inmate running a "store" in most every cell block in the U.S. Penitentiary at Lompoc, California?
a) Timothy Flanagan
b) Esther Hefferman
c) Joseph Fishman
d) David Kalinich
e) Mark Fleischer

16.24. Who studied the State Prison of Southern Michigan in Jackson and found that a market economy provides the goods (contraband) and services not available by prison authorities?
a) Timothy Flanagan
b) Esther Hefferman
c) Joseph Fishman
d) David Kalinich
e) Mark Fleischer

16.25. Which of the following best describes the outward appearance of a women's prison?
a) upper-class country club
b) military institution
c) college campus
d) homeless shelter
e) third world country


## TRUE/FALSE QUESTIONS

16.1. AIDS is not a problem in U. S. prisons.

16.2. Most prisoners are young males.

16.3. Most states have several prison institutions for women.

16.4. There is no difference between men and women prisons

16.5. The number of women incarcerated in the past ten years has increased significantly.

16.6. A good collection of pornography is a survival tip in prison.

16.7. Minding your own business is a survival tip in prison.

16.8. The elderly comprise about twenty percent of the inmate population.

16.9. Classification of prisoners is based on the institution's needs not the prisoner's.

16.10. The Comprehensive Crime Control Act of 1994 increased federal funding to prisoners for post-secondary education.

16.11. Prisoners assigned to education programs are less likely to commit crimes upon release.

16.12. Inmates are usually trained in prison for trades that already have an adequate labor supply or in which new methods have made the skills taught obsolete.

16.13. Most prisons do not have any physicians under contract.

16.14. Japan is one of the safest countries in the developed world.

16.15. Most inmates die in prison.

16.16. Parole release does not impact other parts of the criminal justice system.

16.17. Parolees face many problems when released from prison.

16.18. In most states, ex-felons do not retain the right to vote.

16.19. The pardon power rests with the judicial branch.

16.20. Pardons are used to remove the stigma of a conviction.

Key Terms
1.    Project for Older Prisoners
2.    parole in Japan
3.    mandatory release
4.    halfway house
5.    furlough
6.    civil disabilities
7.    pardon
8.    discretionary release
9.    parole
10.   halfway house
11.   parole officer's roles
12.   parole board
13.   inmate code
14.   doing time
15.   gleaning
16.   jailing
17.   disorganized criminal


Key People
1.    Joseph Fishman
2.    Esther Hefferman
3.    David Kalinich
4.    Timothy Flanagan
5.    Robert Johnson
6.    Mark Fleisher

General Practice Questions
1.    mandatory release
2.    discretionary release
3.    parole board
4.    parole officer


Multiple Choice Answers
16.1.    d
16.2.    a
16.3.    b
16.4.    d
16.5.    d
16.6.    e
16.7.    d
16.8.    a
16.9.    c
16.10.   d
16.11.   d
16.12.   b
16.13.   a
16.14.   c
16.15.   d
16.16.   b

16.17.   a
16.18.   c
16.19.   b
16.20.   d
16.21.   b
16.22.   d
16.23.   e
16.24.   d
16.25.   c

True/False
16.1.    F
16.2.    T
16.3.    F
16.4.    F
16.5.    T
16.6.    T
16.7.    T
16.8.    F
16.9.    T
16.10.   F
16.11.   T
16.12.   T
16.13.   F
16.14.   T
16.15.   F
16.16.   F
16.17.   T
16.18.   T
16.19.   F
16.20.   T

WORKSHEET 16.1      PRISON PROGRAMS

You are in charge of developing programs at a new prison. For each category of possible programs discuss whether you will recommend such programs for your prison. Why? If so, describe the goals and details of those programs.

EDUCATIONAL PROGRAMS _____

_____

_____

_____

_____

_____

_____

VOCATIONAL PROGRAMS _____

_____

_____

_____

_____

_____

_____

PRISON INDUSTRIES _____

_____

_____

_____

REHABILITATIVE PROGRAMS _____

_____

_____

_____

_____

WORKSHEET 16.2    PRISON PROBLEMS

If you were a prison warden, name three things that you would do to address each of the following issues.  How effective do you think your strategies would be?

1.  Racial tensions between groups of inmates_____

_____

_____

_____

_____

_____

_____

2.  Prison gangs controlling the internal economy_____

_____

_____

_____

_____

_____

3.  Mothers of small children serving long sentences in an isolated institution

_____

_____

_____

_____

_____

_____

# CHAPTER 17

## THE JUVENILE JUSTICE SYSTEM

### LEARNING OBJECTIVES

After covering the material in this chapter, students should understand:

1.      the nature and extent of youth crime;

2.      the history of juvenile justice, including the four eras:  Refuge; Juvenile Court; Juvenile Rights; Crime Control;

3.      the juvenile justice system of Norway;

4.      the importance of age and jurisdiction in the juvenile system;

5.      the role of police, intake, case screening, and preliminary discretionary dispositions;

6.      adjudication in the juvenile system;

7.      juvenile corrections, including probation, deinstitutionalization, and community-based treatment settings.

### CHAPTER SUMMARY

This chapter explores the extent and nature of juvenile crime by listing a variety of statistics regarding juvenile crime. It also traces the history of the juvenile justice system from the colonial era to the modern era using five distinct periods: 1) the Puritan period, 2) the Reform period, 3) the Juvenile Court period, 4) the Juvenile Rights period and 5) the Crime Control period. The chapter examines the development of juvenile courts in the United States, the specific rulings by the U. S. Supreme Court that established constitutional protections for juveniles in the 1960s, and the movement to get tough on juveniles that has developed since the 1980s. A comparative perspective is offered by documenting the juvenile system in Norway and, finally, the problems that are faced today within the juvenile justice system are presented such as whether juveniles should be tried as adults in specific circumstances.

### CHAPTER OUTLINE

I.      INTRODUCTION

A.      In October, 2002, four juveniles arrested for arson  in Canaan, Connecticut caused $2 million in damages to an historic landmark and cost many people their jobs. Two of the juveniles were charged in adult court while the two younger juveniles were charged in juvenile court. This example raises the issue of whether juveniles should be treated differently than adults for criminal acts.

II.  YOUTH CRIME IN THE UNITED STATES

A.      <u>Extent and Nature of Crime</u>

1. In all, about 2.4 million juveniles under 18 years are arrested each year; 99,000 for violent crimes. Only 28 percent of arrestees under 18 years of age were females. Youths commit violent crimes out of proportion with their numbers.
2. Some researchers have estimated that one boy in three will be arrested by the police at some point before his eighteenth birthday.
3. Gang violence from youth gangs has exacerbated many problems. Gangs have increased their numbers and moved into suburban and rural areas.
4. There are projections of a huge youth cohort in the coming years that may increase the problems of crime.
5. New Directions in Criminal Justice Policy: Boston's Operation Ceasefire is a coordinated attempt to end gang gun violence. Ceasefire is based on the knowledge that a few offenders account for a substantial portion of all crime and that these offenders are often concentrated in particular city neighborhoods. Operation Ceasefire uses two strategies. First, interagency collaboration identifies individuals and gangs at risk for committing violence. A task force of federal, state, and municipal criminal justice and social service agencies regularly meet to share information. A second strategy is aimed at increasing deterrence through swift and certain sanctions.

III. THE DEVELOPMENT OF JUVENILE JUSTICE

A. Background :The Puritan Period (1646-1824)
1. The English common law had long declared that children under seven years of age were incapable of felonious intent and were therefore not criminally responsible. Children aged seven to fourteen could be held accountable only if it could be shown that they understood the consequences of their actions.
2. Under the doctrine of *parens patriae*, which held the king to be the father of the realm, the chancery courts exercised protective jurisdiction over all children, particularly those involved in questions of dependency, neglect, and property.
   a. These courts, however, had civil jurisdiction, and juvenile offenders were dealt with by the criminal courts.
3. The concept of *parens patriae* was important for the development of juvenile justice, for it legitimized the intervention of the state on behalf of the child.
4. The earliest attempt by a colony to deal with problem children was passage of the Massachusetts Stubborn Child Law in 1646.

B. The Refuge Period (1824-1899)
1. As the population of American cities began to grow in the half century following independence, the problem of youth crime and neglect was a concern for reformers.
2. These reformers focused their efforts primarily on the urban immigrant poor, and sought to have parents declared "unfit" if their children roamed the streets and were apparently "out of control."
3. The state's power was used to create institutions for these children where they could learn good work and study habits, live in a disciplined and healthy environment, and develop "character."
4. The first of these institutions was The House of Refuge of New York, which opened in 1825. It was followed by similar facilities in Boston, Philadelphia, and Baltimore. Children were placed in these homes by court order usually because of neglect or vagrancy. They often stayed there until they reached the age of majority.
5. Some states created "reform schools" to provide the discipline and education needed by wayward youth in a "homelike" atmosphere, usually in rural areas. The first, the Lyman School for Boys, was opened in Westboro, Massachusetts, in 1848. A similar school for girls was opened in Lancaster, Massachusetts, in 1855. Ohio created the State Reform Farm in 1857, and the states of Maine, Rhode Island, New York, and Michigan soon followed suit.

6.      Other groups, such as the Children's Aid Society of New York, were emphasizing the need to place neglected and delinquent children in private homes in the country. Like the reform advocates of adult corrections, the children's aid societies of the 1850s emphasized placement in rural areas, away from the crime and bad influences of the city. The additional hands thus acquired provided an economic incentive for farmers to "take in" these juveniles.

C.      The Juvenile Court Period (1900-1959)
1.      Focus on juvenile criminality.
2.      Members of the Progressive Movement sought to use the power of the state to provide individualized care and treatment of deviants of all kinds--adult criminals, the mentally ill, juvenile delinquents. They pushed for adoption of probation, treatment, indeterminate sentences, and parole for adult offenders and were successful in establishing similar programs for juveniles.
3.      Referred to as the "child savers," these upper-middle class reformers sought to use the power of the state to "save" children from a life of crime.
4.      They were stimulated by: concern over the influence of environmental factors on behavior; the rise of the social sciences, which claimed they could treat the problems underlying deviance; and a belief that state action could be benevolent in serving to rectify social problems.
5.      It was argued that a separate juvenile court system was needed so that the problems of the individual youth could be treated in an atmosphere in which flexible procedures would rid them of thoughts of crime.
6.      The Juvenile Court Act by Illinois in 1899 was first comprehensive system of juvenile justice. By 1920 all but three states provided for a juvenile court.
7.      The philosophy of the juvenile court was the idea that the state should deal with a child who broke the law much as a wise parent would deal with a wayward child. The doctrine of *parens patriae* again helped legitimize the system. Procedures were to be informal and private, records were to be confidential, children were to be detained apart from adults, and probation and social worker staffs were to be appointed.
8.      The term *criminal behavior* was replaced by *delinquent behavior* as it pertained to the acts of children. This shift in terminology serves to underscore the view that these children were wayward; but they could be returned to society as law-abiding citizens. But it also underscores the fact that the juvenile court could deal with behaviors that were not criminal if committed by adults such as smoking cigarettes, consensual sexual activity, truancy, or living a "wayward, idle, and dissolute life": status offenses.
9.      Rejection of due process protections. Because procedures were not to be adversarial, lawyers were unnecessary; psychologists and social workers, who could determine the juvenile's underlying behavior problem, were the main professionals attached to the system.

D.      The Juvenile Rights Period (1960-1979)
1.      During the 1960s period of the "due process revolution" regarding the rights of adult defendants, lawyers and scholars began to criticize the extensive discretion exercised by juvenile justice officials.
2.      In *Kent v. United States* (1966), the Supreme Court extended due process rights to children. In this case a sixteen-year old boy was remanded from the juvenile to the adult court without his lawyer present. The Court ruled that juveniles had the right to counsel at a waiver hearing.
3.      *In re Gault* (1967) extended due process rights to juvenile court. Boy sentenced for making prank phone calls. The U.S. Supreme Court said juveniles should have procedural rights, including notice of charges, right to counsel, right to confront and cross-examine witnesses, and privilege against compelled self-incrimination.

4.	In the case of *In re Winship* (1970) the Court held that proof must be established "beyond a reasonable doubt" before a juvenile may be classified as a delinquent for committing an act that would be a crime if it were committed by an adult.

5.	The Supreme Court held in *McKeiver v. Pennsylvania* (1971) that "trial by jury in the juvenile court's adjudicative stage is not a constitutional requirement."

6.	In *Breed v. Jones* (1975) the Court extended the protection against double jeopardy to juveniles by requiring that before a case is adjudicated in juvenile court, a hearing must be held to determine if it should be transferred to the adult court.

7.	Although the court decisions would seem to have placed the rights of juveniles on a par with those of adults, critics have charged that the states have not fully implemented these rights.

8.	Many states closed juvenile institutions and instead placed children in group homes and community treatment centers.  Other states decreased the number of children held in institutions.

9.	In 1974, Congress passed the Juvenile Justice and Delinquency Prevention Act which included provisions for the deinstitutionalization of status offenders (truants, runaways, etc.).

    a.	Since then efforts have been made to divert such children out of the system, to reduce the possibility of incarceration, and to rewrite the laws with regard to *status offenses.*

E.	Crime Control (1980-Present)

1.	With the public demanding that there be a "crackdown on crime," legislators have responded with changes in the juvenile system.

2.	In *Schall v. Martin* (1984) the Supreme Court significantly departed from the trend toward increased juvenile rights.  The Court confirmed the general notion of *parens patriae* as a primary basis for the juvenile court, equal in importance to the Court's desire to protect the community from crime. Thus, juveniles may be detained before trial if they are found to be a "risk" to the community, even though this rationale is not applicable to adult pretrial detention.

3.	Just as legislators have upped the penalties for adult offenders, juveniles convicted of serious crimes are now spending much longer terms either in youth facilities or adult prisons.  The present crime control policy has resulted in many more juveniles being tried in adult courts, including juveniles facing less serious charges such as alcohol possession.

4.	Public support for a get-tough stance toward older juveniles seems to be growing.

F.	COMPARATIVE PERSPECTIVE: The Hidden Juvenile Justice System in Norway

1.	There is no punishment for crimes in Norway for a child who is under 15.  No special courts have been established with jurisdiction to try criminal cases against juvenile offenders. Older teenagers may be tried in ordinary courts of law and sentenced to prison. Sentences for most crimes, however, consist of only a suspended sentence or probation or several months in an open prison.

2.	The public prosecutor, who represents the police, will transfer the juvenile cases directly to a division of the "social office," the *barnevern*--literally, child protection.

3.	Treatment includes removing child from the home and placing in a juvenile institution.  Once the custody is removed from the parents, the burden of proof is on the parents to retain custody.

4.	In contrast to the American juvenile court, the Norwegian model is wholly social worker dominated.  Placement in an institution is typically for an indefinite period.  No notice of the disposition of the matter is given to the press. This absence of public accountability may serve more to protect the social office than the child.

5.	Children receive far harsher treatments than do adults for similar offenses.  For instance, for a young adult first offender the typical penalty for thievery is a suspended sentence. A child, however, may languish in an institution for years for the same offense.

IV.    THE JUVENILE JUSTICE SYSTEM

A.    Overview
    1.    In general, the states' systems function through many of the existing organizations of the state adult criminal justice system but often with specialized structures for activities having to do with juveniles.
        a.    In many states, special probation officers work with juveniles, but they function as part of the larger probation service.
    2.    Two basic factors characterize the juvenile justice system. These factors are: (1) ages of the clients, and (2) jurisdiction of the system.

B.    Age
    1.    The upper age limit for a juvenile varies from sixteen to eighteen: in thirty-eight states and the District of Columbia it is the eighteenth birthday; in eight states, the seventeenth; and in the remainder, the sixteenth.
    2.    In forty-nine states, judges have the discretion to transfer juveniles to adult courts through a waiver hearing as discussed above. Some state laws permit waiver for children as young as ten years of age.

C.    Categories of Cases Under Juvenile Court Jurisdiction
    1.    Four types of cases enter the juvenile justice system: delinquency, status offenses, neglect, and dependency.
        a.    Delinquent children have committed acts that if committed by an adult would be criminal--for example, auto theft, robbery, and assault.
        b.    Acts that are illegal only if they are committed by juveniles are known as status offenses.
            i.    Rather than having committed a violation of the penal code, status offenders have been designated as ungovernable or incorrigible: as runaways, truants, or persons in need of supervision (PINS).
        c.    Some states do not distinguish between delinquent offenders and status offenders, and label both as juvenile *delinquents*.
        d.    Beginning in the early 1960s, many state legislatures attempted to distinguish status offenders and to exempt them from a criminal record. As previously noted, in 1974 Congress required states to remove noncriminal offenders from secure detention and correctional facilities.
        e.    Juvenile justice also deals with problems of neglect and dependency--situations in which children are viewed as being hurt through no fault of their own, because their parents have failed to provide a proper environment for them.
            i.    Illinois, for example, defines a *neglected child* as one who is neglected as to proper or necessary support, education as required by law, or as to medical or other remedial care recognized under state law or other care necessary for his well being, or who is abandoned by his parents, guardians or custodians, or whose environment is injurious to his welfare or whose behavior is injurious to his own welfare or that of others.
            ii.    A *dependent child* is either without a parent or guardian or is not receiving proper care because of the physical or mental disability of that person.
    2.    Nationally about 75 percent of the cases referred to the juvenile courts are delinquency cases, of which 20 percent are concerned with status offenses; about 20 percent are

dependency and neglect cases; and about 5 percent involve special proceedings, such as adoption.

V.    JUVENILE JUSTICE PROCESS

A.    Overview
    1.    Prevention of delinquency is the system's justification for intervening in the lives of juveniles who are involved in either status or criminal offenses.
    2.    It is still assumed that the juvenile proceedings are to be conducted in a non-adversarial environment, and that the court should be a place where the judge, social workers, clinicians, and probation officers work together to diagnose the child's problem and select a rehabilitative program to attack this problem.
    3.    More discretion is exercised in the juvenile than in the adult justice system.
    4.    Juvenile justice is a particular type of bureaucracy that is based on an ideology of social work and is staffed primarily by persons who think of themselves as members of the helping professions.
    5.    Exchange relations:  The juvenile court must deal not only with children and their parents but also with patrol officers, probation officers, welfare officials, social workers, psychologists, and the heads of treatment institutions. These others all have their own goals, their own perceptions of delinquency, and their own concepts of treatment.

B.    Police Interface
    1.    Many police departments have special units to deal with youth matters, such as drug education, juvenile crime, or gangs.
    2.    Most complaints against juveniles are brought by the police, although they may be initiated by an injured party, school officials, or even the parents.
    3.    The police must make three major decisions with regard to the processing of juveniles:
        a.    Whether to take the child into custody;
        b.    Whether to request that the child be detained following apprehension;
        c.    Whether to refer the child to court.
    4.    The police exercise enormous discretion with regard to these decisions.
    5.    In a study of the police in a metropolitan industrial city of 450,000, it was found that the choice of disposition of juvenile cases depended very much on the prior record of the child, but second in importance was the offender's demeanor.
        a.    Researchers found that only 4 percent of the cooperative youths were arrested, in comparison with 67 percent of those who were uncooperative.
    6.    A number of factors play a role in the way that the police dispose of a case of juvenile delinquency.  These factors include:
        a.    The seriousness of the offense;
        b.    The willingness of the parents to cooperate and discipline their child;
        c.    The child's behavioral history as reflected in school and police records;
        d.    The extent to which the child and his/her parents insist on a formal court hearing;
        e.    The local political and social norms with regard to dispositions in such cases.
    7.    Most jurisdictions now provide the *Miranda* warnings to juveniles, but issues remain as to the ability of juveniles to waive these rights.
        a.    In 1979 the Court ruled in *Fare v. Michael C.* that a child may waive rights to an attorney and to self-incrimination but that juvenile court judges must evaluate the totality of circumstances under which the minor made these decisions.
    8.    Search & Seizure:  State courts interpreted *Gault* to extend these provisions but in 1985 the Supreme Court ruled in *New Jersey v. T.L.O.* that school officials can search

students and their lockers if they have reasonable suspicion that the search will produce evidence of a school or criminal law violation.

    a.      The justices recognized that children do have Fourth Amendment rights yet also noted that under the ancient concept of *in loco parentis*, school officials may act in place of the parent under certain conditions when the child is under their jurisdiction.

9.     Intake: When the police believe that formal actions should be taken by the juvenile justice system, a complaint is filed with a special division of the juvenile probation department for preliminary screening and evaluation.

10.     During this intake stage, a review of the case is made by an officer to determine whether the alleged facts are sufficient to cause the juvenile court to take jurisdiction or whether some other action would be in the child's interest. A petition is filed to move the child into the juvenile system.

11.     In most juvenile justice systems the probation officer plays a crucial role during the intake phase. Because intake is essentially a screening process to determine whether a case should be referred to the court or to a social agency, it often takes place without judicial supervision.

    a.      Informal discussions among the probation officer, the parents, and the child are important means of learning about the child's social situation, of diagnosing behavioral problems, and of recommending treatment possibilities.

12.     The intake hearing is typically presided over by a hearing officer, who is a lawyer, a probation officer, or a social worker.

13.     Some states have moved the intake probation officer under the authority of the prosecuting attorney, thereby showing the trend away from rehabilitation in favor of crime control.

14.     Diversion: the number and types of diversion programs have greatly expanded during the past two decades.

    a.      However, it appears to many observers that the increase in diversion programs has widened the juvenile justice net and that children who in the past would not have been formally handled are so handled now.

15.     Transfer to the Adult Court: Transfer is accomplished either through a *judicial waiver* or by *legislative exclusion*.

    a.      In the past during a waiver hearing the state had to make a case that the youth was not amenable to rehabilitation in the juvenile system before a transfer to the adult court. Now many states place the burden on the youth to show amenability to treatment.

    b.      Although many states exclude from juvenile court only murder, others have extended the range to include rape, armed robbery and other violent crimes.

    c.      A few states place waiver under the control of prosecutorial discretion.

16.     Detention: Decision is usually made by an intake officer of the juvenile court concerning detaining juvenile pending determination of the case.

17.     Although early reformers sought to have juveniles held separately from adults, in some places separate detention facilities do not exist.

18.     Children are held in detention for a number of reasons:

    a.      The possibility that they will commit other crimes while awaiting trial;

    b.      The possibility of harm from gang members or parents if they are released;

    c.      The possibility that they may not appear in court as required;

    d.      There is no responsible adult who is willing to care for them;

    e.      Detention may also be used as punishment, to teach a lesson.

        i.      Although much attention is focused on the juvenile court and the sanctions imposed by judges as a result of the formal processes of adjudication, many more children are punished through confinement in detention centers and jails before any court action has taken place.

ii. An estimated half-million juveniles are detained each year, sometimes for several months; but only about 15 percent are eventually confined to a group home, training school, or halfway house. These figures seem to indicate that detention and intake decisions have a greater impact than the decisions of the court.

19. THE POLICY DEBATE: Should juveniles be tried as adults? Supporters of trying juveniles as adults point to the continuing high levels of violence and the heinous nature of some crimes committed by youths. Opponents of trying juveniles as adults point out that treating adolescents as adults ignores the fact that they are at a different stage of social and emotional development.

VI.    ADJUDICATION

A.    Adjudication
1.    From a formal standpoint, the purpose of the hearing was not to determine a child's guilt but to establish the child's status as either delinquent or not delinquent and to help the child to become law-abiding.
2.    In accordance with the Progressives' belief that adjudication should be informal and noncombative, the normal rules of criminal procedure were modified; the rules of evidence were not strictly followed, hearsay testimony could be admitted, there was no prosecutor (a police or probation officer presented the case), and the sessions were closed to the public.
3.    The changes in criminal proceedings mandated by the due process decisions of the Supreme Court following *Gault* have brought about shifts in the philosophy and actions of the juvenile court.
     a.    Copies of formal petitions with specific charges must be given to the parents and child, counsel may be present and free counsel appointed if the juvenile is indigent, witnesses may be cross-examined, and a transcript of the proceedings must be kept. In about thirteen states, juveniles have a right to a jury trial.
4.    As with other Supreme Court decisions, the reality of local practice may differ sharply from the stipulations in the opinion.
     a.    Juveniles and their parents often waive their rights in response to suggestions made by the judge or probation officer.
     b.    The lower social status of the offender's parents, the intimidating atmosphere of the court, and judicial hints that the outcome will be more favorable if a lawyer is not present are reasons the procedures outlined in *Gault* are not demanded.
     c.    The litany of "treatment," "doing what's right for the child," and "working out a just solution" may sound enticing, especially to people who are unfamiliar with the intricacies of formal legal procedures.
5.    Adjudicatory process: In some jurisdictions the adjudication process is more adversarial than it was before the *Gault* and *Winship* decisions.
6.    Like adult cases, however, juvenile cases tend to be adjudicated in a style that conforms to the crime control (administrative) model: most are settled in preliminary hearings by a plea agreement, and few go on to formal trial.
7.    With the increased concern about crime, prosecuting attorneys are taking a more prominent part in the system.
8.    Juvenile court records and proceedings have traditionally been closed to the public. Judges in adult courts do not necessarily have access to juvenile records and thus cannot tell if adult first offenders actually have a prior juvenile crime record.

9.      Disposition: If the court makes a finding of delinquency, a dispositional hearing is required. This hearing may be held immediately following the entry of a plea or at a later date.

10.      Typically, the judge receives a social history or predispositional report before passing sentence. Few juveniles are found by the court to be not delinquent at trial, since the intake and pretrial processes normally filter out cases in which a law violation cannot be proved.

11.      In addition to dismissal of a petition, four other choices are available:
        a.      alternative dispositions;
        b.      Probation;
        c.      Community treatment;
        d.      Institutional care.

12.      Throughout most of this century judges have sentenced juveniles to indeterminate sentences so that correctional administrators would have the discretion to determine when release was appropriate under a rehabilitation model.

B.      Corrections

1.   Both adult and juvenile systems mix rehabilitative and retributive sanctions.

2.      Differences between adult and juvenile systems flow from the *parens patriae* concept and the youthful, seemingly innocent persons with whom the system deals.

3.      One predominant aim of juvenile corrections is to avoid unnecessary incarceration.
        a.      Placing children in institutions has labeling effects; the children begin to perceive themselves as "bad," because they have received punitive treatment, and children who see themselves as bad are likely to behave that way.
        b.      Treatment is believed to be more effective when the child is living in a normal, supportive home environment.

4.      Alternative Dispositions: Although probation and commitment to an institution are the major dispositional alternatives, judges have wide discretion to warn, to fine, to arrange for restitution, to refer a juvenile for treatment at either a public or a private community agency, or to withhold judgment.

5.      In making this decision, the judge relies on a social background report, developed by the probation department. Often it includes reports from others in the community, such as school officials or a psychiatrist.

6.      When psychological issues are involved, a disposition may be delayed pending further diagnosis.

7.      Judges sometimes suspend judgment, or continue cases without a finding, when they wish to put a youth under supervision but are reluctant to apply the label "delinquent." Judgment may be suspended for a definite or indefinite period of time. The court thus holds a definitive judgment in abeyance for possible use should a youth misbehave while under the informal supervision of a probation officer or parents.

8.      Probation: The most common method of handling juvenile offenders is to place them on probation.

9.      Juvenile probation can be very different from adult probation in two respects:
        a.      Traditionally, juvenile probation has been more satisfactorily funded, and hence caseloads of officers are much lower in number.
        b.      Second, juvenile probation itself is often infused with the sense that the offender can change, that the job is enjoyable, and that the clients are worthwhile. Such attitudes make for greater creativity than is possible with adult probation.

10.      One of the most common probation strategies is to pair the juvenile with a "big brother" or "big sister," who spends time with the offender, providing a positive adult role model.

11.      Community Treatment: Treatment in community-based facilities has greatly expanded during the past decade.

a. In particular, the number of private, nonprofit agencies that contract with the states to perform services for troubled youths has grown.
b. Foster homes developed as a means for implementing a policy of limited intervention into juvenile lives, reflecting the sentiment of the Standard Juvenile Court Act (a model law developed by The National Council on Crime and Delinquency) that when a child "is removed from the control of his parents, the court shall secure for him care as nearly as possible equivalent to [the home]."
c. Group homes are small, often privately run facilities for groups of juvenile offenders. They are usually older houses that have been remodeled to fit the needs of twelve to twenty juveniles.

12. A Question of Ethics: group home that places the emphasis on order rather than treatment and uses older boys to intimidate younger or smaller boys into good behavior.

13. Institutional Care: Large custodial training schools located in outlying areas remain the typical institutions to which juveniles are committed, although during the past decade there has been an increase in the number of privately maintained facilities that accept residents sent to them by the courts.

14. The national incarceration rate per 100,000 juveniles aged ten to eighteen is 368. Nationally, 74 percent of incarcerated juveniles are held in public facilities, the remainder in private facilities

15. Overrepresentation of African-Americans in juvenile facilities.

16. Institutional Programs: Because of the emphasis on rehabilitation that has dominated juvenile justice for much of the past fifty years, a wide variety of treatment programs has been used: counseling, education, vocational training, and an assortment of psychotherapy methods have been incorporated into the juvenile correctional programs of most states.

17. Unfortunately for many offenders, incarceration in a juvenile training institution appears to be mainly preparation for entry into adult corrections.

C. Close-Up: Fernando, 16, Finds a Sanctuary in Crime.
Youthful drug dealer living as if he has no future; difficult childhood in poverty and parental neglect; gang membership.

VII. PROBLEMS AND PERSPECTIVES

A. Overview
1. Much of the criticism of juvenile justice has emphasized the disparity between the treatment ideal and the institutionalized practices of an ongoing bureaucratic system.
2. In many states the same judges, probation officers, and social workers are asked to deal with neglected children as well as with young criminals. Although departments of social services may deal primarily with neglect cases, the distinction is often not maintained.
3. We must acknowledge that our understanding of the causes of delinquency and its prevention or treatment is extremely limited. The array of theories has occasioned an array of proposed--and often contradictory--treatments.
4. Problem of inaccessible juvenile court records blocking access of true records of adult offenders.
5. The conservative crime control policies that have hit the adult criminal justice system-- with their emphasis on deterrence, retribution, and getting tough--have influenced juvenile justice by way of overcrowding in juvenile institutions, increased litigation challenging the abuse of children in training schools and detention centers, and higher rates of minority youth incarceration. All of these problems have emerged during a period of declining youth populations and fewer arrests of juveniles. With the demographic trend now reversing and the increased concern about drugs, one can see a

surge of adolescents going through their criminally high-risk years in a system and community unable to cope with them.

## REVIEW OF KEY TERMS

Fill in the appropriate term for each statement

status offense
*parens patriae*
judicial waiver
legislative exclusion
delinquent
neglected child
dependent child
detention
"child savers"
Progressives
Juvenile Court Period
Crime Control Period
Norwegian juvenile justice
Refuge Period
Juvenile Rights Period
foster home
barnevern
group home
diversion
deinstitutionalization

1. _____ were the early twentieth century reformers who emphasized rehabilitation for juvenile and adult offenders.

2. _____ is the modern period in which retributive and deterrent elements became more influential upon juvenile justice.

3. _____ is a period of temporary custody of a juvenile before disposition of his or her case.

4. _____ is the statutory restriction on crimes for which persons cannot be tried as juveniles.

5. _____ is the movement affecting juveniles, mental patients, and others that put people in community settings instead of under state control and supervision.

6. _____ is the concept of the state as the guardian and protector of juveniles and other citizens who cannot protect themselves.

7. _____ is the period in which constitutional law concerning juvenile justice developed.

8. _____ is a child who has committed a criminal or status offense.

9. _____ is the process of discretionary decisions that move children away from the system's most punitive consequences.

10. _____ involves the placement of a child with a caretaker family on a temporary basis.

11. _____ is the period in which comprehensive juvenile justice institutions developed.

12. _____ is any act committed by a juvenile that would not be a crime if it were committed by an adult but that is considered unacceptable for a juvenile.

13. _____ is the nickname given to Progressive era reformers who sought to reshape the juvenile system.

14. _____ has social workers as central decision makers.

15. _____ involves the placement of the child in a residential setting with a small number of other delinquents.

16. _____ is the method through which a judge decides that a juvenile should be tried in an adult criminal court.

17. _____ is a child whose parents are unable to give proper care.

18. _____ is the period in which juvenile policy focused on urban, immigrant, poor children and the alleged inadequacies of their parents.

19. _____ is the powerful committee in Norway that makes the important discretionary decisions concerning the treatment of a child.

20. _____ is a child who is not receiving proper care because of parental inaction.


## REVIEW OF KEY PEOPLE

Gerald Gault
Julian Mack
Jane Addams
John Irwin
Julia Lathrop
Henry Thurston

1. _____, a social work educator, and the National Congress of Mothers successfully promoted the juvenile court concept

2. _____ was the judge who was an early leader in juvenile justice through his service in the juvenile court in Chicago.

3. _____ was the boy whose case elicited an important decision from the Supreme Court.

4. Activists such as _____ and _____, both of the settlement house movement, also promoted the juvenile court concept, so that by 1904 ten states had implemented procedures similar to those of Illinois.

5. _____ concept of the state-raised youth is a useful way of looking at children who come in contact with institutional life at an early age, lack family relationships and structure, become accustomed to living in a correctional facility, and are unable to function in other environments.

## GENERAL PRACTICE QUESTIONS

Unlike the ____1____, who sought to develop rehabilitation for juveniles during the Progressive era, contemporary critics of juvenile justice who believe that sentences are not tough enough have ushered in a new era, the ____2____, which represents a change from the preceding era, the ____3____, in which the focus was on judicial decisions, such as the fundamental due process case of ____4____, to provide constitutional protections for children.

When a child is declared to be ____5____, he or she may be sent to a residential setting with other juveniles, such as a community-based ____6____, which is among the treatment settings left after the ____7____ movement affected how the government places and treats various troubled populations.

# SELF-TEST SECTION

## MULTIPLE CHOICE QUESTIONS

17.1. In what case did the Court declare that trial court judges must evaluate the voluntariness of confessions by juveniles by examining the totality of circumstances?
a) Fare v. Michael C.
b) McKevier v. Pennsylvania
c) New Jersey v. T.L.O.
d) In re Winship
e) Breed v. Jones

17.2. In what case did the Court declare that there is no constitutional right for a jury trial for juveniles?
a) Fare v. Michael C.
b) McKevier v. Pennsylvania
c) New Jersey v. T.L.O.
d) In re Winship
e) Breed v. Jones

17.3. Which of the following is applicable to juveniles, but not to adults?
a) right to counsel
b) right against unreasonable searches and seizures
c) privilege against self-incrimination
d) right to treatment
e) none of the above are applicable to adults

17.4. In what case did the Court declare that the standard of "proof beyond a reasonable doubt" applies to juvenile proceedings?
a) Fare v. Michael C.
b) McKevier v. Pennsylvania
c) New Jersey v. T.L.O.
d) In re Winship
e) Breed v. Jones

17.5. In what case did the Court declare that juveniles cannot be found delinquent in juvenile court and then waived to adult court without violating double jeopardy?
a) Fare v. Michael C.
b) Schall v. Martin
c) New Jersey v. T.L.O.
d) In re Winship
e) Breed v. Jones

17.6. In what case did the Court declare that juveniles have the right to counsel, to confront and examine accusers, and to have adequate notice of charges when there is the possibility of confinement as a punishment?
a) Fare v. Michael C.
b) McKevier v. Pennsylvania
c) Schall v. Martin
d) In re Gault
e) Breed v. Jones

17.7. Which of the following is NOT applicable to juveniles in most states?
a) right to counsel
b) right to treatment
c) right to a trial by jury
d) right against unreasonable searches and seizures
e) privilege against self-incrimination

17.8. According to the *Uniform Crime Reports*, how many people arrested for an index crime are under 18 years of age?
a) one-fourth
b) one-third
c) one-fifth
d) one-tenth
e) one-half

17.9. According to most Americans, what are the two most important problems facing children?
a) internet and media
b) education and teen pregnancy
c) depression and suicide
d) drugs and crime
e) parental neglect and loneliness

17.10. What legislation was the earliest attempt by a colony to deal with problem children?
a) Georgia Juvenile Delinquent Act of 1678
b) Massachusetts Stubborn Child Law in 1646
c) New York Troubled Child Act of 1702
d) Illinois Juvenile Court Act
e) Virginia Child Protection Act of 1656

17.11. During what period did New York open a half prison and half school house for orphaned and destitute children?
a) The Juvenile Court Period
b) The Juvenile Rights Period
c) The Crime Control Period
d) The Puritan Period
e) The Refuge Period

17.12. Which of the following best describes the House of Refuge?
a) one half prison and one half nursery home
b) one half school house and one house nursery home
c) one half prison and one-half school house
d) school house
e) prison

17.13. During what period did the first reform school, the Lyman School for Boys, open in Westboro, Massachusetts?
a) The Juvenile Court Period
b) The Juvenile Rights Period
c) The Crime Control Period
d) The Puritan Period
e) The Refuge Period

17.14. During what period did Illinois pass the Juvenile Court Act by Illinois?
a) The Juvenile Court Period
b) The Juvenile Rights Period
c) The Crime Control Period
d) The Puritan Period
e) The Refuge Period

17.15. During what period brings the development of upper-middle- class reformers who sought to use the power of the state to "save" children from a life of crime?
a) The Juvenile Court Period
b) The Juvenile Rights Period
c) The Crime Control Period
d) The Puritan Period
e) The Refuge Period

17.16. During what period did Activists such as Jane Addams and Julia Lathrop, successfully promote the juvenile court concept?
a) The Juvenile Court Period
b) The Juvenile Rights Period
c) The Crime Control Period
d) The Puritan Period
e) The Refuge Period

17.17. During what period was the passage of the Massachusetts Stubborn Child Law?
a) The Juvenile Court Period
b) The Juvenile Rights Period
c) The Crime Control Period
d) The Puritan Period
e) The Refuge Period

17.18. During what period did the U. S. Supreme Court expand the rights of juveniles?
a) The Juvenile Court Period
b) The Juvenile Rights Period
c) The Crime Control Period
d) The Puritan Period
e) The Refuge Period

17.19. During what period did the U. S. Supreme Court depart from the trend toward increased juvenile rights?
a) The Juvenile Court Period
b) The Juvenile Rights Period
c) The Crime Control Period
d) The Puritan Period
e) The Refuge Period

17.20. During what period did the doctrine of *parens patriae develop?*
a) The Juvenile Court Period
b) The Juvenile Rights Period
c) The Crime Control Period
d) The Puritan Period
e) The Refuge Period

17.21. In what case did the Supreme Court rule that juveniles had the right to counsel at a hearing at which a juvenile judge may waive jurisdiction and pass the case to the adult court?
a) Fare v. Michael C.
b) McKevier v. Pennsylvania
c) Schall v. Martin
d) Kent v. United States
e) Breed v. Jones

17.22. Which of the following included provisions for taking status offenders out of corrections institutions?
a)  Juvenile and Status Act
b) Massachusetts Stubborn Child Law
c) Delaware Troubled Child Act
d) Illinois Juvenile Court Act
e) Juvenile Justice and Delinquency Prevention Act

17.23. In Norway, for a child who is under fifteen, what is the punishment for a crime?
a) same as for adults
b) one-half the sentence of an adult
c) one-fourth the sentence of an adult
d) there is no punishment
e) twice as severe as an adult

17.24. For which of the following crimes is the percentage of juveniles arrested in lesser proportion than their percentage of the general population?
a) driving under the influence
b) vandalism
c) motor vehicle theft
d) burglary
e) arson

17.25. For which of the following crimes is the percentage of juveniles arrested in greater proportion than their percentage of the general population?
a) arson
b) vandalism
c) motor vehicle theft
d) burglary
e) all of the above

## TRUE/FALSE QUESTIONS

17.1. Youth gangs are a dangerous presence in most American cities.

17.2. Operation Ceasefire was a program developed to prevent date rape.

17.3. A separate juvenile justice system has not yet developed in the U. S.

17.4. England has great influence over the U. S. in the area of juvenile justice.

17.5. For the crime of arson, juveniles are arrested in greater proportion than their percentage of the general population.

17.6. For the crime of vandalism, juveniles are arrested in lesser proportions than their percentage of the general population.

17.7. For the crime of burglary, juveniles are arrested in greater proportions than their percentage of the general population.

17.8. For the crime of prostitution, juveniles are arrested in lesser proportions than their percentage of the general population.

17.9. For the crime of motor vehicle theft, juveniles are arrested in lesser proportions than their percentage of the general population.

17.10. Few states provided services to neglected youth at the end of the nineteenth century.

17.11. "Child savers" were lower-class reformers who fought to "save" children from the state.

17.12. Illinois established the first comprehensive system of juvenile justice in the United States.

17.13. A juvenile under fifteen is harshly punished for a crime in Norway.

17.14. The terminology used in the juvenile justice system reflected the underlying belief that these children could be "cured" and returned to society as law-abiding citizens.

17.15. The U. S. Supreme Court began to afford constitutional protections to juveniles in the 1960s.

17.16. Skipping school is a status offense for a juvenile.

17.17. Murder is a status offense for a juvenile.

17.18. Running away from home is a status offense for a juvenile.

17.19. Since the 1980s, the juvenile justice system has emphasized less crime control.

17.20. Recently, the public has expressed support for a get-tough stance toward older juveniles.

# ANSWER KEY

Key Terms
1.     Progressives
2.     Crime Control Period
3.     detention
4.     legislative exclusion
5.     deinstitutionalization
6.     *parens patriae*
7.     Juvenile Rights Period
8.     delinquent
9.     diversion
10.    foster home
11.    Juvenile Court Period
12.    status offense
13.    "child savers"
14.    Norwegian juvenile system
15.    group home
16.    judicial waiver
17.    dependent child
18.    Refuge Period
19.    barnevern
20.    neglected child

Key People
1.     Henry Thurston
2.     Julian Mack
3.     Gerald Gault
4.     Jane Addams and Julia Lathrop
5.     ohn Irwin

General Practice
1.     "child saver"
2.     Crime Control Period
3.     Juvenile Rights Period
4.     In re Gault
5.     delinquent
6.     group home
7.     deinstitutionalization

Multiple Choice Questions
17.1.    a
17.2.    b
17.3.    d
17.4.    d
17.5.    e
17.6.    d
17.7.    c
17.8.    b
17.9.    d
17.10.   b
17.11.   e
17.12.   c
17.13.   e

17.14.   a
17.15.   a
17.16.   a
17.17.   d
17.18.   b
17.19.   c
17.20.   a
17.21.   d
17.22.   e
17.23.   d
17.24.   a
17.25.   e

True/False
17.1.   T
17.2.   F
17.3.   F
17.4.   T
17.5.   T
17.6.   F
17.7.   T
17.8.   T
17.9.   F
17.10.   F
17.11.   F
17.12.   T
17.13.   F
17.14.   T
17.15.   T
17.16.   T
17.17.   F
17.18.   T
17.19.   F
17.20.   T

WORKSHEET 17.1  HISTORY OF JUVENILE JUSTICE

For each era listed below, assume the role of the listed official.  Describe how much discretionary authority you have to determine which children will be drawn into the system and what will be done with them.  Briefly describe what you would decide to do with such children during that era.

THE REFUGE PERIOD (1824-1899).  Police officer:

_____

_____

_____

_____

_____

_____

JUVENILE COURT PERIOD (1899-1960).  Juvenile Court Judge:

_____

_____

_____

_____

_____

JUVENILE RIGHTS PERIOD (1960-1980).  Social Worker:

_____

_____

_____

_____

_____

CRIME CONTROL PERIOD  (1980-Present).  Prosecutor:

_____

_____

_____

_____

WORKSHEET 17.2  TREATMENT OF DELINQUENTS

Assume each of the following occupational roles.  In each role, formulate a recommendation for what should happen to a fourteen-year-old boy whose seventeen-year-old companion killed a man while the two of them attempted to steal a bicycle.

Social Worker:_____

_____

_____

_____

_____

_____

State Legislator:_____

_____

_____

_____

_____

_____

Director of Group Home for Delinquents:_____

_____

_____

_____

_____

_____

Juvenile Court Judge:_____

_____

_____

_____

_____

_____